A Software Process Model Handbook for Incorporating People's Capabilities

A Software Process Model Handbook for Incorporating People's Capabilities

by

Silvia Teresita Acuña
Universidad Autónoma de Madrid, Spain

Natalia Juristo
Universidad Politécnica de Madrid, Spain

Ana María Moreno
Universidad Politécnica de Madrid, Spain

Alicia Mon
Universidad Nacional de La Matanza, Argentina

 Springer

Silvia T. Acuña
Departamento de Ingeniería Informática
Escuela Politécnica Superior
Universidad Autónoma de Madrid
Avenida Tomás y Valiente 11
28049 MADRID
SPAIN

Natalia Juristo
Facultad de Informática
Universidad Politécnica de Madrid
Campus de Montegancedo
Boadilla del Monte
28660 MADRID
SPAIN

Ana M. Moreno
Facultad de Informática
Universidad Politécnica de Madrid
Campus de Montegancedo
Boadilla del Monte
28660 MADRID
SPAIN

Alicia Mon
Secretaría de Posgrado
Universidad Nacional de La Matanza
Avenida de Mayo 776 - 3° piso
1084AAP - Ciudad de Buenos Aires
ARGENTINA

Library of Congress Cataloging-in-Publication Data

A C.I.P. Catalogue record for this book is available
from the Library of Congress.

**A SOFTWARE PROCESS MODEL HANDBOOK FOR
INCORPORATING PEOPLE'S CAPABILITIES**
by
Silvia Teresita Acuña, Natalia Juristo, Ana María Moreno, Alicia Mon

ISBN 978-1-4419-3746-9   e-ISBN 978-0-387-25489-0

Printed on acid-free paper.

Printed in the United States of America.

9 8 7 6 5 4 3 2 1

springeronline.com

To our parents and our families

As ever forever.

The human relations goals for the software development and maintenance process have to do with the management of people's activities in a way which satisfies the human needs and fulfils the human potential of the people involved in the process.

Poor management can increase software costs more rapidly than any other factor.

- Barry Boehm

Contents

List of Figures   xv

List of Tables   xix

Foreword   xxiii

Acknowledgements   xxvii

1. SOFTWARE PROCESS AND PEOPLEWARE BASICS   1

    1.1. SOFTWARE PROCESS VERSUS LIFE CYCLE   2

    1.2. SOFTWARE PROCESS RESEARCH   3

    1.3. SOFTWARE PROCESS MODELLING   7

    1.4. PEOPLEWARE   9

    1.5. HUMAN COMPETENCIES   12

    1.6. MODELLING PEOPLEWARE IN THE SOFTWARE
       PROCESS   16

    1.7. IMPORTANCE OF PEOPLEWARE IN THE PROCESS   18

    1.8. APPROACH FOR INCORPORATING PEOPLE'S
       CAPABILITIES INTO THE SOFTWARE PROCESS   21

PART ONE SOFTWARE PROCESS MODELS   25

2 OVERVIEW OF SOFTWARE PROCESS MODELS
AND DESCRIPTIVE CRITERIA FOR THEIR
ANALYSIS   27

    2.1. SOFTWARE PROCESS MODELS   27

    2.2. DESCRIPTIVE CRITERIA   30

      2.2.1. Modelling-Related Criteria   30

        2.2.1.1. Elements   31

2.2.1.2. Environments   32

2.2.2. Representation-Related Criteria   32

2.2.2.1. Information Perspectives   33

2.2.2.2. Notational Characteristics   34

2.2.3. Criteria Employed by Other Authors   35

3. ACTIVITY-ORIENTED MODELS   37

3.1. DESCRIPTIVE ACTIVITY-ORIENTED MODELS   37

3.1.1. TAME MODEL   38

3.1.2. FUNSOFT Nets-Based Model   39

3.1.3. STATEMATE Model   40

3.1.4. PRISM Model of Changes   42

3.2. PRESCRIPTIVE ACTIVITY-ORIENTED MODELS   44

3.2.1. Process Models   45

3.2.1.1. TRIAD Model   45

3.2.1.2. Marvel Model   47

3.2.1.3. IPSE 2.5 Model   49

3.2.1.4. SPADE Model   50

3.2.1.5. International Standard ISO/IEC 12207: Software Life-
         Cycle Processes   53

3.2.1.6. IEEE STD 1074: IEEE Standard for Developing
         Software Lifecycle Processes   67

3.2.2. Evaluation Models   76

3.2.2.1. ISO 9001   76

3.2.2.2. CMMI   85

4. PEOPLE-ORIENTED MODELS   93

4.1. DESCRIPTIVE PEOPLE-ORIENTED MODELS   93

4.1.1. Systems Dynamics-Based Model   93

4.1.2. Process Cycle Model 95

4.1.3. Agile Methods 98

4.1.3.1. eXtreme Programming (XP) 99

4.1.4. The Win-Win Spiral Model 106

4.2. PRESCRIPTIVE PEOPLE-ORIENTED MODELS 110

4.2.1. Process Models 111

4.2.1.1. PMDB+ Model 111

4.2.1.2. ALF Model 113

4.2.1.3. SOCCA Model 115

4.2.1.4. Unified Process Model 118

4.2.2. Evaluation Model 121

4.2.2.1. People CMM Model 121

5. SUMMARY OF THE OVERVIEW OF SOFTWARE
PROCESS MODELS 129

PART TWO CAPABILITIES-ORIENTED
SOFTWARE PROCESS MODEL 135

6. ADDING CAPABILITIES TO THE SOFTWARE
PROCESS MODEL 137

6.1. INCORPORATING CAPABILITIES INTO A
SOFTWARE PROCESS MODEL 137

6.2. STRUCTURE OF A CAPABILITIES-ORIENTED
SOFTWARE PROCESS 139

6.3. CAPABILITIES: A KEY ELEMENT OF THE PROCESS
MODEL 143

7. PEOPLE DIMENSION 147

7.1. PEOPLE'S CAPABILITIES EVALUATION ACTIVITIES 149

7.2. CAPABILITIES-PERSON RELATIONSHIP   151

7.3. PEOPLE'S CAPABILITIES EVALUATION METHOD   157

   7.3.1. Stage PCE I.1: Identify Personality Factors   160

   7.3.2. Stage PCE II.1: Determine People's Capabilities   160

   7.3.3. Stage PCE II.2: Validate People Model   163

7.4. COLLATERAL USES OF CAPABILITIES   163

8. ROLES DIMENSION   167

   8.1. IDENTIFYING SOFTWARE ROLES   167

   8.2. CAPABILITIES-ROLE RELATIONSHIP   168

      8.2.1. Software Life Cycle Model Selection Role 170

      8.2.2. Project Management Roles   172

      8.2.3. Pre-Development Roles   175

      8.2.4. Development Roles   177

      8.2.5. Post-Development Roles   179

      8.2.6. Integral Roles   180

9. PRODUCTION DIMENSION   183

   9.1. ASSIGNATION OF PEOPLE TO ROLES   183

      9.1.1. Assignation of People to Roles Activities 184

      9.1.2. Assignation of People to Roles Method   185

10. THE CAPABILITIES-BASED ASSIGNATION
    METHOD IN ACTION   193

   10.1. PEOPLE'S CAPABILITIES EVALUATION METHOD
      IN ACTION   193

10.1.1. STAGE PCE I.1: Identify Personality Factors 194

10.1.2. STAGE PCE II.1: Determine People's Capabilities 194

10.1.3. STAGE PCE II.2: Validate People Model 197

10.2. ASSIGNATION OF PEOPLE TO ROLES METHOD IN ACTION 199

11. BENEFITS OF INCORPORATING PEOPLE'S CAPABILITIES INTO THE SOFTWARE PROCESS 211

11.1. DESIGN OF THE EXPERIMENT ON THE ASSIGNATION OF PEOPLE TO ROLES 212

11.2. RESULTS OF THE EXPERIMENT 214

12. CONCLUSIONS 217

REFERENCES 221

APPENDIX A. PEOPLE'S CAPABILITIES 249

APPENDIX B. 16 PF FIFTH EDITION PERSONALITY FACTOR QUESTIONNAIRE 253

B.1. DESCRIPTION OF THE 16 PF FIFTH EDITION 253

B.2. 16 PF FIFTH EDITION TEST ADMINISTRATION ELEMENTS 256

APPENDIX C. PEOPLE MODELS 261

Index 321

List of Figures

Figure 1.1.   Software process and peopleware   1

Figure 2.1.   Classification used to analyse software process models   28

Figure 2.2.   Surveyed software process models   30

Figure 3.1.   TAME improvement-oriented software process model   39

Figure 3.2.   SPADE Model type hierarchy representation   52

Figure 3.3.   ISO/IEC Standard 12207-1995 structure   54

Figure 3.4.   An example of application of the international standard   63

Figure 3.5.   Software life-cycle processes: roles and relationships   65

Figure 3.6.   Software process according to IEEE STD 1074   68

Figure 3.7.   Model of a process-based quality management system   77

Figure 3.8.   CMMI maturity levels   88

Figure 3.9.   CMMI Model components   88

Figure 4.1.   The Process Cycle   96

Figure 4.2.   XP life cycle   104

Figure 4.3.   Spiral model   107

Figure 4.4.   Win-win model   109

Figure 4.5.   People CMM process areas   124

Figure 6.1.   Overview of the incorporation of people's capabilities into the software
              Process   138

Figure 6.2.   Software process elements   140

Figure 6.3.   Key element, structure and dimensions of the software process   141

Figure 6.4.   Software process model dimension elements   142

Figure 7.1.   Activity groups and roles of the people dimension   148

Figure 7.2.   People's Capabilities Evaluation Method stages   158

Figure 7.3.   People's Capabilities Evaluation Method stages and products   159

Figure 7.4.   Personality Factors Model   161

Figure 7.5.   Capabilities Report   162

Figure 8.1.   Integral software activities and roles   168

Figure 9.1.   Software process model   184

Figure 9.2.   Assignation of People to Roles activities structure   185

Figure 9.3.   Assignation of People to Roles Method   188

Figure 9.4.   Main components of the Assignation of People to Roles Method   191

Figure 10.1.   Personality Factors Model # 4 (RX)   195

Figure 10.2.   Capabilities Report # 4   198

Figure 10.3.   Identification of roles that can be satisfied by RX   200

Figure 10.4.   Identification of roles that GR can play   202

Figure B.1.   Specimen 16 PF Fifth Edition Questions   257

Figure B.2.   Calculating global dimensions   259

Figure B.3.   Primary scales and global dimensions profile   260

Figure C.1.   Personality Factors Model # 4   262

Figure C.2.   Personality Factors Model # 9   269

Figure C.3.   Personality Factors Model # 63   270

Figure C.4.   Personality Factors Model # 17   271

Figure C.5.   Personality Factors Model # 61   272

Figure C.6.   Personality Factors Model # 64   273

Figure C.7.   Personality Factors Model # 7   274

Figure C.8.   Personality Factors Model # 11   275

Figure C.9.   Personality Factors Model # 13   276

Figure C.10.   Personality Factors Model # 12   277

Figure C.11.   Personality Factors Model # 15   278

Figure C.12.   Personality Factors Model # 16   279

Figure C.13.   Personality Factors Model # 40   280

Figure C.14.   Personality Factors Model # 3   281

Figure C.15.   Personality Factors Model # 2   282

Figure C.16.   Personality Factors Model # 6   283

Figure C.17.   Personality Factors Model # 8   284

Figure C.18.   Personality Factors Model # 10   285

Figure C.19.   Personality Factors Model # 1   286

Figure C.20.   Personality Factors Model # 14   287

Figure C.21.   Personality Factors Model # 30   288

Figure C.22. Personality Factors Model # 5   289

Figure C.23. Personality Factors Model # 60   290

Figure C.24. Personality Factors Model # 62   291

Figure C.25. Personality Factors Model # 100   292

Figure C.26. Personality Factors Model # 18   293

Figure C.27. Capabilities Report # 4   294

Figure C.28. Capabilities Report # 9   295

Figure C.29. Capabilities Report # 63   296

Figure C.30. Capabilities Report # 17   297

Figure C.31. Capabilities Report # 61   298

Figure C.32. Capabilities Report # 64   299

Figure C.33. Capabilities Report # 7   300

Figure C.34. Capabilities Report # 11   301

Figure C.35. Capabilities Report # 13   302

Figure C.36. Capabilities Report # 12   303

Figure C.37. Capabilities Report # 15   304

Figure C.38. Capabilities Report # 16   305

Figure C.39. Capabilities Report # 40   306

Figure C.40. Capabilities Report # 3   307

Figure C.41. Capabilities Report # 2   308

Figure C.42. Capabilities Report # 6   309

Figure C.43. Capabilities Report # 8   310

Figure C.44. Capabilities Report # 10   311

Figure C.45. Capabilities Report # 1   312

Figure C.46. Capabilities Report # 14   313

Figure C.47. Capabilities Report # 30   314

Figure C.48. Capabilities Report # 5   315

Figure C.49. Capabilities Report # 60   316

Figure C.50. Capabilities Report # 62   317

Figure C.51. Capabilities Report # 100   318

Figure C.52. Capabilities Report # 18   319

List of Tables

Table 1.1.   Differences between life cycle and software process   4

Table 2.1.   Models of each class found in the literature   29

Table 2.2.   Information perspectives of the process and the applicable language bases 34

Table 3.1.   Characteristics of the PRISM environment architecture components   44

Table 3.2.   ISO/IEC 12207 software process elements   53

Table 3.3.   Structure of International Standard ISO/IEC 12207-1995   55

Table 3.4.   Description, activities and output documents of primary processes   57

Table 3.5.   Description, activities and output documents of supporting processes   58

Table 3.6.   Description, activities and output documents of organisational processes   60

Table 3.7.   Description and activities of the new ISO/IEC 12207-2002 processes   61

Table 3.8.   Tailoring process activities and tasks   64

Table 3.9.   IEEE STD 1074 software process elements   67

Table 3.10.   IEEE STD 1074 structure   69

Table 3.11.   Description, activities and output information of project management
              activity groups   71

Table 3.12.   Description, activities and output information of software development-
              oriented activity groups   72

Table 3.13.   Description, activities and output information of integral activity groups   75

Table 3.14.   ISO 9001 Requirements   78

Table 3.15.   CMMI Model Representations   86

Table 4.1.   Process Cycle sector characteristics   97

Table 4.2.   XP practices   103

Table 4.3.   PMDB+ Model elements   113

Table 4.4.   SOCCA modelling procedure   117

Table 4.5.   Unified Process workflow structure   120

Table 4.6.   Description of People CMM maturity levels   125

Table 5.1.   Assessment of Software Process Models   130

Table 6.1.   Characteristics of people-related activities   139

Table 6.2.   Proposal of capabilities by categories to be used in software
              development   145

Table 7.1.   Activities, and input and output documents for people's capabilities
              evaluation   149

Table 7.2.   Primary and supporting teams for people's capabilities evaluation 150

Table 7.3.   Method for evaluating people's capabilities   151

Table 7.4.   Description of the primary scales by means of adjectives   153

Table 7.5.   Description of dimensions by means of adjectives   153

Table 7.6.   Correspondence between 16 PF personality factors and people's
              capabilities   154

Table 7.7.   Justification (rationale) of the correspondence between the 16 PF
              personality factors test and people's capabilities   155

Table 7.8.   Determining people's capabilities: detail of a focused interview   164

Table 8.1.   Role/capabilities table   169

Table 9.1.   Capabilities/Role profile   186

Table 9.2.   Format of Person/Roles Match Table for a specific person   189

Table 9.3.   Format of Role/People Table   190

Table 10.1.   Extract of the Personality Factors Model (Analytical Report)   196

Table 10.2.   Assignation of RX to Roles   201

Table 10.3.   Assignation of GR to Roles   202

Table 10.4.   Assignation of FR to Roles   203

Table 10.5.   Assignation of CA to Roles   203

Table 10.6.   Assignation of CS to Roles   204

Table 10.7.   Assignation of MA to Roles   204

Table 10.8.   Assignation of EL to Roles   205

Table 10.9.   Assignation of AD to Roles   205

Table 10.10. Assignation of PB to Roles   206

Table 10.11. Assignation of PR to Roles   206

Table 10.12. Assignation of AL to Roles   206

Table 10.13. Assignation of ER to Roles   207

Table 10.14. Assignation of FM to Roles   207

Table 10.15. Assignation of MB to Roles   208

Table 10.16. Assignation of DN to Roles   208

Table 10.17. Assignation of CL to Roles   209

Table 10.18. Role/People Table   209

Table 11.1. Project characterisation   213

Table 11.2. Results for the performance of people in roles criterion   215

Table 11.3. Results for the development time criterion for each activity group and the project   216

Table A.1. Classification of behavioural competencies by categories according to de Ansorena Cao   250

Table A.2. Classification of behavioural competencies by categories according to the Hay Group   250

Table B.1. Description of the 16 PF Fifth Edition primary scales   254

Table B.2. Description of the 16 PF Fifth Edition global dimensions   256

Table C.1. Analytical Report Section of the Personality Factors Model   263

Foreword

A good claim can be made for the statement that in the words of Abraham Lincoln's Gettysburg Address, software engineering is "of the people, by the people, and for the people."

It is "of the people" because it results from people coming together and determining that a software-oriented approach to improve the way that people are currently doing business is worth the investment of their personal and material resources.

It is "by the people" because the software is defined, designed, developed, deployed, and evolved by people.

It is "for the people" because the resulting software helps people spend less time on frustrating, tedious, low-value tasks and more time on meaningful, stimulating, and high-value activities.

In this context, it is amazing how much of past and current software engineering literature is insensitive to people considerations. Other than the little stick figures in use cases, it talks mainly about objects, methods, abstractions, components, connectors, cohesion, coupling, preconditions, postconditions, versions, budgets, schedules, milestones, documents, and various other aspects of software products and projects. As a result, the technical parts of the software are done relatively well, and the major sources of project failure in surveys such as the Standish Report are people-oriented; lack of user input, incomplete and changing user requirements, lack of executive support, inexperienced management, unrealistic expectations, unclear objectives, and unrealistic budgets and schedules.

This book, A Software Process Model Handbook for Incorporating People's Capabilities, adds another valuable contribution to the much-needed literature on people aspects in software engineering. It builds on some of the major contributions of the past, such as Weinberg's Psychology of Computer Programming and other books; the Scandinavian participatory design movement; DeMarco and Lister's Peopleware; Curtis's studies of people factors and People Capability Maturity Model; and the work of the computer-human interaction, computer supported cooperative work, and agile methods communities.

This book focuses on the particular challenge of extending software process definitions to more explicitly address people considerations. Part I of the book provides an extensive survey of the state-of-the-art and state-of-the-practice with respect to the inclusion of people factors in software process models. It identifies criteria for characterizing the models such as process elements represented (agents, activates, artifacts, roles, capabilities, events), process environments covered (organizational, social, technological), information perspectives (functional, behavioral, organizational, informational), and notational characteristics (degree of formality, types of representation). It summarizes the main standardized process models (ISO, IEEE, CMMs) and representative industrial and research process models with respect to the criteria. It concludes that, although some models are good at procedural aspects and others are good at social aspects, none do a thorough job of integrating the procedural and social aspects, particularly with respect to determining how best to staff a project with a given mix of roles when one has a pool of people with a given mix of capabilities.

Part II of the book takes up this challenge. It describes the nature, usage, and positive project results of a people/capabilities extension developed by the authors of the IEEE P-1074 Standard for Developing Software Life Cycle Processes. Chapter 6 describes 20 capabilities (7 intrapersonal, 5 organizational, 5 interpersonal, 3 management) determined to be most significant for evaluating people's abilities to perform the various software engineering roles. Chapter 7 relates these to 16 personality factors, and Chapter 8 relates these to 20 project roles (1 life cycle model selection, 5 management, 3 pre-development, 3 development, 3 post-development, 4 continuing).

Chapter 9 provides analyses of which people capabilities and personality factors are likely to help or hinder performance of the various project roles. Chapter 10 provides a real-project example of how the resulting People's Capabilities Evaluation Method and Assignation of People to Roles Method are applied in practice, and Chapter 11 presents the results of analyzing two comparable samples of four 3-to-6-person projects from the same organization which did or did not use the methods. The results showed statistically significant improvement in on-time delivery and defect density.

Of course, there are risks that should be pointed out of taking an overly simplistic approach to applying the methods in the book. One is overoptimization on project satisfaction. If the same optimal allocation of people to roles is applied on each project, people will get locked into roles, get bored, lose breadth and variety of experience, and overconstrain their career progression opportunities. Another is overfocus on individual capabilities. For example, the role/capabilities table in Chapter 8 has a single line for the designer role. But particularly on larger projects, there may be user interface designers, algorithm designers, and system architects, for whom different combinations of capabilities may be important. A third risk is overfocus on "by the people" project role assignment. Just doing this well does not address the "of the people" concerns of stakeholder identification, negotiation, and collaboration; or the "for the people" concerns of business process reengineering and user interface definition and development.

But these risks need to be compared with the risks of doing nothing. As shown in Chapter 11, an enlightened approach to the overall "of the people, by the people, and for the people" set of considerations led to significant improvement in overall project performance over the "business as usual" projects.

Thus, the methods in the book are well worth learning about and tailoring to your organization's particular environment and project mix. Besides this, the book's contents can be valuable in other ways. Part I provides a handy summary of leading software process models and the degree to which they address a number of important considerations. The role/capability analyses in part II provide a good starting point for working out people's career-path strategies, educating Human Relations Department people on software-people characteristics, and convincing upper management that software development is more than sending over a couple of golden geeks to write a few computer programs.

As a bottom line, I can't think of a better use of your time than to use the material in this book and other sources to help get your organization better focused on how to make the most enlightened use of its people. Your people will thank you for it in the long run.

Barry Boehm
January 2005

Acknowledgements

Thanks to everyone who helped us to "grow" as we wrote this book. We are especially grateful to Rachel Elliott of the Technical University of Madrid for the translation and correction services she has provided throughout the preparation of this book.

Thanks too to the occupational psychologists, managers and developers who all put aside their own paradigms and tried to get into each other's "heads". What we mean here is that they tried to think like the other person (temporarily, "believing and feeling" everything that the other person "believed and felt"). This process of "assuming" someone else's thoughts is not easy, and the generosity and modesty of the people involved led to a fruitful exchange of ideas and the development of the integral methods proposed in this book. We are especially obliged to Marta Aparicio, occupational psychologist of the Complutense University of Madrid, and the psychologists of TEA, Madrid, for processing the 16 PF Fifth Edition questionnaires. Our thanks go to all of them.

We would like to extend these acknowledgements to all our colleagues at the Autonomous University of Madrid and the Technical University of Madrid. We are thankful to them all for their support and the friendly exchange of knowledge.

Thanks too to all the people who have in one way or another helped us to complete this project, people without whose support it would have been very difficult to make this book a reality. Our gratitude goes to our respective friends. Thanks for the gift of your friendship.

We would like to acknowledge and thank our families for their encouragement and patience and for the understanding they have shown for the time we have not been able to spend together. We are profoundly grateful to our parents who have always been there helping us to do better.

Finally, we are indebted to Susan Lagerstrom-Fife and Sharon Palleschi of Kluwer for editing and offering general guidance about this book. Special thanks to you, Barry. Thanks for your insights and your graciousness in honouring us by writing the preface to this book.

Software Process and Peopleware Basics

The software process activities that transform input products into output products are performed by people who have and develop capabilities to play roles within the development organisation. The relationships between the software process and peopleware are shown in Figure 1.1. Peopleware in the software process is an aspect that has not been formally specified, although people and processes are inseparable, as illustrated in Figure 1.1. This chapter aims to give an overview of the software process, including aspects related to peopleware.

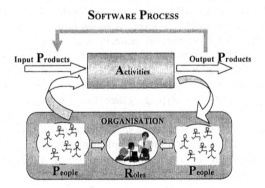

Figure 1.1. Software process and peopleware

In this chapter, we discuss the concept of software process and address the importance of peopleware in the software process. Furthermore, we analyse the three main actions that can be taken with respect to the software process: define or model, evaluate and improve.

1.1. SOFTWARE PROCESS VERSUS LIFE CYCLE

As software and its construction have been examined in further detail, the software process has assumed its own identity and has been the subject of investigation and research (Finkelstein et al., 1994; Hinley, 1996). The term life cycle, not software process, however, was used in the past (Davis, 1993). Although the notion of process was present in all development projects, the concept of development process was not explicitly recognised (Blum, 1992; McChesney, 1995). The concepts of life cycle and process are so closely related that confusion often arises, calling for a clarification of these concepts. The view that we take of these concepts is as follows (Acuña et al., 1999):

1. *Life cycle*: The *states* through which software evolves. The life cycle focuses on the product, defining the state through which a product passes from when it starts to be built (the first state is the user need) to when the software enters into operation (this product state is the delivered system) and is finally retired (the state is the retired system) (Scacchi, 1987; Dowson et al., 1991).

    A *life cycle model* is an abstract representation of the software life cycle. In the case of the software product, there is no one life cycle. A product can pass through different states, depending on the specific circumstances of each project and, hence, there are different life cycle models. For example, if the problem is well defined and well understood and the user need is practically invariable, a *short,* waterfall-like life cycle is likely to be sufficient. However, when we come up against a poorly defined and poorly understood problem and a highly volatile user need, we can hardly expect to output a full requirements specification at the start. In this case, we have to opt for *longer* and more complex life cycles, like the spiral life cycle (Boehm, 1988); prototyping, where the first state will be a prototype (McCracken & Jackson, 1982; Gomaa, 1983); an incremental life cycle, where the first state will be the specification of the system kernel, followed by the kernel design and finally implementation, then going back to specify the next system increment and so on (Hirsch, 1985), etc. So, there are different life cycles for different project circumstances.

    A method for selecting a model from several alternative life cycle models is presented in (Alexander & Davis, 1991). Descriptions of life cycle models are given in (Scacchi, 1987; Comer, 1997; Pressman, 1997; Pfleeger, 1998). Software engineering life cycle models are compared in (Davis et al., 1988; Comer, 1997).

2.   *Software process*: A set of *activities* undertaken to manage, develop and maintain software systems. In other words, the software process focuses on the construction tasks rather than on the output products. The definition of a software process should specify not only the activities, but also the techniques to perform the tasks, the actors who execute the activities, their roles and the artefacts produced. Because the process causes transformations in the products (that is, provokes the life cycle), it may be termed either development process or software life cycle process (IEEE, 1997; Penedo & Shu, 1991; ISO/IEC, 1995). An organisation can define its own way of producing software based on internal and customer characteristics. However, some activities are common to all possible software processes.

The activities that make up a process can be divided according to their purposes into groups, also known as subprocesses or even processes. The software process basically consists of two interrelated groups of activities: the production subprocess and the management subprocess. The first is related to the construction and maintenance of the software product, whereas the second is responsible for estimating, planning and controlling the necessary resources (people, time, technology, etc.) to be able to implement and control the production subprocess. This control makes it possible to generate information about the production subprocess, which can be used later on by the management subprocess with a view to improving the software process and increasing the quality of the developed software.

A *software process model* is an abstract representation of the software process. A variety of software process models have been designed to structure, describe and prescribe the software system construction process. These models are examined in Part I of the book.

Table 1.1 summarises the differences between life cycle and software process, highlighting that these are two different, albeit closely related concepts.

Considering the above definitions, *this book focuses on the software process* and does not refer to the software life cycle.

1.2. SOFTWARE PROCESS RESEARCH

The general objective of software process research (Acuña et al., 2001) is to improve software development practice by proposing: a) better ways of designing the developer organisation processes; b) better ways of assessing the weaknesses of this organisation; and c) better ways of improving this organisation at the level of individual processes and the organisation as a whole. To this end, there are three lines of software process research: software process modelling, software process evaluation and software process improvement. Software process research is comprehensively reviewed in (Derniame et al., 1999), while Fuggetta (2000) presents a critical overall evaluation and possible directions for future research.

CRITERIA	LIFE CYCLE	SOFTWARE PROCESS
Focused on	Product output in each phase	Activity performed during software development
Relationships	The state is transformed by the activity	The activity works on a state
Generality	Multiple life cycle models	Single model for the developer organisation
Domain and scope	Specific, project dependent	General, project independent, organisation dependent

Table 1.1. Differences between life cycle and software process

Software process modelling describes the creation of software development process models. A software process model is an abstract representation of the architecture, design or definition of the software process (Feiler & Humphrey, 1993). Each representation describes, at different detail levels, an organisation of the elements of a finished, ongoing or proposed process, and it provides a definition of the process to be used for evaluation and improvement. A process model can be analysed, validated and simulated, if executable. Process models are used mainly for software process control (evaluation and improvement) in an organisation, but they can be also used for experimenting with software process theory and to ease process automation. The results achieved so far in software process modelling research are reviewed in (Ambriola et al., 1997).

Software process evaluation judges and decides on the quality of the software process of a given organisation, and may propose a process improvement strategy. The efforts of the scientific community in this field have led to quite a number of maturity models and standards, such as ISO 9000 (ISO, 1994; Schmauch, 1995; ISO, 1997) and the updated ISO 9001 (ISO-9001, 2000), CMM (Capability Maturity Model) (Paulk et al., 1995) and the improved CMMI (SEI, 2002e; SEI, 2002f), ISO/IEC 15504 (ISO/IEC 15504, 1998) and Bootstrap (Kuvaja et al., 1994). All these models have two goals: a) to determine the aspects for improvement in a software development organisation; and b) to reach an agreement on what a good process is. This goal stems from the very nature of the evaluation process, as it is essential to use a reference model or yardstick against which to compare the software process of the organisation under evaluation. Therefore, it involves modelling the above process by identifying what sorts of activities have to be carried out by an organisation to assure the quality of the production process and, ultimately, the end product. The software process models on which some of these evaluation methods are based (ISO 9001 and CMMI) will be discussed in Part I of the book.

Software process evaluation involves analysing the activities carried out in an organisation to produce software. The ultimate goal of process evaluation is to improve software production. Development process evaluation and improvement works under the hypothesis that the quality of the software product is determined by the quality of its development process. This strategy is equivalent to the one implemented in other branches of engineering and industry, where the quality of the resulting product is increased by controlling the process used in its production (Humphrey, 1989). Software process evaluation methods introduced innovative concepts that changed the way in which software production activities are perceived.

Software process improvement examines how to improve an organisation's software development practices, once software process evaluation has made clear what the current state of the process is. Software process improvement is not planned as a single step to excellence, but is performed gradually by transitions from one maturity level to another. A capable and mature software development organisation institutionalises the improvement effort.

Looking at the most popular frameworks for software process evaluation, ISO/IEC 15504 and the CMM developed by the Software Engineering Institute (SEI) at Carnegie Mellon University, there is a fundamental difference in the way they help to set improvement goals. While ISO/IEC 15504 deals with processes separately, the CMM organises the processes in a levelled representation that defines a reasonable sequence for improvement. Each level in the CMM groups a set of key process areas, and each key process area groups a set of related activities, which, when performed collectively, help to achieve goals that are considered important for establishing the capability of the software process at a given maturity level. If an organisation is, for instance, at level 2, the CMM recommends that immediate improvement efforts should be directed towards level-3 key process areas. ISO/IEC 15504, on the other hand, provides a detailed snapshot of the current state of each process through process profiles, but makes no suggestions as to how to improve on that state.

The new integrated version of the CMM, which has been prepared and coordinated by the SEI (SEI, 2002e; SEI 2002f), aims to combine both approaches and provide two alternative representations, a continuous and a staged representation. The staged representation clearly orders the maturity levels, while the continuous representation focuses on separate process areas and provides achievement profiles (a list of process areas and their respective capability levels) as a result of the evaluation. Using the continuous approach, the improvement should be planned as target staging, that is, a sequence of target profiles to be achieved by the organisation. An equivalence has been defined between the maturity levels of the staged representation and some target profiles. Thus, the continuous approach allows organisations to set their own improvement goals more flexibly, while staging is a more guided and restricted approach, although it allows for benchmarking between organisations or projects.

There are several improvement models and solutions, like the SEI IDEAL (McFeeley, 1996), the Business Improvement Guides (BIGs) developed by the European Software Institute (ESI) (Satriani et al., 1998; Ostolaza et al., 1999; Ferrer et al., 1999) or the Process Improvement Guide (PIG) developed by the ISO/IEC 15504 project (SPICE, 2003) (called "Software Process Assessment – Part 7: Guide for use in process improvement", working draft V1.00).

While recognising the importance of cultural and people-related issues, all of the above-mentioned models and methods for software process improvement have an organisational focus. They are top-down approaches that require the commitment of senior management and the establishment of an organisational infrastructure for process improvement. Watts S. Humphrey proposed a radically different approach in 1995 with his Personal Software Process (PSP) (Humphrey, 1995; Humphrey, 1997). The PSP is a bottom-up approach focused on individual software engineers, which provides them with a framework to measure and analyse their current software development processes and to identify and implement process improvements for better individual performance.

The rationale behind PSP is that the quality of a software system is determined by the quality of its worst component, and the quality of a software component is determined by the quality of the engineer that developed it. Therefore, an improvement in the quality of software systems can be expected by improving the "quality" of individual software engineers. PSP considers two fundamental improvement areas: the estimation and planning of individual work and the quality of software products.

Filling the gap between the CMM (an organisation-centred approach) and the PSP (an individual-centred approach), the Team Software Process (TSP) (Humphrey, 1998a) came to address the software process improvement problem at the team level. The goal of the TSP is to help establish self-directed teams that are able to plan and track their own work and to set goals, and that own their processes and plans, with a strong motivation for maintaining top-level performance. We refer to (Davis & McHale, 2002) for an analysis of the relationships between the processes, procedures, guidelines and tools for TSP project teams and the key practices of the Software-CMM.

Of these three areas, process modelling, evaluation and improvement, which play a central role in software process research, *this book addresses software process modelling*. Modelling, evaluation and improvement are, however, closely related. Software development process modelling is one of the key factors for improving software productivity and quality (Penedo & Shu, 1991; Conradi et al., 1994a; de Vasconcelos & Werner, 1997). Modelling, which is the foundation for creating the software process prior to any evaluation or control, that is, designing a good process, is possibly the most critical factor for achieving a quality software production process. The objective therefore is to model the process by identifying what elements there should be at a software developer organisation to assure the quality of the production process and, ultimately, the output product. Large-scale software developer organisations are trying to mature their software development processes on the basis of more precise, integral and formalised descriptions of well-established processes (Penedo & Shu, 1991; Hollenbach & Frakes, 1996; Fuggetta, 2000).

1.3. SOFTWARE PROCESS MODELLING

As mentioned above, although, historically speaking, software development was product focused, researchers and developers began to switch their attention to the process dimension about a decade ago (Blum, 1992; Yu & Mylopoulos, 1994). This approach intends to minimise some of the problems encountered in organisations with respect to their development process, such as (Curtis et al., 1992):

a) Dissemination of the description of the software across many documents,

b) Mismatch between the process description and the implemented process,

c) Process description of too high a level for it to be useful in practice,

d) Imprecise, ambiguous or incomprehensible process description and

e) Documentation that does not reflect any changes made.

The extent of these problems is reduced thanks to the specific objectives and advantages of software process modelling, namely (Curtis et al., 1992):

1. *It eases understanding and communication.* To help to understand and enable discussion of the software process, a process model that includes sufficient information for process representation is needed. It formalises the process, establishing a foundation for training.

2. *It supports the process improvement better.* To improve a software process, well-defined and effective processes need to be reused; alternative

processes need to be compared and process evolution needs to be supported.

3. *It supports process management.* To manage a software process, a project-specific software process is needed, upon which follow-up, management and coordination will be based.

4. *It allows automated guidance for process performance.* In this case, an effective software development environment is needed, providing user guidance, instructions and reference material.

5. *It supports automated execution.* For this purpose, automated process parts, cooperative work support, a collection of metrics and process integrity assurance are required.

These benefits mean that, today, software process definition or modelling is an area that plays a central role in software process research. The *definition of the software process* refers to the definition of the processes as models, plus any optional automated support available for modelling and for executing the models during the software process.

Different elements of a process, for example, activities, products (artefacts), resources (personnel and tools) and roles, can be modelled (Huff, 1996). The elements most commonly modelled are artefact or product, agent or actor, activity, role and event (Benali & Derniame, 1992; Finkelstein et al., 1994; McChesney, 1995; Fuggetta & Wolf, 1996; Pfleeger, 1998). Other possible elements are project/organisation, workspace (repository), user viewpoint, model of cooperation, versioning, transactions, quality, etc. Definitions of the process modelling concepts are given in (Conradi et al., 1992; Lonchamp, 1993), and the main software process models that use these concepts are described in (Finkelstein et al., 1994).

There are different types of process modelling. Processes can be modelled at different levels of abstraction (for example, standard models versus tailored models) and they can also be modelled for different purposes (descriptive models versus prescriptive models). The distinguishing features of these models have been described in (Humphrey, 1989; Madhavji, 1991; Lehman, 1991; McChesney, 1995; Pfleeger, 1998). Different process models can define different points of view. For example, one model may define the agents involved in each activity, while another may focus on the relationship between activities. This means that each model observes, focuses on or gives priority to particular points of such a complex world as software construction (Dowson et al., 1990; Feiler & Humphrey, 1993). A model is always an abstraction of reality and, as such, represents a partial and simplified description of reality; that is, a model does not account for all the parts or aspects of the process. Generally, a process model can be divided into several submodels expressing different viewpoints or perspectives.

As we will see in Part I of the book, we suggest the following classification, which we consider to be appropriate for our purposes. There are two viewpoints on software process modelling depending on how the model defines the process elements. The model focuses on:

I. *Activity-oriented modelling*, whose process definition focuses on the functions, activities and information on management, development and/or software process support processes.

II. *People-oriented modelling*, whose process definition focuses on the specifications of the people involved in the software process and their relationships.

Models are divided into two types depending on their objectives:

I. *Descriptive modelling*, whose goal is to specify a process now used within an organisation or to represent a proposed process suitably so as to predict some process features.

II. *Prescriptive modelling*, whose goal is to define how the process needs to or should be enacted.

This book deals with people-oriented prescriptive modelling.

1.4. PEOPLEWARE

One of the main assets of any organisation is its human capital. The intelligent and effective use of the available individuals can lead to some companies gaining a competitive advantage over others. The importance of people is all the more critical in organisations where the production of the goods or services in which they deal depends directly on the performance (good or bad) of their personnel.

Software companies are an obvious example of organisations of this kind, since software construction is a primarily intellectual process. As a matter of fact, several authors have addressed human capital management in software development over the last thirty years or so. For example, back in the 1980s Boehm explicitly mentioned human relations as a key component (alongside adequate resource and program engineering) for achieving a successful software product and conducting a successful software development and maintenance process (Boehm, 1981). As regards the software process, he claimed that "the human relations goals for the software development and maintenance process have to do with the management of people's activities in a way which satisfies the human needs and fulfils the human potential of the people involved in the process". Moreover, Koontz and O'Donnell (1972) defined five basic principles for managing software people that provide guidelines for improving the software organisation's staffing situation with a view to achieving gains in productivity. Such principles can be summarised as:

- The principle of Top Talent (use better and fewer people)

- The principle of Job Matching (fit the tasks to the skills and motivation of the people available)

- The principle of Career Progression (an organisation does best in the long run by helping its people to self-actualise)

- The principle of Team Balance (select people who will complement and harmonise with each other)

- The principle of Phaseout (keeping a misfit on the team doesn't benefit anyone).

It is noteworthy that the ultimate aim of properly managing human capital in software development is to improve software development with respect, for example, to productivity, errors, etc. Note that, for example, the impact of human capital has been dealt with quantitatively in several cost estimation methods, like COCOMO. The first version of the method, dating back to 1981 (Boehm, 1981), identified five factors related to developer capability and experience as effort adjustment factors associated with software system construction. These factors were:

- ACAP Analyst capability

- AEXP Applications experience

- PCAP Programmer capability

- VEXP Virtual machine experience

- LEXP Language experience.

This philosophy of considering the impact of people's characteristics on software development quantitatively as a development effort adjustment factor still applies today. Indeed, the latest update of the COCOMO method, COCOMO II (Boehm et al., 2000), still includes this type of adjustment factors.

It is therefore no wonder that authors like DeMarco and Lister (1999) or Constantine (2001) consider that the major issues of software development are human, and by no means technical. Software development organisations need to understand that dealing with software problems does not only involve the technical dimensions, like introducing a new tool or selecting a method. The human dimension can be considered even more important than the technical side and, as DeMarco and Lister put it, "most software development projects fail because of failures with the team running them".

This is also the underlying idea of People CMM (Curtis et al., 1995b; Curtis et al., 2001), which characterises an organisation on the basis of how it manages its workforce. Accordingly, each progressive level of People CMM produces a transformation in the organisational culture of a software organisation in order to improve the development, organisation, motivation and retention of its workforce.

Against this backdrop, interest in the concept of peopleware is rising in the software community. This concept covers a variety of aspects, like:

a) Development of productive persons (DeMarco & Lister, 1999; Humphrey, 1997),

b) People management (Humphrey, 1998b; DeMarco & Lister, 1999),

c) Organisational culture (Constantine, 2001),

d) Organisational learning (DeMarco & Lister, 1999; Rhue & Bomarius, 2000; Pfahl & Ruhe, 2001),

e) Development of productive teams (Humphrey, 1998a; Constantine, 2001; Slomp & Molleman, 2002) and

f) Modelling of human competencies (Harzallah & Vernadat, 2002).

The process of assigning people to jobs or roles is of unquestionable importance also in software organisations. Proof of this is, for example, that it is part of the process areas of levels 2 and 3 of the People CMM. However, there is a significant shortage of formalised mechanisms for performing this activity in the software industry (Walley & Smith, 1998). Generally, this process of assigning individuals to roles is performed unsystematically in software development projects, depending on the opinion of the project manager or what experience an individual has in particular tasks. This intuitive assignation procedure does not formalise the skills and capabilities of software team members to assure that the project team is effective and efficient (Humphrey, 1998b; Slomp & Molleman, 2002).

There is little work on personnel characterisation in software development. Nevertheless, some attempts have been made at accounting for the individual capabilities of resources with a view to their proper management. One such approach is Qualisem-People (Hass, 2001). This method aims to identify the capabilities of the individuals involved in a software development organisation to identify skill gaps and direct training efforts at filling these gaps. The capabilities of the individuals are identified through questionnaires completed by the individuals concerned and their managers.

The way things are done in the field of software development contrasts with the process followed in other productive organisations, where occupational psychology methods and techniques have been applied since as early as the 1950s to identify personnel capabilities and effectively assign individuals to jobs or roles (Janz et al., 1986; West, 1991). These capabilities-based methods examine the underlying characteristics of individuals that qualify them to perform given roles. For example, management jobs require the performance of planning and organisational tasks. But, do we all have the same planning and organisational capabilities? What makes a person plan and organise efficiently? Psychological research on capabilities has found that there is a group of underlying capabilities causally related to effective planning and organisation: perfectionism (meaning the motivation to achieve); the desire for success (as an invincible longing to raise efficiency); and an analytical mentality (to organise tasks hierarchically, sequentially or in parallel and determine the order in which they should be done). Therefore, by identifying the capabilities needed to produce good results in a given job, we can build capabilities models, which can then be used to establish procedures for selecting personnel and assigning them to the jobs that are best suited to their capabilities.

1.5. HUMAN COMPETENCIES

Human competencies are now a key factor in integrated people management and organisational development (Spencer et al., 1992; Harzallah & Vernadat, 2002). The definition of the concept of competency differs from discipline to discipline (sociology, organisational development, integrated people management, psychology, etc.). The concept of competency is generally associated with other concepts, such as knowledge, skill, ability, know-how, experience, aptitude, capacity, personality feature, behaviour, etc. The meaning of competency, however, now seems to be stabilising and converging towards the following definition (Harzallah et al., 2002). *Competency is the effect of combining and bringing into play resources (i.e. knowledge, know-how, and behaviours) in a given context to achieve an objective or fulfil a specified mission* (Levy-Leboyer, 1996; Le Boterf, 1997; Harzallah & Vernadat, 2002). When exercising a competency, a cognitive process is applied to select the resources, to manage their combination layer by layer and to control the way of bringing them into play (i.e. enacting or putting them into action).

A competency is made up of resources divided into categories. According to the literature, there are three fundamental categories:

1. *Knowledge*: Knowledge is something that we acquire and store intellectually. It includes everything that can be learned in the education system or everything that requires preliminary classroom teaching. This category comprises theoretical knowledge (for instance, knowledge of the second law of thermodynamics), knowledge on existing things (for instance, knowledge of the operation of test-bed equipment for combustion engines), and procedural knowledge (for instance, knowledge of the assembly procedure of an electronic card for a programmable logic-type controller).

2. *Know-how*: Know-how is related to personal experience and working conditions. It is acquired by doing, by practice (for instance, experience in managing certain types of contracts). Synonyms are skills, operational capacities or experience. This category includes formalised know-how (for example, the application of working procedures) and empirical know-how. Empirical know-how is operational know-how that is hard to structure and to formalise. This know-how is generally dependent on the individual; it corresponds to tricks, instinct, tacit know-how, ability, talent, etc.

3. *Behaviour*: Behaviour is individual character or characteristics that lead someone to act or react in a certain way under certain circumstances. Behaviour often conditions the way knowledge and know-how are put into practice. This category includes human traits, qualities and attitudes; examples are initiative, tenacity, creativity, self-confidence, communication, curiosity, etc.

Note that, depending on what resources are mobilised, competencies are sometimes divided into two classes (Baugh, 1997):

I. *Hard Competencies*: Hard competencies identify the basic (and generally technical) resources that are required to perform an activity. These resources are generally expressed in terms of knowledge, skills and abilities (KSA).

II.   *Soft Competencies*: Soft competencies are personal behaviours, personal traits and motives (Woodruff, 1991). Examples of soft competencies are leadership (ability to guide, motivate and influence personnel to meet the organisation's goals), working with others, integrity, persuasiveness, adaptability (ability to readily adapt to new conditions, teams or tasks and to be receptive to new ideas or opinions), etc.

Hard competencies (KSA) are focused on technical aspects, whereas soft competencies make the difference at a given level of KSA. If you picture an iceberg, the soft competencies come below the water line, like the driving forces of an observable behaviour.

In this book, we focus on soft competencies, which we refer to as behavioural competencies or capabilities. Following Boyatzis (1982), these competencies are defined as an underlying characteristic of an individual that is causally related to successful performance of a particular job in a specific organisation. Boyatzis (1982) makes a distinction between differentiating competencies, which are the factors that distinguish a superior from an average performer, and threshold competencies, which are the essential characteristics needed to achieve average or acceptable performance. The differentiating and threshold competencies for a given job lead to a pattern and standard for personnel selection, succession planning, performance evaluation and employee development.

Being personal characteristics underlying behaviour, competencies are divided into five major groups in this approach (Mitrani et al., 1992):

a)   Motive: an underlying need or way of thinking that drives, guides and selects an individual's behaviour; for example, the need to achieve.

b)   Personality trait: a general predisposition to behave or react in a given manner, for example, tenacity, self-control, stress tolerance, etc.

c)   Self-concept (attitudes or values): what a person thinks, values, does or is interesting in doing; for example, inclination towards teamwork.

d)   Knowledge content: an individual's knowledge, both technical and related to interpersonal relationships; for example, knowledge of the market, of products, of processes, etc.

e)   Aptitudes and abilities (cognitive and behavioural capabilities): an individual's ability to perform a given activity type; for example, numerical reasoning, conferencing skill, etc.

These competencies are closely related to, combined with and complement each other in an individual. They can be related to performance through a simple causal flow model that indicates the motives, personality traits, attitudes and values and knowledge mobilised by a situation and are useful for predicting behaviour (aptitudes and abilities), which then forecasts performance. Competencies include an intent, an action and a result. For example, the motivation to achieve (marked interest in doing things better in compliance with an internalised standard of perfection and an interest in doing something original, one-off) will predict enterprising behaviours: setting goals, taking personal responsibility for results, assuming calculated risks. In organisations, these behaviours lead to a continuous improvement in quality, productivity, sales and other financial results, as well as innovation in the development of new products and services. Whereas performance improvement will be lower and ideas for new products or services will be fewer in organisations where the workforce is not motivated to achieve. Hence, the importance of considering these competencies for personnel characterisation in software development, which is a basically intellectual and social activity. We present an original capabilities model for assigning people to roles in software projects in Part II of the book.

A *behavioural competency* or *capability* is defined here as a behavioural skill or personal attribute of an individual that can be considered as characteristic of that person's behaviour and, according to which the activity-oriented behaviour can be classified logically and reliably. Capabilities are the element that integrates the software process area and the peopleware area or the organisational view (peopleware) and the production view (software process).

Note that the logic of core competencies, as we will see later, the theory upon which our book is based, is not a new approach in human resources management. This logic is now practised in many organisations for different purposes, such as personnel selection and recruitment, job analysis, organisational learning or financial evaluation (Hamel & Prahalad, 1994; Molleman & Broekhuis, 2001). However, this logic is not routinely applied yet in the context of the software process. Although there are interesting ad hoc solutions, such as the PARYS system (West, 1991) for the Automobile Association and Fraunhofer-IESE's Qualisem-People system (Hass, 2001), these are particular solutions for specific cases rather than general-purpose solutions. There are several accepted competency-based frameworks within the field of software engineering, for example:

- The Career-Space framework is a set of generic skills profiles covering the main job areas for which the European-wide ICT industry is experiencing skills shortages (http://www.career-space.com).

- APO-profiles, a German-wide initiative that is focusing on the description of job profiles in terms of work processes, associated activities and required competencies (http://www.apo-it.de).

- ESF-Baukasten (http://www.iese.fhg.de/ESF-Baukasten/) describes role-oriented competency profiles for the field of software engineering.

As mentioned in section 1.4, the process of assigning capabilities to roles used generically in productive organisations is based on the use of techniques and conceptual tools founded on well-established principles of psychology and, in particular, occupational psychology. One of the most commonly used methods is the Assessment Centre Method (Moses & Byham, 1997), which dates back to research into the best selection of officers in World War I and World War II. The use of this method in different disciplines has led to a number of benefits that have been repeatedly observed by researchers (Boam & Sparrow, 1992; Harzallah & Vernadat, 2002):

a) Better predictions of the behaviour of the person's on the job performance,

b) Lower level of inference by the evaluator or the person who is selecting,

c) Participation of managers in the evaluation process and

d) More powerful identification of weaknesses in specific skills.

The process model proposed here should be considered as a contribution to developing this logic of core competencies for the software field. Unlike the People CMM (Curtis et al., 2001), our model uses an adaptation of capabilities validated by the Assessment Centre Method (Moses & Byham, 1997) to deal with the more subjective part of the software process: people. The application of methods for assigning jobs to people based on matching their personal characteristics to the characteristics of the jobs in question can be divided into several steps. First, the roles to be performed in the activity in which the organisation is involved need to be characterised, as do the individuals available to an organisation. Second, a process of assignation needs to be run to match the individuals to the roles for which they are best suited. We will look at how to do this in software development organisations in Part II of the book.

1.6. MODELLING PEOPLEWARE IN THE SOFTWARE PROCESS

There are several problems related to the process descriptions in the models proposed to date (de Vasconcelos & Werner, 1997). For example, they do not cover all the subprocesses across the whole software construction process, they do not handle all the basic development elements (that is, organisation of work, projects, processes, activities, products, people, capabilities, roles and application tools) and the approach used is not structured enough to serve as a guide. To be useful, a process description needs to clearly establish and organise all the details related to the real or proposed process. The creation of such a description is not an easy task.

Traditionally, software process model representations have focused on three elemental process features: the activity, the artefact and the agent (human and computerised) (McChesney, 1995). However, other characteristics have been empirically proven to have a big influence on the production process: human roles and the organisation of work among human beings (Boehm, 1981; Adelson & Soloway, 1985; Curtis et al., 1988; Sherdil & Madhavji, 1996; Kawalek & Wastell, 1996; Humphrey, 1997; Humphrey, 1998a). Roles are partially dealt with by existing software process models (Finkelstein et al., 1994). The organisation of work is considered to be independent from the characteristics applied to model the software process (Min & Bae, 1997) or is ignored (Engels & Groenewegen, 1994), since the organisation of work is an organisational concern and, therefore, forms the environment of the software process and does not need to be explicitly modelled. Consequently, the approaches of current models do not integrally and jointly model the technical and organisational characteristics of the software process.

The need for highly trained personnel to develop software has been a subject of discussion since the 80s (Cougar & Zawacky, 1980; Whitaker, 1994; DeMarco & Lister, 1999). In the area of software process evaluation and improvement, there is now:

1.   The People CMM (Curtis et al., 1995a; Curtis et al., 2001), focused on the human resource factor.

2.   The Personal Software Process (Humphrey, 1997), focused on individual performance.

3.   The Team Software Process (Humphrey, 1998a), which deals with software process improvement at the team level.

In the area of software process modelling, however, the inclusion of people and their capabilities and the interaction in which they participate is not at all conceptualised or formalised (Min & Bae, 1997; Fuggetta, 2000).

Despite all the efforts and progress made in recent years, we are still without:

a)   A conceptualisation and formalisation of the inclusion of people and the interaction in which they participate (Engels & Groenewegen, 1994; Min & Bae, 1997; Pan et al., 1997; Leveson, 2000; Zhuge & Shi, 2001) and

b)   A systematic and disciplined process for including organisational aspects in software process modelling (Seaman & Basili, 1994; Kawalek & Wastell, 1996; Nguyen & Conradi, 1996; Crabtree, 2000).

On the one hand, the traditional models like IEEE STD 1074 (IEEE, 1997) and ISO/IEC 12207 (ISO/IEC, 1995; ISO/IEC, 2002), TRIAD (Ramanathan & Sarkar, 1988), Marvel (Kaiser et al., 1988), IPSE 2.5 (Warboys, 1989), SPADE (Bandinelli et al., 1993) do not specify the human parts of the software process in detail, or at least not as formally as the technical parts. On the other hand, the advanced models, like PMDB+ (Penedo & Shu, 1991), SOCCA (Engels & Groenewegen, 1994), ALF (Canals et al., 1994) and the Unified Process (Jacobson et al., 1999), which do explicitly include the technical and human parts and the interaction in which they are involved, do not define a method for including the people and their capabilities in the process model. Part I of this book will deal with these models in detail.

Therefore, as we will see from Part I of the book, the problems with the current software process models are:

a)   No definition of a model that covers the joint representation of processes, products, people and organisation,

b)   No formalisation in the software process of aspects like the organisation of work, people and their interactions and

c)   No defined process to include both the technical and human parts of the process in the model.

This book aims to remedy these weaknesses. The primary objective is to *define a group of peopleware activities*, which are normally missing from traditional software process models, to take into account the capabilities of the people who play roles in the software process. Additionally, it should represent the interactions between the original elements: people's capabilities and role capabilities. Another objective is to *define a method for including* peopleware issues in a software process model.

1.7. IMPORTANCE OF PEOPLEWARE IN THE PROCESS

The productivity of software developers and the quality of the software products and services provided are intrinsically dependent on the effectiveness of the associated processes. This view has driven work on software productivity and quality towards software process modelling, management and improvement upon the hypothesis that software product quality is determined by the quality of the production process (Tully, 1989; Sanders & Curran, 1994; Druffel, 1994; McDowell, 1994; Hinley, 1996). This hypothesis is added to in this book: the inclusion of people and organisations in the software process will improve the quality of the process (Sommerville & Rodden, 1995; Fuggetta, 2000) and, ultimately, of the resulting product.

The three lines of research discussed earlier, software process modelling, evaluation and improvement, are based on the hypothesis that the process influences product quality. Although leading researchers have suggested that the organisation and people influence software product quality, it is not a subject that the community is researching in depth. For example, Curtis et al. (1988) reached the conclusion that the "development of large software systems should be dealt with, at least partly, as a process of learning, communication and negotiation". Additionally, Curtis (1989) and Fuggetta (2000) maintain that few process models discuss how to organise and manage large development groups to maximise their coordination. This is, nevertheless, just as important as managing the software process.

The idea that it is essential to include the human parts and the interaction in which they participate in software process modelling is shared by (Curtis et al., 1988; Minsky & Rozenshtein, 1990; Humphrey, 1989; Abdel-Hamid & Madnick, 1991; Gruhn, 1992; Lonchamp, 1992; Seaman & Basili, 1994; Engels & Groenewegen, 1994; Yu & Mylopoulos, 1994; Humphrey, 1995; Kawalek & Wastell, 1996; Fuggetta, 2000). These researchers have determined some characteristics that should be considered from the modelling viewpoint:

- *The inclusion of the human parts should have the same abstract characteristics as the non-human parts.* Therefore, the data-related, behaviour-related and algorithm-related aspects should be clearly recognisable in the specification of the human parts. The inclusion of the human parts and the interaction in which they participate within an automated system is highly unusual in software engineering. It should be noted that the question of how to include the human parts of the system within the specification is being examined within the more general framework of Computer Supported Cooperative Work (CSCW), but remains an open question. As software process modelling can be considered as a special class of CSCW, whose non-human parts are easier to structure due to their technicality, the findings of such an approach are applicable or adaptable to this more general framework. What is required (Engels & Groenewegen, 1994) is a specification formalism for software process modelling that explicitly includes both the human parts and the interaction in which they are involved.

- *The inclusion of the human parts should consider what capabilities or behavioural competencies a person has to perform a given role in the software process.* People's capabilities are the least formalised factor in current software process models. However, their importance is evident (Yu & Mylopoulos, 1994; Sommerville & Rodden, 1995; Acuña & Juristo, 2004): people behave non-deterministically and subjectively, which has a decisive bearing on the result of software production that is an inherently intellectual and social activity. The knowledge of the capabilities of these people would mean that the software process could be designed and managed effectively, as deficient design and management are often rooted in the lack of commitment, interest and participation of the people involved. Human action is fundamental for the success and effectiveness of both the software process and the organisational process. Additionally, failure to specify the capabilities of the human beings means that the process does not reflect the actual state of the software process of the modelled organisation, with the added risk of processes being enacted that are not suited to the capabilities of the organisation's human resources (Seaman & Basili, 1994; Ellmer, 1996; Pan et al., 1997; Leveson, 2000; Stallinger & Grünbacher, 2001; Zhuge & Shi, 2001).

- *The inclusion of people should also consider how personal work is organised in the software process model,* as, to work effectively, people should have a clear understanding of their activities and organisational development. This determines what class of requirements need to be satisfied, eases understanding and representation of these requirements and identifies what changes are possible (Flood & Jackson, 1991; Ellmer, 1996; Checkland & Holwell, 1998; Checkland & Scholes, 1999; Baresi et al., 1999); that is, organisational aspects are essential in the software process requirements elicitation and analysis processes (Madhavji & Schäfer, 1991; Finkelstein et al., 1994). One of the reasons for considering organisational aspects in software process models is that software processes originate, and are applied and evaluated within the organisation. Another reason is that the information generated and structured during the elicitation and analysis process should serve as a starting point for the construction of the software process. Therefore, incorrect decisions, misinterpretations or any other mistakes made during this process have a critical impact on the design and construction and later enactment of the software process and, consequently, on the software product under construction. Finally, a process model that accounts for the motivations, cultural aspects, values, intuitions, reasoning and capabilities of the people involved and the organisational structure of work provides a better basis for the process engineer to model the broad implications of a process.

The view of software development as a process carried out by teams of people who have to be coordinated and managed within an effective organisational structure helps to identify the different dimensions of software development and the problems that need to be dealt with to establish effective practices. This view has switched from "software processes are software too" (Osterweil, 1987) to "software processes are processes too" (Fuggetta, 2000) in the understanding that dealing with the problems and questions of software development is not confined to the technological dimension, such as, for example, the introduction of an effective environment or the selection of a suitable life-cycle strategy. These questions are necessary but not sufficient. The organisational dimension, that is, the discipline of organisational and personal behaviour, should also be considered. Moreover, attention should be paid to the complex interrelationship between several organisational, cultural, technological and financial factors within the software development process. Fuggetta (2000) remarks upon the preconception that the software process was a special and unique sort of process and that, therefore, it was inappropriate or impossible to reuse the approaches and results produced by other communities (for example, CSCW, organisational behaviour, human resources management, etc.). This attitude has led to an even bigger problem. The software process community has redone part of the work carried out by other communities, without having benefited from their experience. This inability to analyse the results and contributions of other areas has considerably lowered the innovation rate. Additionally, the software community has missed out on the chance to learn from the mistakes of other researchers.

1.8. APPROACH FOR INCORPORATING PEOPLE'S CAPABILITIES INTO THE SOFTWARE PROCESS

The objective of this book is to incorporate the management of people's capabilities into the software development process. The inclusion of these aspects will make it possible to output software process models that meet the specified organisational, cultural and technological requirements, providing an exhaustive analysis of the people in the software process, as well as a modelling process and method, which is missing from the models now defined.

The approach taken to achieve this goal is based on incorporating people-oriented aspects into a traditional process model, such as IEEE STD 1074, to give it a wider scope and applicability range. As mentioned earlier, Part II of the book addresses this aim.

Two new activities need to be defined to incorporate people's capabilities into the process model. These activities are:

- *People's Capabilities Evaluation,* for modelling the capabilities of the people in the organisation, that is, the workforce profile. This activity is located within the *Organisational Activity Groups.* Unlike ISO/IEC 12207, which considers the organisational subprocesses of the life cycle, including the management infrastructure and training activities, IEEE STD 1074 does not include the organisational activity groups. The People's Capabilities Evaluation Activities are an original proposal, having required adaptation from the science of organisational and personal behaviour to software development. Chapters 6 and 7 discuss the original elements of these activities in detail, as they are the foundations for later assigning people to software project roles.

- *Assignation of People to Roles,* for assigning people to roles depending on their capabilities (determined in the People's Capabilities Evaluation Activities) and the capabilities required by each role defined in the software process. These activities are located within the *Project Management Activity Groups,* which creates the project and work team structure in IEEE STD 1074. Apart from the traditional activities, we include these activities of assigning people to roles. Chapters 8 and 9 discuss the original elements of these activities in detail, as they are the pillars for incorporating people's capabilities into the software process.

These two people-oriented activities (People's Capabilities Evaluation and the Assignation of People to Roles) should be independent from the software process model in use, allowing the modelling of people, roles and capabilities in the construction of software systems. The activities should be maintained within the organisational and project management view, respectively, in any software process model. This model allows the software process to be engineered, managed and enacted in relation to the organisation and in the profound understanding that software is the result of a complex process of communication.

The People's Capabilities Evaluation and the Assignation of People to Roles Activities are implemented by two methods: one for determining the capabilities of the members of the team, designed to represent the general software process models that include these people-related aspects (People's Capabilities Evaluation Method), and another for assigning and/or reallocating people to software project roles (Assignation of People to Roles Method).

We use concepts and techniques from the science of organisational and personal behaviour. In particular, we have recourse to two of the fields of behavioural science: organisational development and integrated people management.

Organisational development is a planned and systematic process of organisational change (Woodman, 1995; Hellriegel et al., 1998) and integrated people management is a planned and systematic process of competencies acquisition, human resource evaluation and competencies development within an organisation (Morales Gutiérrez et al., 1999; Pereda & Berrocal, 1999). Both areas are based on behavioural science research and theory. The goal of organisational development is to create adaptable organisations, capable of repeatedly transforming and reinventing themselves, as needed, to preserve effectiveness. Human resources management aims to optimise the person/job/results triad, develop the integration of people within the organisation and consider the needs of the people as well as the possibilities of the organisation. In particular, we take the approach of integrated people management by competencies, which defines the job profile depending on how people should behave to effectively perform a job (Morales Gutiérrez et al., 1999). Based on this approach, we put forward a definition of a profile for each role considered in software construction and a set of methods that can be used to define the capabilities of people and assign these people to the roles that they are best suited for. These fields of organisational behaviour borrow heavily from psychology, generally, and occupational psychology in particular and also feed off sociology. They are based on information from the theory of personality, the theory of learning and the theory of motivation and from research into group dynamics, power, leadership and organisational design. In other words, they are based on many well-established principles related to the behaviour of individuals and groups in organisations.

In Part II of this book, we also formalise the method for assigning people to roles according to people's capabilities and the capabilities demanded by the roles involved in the software process. A software tool has been developed to assign people to roles in software projects following the approach described in the book. The tool is called capabilityware. The process model has been formalised in UML (Acuña, 2002) and implemented as a tool that is available at http://www.ls.fi.upm.es/spt/. This tool is being used in two organisations in Argentina and one in Spain as an exploratory system for distributing roles in medium-sized software development projects. In this book, however, we will focus on people and their capabilities.

Part

Software Process Models

This part of the book focuses on describing the most representative software process models, which are analysed and compared with respect to their strengths and weaknesses. The software process models will be analysed from different perspectives: software process model type and guidance required for designing the models. In this chapter, we present the main software process models. These models are divided, according to how the model defines the process elements, into activity-oriented and people-oriented and, within these classes, according to their approach, into descriptive and prescriptive models. Chapter 2 gives an overview of the different models considered, whereas Chapters 3 and 4 describe activity-oriented and people-oriented models, respectively. Finally, Chapter 5 summarises the main benefits and drawbacks of the surveyed models. Readers interested in modelling only human roles and capabilities and not in particular process models can skip Part I.

Overview of Software Process Models and Descriptive Criteria for their Analysis

In this chapter, we present an overview of the process models that will be detailed in the following chapters. Depending on their focus, these models have been divided into two groups: activity-oriented and people-oriented models. Also we describe the criteria used to analyse the models, which will serve to ascertain their advantages and disadvantages.

2.1. SOFTWARE PROCESS MODELS

The parameter used here to classify the process models is based on defining what process elements the model covers. Specifically, the models analysed have been classified as shown in Figure 2.1.

The *Activity-Oriented Models* focus on defining the functions, activities and information of the software process management, development and/or supporting processes. The *People-Oriented Models* focus on defining the people involved in the software process and their relationships.

These two model categories are further divided into two alternatives depending on the goal for which the model was developed:

- Descriptive Models

- Prescriptive Models.

Descriptive Models are mainly concerned with specifying a process now used within an organisation or with representing a proposed process to be able to predict some process features. Descriptive models answer the question, "How is software now developed?" Or how has software been developed? (Lonchamp, 1993). *Prescriptive Models* focus on defining how the process should be enacted. Prescriptive models answer the question "How should software be developed?" (Lonchamp, 1993).

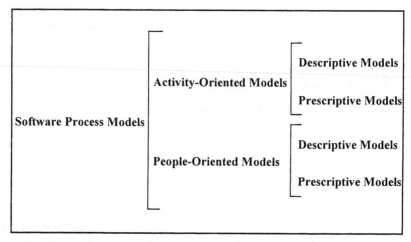

Figure 2.1. Classification used to analyse software process models

Table 2.1 lists the models belonging to each category. We have selected the most significant and representative models according to (Lonchamp, et al., 1990; Armenise et al., 1992; Lonchamp, 1994; McChesney, 1995; Ambriola et al., 1997; Fuggetta, 2000) for more detailed description in Chapters 3 and 4. They are listed in Table 2.1 under the surveyed models column. The selected models have served as a source of inspiration for most of the other models in this area (Finkelstein et al., 1994; Derniame et al., 1999; Acuña et al., 2001) or else somehow represent general features of other models (Beck et al., 2001).

In the following chapters, we will analyse the models that are representative of each class from the viewpoint of the software process dimensions described in the following section. It should be noted that this review includes both models that are designed to simply model the process and models that pursue other objectives, such as process evaluation, improvement or prediction. These models are also considered, because, to achieve their specific objectives, they model the process and are, therefore, of interest. The models surveyed in this part of the book are illustrated in Figure 2.2.

CLASS	SUBCLASS	SURVEYED MODELS	OTHER MODELS
Activity-Oriented Model	Descriptive	- TAME (Basili & Rombach, 1988) - FUNSOFT Nets-Based (Deiters & Gruhn, 1991) - STATEMATE (Kellner, 1991) - PRISM model of changes (Madhavji, 1992)	- Amadeus (Selby et al., 1991) - Wolf & Rosenblum (1993) - Conradi et al. (2000)
	Prescriptive	- TRIAD (Ramanathan & Sarkar, 1988) - Marvel (Kaiser, 1988a; Kaiser, 1988b) - IPSE 2.5 (Ould & Roberts, 1988; Warboys, 1989) - SPADE (Bandinelli et al., 1994) - ISO/IEC 12207-1995 (ISO/IEC, 1995; ISO/IEC, 2002) - IEEE 1074 (IEEE, 1997) - ISO 9001 (ISO-9001, 2000) - CMMI (SEI, 2002c; SEI, 2002d)	- GRAPPLE (Huff & Lesser, 1988) - HFSP (Katayama, 1989) - Appl/A (Sutton et al., 1990) - Articulator (Mi & Scacchi, 1990) - Minsky & Rozenshtein (1990) - Oikos (Ambriola & Jaccheri, 1991) - EPOS (Conradi et al., 1991b; Jaccheri et al., 1992; Conradi et al., 1994b) - Adele-Tempo (Belkhatir et al., 1993) - Hakoniwa (Iida et al., 1993) - LOTOS/SPD (Yasumoto et al., 1994) - E3 (Baldi et al., 1994) - Trillium (Bell, 1994) - DoD 2167A-1995 (DoD, 1995) - TickIT (BSI, 1995) - WADP (Weske et al., 1999)
People-Oriented Model	Descriptive	- Systems Dynamics Based (Abdel-Hamid & Madnick, 1989) - Process Cycle (Madhavji, 1991) - Agile Methods: eXtreme Programming (Beck, 1999) - WinWin (Boehm et al. 1998)	- Spiral Model (Boehm, 1988) - Cain & Coplien (1993) - Actor Dependency (Yu, 1993; Yu & Mylopoulos, 1994) - SCRUM (Schwaber, 1995) - DSDM (Stapleton, 1997) - Evo (Gilb, 2002)
	Prescriptive	- PMDB+ (Penedo & Shu, 1991) - ALF (Canals et al., 1994) - SOCCA (Engels & Groenewegen, 1994) - Unified Software Development Process or Unified Process (Jacobson et al., 1999) - People CMM (Curtis et al., 2001)	- CHAOS (De Cindio et al., 1988) - COSMOS (Yeh et al., 1991; Mittermeir & Schlemmer, 1992) - Conversation Builder (Kaplan et al., 1992) - MERLIN (Junkermann et al., 1994) - PADM (Bruynooghe et al., 1994) - PEACE (Arbaoui & Oquendo, 1994) - OPEN (Graham et al., 1997) - Personal Software Process (Humphrey, 1997) - ISO/IEC 15504 (ISO/IEC 15504, 1998) - Team Software Process (Humphrey, 1998a)

Table 2.1. Models of each class found in the literature

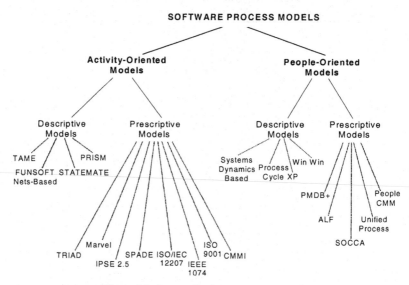

Figure 2.2. Surveyed software process models

Two dimensions are used to evaluate and compare the models shown in Figure 2.2. These are the modelling dimension and the representation dimension. The two dimensions (modelling and representation) have been established on the basis of the features of the existing models and the features that software process models should ideally have, with the aim of providing a good understanding, organisation and evaluation of the state of the art in software process modelling.

The criteria examined for each model are described below.

2.2. DESCRIPTIVE CRITERIA

2.2.1. Modelling-Related Criteria

The modelling dimension is divided into two top-level criteria. These criteria determine the process features that a model can model. Any individual model will explicitly model a given range of process features, which make up a range of descriptors associated with the model. The process features that can be explicitly modelled by existing approaches are:

- Process elements represented by the model. The possible values are one or more agents, activities, artefacts, roles, capabilities and events.

- Process environments covered by the model. The possible values are organisational environment, social environment and technological environment.

The meaning of the different values is described in the following.

2.2.1.1. Elements

The basic process-related *Elements* are outlined below:

- *Agent* or *Actor*: an entity (person or system) that enacts a process. Actors can be divided into two groups as regards their relationship to the computer: a) human actors, who are the people who develop software or are involved in the software *process* and are possibly organised as teams; and b) system actors or system tools, which are the computer software or hardware components. An actor is characterised by the properties of its role and its availabilities. An actor can play several roles, which are composed of consistent sets of activities. A role can be played by several co-operative actors.

- *Role*: a description of a set of agent or group responsibilities, rights, skills and capabilities required to perform a specific software process activity. This is an association between agents and activities in terms of a defined set of responsibilities executed by agents.

- *Capability*: an underlying trait of a person, which is causally related to good or excellent performance in a particular role in a particular organisation. Personal capabilities determine behaviours, indicating the person's general predisposition to *behave* or react in a given way, for example, tenacity, self-control, stress tolerance, etc.

- *Activity*: the stage of a process that produces externally visible changes of state in the software product. An activity can have an input, an output and some intermediate results, commonly termed products (for example, requirements specification documents, database schemata, etc.). The activity includes and implements procedures, rules, policies and goals to generate and modify a set of given *artefacts*. An activity can be performed by a human agent or using a tool. The activities can be divided into more elementary activities; that is, there are elementary or compound activities. The activities can be organised in networks with both horizontal (chained) and vertical (decomposition) dimensions. The activities are associated with roles, other activities and artefacts.

-   *Artefact* or *Product*: the output and input of an activity. The products can be created, accessed or modified during a process activity. An artefact produced by an activity can be used later as raw material for the same or another activity to produce other artefacts. An artefact can have a long lifetime, and there may be different versions of each artefact as the software process evolves.

-   *Event*: a noteworthy occurrence happening at a specific moment in time. Event-based models provide a different view of the activities, thereby evidencing process dynamism.

2.2.1.2. Environments

The *Environment* criterion identifies the contexts that influence and are influenced by the software process. Software process models should consider three interrelated environments: the organisational environment, the social environment and the technological environment. These environments are described as follows:

-   *Organisational environment*: this criterion indicates whether the models account for organisational issues, such as the culture, behaviour, design, development and evolution of the organisation.

-   *Social environment*: this criterion indicates whether the models cover the people involved, the relationships between these people and with the organisation, that is, capabilities such as creativity, social interaction within a team and flexibility of the organisation with respect to the environment, etc.

-   *Technological environment*: this criterion indicates whether the models cover the software techniques, tools, infrastructure, environments and methodologies for both the production of software and the management, improvement and control of the software process.

2.2.2. Representation-Related Criteria

This second dimension has to do with what guidance is provided for organising the information in a model, what properties the process modelling notation has and what quality of information the software process model representation affords. There are two types of representation-related criteria:

-   Information perspectives

-   Notational characteristics.

The information perspectives are related to the organisation of the information captured within a process model by applying different viewpoints: functional, behavioural, organisational and informational. These viewpoints can be combined to provide an integrated, consistent and complete process description. The notational characteristics are also presented from different viewpoints: a) information quality, which refers to the manner in which the software process model components are represented: informal, formal or automated, and b) formalised notation, which refers to the format: text or graphic.

The meaning of the possible values of the representation-related criteria is described below.

2.2.2.1. Information Perspectives

The information in a process model can be structured from different viewpoints. Curtis lists the following *Information Perspectives* commonly found in the literature (Curtis et al., 1992):

- *Functional perspective*: This represents what process elements are being executed and what information item flows are relevant for these elements.

- *Behavioural perspective*: This represents when (that is, order) and under which conditions the process elements are triggered.

- *Organisational perspective*: This represents where and by whom in the organisation the process elements are executed.

- *Informational perspective*: This represents the information items output or manipulated by a process, including their structure and relationships.

The models are built according to the languages, abstractions or formalisms created for representing the specific information about these information perspectives. The most commonly used language in practice is (structured) natural language due to its flexibility. Table 2.2 lists the representation abstractions (excluding natural language) organised according to the above-mentioned perspectives. These are the most popular abstractions used in software process research. None of these abstractions covers all the information perspectives. Therefore, most of the models found in the literature employ languages based on more than one of these abstractions. These models integrate multiple representation paradigms (that is, different process models), although this generally makes the model definition more complicated (de Vasconcelos & Werner, 1997).

LANGUAGE BASE	INFORMATION PERSPECTIVES
Procedural programming language (Ramanathan & Sarkar, 1988)	Functional Behavioural Informational
Systems analysis and design, including data flow diagram (Frailey, 1991), structured analysis and design technique (SADT) and structure diagrams (McGowan & Bohner, 1993)	Functional Organisational Informational
Artificial intelligence languages and approaches, including rules and pre-/postconditions (Barghouti et al., 1995)	Functional Behavioural
Events and triggers // Control flow (Finkelstein et al., 1994)	Behavioural
State transition and Petri nets (Deiters & Gruhn, 1991; Bandinelli et al., 1995) // Statecharts (Kellner & Hansen, 1989; Kellner, 1991; Harel & Politi, 1998; Raffo & Kellner, 1999)	Functional Behavioural Organisational
Functional languages // Formal languages (Curtis et al., 1992; Huff, 1996)	Functional
Data modelling, including entity-relationship diagrams, relationship declarations and structured data (Penedo & Shu, 1991)	Informational
Object modelling, including class and instance types, hierarchy and inheritance (Engels & Groenewegen, 1994)	Organisational Informational
Quantitative modelling, including quantitative operational research and systems dynamics techniques (Abdel-Hamid & Madnick, 1991)	Behavioural
Precedence networks, including actor dependency modelling (Yu & Mylopoulos, 1994; Briand et al., 1995)	Behavioural Organisational

Table 2.2. Information perspectives of the process and the applicable language bases

2.2.2.2. Notational Characteristics

As mentioned earlier, this aspect is addressed from two viewpoints: information quality and formalised notation.

Information quality indicates whether the models provide informal, formal or automated specifications of the software process modelling elements. These values are:

- *Informal specifications*: manual, qualitative, subjective and informal representation of the process.

- *Formal specifications*: formal representation of the process, related to the formal description or prescription of the process.

- *Automated specifications*: computerised representation of the process. Automated models may include the features and principles of their manual counterparts, but they are automated to some extent and the recommended set of possible steps are restricted to the ones permitted by the model.

From the viewpoint of *Formalised notation*, some models adopt a *text*-based representation for the process model, whereas others take a *graphic*-based approach.

2.2.3. Criteria Employed by Other Authors

There are a number of reference frameworks for classifying and characterising software process models (Madhavji, 1991; Conradi et al., 1991a; Mi & Scacchi, 1991; Curtis et al., 1992; Benali & Derniame, 1992; Armenise et al., 1993; Lonchamp, 1993; Lonchamp, 1994; McChesney, 1995; Ambriola et al., 1997). Traditionally, classification schemas have focused on the process modelling language style (Madhavji, 1991; Kellner, 1991; Conradi et al., 1991a; Mi & Scacchi, 1991; Armenise et al., 1993). The selection of one or more styles depends principally on the information perspectives (Curtis et al., 1992) according to which the model elements are organised and on the notational characteristics used (Lonchamp et al., 1990). This book uses these two criteria.

Benali and Derniame (1992) presented an informal basis for assessing the scope of a software process model, highlighting the essential properties of the software process that a modelling formalism should represent. This basis takes into account three aspects: "what does the software process model?", "who are the process actors?" and "when do the actors intervene in the process?" Later, more systematic software process model classifications were developed. McChesney (1995) proposed a classification schema for comparing, characterising and applying different software process modelling approaches. This schema considers four dimensions on the basis of which these approaches can be characterised (McChesney, 1995): a) the objectives for which the model is used; b) the properties of the process modelling language; c) the process features that can be modelled; and d) the world view associated with the approach. This schema allows a more rigorous comparison of the existing process models. However, it does not include the ideal or required characteristics for comparing and evaluating models. To give a better understanding of the field of software process modelling, Lonchamp (1994) developed a four-part assessment grid: a) software process modelling approaches, b) process modelling language, c) metaprocesses, and d) representation engine. Ten European universities who were involved in projects related to software process modelling and technology completed this grid.

However, the existing classification schemas do not systematically address the features of a model considered in the context of its relationships to other entities: organisations, social interaction activities and modelling procedures. The traditional classification criteria focus on the technological dimension and do not include the organisational dimension, whose presence, although its development within software modelling is in its early days, has grown in more recent research. This transition is taking place as process engineers become aware of the importance of the social and cultural environment on the initiation, development, application and evaluation of high-quality software processes.

Chapter 3

Activity-Oriented Models

In this chapter, we describe both the descriptive and prescriptive activity-oriented models shown in the previous chapter (Table 2.1). For each model, the values of the criteria considered are highlighted in italic print.

3.1. DESCRIPTIVE ACTIVITY-ORIENTED MODELS

The models belonging to this category generally pursue one the following objectives:

- *Process Evaluation*, which aims to identify the characteristics of the process in the course of or after process enactment, for the purpose of comparing the main process features against an ideal process.

- *Process Improvement*, which is implicit in process evaluation, as data collected from the assessment are recorded and are systematically available for future projects. At present, however, as research into product and process metrics (López Fernández, 1998) to evaluate the product and process quality for improving software quality is prominent, a descriptive model can be developed explicitly for the purpose of improvement.

- *Process Prediction*, which refers to analysing the software process to predict its future behaviour. Some specific aspects of the process that can be predicted are: development time, manpower, bottlenecks and deadlocks, etc.

The descriptive activity-oriented models analysed in this book are presented below. As mentioned in Table 2.1, the most representative of this group are as follows:

- TAME model (Basili & Rombach, 1988)

- FUNSOFT Nets-based model (Deiters & Gruhn, 1991)

- STATEMATE model (Kellner, 1991)

- PRISM model of changes (Madhavji, 1992).

3.1.1. TAME Model

The TAME model (Tailoring A Measurement Environment) (Basili & Rombach, 1988) and the associated TAME system are the result of a project of the same name developed at the University of Maryland, which is based on the Quality Improvement and Goal-Question-Metric (GQM) paradigm. The objective of the TAME model is to gather, validate and analyse the process data to assess the characteristics of the process in place, identify problems and give recommendations on software product and process improvement.

The model sets out a goal-question-metric process enactment. This model is composed of: a) a set of templates designed to establish the project goals (suited to the specific needs of an organisation), and b) a set of guidelines for deriving the questions and metrics. The goals are defined in terms of purpose, perspective and environment. There are different sets of guidelines for defining the product- and process-related questions. The product-related questions are formulated for the purpose of defining the product (for example, physical attributes, cost, changes, defects, context), defining the quality perspective (for example, reliability, usability) and providing feedback. The process-related questions are formulated for the purpose of defining the process (for example, quality of use, domain of use), defining the quality perspective (for example, defect reduction, cost effectiveness) and for providing feedback. The GQM model has been applied at numerous organisations to specify what data should be collected to evaluate different aspects of the process and product (Basili, 1985; Basili & Rombach, 1987b; Grady, 1987; Rombach & Basili, 1987; Selby et al., 1987).

Basili and Rombach (1988) formalised the GQM paradigm for the following tasks: characterisation of the current state of the project environment and project planning construction, analysis, learning and feedback. Each of these tasks is dealt with from a constructive and analytical viewpoint, that is, the model integrates methods and tools for building the products (constructive viewpoint) and methods and tools to analyse the construction processes and products output (analytical viewpoint). The TAME model is shown in Figure 3.1, where the relationships (arcs) between the process model tasks represent information flows. The experience base is the body of the experience gathered within a project or organisational environment. The project personnel includes engineers (that is, designers, coders, etc.) and software development managers.

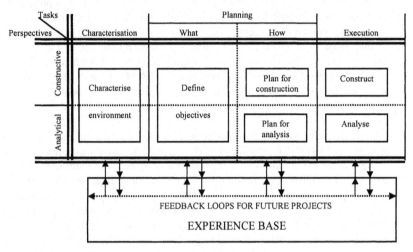

Figure 3.1. TAME improvement-oriented software process model (Basili & Rombach, 1988)

The model represents the following process elements: *agent, activity* (called task in TAME) and *artefact*. This model accounts for the *organisational* and *technological environments*. It does not cover the characteristics of the social environment or the methods and tools for its identification. TAME employs the *functional, behavioural* and *informational* perspectives to organise the information in the model, interpreting the process generally as a software-solvable problem and particularly as a sequential problem (Basili & Rombach, 1987a). As regards its notational characteristics, from the viewpoint of the quality of the information represented, it is *formalised* and from the viewpoint of the notation, it has a *text*-based format.

3.1.2. FUNSOFT Nets-Based Model

The goal of Deiters and Gruhn's model (1991) is to analyse the properties of the software process elements based on FUNSOFT nets to predict the future behaviour of the process. This model predicts specific aspects of the basic elements of the modelled process, for example, the time it takes to do each activity, bottlenecks and process deadlocks. These predictions are made on the basis of the representation and enactment of the process by means of FUNSOFT nets. FUNSOFT nets (Gruhn, 1991; Deiters & Gruhn, 1990) are based on a high-level Petri net notation founded on predicate/transition nets (Genrich & Lautenbach, 1981; Genrich, 1986). These nets provide extensions that are useful for supporting software process modelling, including, for example, the ability to connect a policy with places (random, FIFO, LIFO) to each software product. Being a Petri net-based formalism, FUNSOFT nets naturally represent non-determinism and parallelism. A value can also be associated with a transition to model the duration of the activity represented by that transition. This information is then used to simulate the behaviour described by the net in the simulation process. The process elements, such as agent, activity and artefact, are described using an extendible set of object types. FUNSOFT nets are suitable for representing complex activities. These nets support the analysis of the properties of the modelling process, and dynamic process simulation and modification.

The model represents the following process elements: *agent, activity, artefact* and *event*. FUNSOFT nets can model, analyse and enact the software process using a *graphic notation*, where the information quality is *formalised*. While this extended formalism improves software process modelling, Petri nets were not originally developed for this purpose. Consequently, the constructs or abstractions (transitions, states, arcs) of the modelling process supported by the formalism do not match the entities of the software process elements at equivalent levels of abstraction (Min & Bae, 1997). The model information is organised from the *functional, behavioural* and *organisational perspectives.* This representation has no informational perspective.

As regards the process environments, this model only considers the *technological environment*. It does not specify the process roles, the organisational aspects or the sociocultural characteristics of the people involved; it omits the organisational and social environments.

3.1.3. STATEMATE Model

This formalism was not originally developed to model the software process. The STATEMATE system was designed as an aid for specifying and designing real-time reactive systems (Harel et al., 1990). It was later used by the Software Engineering Institute at Carnegie Mellon University to model software processes (Humphrey & Kellner, 1989; Kellner, 1989; Kellner, 1990; Kellner, 1991). Its goal is to analyse and simulate process models to provide process predictions, such as development time and effort. These predictions are made by modelling the process elements and their properties, for example, activity duration, time required per person for each activity, etc., by means of interrelated statecharts, activity charts and module charts, implementing this process on a software system, and enacting and simulating the process.

STATEMATE uses module charts to describe an artefact or product as a data item. This formalism does not provide data typing. The data items can be added, but there is no visible construct for the composition. This reduces the product analysis capability. As STATEMATE does not support typing, it cannot represent different types of project resources (people, tools, etc.).

STATEMATE can represent the processes at different levels of abstraction. Refinement into less complex processes and their relationships are documented in the activity charts. The state and event matrix is represented by statecharts. Therefore, this formalism represents the process hierarchy and operation. Because of the specific (structured) use of statecharts, this formalism does not have special constructs for representing the software process-dependent particularities and can only give a general description (Kellner, 1991).

On the one hand, the product flow, that is, the order of the activities performed to modify or transform all or part of the product, is described by means of statecharts. The functional parts of a process are connected or related by means of data flows from STATEMATE's functional perspective. Any direct connection is labelled with the respective data item. On the other hand, the control flow, that is, the order of software process enactment, is represented explicitly by a special language called activity charts. The descriptive form of this document and the explicit representation of the relationships allows the process to be analysed from the behavioural viewpoint.

Processes and resources are mapped by means of connections between the functional and organisational charts in STATEMATE. These connections are labelled "responsibility" and express who is responsible for performing a given process. STATEMATE provides this mechanism, provided that the resources are fully modelled in the module charts. But STATEMATE cannot express tool invocation. Additionally, although the organisational chart is used to describe and aggregate the people involved in the project, the module charts do not satisfactorily support all classes of resources (Rombach & Verlage, 1993).

The process elements represented by the model are: *agent, activity, artefact* and *event.* People's capabilities, such as creativity, social interaction and flexibility, are not specified. Consequently, the model does not account for the social environment of the process. On the other hand, this model does address the *organisational* and *technological environments.*

STATEMATE uses three different models to represent three software process aspects: *functional* (what is to be done), *behavioural* (when and how something is to be done) and *organisational* (where a task is done and by whom). From the functional perspective, the model specifies the functions similarly to structured analysis methods, using statecharts. From the behavioural perspective, the process model is represented by means of activity charts. From the organisational perspective, the module charts aid the specification of the organisational aspects of the system (Kellner & Hansen, 1988). The separate views of a software process are later related to provide a comprehensive model of real-life activity. As regards STATEMATE's notational characteristics, the notation emulates these three representation languages, and is *formalised* and *graphic*.

The model information is organised from four perspectives: *functional, organisational, informational* (present in the product flows of the modified statecharts) and *behavioural*. Unlike the other approaches that we have looked at so far, STATEMATE does consider all the information representation perspectives in the software process model.

3.1.4. PRISM Model of Changes

The PRISM Model of Changes, designed within a project of the same name, is an abstract description of a software environment that specialises in the problem of change within a software project (Madhavji, 1992). It formalises the change process of the principal software process element types: people, policies, laws, resources, processes and results. The PRISM model was developed on the basis of this model of change management, within the framework of the PRISM project (Madhavji & Schäfer, 1991). This model is an experimental process-oriented environment, which supports the methodology, development, instantiation and enactment of software processes. Process-oriented environment means the development process model, the description and relationship between process components, and process storage, enactment and improvement.

The PRISM model is composed of four vertices: methodology, development, instantiation and execution. The methodology vertex states the methods used during the engineering process, assuring that this process is not ad hoc (Madhavji & Schäfer, 1991). The development, instantiation and enactment vertices (Tully, 1989) are specified for the development, instantiation and execution of the processes. These three central vertices are explicitly interrelated to highlight how the key elements of a process-oriented environment are related. These iterative relationships underlying the model, called simulation, initialisation and operation in PRISM, show the main cycles involved in the incremental and methodological development, instantiation and enactment of processes:

- Simulation cycle, where a generic process model is constructed, which may be meant to be embedded in the process that is executed in the operation phase. A generic model is not restricted by real parameters, such as company resources, and is based on the user requirements and software project documents.

- Initialisation cycle, where the process model is incrementally instantiated in the process-oriented environment. The right real parameters are assigned at this stage. The initialisation cycle can partially remodel and re-tailor the instantiated process model.

- Operation cycle, where real software is produced. It provides for the evaluation and improvement of the software process being executed.

The three cycles of the metaprocess described (simulation, initialisation and operation) are supported by three components of the same name in the PRISM environment architecture (Madhavji & Schäfer, 1991). Additionally, this architecture has three interfaces: user, tool and objectbase interfaces. These interfaces allow: a) environment users to interact with the components depending on their software project roles; b) the appropriate tools to be invoked by the components in all three metaprocess cycles; and c) the tools to access an objectbase to store and retrieve information if and when required in each of the three cycles.

The metaprocesses enacted by the simulation, initialisation and operation components are respectively referred to as simulation, initialisation and operation metaprocesses. Each of these components is composed of two basic items: an explicit representation of an appropriate metaprocess description and an interpreter for this description. The operation component also contains a description of the product software process and its interpreter (Madhavji & Schäfer, 1991).

The characteristics of the metaprocesses of simulation, initialisation and operation and the objectbase of the PRISM environment architecture are briefly analysed in Table 3.1. This table states the values for the following criteria: process elements that the model represents and characteristics of the formalised notation.

As Madhavji states, the model explicitly determines the dependencies between traditional elements of change (software products, processes and resources) and non-traditional elements of change, such as software project people, policies and laws. Therefore, the model represents the *technological environment*, where the process policies, laws, infrastructures and standardisation are generated, and the *organisational environment*, where the process engineers, managers and developers create, tailor and execute models. But, the PRISM model does not specify the social environment, as it does not cover the capabilities of the people involved in the process.

As regards the information perspectives, the PRISM model integrates the *organisational, informational* and *functional* approaches, which drive the construction of the software process models. The description of both the metaprocess and the product software process is represented in a language called FUNSOFT, (Deiters et al., 1989), where the *quality of the information represented is automated*. The notational format of this language is both *text* and *graphic*.

COMPONENTS		CHARACTERISTICS
Simulation, Initialisation and Operation	Metaprocess programs	A metaprocess description contains the following basic components, some of which have a *graphic notation* and others a *text notation*: (a) *element types (artefacts, agents)*, (b) *activity types*, (c) *safeguard activities*, (d) *relationships between activity types*, and (e) *exception-handling mechanisms*. The text parts are incrementally translated to the function nets version for description interpretation.
	Interpreter	The function nets are interpreted by *executing the pre- and postconditions of several activities and invoking the specified tools*. As there may be several activities that should be permitted in a given context, the interpreter visualises a user agenda. The process can be executed sequentially and concurrently for software development.
Objectbase		It includes fragments of software process descriptions, specific data on *tools*, such as their functionality, performance, reliability, portability and compatibility with other tools, personal particulars and software components and documents.

Table 3.1. Characteristics of the PRISM environment architecture components

3.2. PRESCRIPTIVE ACTIVITY-ORIENTED MODELS

These models are manual standards or automated prescriptions that specify the processes for developing and maintaining or managing software or for evaluating these processes. As many different models were analysed in this class, the prescriptive activity-oriented models have been divided for description and analysis into:

- Process Models

- Evaluation Models.

The group named *process models* includes both the main manual process standards that can be applied to initiate, plan, manage, support, develop, operate, maintain and evaluate the software products and some automated software process prescriptions. These models provide a common framework that can be used by all the people who participate in the software process.

Within the prescriptive activity-oriented process models, a variety of multiparadigm approaches have been proposed for modelling software processes. Most are structured around a primary paradigm, like rules (for example, Marvel), imperative programs (for example, TRIAD/LMC), object-orientation (IPSE 2.5) or Petri nets (for example, SPADE). These models are computerised prescriptive specifications of the software process activities.

The process models examined in the section are:

- Automated prescriptive software process activity-oriented models: TRIAD (Ramanathan & Sarkar, 1988), Marvel (Kaiser, 1988a; Kaiser, 1988b), IPSE 2.5 (Ould & Roberts, 1988; Warboys, 1989) and SPADE (Bandinelli et al., 1994).

- Development process standards. The models reviewed here are: ISO/IEC 12207 (ISO/IEC, 1995; ISO/IEC, 2002) and IEEE STD 1074 (IEEE, 1997).

The group called *evaluation models* rises to the aim of defining a model of an ideal software process as a yardstick against which to evaluate a process and thus identify the aspects for improvement in an organisation. Under the heading of prescriptive activity-oriented models designed for evaluation, we describe the software process that the evaluation method uses as a yardstick.

The evaluation models examined in this section are methods based on standards or on software process evaluation models applied internationally, which are the most widespread and most commonly used at present. The models reviewed here are: ISO 9001 (ISO-9001, 2000) and CMMI (SEI, 2002c; SEI 2002d).

3.2.1. Process Models

3.2.1.1. TRIAD Model

TRIAD is a research prototype of a third-generation integrated project support environment (IPSE) based on a model with prescriptions expressed in an imperative style (Ramanathan & Sarkar, 1988). It uses a conceptual modelling language (CML), which includes the following four related models:

- Process model, which represents the hierarchy of communication of sequential activity types.

- Data model, which specifies a semantic object-oriented data model.

- Tool model, which describes the function of each tool and defines the appropriate invocation paradigm.

- User model, which represents the roles of the members of the project staff and their relationships.

TRIAD provides a hierarchical structure of activity types. Each activity type includes: a) a precondition and a postcondition, b) zero or more attributes, including references to objects and database tools, c) zero or more subactivities, d) a number of local variables, and e) an action part that contains imperative code.

The following sentences can be used to control the process model execution:

- Create task, delete task: dynamically create and delete instances of (sub)activities.

- Begin subactivities: starts the execution of the subactivities of an activity instance.

- Wait for user, send task and wait for task, wait for subactivities: assure data synchronisation and/or exchange between a user and an activity, between two activities and between an activity and its subactivities.

A typical execution starts with an explicit command from the project manager. This execution involves the following aspects (Lonchamp et al., 1990): a) the action part of the principal activities originates the subactivities for the main development phases (for example, requirements, design), associates these subactivities with the manager (owner) and begins execution; b) the sequence and overlap of these subactivities are determined by their preconditions; and c) each phase recursively creates subactivities for the tasks within the phase up to the desired detail level. There is an elementary form of reasoning on the database rules, which generates a forward-chaining control paradigm. These rules are exclusively appended to the primitive data operations.

This model characterises the three software process roles: process model designer, manager and developer. The designer role of the software process model describes a specific assistant for a project in CML. The TRIAD approach does not establish a standard model (for example, the description of a development method) and how to tailor it for a particular context. The software process model manager role compiles the CML description into an intermediate representation that can be interpreted by a generic machine. The model can only be adapted and changed during the process lifetime within the limits of the predefined program specifications (for example, the creation of activity instances that are coded for each programmer designed by the manager of the programming phase). Any structural change (for example, the creation of new activity types or the change of a precondition) involves updating and recompiling the model; there is no information on the retrieval of the current state of the development process in such circumstances. The TRIAD model developer role is a "human device", driven by explicit synchronisation/communication sentences in the program (for example, the sentence "wait for user"). These sentences allow the system: a) to take the developer through the steps by presenting a selection of options from the activity-specific menu, and b) return control to the user to perform the creative aspects of a task.

This model represents the following elements: *agent (human and system tool), activity* and *role*. This model addresses the *technological environment*, but not the organisational and social environments, which are missing.

TRIAD employs the *functional, behavioural* and *informational perspectives* to organise the information in the model. The quality of the information of the guidance or assistance representation that it provides is *automated*. The formalised notation of this representation is *text*-based.

3.2.1.2. Marvel Model

The Marvel model is a third-generation IPSE architecture with a heuristic software process modelling approach. Its concepts and its rule-based metalanguage have been validated by three different research prototypes (Kaiser, 1988a; Kaiser, 1988b). This model uses the Marvel strategy language (MSL) to specify three classes of knowledge:

- Software engineering artefact types and relationships between them.

- Computerised tools with inputs, outputs and secondary effects with respect to the artefacts.

- Rules that regulate the software project progress and allow the controlled automation of minor activities.

Marvel rules are composed of a name, followed by parameters and by a three-part body: a) a precondition, which should be true before the activity can be executed; b) an activity, which names a tool (for example, compiler) and an operation (for example, compile or optimise) with arguments; and c) a set of postconditions (where only one will be true after the activity has been completed), which describe the successful completion and error classes that can be detected by the tool. The preconditions and postconditions are written as formulas founded on first-order logic.

Marvel's generic engine interprets the rules to provide the controlled automation of activities: a) by forward chaining, when the preconditions of the activities are satisfied, and b) by backward chaining, when one of the postconditions of a tool is required (for example, to force satisfaction of the precondition of an operation required by a user). This class of automation is called opportunistic processing, because Marvel invokes the tools when the opportunity arises. The reasoning engine is unable to consider effects not described in the postconditions. In some descriptions of Marvel (Kaiser & Feiler, 1987; Kaiser, 1988a), the preconditions of the options activities can be expressed by rules without postconditions. These rules are used to guide the inference engine during forward chaining (for example, so that an activity can be used under different circumstances in the same process).

However, the Marvel implementation describes an inference engine that works in a rigid and predefined fashion (Lonchamp et al., 1990). For example, when an activity is triggered by the planner, Marvel can never undo it, even if the plan fails and the engine goes back. Additionally, Marvel has no decomposition of activities; it uses a flat representation of each activity, which is directly implemented by a tool.

This model characterises the three software process roles: process model designer, manager and developer (called "users" in Marvel). With respect to the role of software process model designer, a "superuser" writes a "strategies" library. A strategy is a module with a strict interface, which includes entities, tools and rules suited for a particular phase of a project, for a particular category of users, etc. Some strategies are self-contained, others are incomplete and must be combined with one or more other strategies to provide an executable model. Generic strategies can be written, although most papers describe project-related strategies (strategies do not have parameters). The Marvel model does not explicitly specify the software process model manager role. However, there are functions corresponding to the manager role. For example, before the process starts: a) load a subset of the strategies library to initiate a Marvel environment with the descriptions of the representation language it uses (these strategies are combined after verification by the MSL consistency checker); and b) save the initiated environments. The strategies can be dynamically loaded, combined and unloaded during the process lifetime. Extendibility and dynamic adaptability are supported provided that consistency is preserved. The software process developer role uses an instantiated Marvel environment similar to a classical environment by invoking tools. However, this environment has other assistance facilities. For example, if a user invokes a tool that is not executable, Marvel tries to automatically satisfy the false precondition; when a tool terminates, Marvel can execute complementary minor activities; object and activity searching and querying, explanations when a backward chaining fails, etc.

The Marvel model represents the following elements: *artefact, agent (system tool)* and *activity*. This model only considers *technological aspects*. It does not explicitly address organisational characteristics or the capabilities of the people involved. Therefore, the organisational and social environments are rated as not covered.

Marvel model information is organised from the *functional* and *behavioural perspectives*. The quality of this information determines an *automated* representation of the software process activities. But, the assistance provided by this representation through controlled automation of the elementary activities during the implementation, testing and maintenance phases of software development is weak. The formalised notation adopted is *text*-based.

3.2.1.3. IPSE 2.5 Model

This third-generation IPSE approach is based on a conceptual view of object-oriented software processes (Ould & Roberts, 1988; Warboys, 1989). So, a software process consists of a number of distinct, concurrent activities corresponding to many collaborating roles. These roles and their interactions are objects that should be modelled.

The process modelling language permits an object-oriented style description of these aspects. The notions of classification/instantiation, specialisation and aggregation/decomposition are part of the process modelling language. The model is structured as five classes, which are primitive object groups whose behaviour is constructed in the language. Each class defines a set of property categories that determine what property types the classes of each category can contain. The primitive classes are as follows:

- Role, with the resources of the property categories (the data of the objects that belong to the role), associations (the interaction of objects with which the role communicates), actions and interactions that operate in the role, role start and stop conditions.

- Action, manual or automatic.

- Interaction, that is, multiparty, two-way, synchronised communication; cooperation is not assured in IPSE 2.5 because of object sharing.

- Entity, resources belonging to roles.

- Statements, set of Boolean expressions with arguments, used, for example, to define roles, action start and stop conditions and interactions. They initiate or fire activities; the action orderings are expressed by the start and stop conditions.

The IPSE 2.5 model identifies the roles of software process designer, manager and developer. The designer role constructs a model by creating subclasses of primitive classes, subclasses of these classes and, so on, in the usual object-oriented manner. The role of manager (model user in IPSE terminology) specialises, for example, a generic role, an entity, action classes, etc., defined by the designer according to the needs of an individual project. To execute the model, the user (administrator or developer) instantiates roles and assigns values to the entities. Users can dynamically extend the model. The developer role interacts with the environment when manual actions are initiated or fired through model execution by the process control engine. The engine is limited only by the statements present in the model at the time of interaction. The automated actions can be initiated as needed.

This model represents the following process elements: *agent (human and system tool), activity, artefact* and *role*. The model addresses the *technological aspects*. The organisational characteristics are only considered implicitly, and creativity, social interaction and flexibility of the people involved in the process are missing. Therefore, the organisational and social environments are rated as not covered.

IPSE 2.5 organises the process information according to the *organisational* and *informational perspectives*, as an IPSE 2.5 process model is a net of primitive class and/or subclass instances that specialise the primitive classes (Lonchamp et al., 1990). From the viewpoint of information quality, the IPSE 2.5 model provides a *formalised* representation of the process with a *text-based* notation.

3.2.1.4. SPADE Model

The SPADE project (whose name comes from a contraction of the initials Software Process Analysis, Design and Enactment), developed at Politecnico de Milano and CEFRIEL, provides an IPSE to guide and support the analysis, design and enactment of a software process (Bandinelli et al., 1992; Bandinelli et al., 1993; Bandinelli & Fuggetta, 1993; Bandinelli et al., 1994). The SPADE environment is based on a process modelling language called SLANG (Spade LANGuage), which is a high-level timed Petri net-based formalism, called ER nets (Ghezzi et al., 1991).

SLANG permits both the modelling, enactment and evolution of processes and the description of the interaction with external tools and people. This language is defined at two levels: a) Kernel SLANG, which is a low-level notation, and b) Full SLANG, which is high-level notation. Kernel SLANG is a powerful formal notation, which provides the basic constructs and mechanisms for process modelling. This is a minimum set on top of which new process-specific constructs may be defined (by giving semantics in terms of primitive SLANG constructs) and incorporated into the language. Full SLANG is the language augmented with these new constructs.

The SPADE model models the following characteristics by means of the SLANG language:

- Process model, modular structure of process activities. The activities are dynamically instantiated. They can be handled as data by other activities (reflexive computing).

- Process products, including the process models saved and maintained in an object-oriented database.

- Tools (human and system) manipulated as data.

The SPADE model identifies the roles of software process designer, manager and developer. The software process model designer role constructs a development model by means of Kernel SLANG. The Kernel SLANG offers a rich type system for modelling the variety of data produced, used and manipulated in the software process. These data can be of different kinds, including, for example, graphical software specifications, failure reports, test data and executable code. A type definition contains the type name (which uniquely identifies the type); the specification of types, from which the type inherits the list of attributes and the list of operations to access the instances of the type. These definitions follow an object-oriented style, organised in a type hierarchy defined by an "is-a" relationship. The Kernel SLANG contains a set of basic types, including integer, real, string, Boolean, text, bitmap, etc. The types can be combined using type constructors: tuple, set, list, etc. Being based on high-level Petri net notation, the process data are represented by tokens. Each token is a typed object, upon which the operations in a type description or inherited from its super types are applied. The SPADE type hierarchy provides a predefined type token. All the tokens in the Kernel SLANG process model are of type token or of one of its subtypes.

The process model manager role (called user in SPADE) can define specific types of process tokens, which characterise the particular process model. They are represented by a token subtree, Figure 3.2, in the hierarchical type path "is-a" of ModelType (Bandinelli et al., 1994).

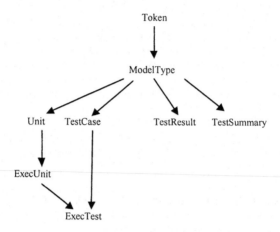

Figure 3.2. SPADE Model type hierarchy representation (Bandinelli et al., 1994)

The software process model developer role (user in SPADE terminology) interacts with the process through a set of integrated tools. These tools are classed as:

a) Black box tools: they are viewed by the process machines as functions performed on some inputs and which produce some outputs; the process has no control over the tools, while they are working and

b) Structured tools: they are decomposed into fragments that are visible through the programmatic interface.

The interaction with tools and users is modelled by black transitions and user places. Black transitions are a special type of transition that represent the asynchronous execution of a tool. User places are used to capture events that may occur in the external environment. Depending on how the process is modelled, the token may produce the firing of one or more transitions in the net.

The SPADE model represents the following elements: *activity, artefact* and *agent*. It also represents *events* using a Petri net-based language. This model only considers the *technological environment*. It does not cover the organisational and social environments.

The model information is organised from the *functional, behavioural* and *organisational perspectives*. The information quality determines an *automated* representation of the process and its formalised notation is *graphical*.

3.2.1.5. International Standard ISO/IEC 12207: Software Life-Cycle Processes

The International Standardisation Organisation (ISO) and the International Electrotechnical Commission (IEC) established a joint technical committee, ISO/IEC JTC 1. This committee developed international standard ISO/IEC 12207, which specifies the software life cycle processes for software development and maintenance (ISO/IEC, 1995). Additionally, this committee prepared Amendment 1 to International Standard ISO/IEC 12207-1995 based on lessons learned from using this standard separately and integrated with ISO/IEC 15504 (ISO/IEC 15504, 1998). This amendment is detailed in (ISO/IEC, 2002). This international standard is a static and dynamic prescriptive model that aims to provide manual guidance for the management and development of software. It provides a common framework for the software life cycle process, with well-defined terminology, which can be used by all the people participating in the software process to create and manage the software. The framework covers the software life cycle from the conception of the ideas to the retirement of the software and contains the principal processes that can be applied to acquire, supply, develop, operate and maintain the software products and services. Also it includes a process that can be used to define, control and improve software development processes. ISO/IEC 12207 models the elements and their relationships shown in Table 3.2.

PRESCRIBED SOFTWARE PROCESS ELEMENTS AND INTERRELATIONSHIPS
- Processes, activities and tasks.
- Artefacts: software products, including documents, to which no specific name is attached.
- Roles:
· Principal roles: software product acquirer (buyer, client, user or owner), supplier, developer, operator, and maintainer.
· Supporting roles: configuration manager, evaluator, auditor, usability specialist.
· Organisational roles: manager, asset manager, knowledge manager, reuse program administrator, domain engineer.
- Hierarchical processes/activities/tasks interaction.
- Processes-organisations interaction (roles).

Table 3.2. ISO/IEC 12207 software process elements

This international standard should be tailored for each software development project. The tailoring process involves the justified omission of inapplicable processes, activities and tasks and/or the addition of special processes, activities and tasks. This standard is designed to be used in a situation that involves two parties and is equally applicable if the two parties are from the same organisation. Like IEEE STD 1074, this standard does not prescribe a particular life cycle. The parties applying this standard are responsible for selecting a life-cycle model for the software project and for instantiating the processes, activities and tasks included in the international standard within their own development process.

The software process according to ISO/IEC 12207-1995, illustrated in Figure 3.3, separates the activities that can be performed during the software life cycle into five primary processes, eight supporting processes and four organisational processes. Each life-cycle process is divided into a set of activities; each activity is further divided into a set of tasks. The three life cycle processes are:

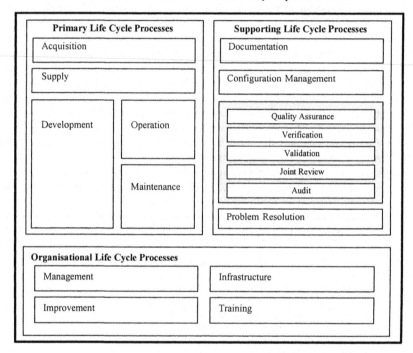

Figure 3.3. ISO/IEC Standard 12207-1995 structure (ISO/IEC, 1995)[1]

---

[1] The terms and definitions taken from ISO/IEC 12207-1995, Information technology – Software life cycle processes, Figure 1 are reproduced with the permission of the International Organization for Standardization, ISO. This standard can be obtained from any ISO member and from the Web site of the ISO Central Secretariat at the following address: www.iso.org. Copyright remains with ISO.

- *Primary life cycle processes.* These processes initiate or perform the development, operation or maintenance of software products. The primary parties (the acquirer, supplier, developer, operator and maintainer of the software product) carry out these processes.

- *Supporting life cycle processes.* These processes support another process as an integral part with a distinct purpose and contribute to the success and quality of the software project. A supporting process is employed and executed, as needed, by another process.

- *Organisational life cycle processes.* These processes establish and implement an underlying structure made up of associated life cycle processes and personnel and continuously improve the structure and processes.

This overview of the structure of the software process model according to ISO/IEC 12207-1995 illustrates: a group of primary processes, which structure and cover the software life cycle; another group of supporting processes, which aid their enactment, and another group of organisational processes, which are of assistance in the management of the software life cycle. The supporting processes also assist performance of the organisational processes, which, in turn, allow management of the performance of the supporting processes. The subprocesses associated with these software life cycle processes and the tailoring process, also included in this standard, are described in Table 3.3.

PROCESS	SUBPROCESS	DESCRIPTION
Primary life cycle processes	Acquisition process	This process defines the activities and tasks of the acquirer: the organisation that acquires a software system, product or service.
	Supply process	This process defines the activities and tasks of the supplier: the organisation that supplies the software system, product or service.
	Development process	This process defines the activities and tasks of the developer: the organisation that defines and develops the software product.
	Operation process	This process defines the activities and tasks of the operator: the organisation that provides the software system operating service in its living environment for its users.
	Maintenance process	This process defines the activities and tasks of the maintainer: the organisation that provides the software product maintenance service, that is, the management of any software product modifications needed for improvement or adaptation. This process includes software product migration and retirement.

Table 3.3. Structure of International Standard ISO/IEC 12207-1995

PROCESS	SUBPROCESS	DESCRIPTION
Supporting life cycle processes	Documentation process	This process defines the activities for recording the information produced by a life cycle process.
	Configuration management process	This process defines the configuration management activities.
	Quality assurance process	This process defines the activities for adequately assuring that the software products and processes conform to the specified requirements and adhere to the established plans. Quality assurance may make use of the results of other supporting processes, such as verification, validation, joint review, audit and problem resolution.
	Verification process	This process defines the activities (for the acquirer, supplier or an independent party) for verifying the software products at varying levels of thoroughness depending on the software project.
	Validation process	This process defines the activities (for the acquirer, supplier or an independent party) for validating the software project software products.
	Joint review process	This process defines the activities for evaluating the status and products of an activity. This process may be employed by any two parties, where one party (reviewing party) reviews the other party (reviewed party).
	Audit process	This process defines the activities for determining compliance with the requirements, plans and contract. This process may be employed by any two parties, where one party (auditing party) audits the software product or activities of the other party (audited party).
	Problem resolution process	This process defines a process for analysing and resolving the problems (including non-conformance), whatever their nature or source, that are discovered during the execution of development, operation, maintenance or other processes.
Organisa-tional life cycle processes	Management process	This process defines the generic management activities, including project management, during a life cycle process.
	Infrastructure process	This process defines the activities for establishing the underlying structure of a life cycle process.
	Improvement process	This process defines the basic activities of an organisation (that is, acquirer, supplier, developer, operator, maintainer or the manager of another process) for establishing, measuring, controlling and improving its life cycle processes.
	Training process	This process defines the activities for providing adequate personnel training.
Tailoring process		This process defines the basic activities needed to tailor this international standard to software projects. For example, variations in organisational policies and procedures, acquisition methods and strategies, project size and complexity, system requirements and development methods influence how a software system is acquired, developed, operated or maintained. This standard has been defined for a general software process that accommodates such variations. Therefore, in the interest of cost reduction and quality improvement, it should be tailored for an individual project.

Table 3.3. Structure of International Standard ISO/IEC 12207-1995 (cont'd)

The subprocesses of each set of ISO/IEC 12207-1995 processes (primary processes, supporting process and organisational processes) are described at the level of functions, activities and principal output documents in Tables 3.4, 3.5 and 3.6, respectively.

DESCRIPTION OF PRIMARY PROCESSES	ACTIVITIES	OUTPUT DOCUMENTS
The *Acquisition Process* begins with the definition of the need to acquire, develop or enhance a system, software product or software service. The process continues with the preparation and issue of the request for proposal, selection of a supplier, and management of the acquisition process through to the acceptance of the system, software product or software service.	*1) Initiation* *2) Request-for-proposal (tender) preparation* *3) Contract preparation and update* *4) Supplier monitoring* *5) Acceptance and completion*	*Acquisition plan; Request for proposal; Contract between acquirer and supplier*
The *Supply Process* may be initiated either by a decision to prepare a proposal to answer an acquirer's request for proposal or by signing and entering into a contract with the acquirer to supply the system or software product or service. The process continues with the determination of the procedures and resources needed to manage and assure the project, including development of project plans and the execution of the plans through to delivery of the system, software product or service.	*1) Initiation* *2) Preparation of response* *3) Contract* *4) Planning* *5) Execution and control* *6) Review and evaluation* *7) Delivery and completion*	*Proposal of response to request for proposal; Reviewed contract; Project management plans; Software product or service*
The *Development Process* contains the activities for requirements analysis, design, coding, integration, testing and installation and acceptance related to the software products. It may contain system-related activities if stipulated in the contract. The developer performs or supports those activities in this process in accordance with the contract. If not stipulated in the contract, the developer will define or select a software life cycle model appropriate to the scope, magnitude and complexity of the project. The activities and tasks of the development process will be selected and mapped to the life cycle model. These activities and tasks may overlap or interact and may be performed iteratively or recursively.	*1) Process implementation* *2) Requirements elicitation* *3) System requirements analysis* *4) System architectural design* *5) Software requirements analysis* *6) Software architectural design* *7) Software detailed design* *8) Software coding and testing* *9) Software integration* *10) Software qualification testing* *11) System integration* *12) System qualification testing* *13) Software installation* *14) Software acceptance support*	*Plans* to manage the development process activities. The plans should include specific standards, methods, tools, actions and the responsibility associated with development and qualification of all the requirements including prevention and security. If necessary, separate plans can be developed. *System requirements specification; System architectural design; Software requirements specification; Software architectural design; Detailed design specification; Testing plan; Code; Test results; User documentation; Evaluation results; Qualification test results; Installed software*

Table 3.4. Description, activities and output documents of primary processes

DESCRIPTION OF PRIMARY PROCESSES	ACTIVITIES	OUTPUT DOCUMENTS
The *Operation Process* covers the software product operation and operational support to users. Because the operation of software products is integrated into the operation of the system, the activities and tasks of this process refer to the system.	*1) Process implementation* *2) Operational testing* *3) System operation* *4) User support*	*Operation plan*
The *Maintenance Process* is activated when the software product undergoes modifications of code and associated documentation due to a problem or the need for improvement or adaptation. The objective is to modify the existing software product while preserving its integrity. This process includes the migration and retirement of the software product. The process ends with the retirement of the software. The maintenance process may utilize other processes. If the development process is utilized, the term developer there is interpreted as maintainer.	*1) Process implementation* *2) Problem and modification analysis* *3) Modification implementation* *4) Maintenance review/acceptance* *5) Migration* *6) Software retirement*	*Maintenance plan; Migration plan; Retirement plan*

Table 3.4. Description, activities and output documents of primary processes (cont'd)

DESCRIPTION OF SUPPORTING PROCESSES	ACTIVITIES	OUTPUT DOCUMENTS
The *Documentation Process* contains the set of activities that plan, design, develop, produce, edit, distribute and maintain the documents needed by all concerned, such as managers, engineers and users of the system or software product. Execution of this process by an organization results in the establishment of internal documentation standards (such as standards for program management plan and software design document) in a suitable medium.	*1) Process implementation* *2) Design and development* *3) Production* *4) Maintenance*	*Documentation plan*
The *Configuration Management Process*, modified in (ISO/IEC, 2002) is a process of applying administrative and technical procedures throughout the software life cycle to: identify and define software items in a system; control modifications and releases of the items; record and report the status of the items and modification requests; ensure the completeness, consistency and correctness of the items and control storages, handling and delivery of the items.	*1) Process implementation* *2) Configuration identification* *3) Configuration control* *4) Configuration status accounting* *5) Configuration evaluation* *6) Release management and delivery*	*Configuration management plan Software item releases*

Table 3.5. Description, activities and output documents of supporting processes

DESCRIPTION OF SUPPORTING PROCESSES	ACTIVITIES	OUTPUT DOCUMENTS
The *Quality Assurance Process* provides adequate assurance that the software products and processes in the project life cycle conform to their specified requirements and adhere to their established plans. To be unbiased, quality assurance needs to have organisational freedom and authority from persons directly responsible for developing the software product or executing the process in the project. Quality assurance may be internal or external.	*1) Process implementation* *2) Product assurance* *3) Process assurance* *4) Assurance of quality* * systems*	*Quality assurance plan*
The *Verification Process* is a process for determining whether the software products of an activity fulfil the requirements or conditions imposed on them in the previous activities. For cost and performance effectiveness, verification should be integrated, as early as possible, with the process (such as supply, development, operation or maintenance) that employs it. This process may include analysis, review and testing.	*1) Process implementation* *2) Verification*	*Verification plan*
The *Validation Process* is a process for determining whether the requirements and the final as-built system or software product fulfils its specific intended use. Validation may be conducted in earlier stages. This process may be conducted as part of software acceptance support.	*1) Process implementation* *2) Validation*	*Validation plan*
In the *Joint Review Process*, the joint reviews are at both project management and technical levels and are held throughout the life of the contract. This process may be employed by any two parties, where one party (reviewing party) reviews the other party (reviewed party).	*1) Process implementation* *2) Project management* * reviews* *3) Technical reviews*	*Review results*
The *Audit Process* may be employed by any two parties, where one party (auditing party) audits the software products or activities of another party (audited party).	*1) Process implementation* *2) Audit*	*Audit results*
The objective of the *Problem Resolution Process* is to provide a timely, responsible and documented means to ensure that all discovered problems are analysed and resolved and trends are recognised.	*1) Process implementation* *2) Problem resolution*	*Problem report*

Table 3.5. Description, activities and output documents of supporting processes (cont'd)

DESCRIPTION OF ORGANISATIONAL PROCESSES	ACTIVITIES	OUTPUT DOCUMENTS
The *Management Process* contains the generic activities and tasks that may be employed by any party that has to manage its respective process(es). The manager is responsible for product management, project management, and task management of the applicable process(es), such as acquisition, supply, development, operation, maintenance or supporting processes. These management activities also include making measurements in (ISO/IEC, 2002). For example, apart from the above, the manager must establish and maintain measurement commitment, plan the measurement process, perform measurement in accordance with the plan, and evaluate measurement to create and maintain a "Measurement Experience Base".	*1) Initiation and scope definition* *2) Planning* *3) Execution and control* *4) Review and evaluation* *5) Closure* *6) Measurement*	*Plans* for the execution of the process, which include, but are not limited to, the following: *a) Schedules for the timely completion of tasks;* *b) Estimation of effort;* *c) Adequate resources needed to execute the tasks;* *d) Allocation of tasks;* *e) Assignment of responsibilities;* *f) Quantification of risks associated with tasks or the process itself;* *g) Quality control measures to be employed throughout the process;* *h) Costs associated with process execution;* *i) Provision of environment and infrastructure.*
The *Infrastructure Process* establishes and maintains the infrastructure needed for any other process. The infrastructure may include hardware, software, tools, techniques, standards and facilities for development, operation or maintenance.	*1) Process implementation* *2) Establishment of the infrastructure* *3) Maintenance of the infrastructure*	*Infrastructure plan*
The *Improvement Process* is a process for establishing, assessing, measuring, controlling and improving a software life cycle process.	*1) Process establishment* *2) Process assessment* *3) Process improvement*	*Process documents*
The *Training Process*, called Human Resource Process in (ISO/IEC, 2002), is a process for providing and maintaining trained personnel. The acquisition, supply, development, operation or maintenance of software products is largely dependent upon knowledgeable and skilled personnel, e.g., developer personnel should have essential training in software management and software engineering. It is imperative that personnel training be planned and implemented early so that trained personnel are available as the software product is acquired, supplied, developed, operated or maintained.	*1) Process implementation* *2) Training material development* *3) Training plan implementation*	*Training plan* *Training manuals*

Table 3.6. Description, activities and output documents of organisational processes

Each subprocess within the primary processes and supporting processes is managed at the project level following the management process, an infrastructure is established following the infrastructure process, which is tailored to the project following the tailoring process and is managed at the organisational level following the improvement process and training process.

Amendment 1 of ISO/IEC 12207 (ISO/IEC, 2002) has defined a Process Reference Model at a high level of abstraction, specifying the purpose and the main outcomes for each process. These outcomes include artefact production, a significant change in state or constraints, for example, requirements, goals, etc., or meeting of specified process. These purposes and outcomes are a statement of the goals for process performance and allow a more formalised assessment of the process effectiveness. The Process Reference Model is applicable to an organisation that is assessing its processes in order to determine the capability of the processes, using the latest version of ISO/IEC 15504. This Process Reference Model is not described in this book, because we are concerned with the process modelling area and not the process evaluation and improvement area. This model has included new subprocesses, activities and tasks, has extended the scope of particular activities or has regrouped ISO/IEC 12207-1995 activities. For a full description, see (ISO/IEC, 2002). However, Table 3.7 does include the new processes and their associated activities that are added to ISO/IEC 12207-1995 (ISO/IEC, 2002).

DESCRIPTION OF NEW PROCESSES	ACTIVITIES
Supporting Processes	
The *Usability Process* contains the iterative activities and tasks of the usability specialist. The process contains the activities that take account of the interests and needs of the stakeholders, throughout development and operation of the software or system. The usability process ensures the quality in use of the software. The developer manages the Usability Process at the project level. The usability specialist integrates usability activities and the results from usability activities with Development and Operation (within the Primary Processes) and Quality Assurance, Verification and Validation (within the Supporting Processes).	*1) Process implementation* *2) Human-centred design* *3) Human aspects of strategy, introduction and support*
The *Product Evaluation Process* is not a completely new process, but extends evaluation activities in order to ensure, through systematic examination and measurement, that a product meets the stated and implied needs of the users of that product.	*1) Process implementaiton* *2) Establish evaluation requirements* *3) Identify product evaluation criteria and methods* *4) Planning, execution and control* *5) Collect measures and assess results against defined criteria* *6) Make available results of product evaluation activities to the interested parties*

Table 3.7. Description and activities of the new ISO/IEC 12207-2002 processes

DESCRIPTION OF NEW PROCESSES	ACTIVITIES
Organisational Processes	
The *Human Resource Process* replaced the Training Process in ISO/IEC 12207-1995. This process has included new activities, apart from Training process activities. The Human Resource Process provides the organisation and projects with individuals who possess skills and knowledge to perform their roles effectively and to work together as a cohesive group. It requires a review of the organisation and project requirements to establish and make timely provision for acquiring or developing the resources and skills required by the management and technical staff. These needs may be met through training, recruitment or other staff development mechanisms. It involves drawing up and implementing a training plan, establishing a systematic programme of recruitment of staff who are qualified to meet the needs of the organisation and projects, the evaluation of staff achievement, building teams with shared views and appropriate intra and inter-team communication mechanisms, and knowledge management implementation to assure that individual knowledge, information and skills are collected, shared, reused and improved throughout the organisation.	*1) Process implementation* *2) Define training requirements* *3) Recruit qualified staff* *4) Evaluate staff performance* *5) Establish project team requirements* *6) Knowledge management*
The *Asset Management Process* involves the application of administrative and technical procedures throughout the life of an asset to identify, define, certify, classify and baseline the asset, track modifications, migrations and versions of the asset, record and report the status of the asset, and establish and control storage and handling of the asset, delivery of the asset to its reusers, and retirement of the asset. The activities and tasks associated with this process are implemented by the asset manager.	*1) Process implementation* *2) Asset storage and retrieval definition* *3) Asset management and control*
The *Reuse Program Management Process* includes the planning, establishment, management, control and monitoring of a organisation reuse programme. These activities and their associated tasks are performed by the reuse programme administrator.	*1) Initiation* *2) Domain identification* *3) Reuse assessment* *4) Planning* *5) Execution and control* *6) Review and evaluation*
The *Domain Engineering Process* contains the activities and associated tasks of the domain engineer. This process covers the development and maintenance of the domain models, domain architecture, and other assets for this domain. It includes activities such as domain definition, domain analysis, developing the domain architecture and domain implementation, which includes building the assets (for example, requirements, designs, software code, documentation) for a class of systems, subsystems or applications.	*1) Process implementation* *2) Domain analysis* *3) Domain design* *4) Asset provision* *5) Asset maintenance*

Table 3.7. Description and activities of the new ISO/IEC 12207-2002 processes (cont'd)

The *Tailoring Process* is a process for performing basic tailoring of this international standard for a software project. Figure 3.4 illustrates an application of the standard. The activities and tasks of the tailoring process are described in Table 3.8.

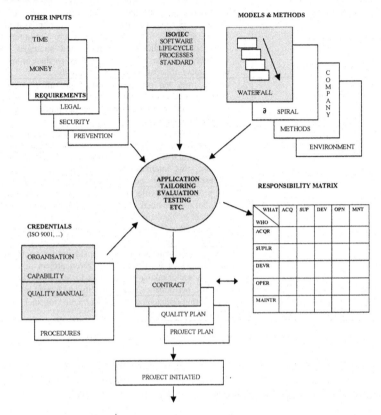

Figure 3.4. An example of application of the international standard (ISO/IEC, 1995)[2]

---

[2] The terms and definitions taken from ISO/IEC 12207-1995, Information technology – Software life cycle processes, Figure B.1 are reproduced with the permission of the International Organization for Standardization, ISO. This standard can be obtained from any ISO member and from the Web site of the ISO Central Secretariat at the following address: www.iso.org. Copyright remains with ISO.

ACTIVITIES	TASKS
1) Identifying project environment	1.1) Characteristics of the project environment that are going to influence tailoring shall be identified. Some of the characteristics may be: life cycle model; current system life cycle activity; system and software requirements; organisational policies, procedures and strategies; size, criticality and types of system, software product or service; and number of personnel and parties involved.
2) Soliciting inputs	2.1) Inputs from the organisations that are affected by the tailoring decisions shall be solicited. Users, support personnel, contracting officers, potential bidders should be involved in tailoring.
3) Selecting processes, activities and tasks	3.1) The processes, activities and tasks that are to be performed shall be decided. These include the documentation to be developed and who are to be responsible for them. For this purpose, this international standard should be evaluated against relevant data gathered in activities 1) and 2).
	3.2) The processes, activities and tasks that were decided upon in 3.1), but not provided in the international standard shall be specified in the contract itself. Organisational life cycle processes should be evaluated to determine whether they could provide for these processes, activities and tasks.
	3.3) These tasks should be carefully considered for whether they should be kept or deleted for a given project or a given business sector taking into account for example, risk, cost, schedule, performance size, criticality and human interface.
4) Documenting tailoring decisions and rationale	4.1) All tailoring decisions shall be documented together with the rationale for the decisions.

Table 3.8. Tailoring process activities and tasks

Figure 3.5 shows the processes and the relationships between processes and between processes and organisations (roles) in ISO/IEC 12207-1995. This approach is still valid in the new version of ISO/IEC 12207-2002:

- *Contract view*. The acquirer and supplier parties negotiate and sign a contract, employing the acquisition process and the supply process.

- *Management view*. The acquirer, supplier, developer, operator and maintenance personnel manage their respective processes for the software project.

- *Operation view*. The operator provides the service of operating the software for users.

- *Engineering view*. The developer or maintainer perform their respective engineering tasks to produce or modify the software product.

-   *Supporting view*. The parties (such as configuration management quality assurance) provide supporting services in compliance with specific single tasks.

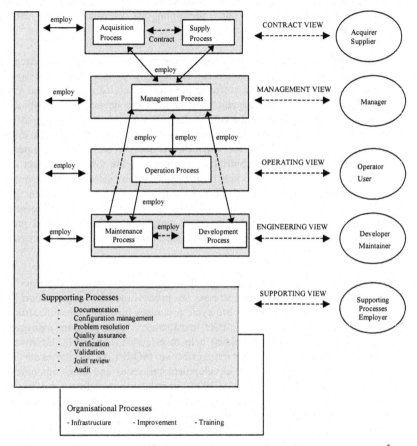

Figure 3.5. Software life-cycle processes: roles and relationships (ISO/IEC, 1995)[3]

---

[3] The terms and definitions taken from ISO/IEC 12207-1995, Information technology – Software life cycle processes, Figure C.1 are reproduced with the permission of the International Organization for Standardization, ISO. This standard can be obtained from any ISO member and from the Web site of the ISO Central Secretariat at the following address: www.iso.org. Copyright remains with ISO.

In this international standard, the relationships between the processes are static only. The more important dynamics, the real-life relationships between the processes, between the parties and between the processes and the parties are automatically established when this international standard is applied on software projects. Each process (and party performing it) contributes to the software process in its own unique way.

The acquisition process (and the acquirer) contributes by defining the system that is to contain the software product. The supply process (and the supplier) contributes by providing the software product or service on which the system would depend. The development process (and the developer) contributes by "looking" to the system for the correct derivation and definition of the software product, by supporting proper integration of the software product back into the system and by developing the software product in between. The operation process (and the operator) contributes by operating the software product in the system's environment for the benefit of the users, the business, and the mission. The maintenance process (and the maintainer) contributes by maintaining and sustaining the software product for operational fitness and by providing support and advice to the user community. Each supporting or organisational process contributes by providing unique, specialised functions to other processes as needed.

The ISO/IEC 12207 considers only three elementary process characteristics: *activity, artefact* and *roles* and stresses the process (activity)-organisation (role) interaction. The organisational life cycle processes (management, infrastructure, improvement, human resource, asset management, reuse program management and domain engineering processes) help to establish, implement, improve and reuse an organisation, making it more effective. ISO/IEC 12207 allows developer organisations to improve their development processes and eases attainment of ISO 9001 certification (ISO-9001, 2000), as it establishes a framework in which all the elements needed for the purpose can be inserted: development methodology, project management, configuration management, quality assurance, human resource management, continual improvement, etc. This software process model explicitly specifies a software life cycle process improvement process that can establish, assess, measure, control and improve these processes. Therefore, the specification, albeit informal, of the *organisational* and *technological environments* through the specification of human resources and improvement processes and the management and infrastructure processes, respectively, can be considered to be complete. It focuses on the improvement of the competencies of the personnel involved in the software projects of the developer and user organisation and on the improvement of the developer organisation itself. Accordingly, this model accounts for the *social environment*, as it encourages the creativity of the people and teams involved in the software project and the organisation.

This model qualitatively describes the structure of the software development processes, but does not specify the details of how to implement or perform the activities and tasks included in the processes. Therefore, the quality of the information of the representation is extremely *informal*. This representation organises the information from the *functional perspective*. The representation is incomplete, as it fails to organise the information from the behavioural, organisational and informational perspectives.

3.2.1.6. IEEE STD 1074: IEEE Standard for Developing Software Lifecycle Processes

The IEEE first published this standard in 1991 (IEEE, 1991). Since the original publication of this standard, considerable worldwide attention has been paid to software life cycle processes. Use of IEEE STD 1074-1991, IEEE 1074-1995 (a minor revision to correct specific errors found in the 1991 version) (IEEE, 1995) and other quality system and life cycle standards activity has been carefully considered in preparing a major revision of this standard. The result was IEEE STD 1074-1997, referred to here simply as IEEE STD 1074. IEEE STD 1074 specifies the software life cycle processes for developing and maintaining software (IEEE, 1997). It identifies a non-ordered set of essential activities that should be included within software product development. These activities are arranged as logical and cohesive groupings, called Activity Groups.

IEEE 1074 describes a prescriptive static model designed as manual guidance for managing and developing software. It provides a common framework for the development activity groups, including well-defined terminology, which can be used by all the people participating in the software process. These activity groups cover the software life cycle from the identification of the need or idea to its retirement. The standard covers the main activity groups that can be applied to initiate, plan, manage, support, develop, operate, maintain and evaluate software products and services. The elements and their interrelationships in the software process modelled by IEEE STD 1074 are shown in Table 3.9.

PRESCRIBED SOFTWARE PROCESS ELEMENTS AND INTERRELATIONSHIPS
- Processes (called activity groups in IEEE STD 1074) and activities.
- Artefacts: software products, including input and output documents (called information in IEEE STD 1074) for each activity, which are assigned a standard name.
- Activity-artefact interaction.
- Activity-activity interaction.

Table 3.9. IEEE STD 1074 software process elements

IEEE STD 1074 should be tailored to each particular software project. The tailoring process involves the justified omission of inapplicable activity groups and activities and/or the addition of special activity groups and activities. Initially, the project manager (called process architect in IEEE STD 1074) should identify and select a software life cycle model (SLCM) that best satisfies the project attributes and constraints, create the software life cycle, that is, map the IEEE STD 1074 activities to the SLCM, determine their source, develop and justify a list of unused activities and verify the map and, finally, establish a software life cycle process, that is, apply the organisational process assets (policies, standards, procedures, metrics, tools, methodologies, etc.) to the software life cycle activities and assign the standard output information to the specific project documents. These three steps are performed in the create software life cycle process within the project initiation activities. According to IEEE STD 1074, illustrated in Figure 3.6, the software process is composed of 17 activity groups, each of which contains activities that are responsible for satisfying their associated requirements. The process is composed of a total of 65 activities. IEEE STD 1074 covers the following families of activities:

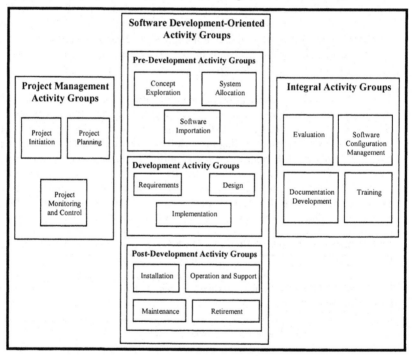

Figure 3.6. Software process according to IEEE STD 1074

- *Project Management Activity Groups.* These activities create the project framework and assure the right level of project management throughout the entire software life cycle.

- *Software Development-Oriented Activity Groups.* These activities produce, install, operate and maintain the software and retire it from use. They are divided into pre-development, development and post-development activity groups.

  - *Pre-Development Activity Groups.* These are the activities that should be performed before starting actual software development.

  - *Development Activity Groups.* These are the activities that should be performed to build the software product.

  - *Post-Development Activity Groups.* These activities are performed after the software has been constructed, that is, are applied in the later phases of the software life cycle phases.

- *Integral Activity Groups.* These activities are needed to successfully complete the software project activities. They are simultaneous with the software development-oriented activities and include non-development activities.

The activity groups of which the IEEE STD 1074 software process is composed are described in Table 3.10.

ACTIVITY GROUPS	ACTIVITY SUBGROUPS	DESCRIPTION
Project Management Activity Groups	Project Initiation	This activity group contains the activities that create the framework for the development or maintenance.
	Project Planning	The goal of this activity group is to plan for all project management, including contingencies.
	Project Monitoring and Control	This is an iterative process of tracking, reporting and managing project costs, problems and performance throughout its development.
Pre-Development Activity Groups	Concept Exploration	This activity group defines the preliminary activities of the software system development effort.
	System Allocation	This activity group is performed when the system requires both hardware and software development or there is no assurance that only software development is required.
	Software Importation	This activity group is performed when some or all the software requirements may best be satisfied by reusing existing software or by acquiring software from outside the project.

Table 3.10. IEEE STD 1074 structure

ACTIVITY GROUPS	ACTIVITY SUBGROUPS	DESCRIPTION
Development Activity Groups	Requirements	This activity group includes the iterative activities directed toward the development of the software requirements specification.
	Design	This is the central process that unites the software development and maintenance activity groups. Its objective is to develop a coherent and well-organised representation of the software system that meets the software requirements specification. The quality of this representation can be evaluated.
	Implementation	This activity group transforms the detailed design representation of a software product into a programming language realisation.
Post-Development Activity Groups	Installation	This activity group verifies that the correct software configuration has been implemented and ends with the formal customer acceptance of the software in conformance with the specifications of the Software Project Management Planned Information and the successful performance of the user acceptance test.
	Operation and Support	This activity group defines the activities to assure proper use of the software system by the user and ongoing user support, which includes technical assistance and consulting with the user.
	Maintenance	This activity group is concerned with software errors, defects, improvements and changes.
	Retirement	This activity group defines the basic activities for the removal of an existing system from its active support or use.
Integral Activity Groups	Evaluation	This activity group includes planning and performing all the verification and validation tasks that are executed throughout the software life cycle to assure that all the software requirements are satisfied.
	Software Configuration Management	This activity group includes a set of activities developed to manage the changes throughout the software life cycle.
	Documentation Development	This activity group defines the activities that plan, design and distribute the documents required by developers and users.
	Training	This activity group defines the activities that plan, develop, validate and implement the training programme.

Table 3.10. IEEE STD 1074 structure (cont'd)

The Project Management Activity Groups establish the conditions for project development. They involve the activities of project initiation, resource allocation, planning, monitoring and control throughout the software life cycle. The Software Development-Oriented Activity Groups initiate the development effort with the identification of a need for automation. A new application or a change of all or part of an existing application may be necessary to satisfy this need. On the basis of the statement of need, the Development Activity Groups produce the software (code and documentation) with the support of the Integral Activity Groups and according to the Software Project Management Planned Information.

Finally, the activities to install, operate, support, maintain and retire the software product should be performed. The Integral Activity Groups are simultaneous and complementary to the development-oriented processes. They include activities that are essential to assure that the constructed system is reliable and used to the utmost of its potential.

Tables 3.11, 3.12 and 3.13 describe the subgroups of activities for each of the three main sets of activity groups at the level of functions, activities and principal information, respectively.

DESCRIPTION OF MANAGEMENT ACTIVITY GROUPS	ACTIVITIES	OUTPUT INFORMATION
In *Project Initiation*, the software life cycle process is created for this project. The resources are estimated and allocated, which involves determining the costs and resources required to perform all the tasks required by the project. Project product and process metrics are defined throughout the software life cycle. For each defined metric, the data collection and analysis methods are specified.	*1) Create a software life cycle process* *2) Perform estimations* *3) Allocate project resources* *4) Define metrics*	*- Software Life Cycle Process* *- List of Activities Not Used* *- Project Estimates* *- Estimation Assumptions* *- Resource Allocations* *- Defined Metrics* *- Collection and Analysis Methods*
Project Planning establishes all the plans for project management. Plans are prepared and established for timely project implementation, including milestones and reviews. Technical, financial, operational, and support and schedule risks are analysed, identifying potential problems, the likelihood of them materialising and their potential impact and establishing the steps to be taken for their management. The identified risks and their management are documented in the contingency planned information. This involves planning evaluations, configuration management, system transition, installation, documentation, training, project management and integration.	*1) Plan Evaluations* *2) Plan Configuration Management* *3) Plan System Transition (if applicable)* *4) Plan Installation* *5) Plan Documentation* *6) Plan Training* *7) Plan Project Management* *8) Plan Integration*	*- Evaluation Planned Information* *- Software Configuration Management Planned Information* *- Transition Planned Information* *- Transition Impact Statement* *- Software Installation Planned Information* *- Documentation Planned Information* *- Training Planned Information* *- Software Project Management Planned Information* *- Problem Reporting and Resolution Planned Information* *- Retirement Planned Information* *- Support Planned Information* *- Integration Planned Information*
In *Project Monitoring and Control*, the project is tracked and managed. Risks are managed. Project progress is reviewed and measured against the milestones established in the Software Project Management Planned Information. Additionally, the project software metrics are collected and analysed, the project records are retained and opportunities for software life cycle process improvement are identified.	*1) Manage risks* *2) Manage project* *3) Identify software process improvement needs* *4) Retain records* *5) Collect and analyse metric*	*- Risk Management Reported Information* *- Project Management* *- Anomalies* *- Environment Improvement Needs* *- Historical Project Records* *- Analysis Reported Information*

Table 3.11. Description, activities and output information of project management activity groups

For a full description of the input information and its source activity groups and activities that are processed for each IEEE STD 1074 activity to get the respective output information together with its target activity groups and activities, see (IEEE, 1997).

DESCRIPTION OF DEVELOPMENT-ORIENTED ACTIVITY GROUPS	ACTIVITIES	OUTPUT INFORMATION
Concept Exploration includes the identification of an idea or need for a system to be developed (whether it be a new effort or a change to all or part of an existing application), the formulation of potential solutions, their evaluation (feasibility study) and refinement at system level. Having established its scope, a statement of need is generated for the system under development. This report initiates the system allocation and/or the requirements activities and feeds the project management activities. The statement of need is a document that constitutes the basis of all the later engineering work.	*1) Identify ideas or needs* *2) Formulate potential approaches* *3) Conduct feasibility studies* *4) Refine and finalise idea or need*	*- Preliminary Statement of Need* *- Constraints and Benefits* *- Potential Approaches* *- Recommendations* *- Statement of Need*
In *System Allocation,* the statement of need is analysed to identify the inputs, input processing, required outputs and functions of the total system, permitting the development of the system architecture and identification of the hardware and software functions and the interfaces. This activity group ends with the system functional hardware, software and interface requirements.	*1) Analyse functions* *2) Develop system architecture* *3) Decompose system requirements*	*- Functional Description of the System* *- System Architecture* *- System Functional Human &Hardware Requirements (if applicable)* *- System Functional Software Requirements* *- System Interface Requirements (if applicable)*
Software Importation covers the elicitation of the software requirements that will be satisfied through importation, the evaluation of candidate sources from which the imported software might be obtained, the determination of the method of importation and the importation of the software, including documentation, into the project.	*1) Identify imported software requirements* *2) Evaluate software import sources (if applicable)* *3) Define software import method (if applicable)* *4) Import software (if applicable)*	*- Imported Software Requirements* *- Selected Software Import Sources* *- Candidate Software Import Methods* *- Selected Software Import Method* *- Imported Software* *- Imported Software Documentation*

Table 3.12. Description, activities and output information of software development-oriented activity groups

DESCRIPTION OF DEVELOPMENT-ORIENTED ACTIVITY GROUPS	ACTIVITIES	OUTPUT INFORMATION
In the *Requirements* activities, the analysis of requirements stresses the resulting output, data decomposition, data processing, databases (if any) and the user, software and hardware interfaces to assure a full and consistent determination of the software requirements. The Software Requirements specification is the concise and precise establishment of a set of requirements that should be met by a software product, indicating, if applicable, the procedure by means of which it can be determined whether it satisfies the given requirements. It describes the software functional, performance and interface requirements and defines the operation and support environments. This document is the output that culminates this process.	*1) Define and develop software requirements* *2) Define interface requirements* *3) Prioritise and integrate software requirements*	*- Preliminary Software Requirements* *- Installation Requirements* *- Software Interface Requirements* *- Software Requirements*
Design translates the "what to do" of the requirements specifications into the "how to do it" of the design specifications. Initially, the representation describes a systematic and holistic view of the software. Later design refinements lead to a representation closer to source code.	*1) Perform architectural design* *2) Design data base (if applicable)* *3) Design interfaces* *4) Perform detailed design*	*- Software Architectural Design* *- Database Design* *- Interface Design* *- Software Detailed Design*
Implementation produces the source code, database code (if applicable) and the documentation constituting the physical manifestation of the design according to the project standards and methodologies. Additionally, the code and the database should be integrated. If the system is composed of hardware and software components, system integration should be planned and implemented. The output of this process is subject to the appropriate verification and validation tests. The code and the database together with the documentation produced during this process are the first full representation of the software product.	*1) Create executable code* *2) Create operating documentation* *3) Perform integration*	*- Source Code (if required)* *- Executable Code* *- Database (if applicable)* *- Operating Documentation* *- Integrated Software*

Table 3.12. Description, activities and output information of software development-oriented activity groups (cont'd)

DESCRIPTION OF DEVELOPMENT-ORIENTED ACTIVITY GROUPS	ACTIVITIES	OUTPUT INFORMATION
Installation consists of the transportation and installation of a software system from the development environment to the target environment. It includes database loading, if necessary, the necessary software modifications, checkout in the target environment and customer acceptance. If a problem arises during installation, it is identified and reported.	*1) Distribute software* *2) Install software* *3) Accept software in the operating environment*	*- Packaged Installation Planned Information* *- Packaged Software* *- Packaged Operating Documentation* *- Installation Reported Information* *- Customer Acceptance* *- Installed Software System*
Operation and Support involves user operation of the system and ongoing support, including technical assistance, consulting with user and recording the user support requests in a support request log. Accordingly, this process may trigger the maintenance process that provides information re-entering the software life cycle.	*1) Operate the system* *2) Provide technical assistance and consulting* *3) Maintain support request log*	*- Operation Logs* *- Anomalies* *- Support Response* *- Support Request Log*
In *Maintenance*, a software maintenance requirement initiates software life cycle changes. The software life cycle is remapped and executed. The output of this process is maintenance recommendations that enter the software life cycle at the concept exploration process to improve the software system quality.	*1) Identify software improvement needs* *2) Implement problem reporting method* *3) Reapply software life cycle*	*- Software Improvement Recommendations* *- Out-Of-Scope Anomalies* *- Report Log* *- Enhancement Problem Reported Information* *- Correction Problem Reported Information* *- Maintenance Recommendations* *- Resolved Problem Reported Information* *- Updated Report Log*
Retirement is the removal of an existing system from its active support or use either by ceasing its operation or support or by replacing it by a new system or an upgraded version of the existing system. If the manual or automated system is being replaced by a new system, a period of dual operation is required, called parallel trial. In this period, the retiring system is used for official results, while completing the preparation of the new system for formal operation. It is a period of user training on and validation of the new system.	*1) Notify user* *2) Conduct parallel operations (if applicable)* *3) Retire system*	*- Official Notification* *- Parallel Operations Log* *- Archive Reported Information* *- Post-Operation Review Reported Information*

Table 3.12. Description, activities and output information of software development-oriented activity groups (cont'd)

DESCRIPTION OF INTEGRAL ACTIVITY GROUPS	ACTIVITIES	OUTPUT INFORMATION
Evaluation includes planning and performing all the verification tasks, including tests, reviews and audits, and all the validation tasks, including tests, that are conducted during the software life cycle to assure that all the software requirements are satisfied. This process addresses each software life cycle process and product.	*1) Conduct reviews* *2) Create traceability maps* *3) Conduct audits* *4) Develop test procedures* *5) Create test data* *6) Execute tests* *7) Report evaluation results*	- *In-Process Review Results* - *Post-Implementation Review Reported Information* - *Process Improvement Recommendations* - *Management Status Reported Information* - *Traceability Analysis Reported Information* - *System Allocation Change Reported Information* - *Traceability Matrix* - *Audit Results Information* - *Test Procedures* - *Stubs and Drivers (if applicable)* - *Test Data* - *Test Summary Reported Information* - *Tested Software* - *Anomalies* - *Evaluation Reported Information*
Software Configuration Management identifies the structure of a system (what routines, modules, data, files, etc., it is composed of) at any given time (including when it is under development), which is called the system configuration. Its goal is to control the changes to the system, maintain its coherence and its "traceability" and be able to run control audits on the evolution of the configurations	*1) Develop configuration identification* *2) Perform configuration control* *3) Perform status accounting*	- *Configuration Identification* - *Controlled item* - *Change Status* - *Status reported information*
The *Documentation Development* for software development and usage is a set of activities that plan, design, implement, edit, produce distribute and maintain the documents required by developers and users.	*1) Implement documentation* *2) Produce and distribute documentation*	- *Document* - *Published documents*
Training includes the planning, development, validation and implementation of training programmes for developers, technical support staff and customers and prepares the appropriate training materials.	*1) Develop training materials* *2) Validate the training programme* *3) Implement the training programme*	- *Training Manual* - *Training Materials* - *Prepared Presentations* - *Training Feedback* - *Updated Training Manual* - *Updated Training Materials* - *Updated Skills Inventory* - *Trained Personnel*

Table 3.13. Description, activities and output information of integral activity groups

It follows from the above description that the process elements represented by the IEEE STD 1074 model are: *activity* and *artefact*. This standard gives a very detailed (supposedly complete) decomposition of the activities, as well as the transformed products of the software process. It is the most complete model with regard to the definition of these two process elements.

However, it is an *informal* model, which focuses qualitatively on the activity-artefact interaction and, therefore, on the activity-activity interaction. Therefore, this model only considers the *technological environment* and does not address either the organisational or the social environments.

The information is organised from the *functional perspective*. The representation is, therefore, incomplete, as it fails to organise the information from the behavioural, organisational and informational perspectives. It does not establish a process for constructing the software process model in line with the characteristics and needs of the participant organisation, that is, for tailoring the software process models. It does not include other elements or aspects directly, such as agent roles, technological resources, other strategic level processes (related to the organisation's internal structure and organisation), or the improvement of management and development processes to allow the establishment, assessment, measurement, control and improvement of these processes.

3.2.2. Evaluation Models

3.2.2.1. ISO 9001

The ISO 9001 international standard was prepared by Technical Committee ISO/TC 176, Quality Management and Assurance, Subcommittee SC 2, Quality Systems. This third edition of ISO 9001 replaces the second edition (ISO 9001:1994), as well as standards ISO 9002:1994 and ISO 9003:1994 (ISO, 1994; ISO-9002, 1994; ISO-9003, 1994; ISO, 1997). This is a technical revision of these documents. Organisations that have used standards ISO 9002:1994 and ISO 9003:1994 can use this international standard by excluding some requirements, as established in (ISO-9001, 2000).

This international standard can be used by internal and external parties, including certification institutions, to evaluate the capability of a organisation to meet customer requirements, regulatory requirements and organisational requirements. Quality management principles set out in ISO 9004 (ISO, 1993) have been taken into account to develop this international standard. The current editions of standards ISO 9001 and ISO 9004 have been developed as a coherent pair of standards for quality management systems, which have been designed to be complementary, but which can be likewise used as separate documents. Although the two standards have different purposes and scopes, their structure is similar to ease their application as a coherent pair.

ISO 9001 specifies the requirements for a quality management system that can be applied internally by organisations for certification or contractual purposes. It focuses on quality management system effectiveness in meeting customer requirements. ISO 9004 provides guidance on a wider range of quality management system goals than ISO 9001, especially for an organisation's global continual performance and efficiency improvement, as well as its effectiveness. ISO 9004 is recommended as a guideline for organisations whose senior management intends to go beyond the ISO 9001 requirements in pursuit of continual performance improvement. However, it is not intended for use for contractual or certification purposes.

This section focuses on the description of the software process model, illustrated in Figure 3.7 (yardstick according to software process evaluation terminology (López Fernández, 1998)) and not the associated evaluation and improvement process, as this book is concerned with software process modelling, not software processes evaluation and improvement.

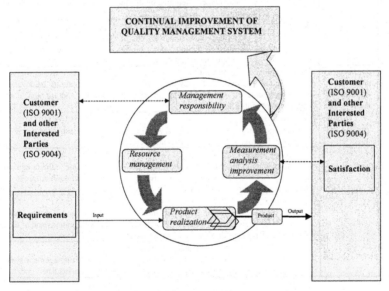

Figure 3.7. Model of a process-based quality management system
(www.iso.ch/iso/en/iso9000-14000/iso9000/2000rev9.html)

The evaluated organisation must define and implement its quality management system based on the requirements specified in ISO 9001, taking into account at all times that it must be able to demonstrate that the processes used are efficient and effective. The evaluation method verifies these two characteristics (use and demonstrability) of each of the requirements or criteria it covers.

The requirements prescribed by ISO 9001 (ISO-9001, 2000) are detailed in Table 3.14.

REQUIREMENTS DESCRIPTION		
4 Quality manage-ment system	4.1 General requirements The organisation needs to identify, organise, plan, implement, monitor and control a quality management system and continually measure and improve its effectiveness.	
	4.2 Docu-mentation require-ments	4.2.1 General The quality management system documentation should include documentation of quality policy, quality objectives, a quality manual, the written procedures required by ISO 9001, documents needed by the organisation to assure effective process planning, operation and control, and records required by ISO 9001.
		4.2.2 Quality manual The organisation needs to establish and maintain a quality manual that includes the system scope, the written procedures and a description of the interaction between the quality management system processes.
		4.2.3 Control of documents The documents required by the quality management system need to be controlled.
		4.2.4 Control of records A written procedure needs to be established to define the controls required to identify, store, protect, retrieve records and define their retention and disposal times.
5. Manage-ment respons-ibility	5.1 Management commitment The top management needs to provide evidence of its commitment to the development and implementation of the quality management system and to the continual improvement of its effectiveness.	
	5.2 Customer focus Top management must ensure that customer requirements are established and met with the goal of improving customer satisfaction (see 7.2.1 and 8.2.1).	
	5.3 Quality policy Top management must ensure that the quality policy is appropriate to the organisation's purpose, establish a commitment to meet requirements and continually improve quality management system effectiveness.	
	5.4 Planning	5.4.1 Quality objectives The quality objectives must be measurable and coherent with the quality policy and be established in the right functions and at the right levels throughout the organisation.
		5.4.2 Quality management system planning Top management must assure that the quality management system is planned and integrated to meet all the requirements listed under 4.1.

Table 3.14. ISO 9001 Requirements (ISO-9001, 2000)

REQUIREMENTS DESCRIPTION		
5. Management responsibility	5.5 Responsibility, authority and communication	5.5.1 Responsibility and authority Top management must assure that responsibility and authority are defined and communicated within the organisation.
		5.5.2 Management representative Top management must appoint a manager who must assure that the processes needed for the quality management system are established, implemented and maintained.
		5.5.3 Internal communication Top management needs to set up an effective system of communication to ensure effective operation of the quality management system.
	5.6 Management review	5.6.1 General Top management must regularly review the organisation's quality management system to evaluate opportunities for improvement and changes to the quality management system, including the quality policy and quality objectives.
		5.6.2 Review input The input for the management review must include: internal audit results, customer feedback, how well processes have been working and how well products have been meeting requirements, status of corrective and preventive actions, earlier management review follow-up actions, changes that could effect the quality management system, and recommendations for improvement.
		5.6.3 Review output The management review must result in all the decisions and actions related to improving the effectiveness of the quality management system and its processes, improving the product in line with customer requirements and the need for resources.
6 Resource management	6.1 Provision of resources The organisation must determine and provide the resources for implementing and maintaining the quality management system and continually improving its effectiveness and raising customer satisfaction by meeting their requirements.	
	6.2 Human resources	6.2.1 General People performing work affecting product quality must be competent and have appropriate education, training, skills and experience.
		6.2.2 Competence, awareness and training The organisation must determine what capabilities or training people need to do jobs that affect product quality or otherwise assist people to meet these needs, assess the effectiveness of the actions taken, make sure people understand how important their activities are and how they contribute to achieving the quality objectives and keep records of education, training, skills and experience (see 4.2.4).
	6.3 Infrastructure The organisation must determine, provide and maintain the infrastructure required to meet the product requirements. The infrastructure includes buildings, workspace and associated services, processing equipment (hardware and software) and supporting services (such as transport and communication).	
	6.4 Work environment The organisation must determine and manage the work environment necessary to meet the product requirements.	

Table 3.14. ISO 9001 Requirements (cont'd) (ISO-9001, 2000)

REQUIREMENTS DESCRIPTION		
7 Product realisation requirements	7.1 Planning of product realisation The organisation must plan and develop the processes required to realise the product. The planning of product realisation must be coherent with the requirements of other quality management system processes (see 4.1). During planning, the organisation must determine the quality objectives and product requirements, needed to establish processes, documents and provide resources needed for product realisation; required verification, monitoring, inspection and test activities, as well as product acceptance criteria; and the records to be kept to demonstrate that the realisation processes and resulting product meet the requirements (see 4.2.4).	
	7.2 Customer-related process	7.2.1 Determination of requirements related to the product The organisation must determine: the requirements specified by the customer, including the requirements for delivery and post-delivery activities; requirements not established by the customer but necessary for the specified use; legal or statutory requirements related to the product; any additional requirement determined by the organisation.
		7.2.2 Review of requirements related to the product The organisation must review the requirements related to the product. This review should be conducted before the organisation is committed to supplying the customer with a product. Records of the results of the review, the modifications and actions taken as a result of the review must be kept (see 4.2.4).
		7.2.3 Customer communication The organisation must establish and implement effective communication channels with customers concerning the product information, questions about contracts, order handling, changes and customer feedback.
	7.3 Design and development	7.3.1 Design and development planning The organisation must plan and control product design and development. During design and development planning, the organisation must determine the design and development stages, review, verification and validation for each design and development stage and the responsibility and authority for design and development.
		7.3.2 Design and development inputs The inputs related to product requirements must be determined and records kept (see 4.2.4). These inputs should be reviewed to verify their appropriateness. The requirements must be complete, without ambiguity and not contradictory.
		7.3.3 Design and development outputs The output of design and development must include sufficient information to verify that design output meets design input requirements and should be approved before release.

Table 3.14. ISO 9001 Requirements (cont'd) (ISO-9001, 2000)

REQUIREMENTS DESCRIPTION		
7 Product realisation require-ments	7.3 Design and develop-ment	7.3.4 Design and development review Systematic reviews of design and development must be conducted as planned in each stage (see 7.3.1). The participants must include representatives from each function concerned with the design and development stage being reviewed. Records of the results of the verification activities and any action required must be kept (see 4.2.4).
		7.3.5 Design and development verification The design output must be verified to assure that it meets design input requirements (see 7.3.1). Records must be kept of the results of verification and any required action (see 4.2.4).
		7.3.6 Design and development validation The design and development must be validated as planned (see 7.3.1) to assure that the resulting product is capable of meeting the requirements for its specified application or intended use, if known. Whenever possible, the validation should be performed prior to product delivery or implementation. Records must be kept of the validation results and any required action (see 4.2.4).
		7.3.7 Control of design and development changes The design and development changes must be identified and records must be kept. The changes must be reviewed, verified and validated, as appropriate, and approved before they are carried out. The review of design and development changes must include the evaluation of the impact of the changes on the constituent parts and delivered product. Records must be kept of the changes review and any required action (see 4.2.4).
	7.4 Purchasing	7.4.1 Purchasing process The organisation must ensure that purchased products meet the specified purchasing requirements. The extent of the controls applied to the supplier and the purchased product must depend on the importance of the purchased products in the later product implementation or on the finished product. The organisation must evaluate and select suppliers depending on their ability to provide products that meet the organisation's requirements. Criteria for selection, evaluation and re-evaluation must be established. Records must be kept of the evaluation results and any required action (see 4.2.4).
		7.4.2 Purchasing information The purchasing information must describe the product being ordered, including, if appropriate, requirements for product, procedure, process and equipment approval, requirements for personnel competencies and quality management system requirements.
		7.4.3 Verification of purchased product The organisation must establish and carry out the inspection and other activities required to ensure that the purchased product meets the specified purchasing requirements.

Table 3.14. ISO 9001 Requirements (cont'd) (ISO-9001, 2000)

REQUIREMENTS DESCRIPTION		
7 Product realisation require- ments	7.5 Production and service provision	7.5.1 Control of production and service provision The organisation must plan and carry out the production and provision of service under controlled conditions. The controlled conditions must include, if applicable, information regarding product specifications, instructions for carrying out the work, suitable equipment, use and implementation of adequate tools for monitoring and measuring, criteria for product release, delivery and post-delivery servicing activities.
		7.5.2 Validation of processes for production and service provision The organisation must validate the production processes and service provision where the resulting products cannot be verified through monitoring or measurement. This includes any process where deficiencies are not identified until the product is in use or the service is delivered. Validation must demonstrate that the operation of the processes achieves the planned results.
		7.5.3 Identification and traceability Where appropriate, the organisation must establish appropriate procedures to identify the product and its status as it moves through the production process. When traceability is a requirement, the organisation must control and record the unique serial identification of the product (see 4.2.4).
		7.5.4 Customer property The organisation must take special care of the customer's property when it is under the organisation's control or is being used by it. The organisation must identify, verify, protect and safeguard property provided by the customer for use or inclusion in the product.
		7.5.5 Preservation of the product The organisation must preserve product conformity during the internal process and delivery at the intended destination. This preservation must include the identification, handling, packaging, storage and protection of parts and products.
7.6 Control of monitoring and measuring devices The organisation must determine the monitoring and measurement to be taken and the measuring and monitoring devices required to provide evidence of product compliance with the specified requirements (see 7.2.1). The organisation must establish processes to assure that monitoring and measuring can be carried out and are carried out in compliance with the monitoring and measuring requirements. The ability of computer programs to satisfy their intended purpose must be confirmed when they are used in monitoring and measuring activities of the specified requirements. This must be carried out before they are used and again confirmed whenever necessary.		

Table 3.14. ISO 9001 Requirements (cont'd) (ISO-9001, 2000)

REQUIREMENTS DESCRIPTION		
8 Measurement, analysis and improvement	8.1 General The organisation must plan and implement the inspection, measuring, analysis and improvement activities needed to demonstrate that the product meets the requirements, assure the quality management system works as planned, and continually improve the effectiveness of the quality management system. This must include the determination of the applicable methods, including statistical techniques and the scope of their use.	
	8.2 Monitoring and measurement	8.2.1 Customer satisfaction As one of the quality management system performance measures, the organisation must monitor information concerning the customer's perception of whether the organisation meets its requirements. Methods to gather and use this information must be determined.
		8.2.2 Internal audit The organisation must carry out internal audits regularly to determine how well the quality management system meets the plans (see 7.1). Audits address conformity with the quality management system, the requirements of ISO 9001:2000, and the effectiveness of the implementation.
		8.2.3 Monitoring and measurement of processes The organisation must apply appropriate methods to monitor, and when applicable, measure the quality management system processes. These methods must demonstrate that the processes are able to achieve the planned results. If they do not achieve the planned results, corrective action must be taken to make sure the product meets requirements.
		8.2.4 Monitoring and measurement of product The organisation must measure and monitor the product features to verify that they meet the product requirements. This must be done in the appropriate stages of the product realisation process according to the plans (see 7.1). Records must be kept showing the product meets acceptance criteria and the name of the person who authorised release of the product (see 4.2.4).
	8.3 Control of nonconforming product The organisation must ensure that any nonconforming product is identified and controlled to prevent its unintended use or delivery. The controls, responsibilities and authorities related to dealing with the nonconforming product must be defined in a written procedure. Any corrected products must be reinspected to assure that they meet the requirements. The organisation must take the appropriate action with regard to the effects or potential effects of any product that has been found to be defective after its release to the customer.	

Table 3.14. ISO 9001 Requirements (cont'd) (ISO-9001, 2000)

REQUIREMENTS DESCRIPTION		
8 Measure-ment, analysis and improve-ment	8.4 Analysis of data The organisation must determine, collect and analyse the appropriate data to ensure the suitability and effectiveness of the quality management system and to evaluate opportunities for continual improvement of quality management system effectiveness. This must include data generated from the result of monitoring and measurement and any other relevant sources. The analysis of data must provide information on customer satisfaction (see 8.2.1), whether the product meets the requirements (see 7.2.1), process and product characteristics and trends, including opportunities for preventive actions, and suppliers.	
	8.5 Improve-ment	8.5.1 Continual improvement The organisation must make use of the quality policy, the quality objectives, the audit, results, data analysis, corrective and preventive actions and management review to continually improve the effectiveness of the quality management system.
		8.5.2 Corrective action The organisation must take action to fix the root causes of nonconformities to prevent them from occurring again. The corrective actions must be proportional to the effects of the detected nonconformities.
		8.5.3 Preventive action The organisation must take action to do away with the root causes of nonconformities that have yet to occur. Preventive actions must be proportional to the effects of the potential problems.

Table 3.14. ISO 9001 Requirements (cont'd) (ISO-9001, 2000)

From the above description, it follows that ISO 9001 (ISO-9001, 2000) is an *informal model*. It focuses on the organisation's quality management system and on the quality standards that the analysed processes should meet. The only process element represented by the model is *activity*. This model does not include other elements like agents, technological resources, other strategic processes (related to the internal structure and organisation of the company) and, generally, other criteria that do not focus on the company's quality system. The model covers the *organisational* and *technological* environments. The characteristics of the social environment are not explicitly mentioned. Even though the model does specify training requirements for the organisation's staff, there is no investigation of cognitive processes, motivations or group dynamics, which means that the model cannot be classed as accounting for the social environment.

With respect to the model features, ISO 9001 development follows a standard production process, applicable to any type of organisation. It is just a list of activities to be performed and the requirements that they should meet. The standard does not identify either the relationships between these tasks or how to implement a task that is not in place at the company. However, it attaches special importance to monitoring and customer satisfaction after product delivery. This information is only organised from the *functional perspective* in the representation.

3.2.2.2. CMMI

The Software Engineering Institute at Carnegie Mellon University started to develop the Capability Maturity Model (CMM) in 1986 (Paulk et al., 1995) to analyse the capability of an organisation to produce high quality software consistently and predictably and to improve the organisation's software process. Its development was based on incorporating the principles of Total Quality Management into the software process (Fox & Frakes, 1997). The list of the processes included in the model was based on DoD standard 2167A (Kuvaja et al., 1994; DoD, 1988; DoD, 1995).

With the aim of evaluating other factors that influence the software process and, above all, developing a framework to integrate a range of production processes, the SEI developed a series of maturity models, which, in principle, materialised as independent evaluation methods (Curtis et al., 1995a): a) Software CMM, b) People CMM, c) Systems Engineering CMM, d) Software Acquisition CMM, and e) Integrated Product Development CMM.

Later the Department of Defense sponsored the development of an integrated model based on this set of models to unify the use of multiple standards in practice. This is called Capability Maturity Model Integration (CMMI). The method analysed in this section is what is referred to as Software CMMI, but which, for the sake of simplicity, is referred to here as CMMI. So, the CMMI project combines three source models (the Capability Maturity Model for Software (SW-CMM) Version 2.0 Draft C, Electronic Industries Alliance Standard (EIA/IS) 731, and the Integrated Product Development Capability Maturity Model (IPD-CMM) Version 0.98) to generate an improved single framework for use in organisations.

The purpose of the model is to provide guidance for improving the organisation's processes and capabilities to manage product or service development, acquisition and maintenance. An organisation can use the CMMI model to start to improve goals and priorities, improve processes and provide guidance for assuring process stability and maturity. There are several available CMMI models, which means that each organisation has to decide which to adopt depending on its needs. First, a choice should be made between a continuous or a staged representation, each of which has the benefits listed in Table 3.15.

CMMI REPRESENTATIONS	
Continuous	**Staged**
Allow you to select the order of improvement that best meets the organization's business objectives and mitigates the organization's areas of risk.	Provide a proven sequence of improvements, beginning with basic management practices and progressing through a path of successive levels, each serving as a foundation for the next.
Enable comparisons across and among organizations on a process area.	Permit comparisons across and among organizations by the use of maturity levels.
Provide an easy migration from EIA/IS 731 to CMMI.	Provide an easy migration from the SW-CMM to CMMI.
Afford an easy comparison of process improvement to ISO/IEC 15504, because the organization of process areas is similar to ISO/IEC 15504.	Provide a single rating that summarizes appraisal results and allows comparisons among organizations.

Table 3.15. CMMI Model Representations

Next the body of knowledge needs to be selected. There are now four options: systems engineering, software engineering, integrated process and product development and supplier sourcing (SEI, 2002a; SEI, 2002b; SEI, 2002c; SEI, 2002d; SEI, 2002e; SEI, 2002f).

Since our primary concern is software process modelling, this section describes the model, and not the assessment techniques used or its methods of evaluation. The CMMI model with staged representation provides an evolutionary framework that organisations can adopt to continually improve their process, including or improving given activities rather than introducing large-scale changes. It was developed upon the concept of maturity, meaning the extent to which a given process is explicitly defined, managed, measured and controlled. Its hierarchical structure is composed of five maturity levels (initial, managed, defined, quantitatively managed and optimising), associated with a particular behaviour of the organisation and its software process. With the exception of level 1, each level provides the basis upon which the improvement actions of the next level should be taken. These maturity levels define an ordinal scale that roughly corresponds to software process evolution from an ad hoc (unpredictable and unmanaged) state, through an intuitive state (basic process management and repeatability of some projects), a qualitative state (well-defined and institutionalised processes), a quantitative state (measured and controlled processes) to the optimising state, where the processes will be continuously improved thanks to their quantitative control.

Each maturity level is decomposed into the following set of elements, which conforms the underlying structure of the model:

- Process areas are a cluster of activities associated with a level. They constitute the core tasks that should be improved, if they exist and are already executed at the organisation, or implemented, if they do not exist. At this level of definition, they are the criteria that the company should meet to qualify for the level in question. All CMMI process areas are common to both continuous and staged representations. In the staged representation, process areas are organized by maturity levels, as shown in Figure 3.8.

- Specific goals apply to a process area and address the unique characteristics that describe what must be implemented to satisfy the process area.

- A specific practice is an activity that is considered important in achieving the associated specific goal.

- Common features are a schema that organises the generic practices of each process area.

- Generic goals are called "generic" because the same goal statement appears in multiple process areas. In the staged representation, each process area has only one generic goal.

- Generic practices provide institutionalisation to ensure that the processes associated with the process area will be effective. Generic practices are categorized by generic goals and common features.

A CMMI model with a staged representation is illustrated in Figure 3.9. CMMI models are designed to describe discrete levels of process improvement. In the staged representation, maturity levels provide a recommended order for undertaking process improvement in stages. As illustrated in Figure 3.9, maturity levels organise the process areas. Within the process areas are generic and specific goals as well as generic and specific practices. Common features organise generic practices.

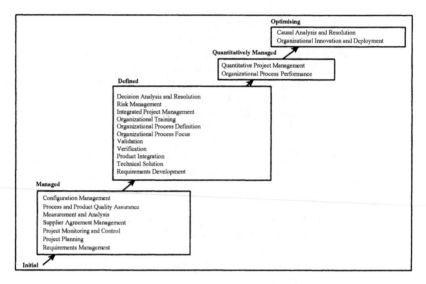

Figure 3.8. CMMI maturity levels (SEI, 2002c)[5]

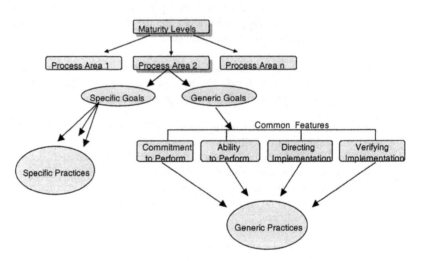

Figure 3.9. CMMI Model components (SEI, 2002c)[4]

---

[5] Special permission to use Capability Maturity Model Integration for Software Engineering version 1.1 © 2002 by Carnegie Mellon University in A Software Process Model Handbook for Incorporating People's Capabilities is granted by the SEI.

The maturity levels specified by the CMMI model with a staged representation are:

1. *Initial*: at maturity level 1, processes are usually ad hoc and chaotic. The organisation usually does not provide a stable environment. Maturity level 1 organisations often produce products and services that work; however, they frequently exceed the budget and schedule of their projects.

2. *Managed*: at maturity level 2, an organization has achieved all the specific and generic goals of the maturity level 2 process areas. In other words, the projects of the organisation have ensured that requirements are managed and that processes are planned, performed, measured, and controlled. Commitments are established among relevant stakeholders and work products are reviewed with stakeholders to check that they satisfy their specified requirements, standards, and objectives.

3. *Defined*: at maturity level 3, an organisation has achieved all the specific and generic goals of the process areas assigned to maturity levels 2 and 3. At maturity level 3, processes are well characterised and understood, and are described in standards, procedures, tools, and methods. The process standards for a project are tailored from the organization's set of standard processes to suit a particular project.

4. *Quantitatively managed*: at maturity level 4, an organisation has achieved all the specific goals of the process areas assigned to maturity levels 2, 3, and 4 and the generic goals assigned to maturity levels 2 and 3. Subprocesses are selected that significantly contribute to overall process performance. These selected subprocesses are controlled using statistical and other quantitative techniques. Quantitative objectives for quality and process performance are established and used as criteria in managing processes. Quantitative objectives are based on the needs of the customer, end users, organisation, and process implementers. For these processes, data analysis can identify causes of process variation and the sources of special causes are corrected. All this information is kept in repositories for future reference.

5. *Optimising*: at maturity level 5, an organisation has achieved all the specific goals of the process areas assigned to maturity levels 2, 3, 4, and 5 and the generic goals assigned to maturity levels 2 and 3. Processes are continually improved based on a quantitative understanding of the common causes of variation inherent in processes. Improvements are selected based on a quantitative understanding of their expected contribution to achieving the organisation's process-improvement objectives versus the cost to and impact on the organisation.

The continuous representation, which uses capability levels to measure processes, has six levels numbered from 0 to 5: incomplete, performed, managed, defined, quantitatively managed and optimising (SEI, 2002d). Each level corresponds to a generic goal and a set of generic and specific practices.

This representation has more specific practices than the staged representation because the continuous representation has two types of such practices: base practices and advanced practices. In the continuous representation, there are generic practices for levels 1 to 5, whereas they only appear for levels 2 and 3 in the staged representation.

When a company needs to develop a software project, the process to be used will be derived from the organisation's standard software process, always taking into account the project characteristics: requirements and the life cycle to be applied. The final result will be the definition of what is known as "software process defined for the project", which sets out all the stages and activities that will be performed, plans and controls needed for management and results to be achieved. Therefore, this model allows the development of a detailed description of the process in compliance with the general definition and with planned control for proper tracking. The definition and implementation of this conceptual framework constitutes the core upon which the CMMI defines the process areas of the process management and engineering processes that will be developed at maturity levels 3 (defined), 4 (quantitatively managed) and 5 (optimising).

The process areas that the CMMI identifies correspond to the generic criteria that are assessed. They are divided into four categories:

- Process management: process management process areas contain the cross-project activities related to defining, planning, resourcing, deploying, implementing, monitoring, controlling, appraising, measuring, and improving processes.

- Project management: project management process areas cover the project management activities related to planning, monitoring, and controlling the project.

- Engineering: engineering process areas cover the development and maintenance activities that are shared across engineering disciplines (e.g., systems engineering and software engineering). The six process areas in the engineering process area category have inherent interrelationships. These interrelationships stem from applying a product development process rather than discipline-specific processes such as software engineering or systems engineering.

- Support: support process areas cover the activities that support product development and maintenance. The support process areas address processes that are used in the context of performing other processes. In general, the support process areas address processes that are targeted towards the project, and may address processes that apply more generally to the organisation. For example, process and product quality assurance can be used with all the process areas to provide an objective evaluation of the processes and work products described in all of the process areas.

The CMMI focuses exclusively on the organisational processes of software process management and control, representing *activities*. Some of the criticisms of CMM, such as it does not consider how to evaluate other factors influencing the process, for example, agents, like human resources (Mogilensky & Deimel, 1994; Bamberger, 1997), technological resources (Bollinger & McGowan, 1991), and strategic level processes (Cattaneo et al., 1995), related to the internal structure and organisation of the company, still apply to CMMI.

The CMMI covers the *organisational* and *technological environments* because the internal process of evaluation leads to changes to the organisational design and technological innovation. This model does not address the social environment of the organisation.

What the CMMI denotes as a maturity model is a model or yardstick used in evaluations. It was developed as a static structure: maturity levels, process areas, common features, specific goals, specific practices, generic goals and generic practices. It places each process area at a given level and proposes a strategy for implementing the areas from a *functional perspective* and on the basis of heuristics, which means that information quality of the software process model representation is *informal*.

People-Oriented Models

In this chapter, we present the software process models grouped under the name of people-oriented models. As mentioned earlier, these models can be either descriptive or prescriptive. In the following, we describe the models belonging to each of the categories that consider people according to Table 2.1. The results of the criteria described in Chapter 2 are highlighted in italics for each model.

4.1. DESCRIPTIVE PEOPLE-ORIENTED MODELS

These models are manual or automated descriptions that pay special atention to the roles that people perform or the capabilities of the people involved in the software development process. The models belonging to this category are typified as being a means for understanding and reasoning about the people and the roles of a process or for achieving more ambitious goals, such as automating and predicting the behaviour of the organisation's human resources and, consequently, the software process.

In particular, the descriptive people-oriented models examined in this section are: the Systems Dynamics-Based Model (Abdel-Hamid & Madnick, 1989), the Process Cycle Model (Madhavji, 1991), the Agile Methods and in particular eXtreme Programming (XP) (Becker, 1999) and Win Win (Boehm et al., 1998).

4.1.1. Systems Dynamics-Based Model

The Systems Dynamics approach to process modelling is used as a means to simulate proposed processes, predict the dynamic behaviour of the software process and report the appropriate policies and procedures to the project management. Abdel-Hamid and Madnick (1989) developed an automated comprehensive systems dynamics model of the software development process. This dynamic feedback model considers the management processes (for example, human resources planning, tracking and control, and management) and the technical processes of software production (for example, design, coding, quality assurance review, testing). It also addresses the capabilities (depending on the specific knowledge domain) of the people in the organisation. Its goal is to predict the dynamic behaviour of the software development processes and the consequences of the software development-related management policies and procedures.

This model proposes integrating knowledge of the software development processes and of the project personnel to predict the consequences on the behaviour of the overall software process. The simplified model is composed of four subsystems: human resource management, software production, controlling and planning.

This model was developed on the basis of a field study, conducted by interviewing (structured) software project managers from five organisations and based on the review and analysis of the literature on how to manage software projects in software development organisations. Each subsystem was represented using the causal loop diagram technique and Forrester's systems dynamics diagrams, and the global model was designed to arrive at the mathematical model and, finally, the computerised simulation model (Forrester, 1961). The human resource management subsystem captures the recruitment, training and transfer of the human resource. Employees can be characterised, for example, as novice and experienced, to ascertain effort and determine the total project workforce.

The software production subsystem models the software development process, which includes the design, coding and testing phases. The initial requirements definition and the final operation and maintenance phases are excluded. This is mainly due to the fact that the model focuses on analysing and simulating how the policies, decisions, actions, etc., of the project managers and software developers affect software development success or failure. So, the requirements phase was omitted, because, in many environments, the software development group is not in charge of defining user requirements (Abdel-Hamid, 1989). The formulation of software productivity is based on the work of the psychologist Ivan Steiner (1972). Steiner's model can be simplified as:

Real Productivity = Potential Productivity − Losses due to defective process.

Potential productivity is defined as the maximum level of productivity that can occur when an individual or a group... makes the best possible use of their resources (Abdel-Hamid, 1989). It is a function of two sets of factors, the nature of the task (for example, product complexity, database size) and the resources of the group (for example, people's capabilities, experience level, software tools). The losses induced by defective processes refer to losses in productivity due to communication and coordination impediments and/or low motivation.

The planning subsystem defines initial project estimates (for example, project duration, manpower, etc.) (Kemerer, 1987), which are reviewed during project development for redefinition. Finally, the controlling subsystem measures the deviations in real project variables against the planned or expected variables.

The model represents the following elements: *agent, activity* and *capability*. It is the first model analysed so far that considers the software process as a socio-technical process, including the capabilities of the people involved in software development. As regards the process environments covered by the model, the *social environment* is present, as it explicitly considers the characteristic of creativity. Additionally, the model addresses the *organisational environment* and the *technological environment*, albeit informally.

This systems dynamics model organises information from the *behavioural* perspective only. Accordingly, the representation is incomplete, as it fails to organise information from the functional, organisational and informational perspectives. As regards the notational characteristics, from the viewpoint of information quality, it is *automated* and from the viewpoint of formalised notation, its format is *text-based*.

Note that this is one of the few integral models, as it considers both the management and technical processes of software production, and the capabilities of the members of the organisation. However, it remains to formalise the requirements analysis phase and, consequently, the capabilities of developers, such as user interaction and flexibility in adapting to the user organisation, for it to be complete. This systems dynamics-based model offers a quantitative and deterministic description of the organisation's human resources from the viewpoint of human resource recruitment, training, transfer and experience level and not as regards the logic of competencies of the human resources and roles.

4.1.2. Process Cycle Model

The Process Cycle, shown in Figure 4.1, is a concise and integrated model of the software process engineering, management, implementation and improvement processes (Madhavji, 1991). The Process Cycle, formed by sectors A (engineering process models), B (managing software processes) and C (performing software processes), defines the scope of the entire set of process steps needed to develop and evolve software processes. This model describes the key roles performed by agents, the categories of tools used, the goals and policies that drive the processes and interrelationships and feedback between different roles.

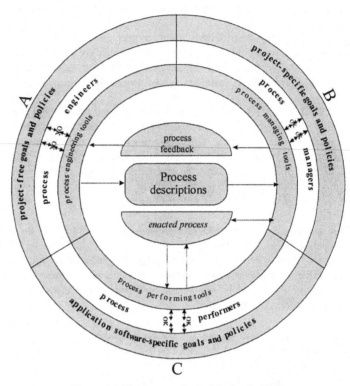

Figure 4.1. The Process Cycle (Madhavji, 1991)

In the standard model construction, tailoring and execution cycle (Figure 4.1), the communication, that is, the feedback between the sectors, from developers to managers and from managers to engineers, is continuous, leading to improvements in the models, from the application software-dependent models to the project-dependent models and from the project-dependent models to the project independent-models, respectively (Madhavji, 1991). In Figure 4.1, this communication is illustrated by a dashed directed line and a solid line from the process enactment tools to the process management tools. These tools would also provide feedback, producing qualitative and quantitative data on the active process. The feedback, generated or received by any sector does not necessarily remain within the process cycle. This feedback passes on to the corporate levels to improve the organisational goals and policies through osmosis with the outer ring of the cycle. The three sectors of this model are detailed in Table 4.1.

This model describes the following elements: both human (process engineer, manager and developer) and automated (tools of each sector of the model) *agents*, *activities* of the process cycle and *roles* of the process agents. The software development management, technical and support processes and their associated elements are not specified.

SECTOR	NAME	GOAL/GOAL & POLICY SCOPE	AGENTS	ROLES	TOOLS
A	Engineering process models	Explain the software process Software project independent and software process dependent	Process engineers	Design, construct & improve standard software processes	Design oriented
B	Managing software processes	Organise the software process Application software independent, project dependent	Process managers	Manage specific software process models	Management oriented
C	Performing software processes	Apply the software process Application software dependent	Process developers	Design, construct & improve application software	Software development specific

Table 4.1. Process Cycle sector characteristics

The Process Cycle model considers the technological aspects of software process engineering (Table 4.1), as the software process is described in the context of software development environments and the process cycle including the goals and policies of the organisation, the process and the application software. Therefore, this model covers the *technological environment*. The human agents and engineering tools permit the creation of new standard and specific software process models and software life cycle models. However, the model does not specify the social characteristics of the organisation and the people involved. Consequently, this model does not represent the organisational and social environments.

As mentioned above, the model identifies the role of the software process engineers, managers and developers, who perform design and improvement, process instantiation and enactment activities, respectively, and the flow of communication and control between the process elements. Therefore, the *information perspective* of this *informal* model is *behavioural* and *organisational*. As the notation is informal, the criterion of formalised notation is not analysed.

4.1.3. Agile Methods

The software process models developed in recent years, known as agile methods (AMs) (Beck et al., 2001; Fowler, 2001; Jeffries et al., 2001; Cockburn & Highsmith, 2001b) emerged especially in response to the complexity of traditional software development models and propose to strike a balance between a non-existent process and too complex a process. For this purpose, they suggest altering some principles that software development methods have traditionally used, such as the production of a lot of documentation for each activity or the detailed definition of tasks and task interdependency.

AMs are, therefore, proposed as *people-oriented adaptable models*. AMs are characterised as *adaptable* rather than *predictable* models, because they assume change to be an inherent part of the actual development process. Therefore, these models try to adapt and grow through change, even to the point of changing themselves.

Iterative development is a must in adaptable processes to be able to deal with the permanent changes required by the actual process. Each iteration should be as short as is manageable, generating frequent feedback. These short iterations mean that software errors or modifications tend to appear earlier on, ruling out the need for modifications later on that raise the cost of development. Additionally, such iterative development leads to a planning style where long-term plans are fuzzy and the only stable plans are short term, put together for just one iteration. In each iteration, iterative development provides a solid foundation that can be used to develop later plans.

Such an adaptable process calls for a different type of relationship with customers, where the actual customer works together with the development team in the same physical space throughout the entire project. The customer is involved in development rather than development being driven by a negotiated contract, which means that the customer works together with the development team, irrespective of the commitments established by means of a contract. This makes the genuine state of the project clearer to the customer.

Another major trait of AMs is that they advocate a *people-oriented* process (Cockburn & Highsmith, 2001a). In this respect, agilists (AM practitioners) state that no process should consider the people involved in development as replaceable parts, meaning that the process role should focus on supporting the work of the actual development team and not the generic process roles. The reason is that a very effective team of creative developers, focused on the quality of the individuals as well as how they work together as a team, is needed to enact an adaptable process.

The people focus is manifested in different ways in agile processes. One key element is the *acceptance* rather than the *enforcement* of a process. Agilists consider that management often enforces software processes, but acceptance of a process calls for commitment from and, consequently, the active involvement of the whole development team. In this approach, there needs to be acceptance that developers and project management share the same decision-making responsibilities, thereby acknowledging the importance of developers.

There are a lot of AMs that share many of the above-mentioned features, of which the most well known according to (Glass, 2001; Cohen et al., 2003; Larman, 2004) are: eXtreme Programming (XP), Scrum, Dynamic Systems Development Method (DSDM), Evo, Crystal Methods, Adaptive Software Development, Agile Modeling and Lean Development.

Of this range of agile methods, eXtreme Programming (XP) is ranked by the Cutter Consortium as the most commonly used AM, accounting for 38% of the agile market (Charette, 2004; Riehle, 2000). Therefore, this chapter focuses on this method.

4.1.3.1. eXtreme Programming (XP)

As an agile software development strategy, XP is a people-oriented adaptable model founded on iterative practices. These practices target features and releases and are focused on an intensive communication obliging customers to get directly involved in development.

In the mid 1980s, a research group at Tektronix formed by Kent Beck and Ward Cunningham conceived CRC ("Class/Responsibilities/Collaborators") cards (Beck & Cunningham, 1989). They were simply 4x6-inch index cards on which the responsibilities (high-level description of the purpose of a class) and primary dependencies (existing between the different responsibilities) were written. No more could be written than what fitted on these cards, and they became a substitute technique for diagrams in model representation. As regards their syntactic economy and abstraction, these cards were the precursors of what XP storycards would later be.

XP uses paper storycards on which brief requirements of a product feature or characteristic are written. They have a granularity of 10 to 20 days, that is, the scope of the requirements contained on these cards will be developed in this period of time. Storycards are used to estimate priorities, scope and development time (time boxing).

The customer continuously works together with developers and comes up with details for writing storycards and the respective acceptance tests. In release planning, the customers together with the development team complete the storycards and time estimates and decide what implementation and release priorities there are (Beck, 1999).

XP teams are small, composed of from three to 20 people at most. The roles required for an XP development are defined as follows:

Customer
- Writes the stories and acceptance tests
- Selects the stories for each iteration

Developer
Programmer
- Designs, codes and writes test cases
- Refactors
- Identifies tasks and makes estimates

Tester or verifier
- Helps the customer to write and develop the acceptance tests

Management
Coach or advisor
- Intervenes and teaches

Tracker
- Takes measurements
- Reports project progress
- Provides feedback on estimates

Others
Technical advisor

XP is based on four values: communication, feedback, simplicity and courage. XP builds and encourages a series of practices based on these values that agile development teams should follow. These practices are old, tried and tested techniques, although XP unites them in such a way that each one strengthens the other. It does not require any tool outside the programming and testing field, nor does it require modelling. All it needs is storycard-based oral communication for both requirements definition and design.

The practices proposed initially for XP are as follows:

- Release planning. Programmers estimate the effort required to implement the customer stories, and the customer decides on the release scope and schedule. This practice aims to rapidly determine the scope of the next release, combining the business priorities defined by the customer and programmers' technical estimates. The spikes are an experiment in dynamic coding and are used to estimate how difficult the task at hand is and how long it will take. They are the agile version of a prototype.

- Small and frequent releases. A small system is rapidly developed at least every two or three months, and new deliverables to which a few items are added each time may be released every day.

- System metaphors. The system should be defined using a metaphor: story shared by the customer, managers and programmers that drives the whole system. The metaphor should describe very generically how the system should work.

- Simple design. Development is driven by the need to design the simplest solution that can be implemented at any time. Unnecessary complexities and extra code are removed, code should not be duplicated and as few classes as possible are defined. The design is built by defining cards written in short sessions, and nothing is designed that is not needed at the time in an attempt to minimise the use of diagrams and documents.

- Continuous testing. Testing drives the integration of the development. The purpose of the code is not to meet a requirement, but to pass the tests. There are two types of tests: unit tests, which verify just one class, and acceptance tests, which integrate and check the whole or a large part of the system. All the points under development should have automatic unit and acceptance tests to rule out inspection work. The customer helps to write the functional tests before the code is written. Although the tests and code are written by the same programmer or pair of programmers, the tests should be carried out automatically without human intervention.

- Continuous refactoring. This practice involves enacting a process by making small changes that modify the internal structure of the system without altering the external and apparent behaviour of the code. Assertions (invariants, pre- and postconditions) are habitually used to express properties that should be conserved, or graph transforming techniques, software metrics, program refinement and formal analysis of concepts. There is a long catalogue of the most common refactorings: replacement of iteration by recursion; class, interface or method extraction; replacement of one by another clearer algorithm; decomposition of conditionals, etc.

- Pair programming. All the code should be written by pairs of programmers. Jointly, two people seated at one computer write code, taking it in turns to use the mouse and keyboard. Whereas one thinks from a more strategic viewpoint and does what could be termed real-time code inspection, the other programmer writes the code directly, and they switch roles several times a day.

- Collective code ownership. The code is open and accessible to all the programmers. Any programmer can change any part of the code at any time, provided they first write the respective test.

- Continuous integration. Each developed part is integrated into the code base as soon as it is ready. This process can be performed several times a day, for which purpose a machine is set aside exclusively for this process.

- Sustainable pace, maximum 8-hour working day. As software development is considered a creative process, the team members should be fresh and relaxed to work efficiently. This motivates programmers, lowers staff turnover and improves product quality.

- On-site customer. The customer should be present at the development site and available full time for the team to define requirements and run continuous testing.

- Coding standards. Development is driven by code rules and code-mediated communication, with defined notation styles, indentation and nomenclature. As there is some code purism in XP, comments are not well looked upon. If code is so obscure as to need explanation, it should be rewritten.

- Open plan. The physical arrangement of the team is essential for the integration of XP work. The site should be large and open, without divisions. The programmer pairs should be placed in the centre, there should be a blackboard that everyone can see, and private machines should be arranged on the outside.

- Fair rules. The team should define its own rules to follow, which may change at any time. Each project is a one off, there being no process that is suitable for all projects, and the set of practices should be tailored to the features of each individual project.

One of the most significant practices is the strong emphasis placed on testing, as a foundation for development, change control and joint work between the customer and developer. Additionally, before they write any code, each programmer pair must write the unit tests from the acceptance tests, which, as already mentioned, are written with the active participation of the customer. The tests are run within a process of continuous integration and construction that provides a stable platform for future development.

Upon this platform, XP builds an evolutionary development process that is based on refactoring the system in each iteration (Fowler et al., 1999). Refactoring means modifying the code of a software product to improve its internal structure without altering its external behaviour. This is a disciplined code restructuring technique. All design focuses on the current iteration and nothing that could be needed in the future is designed beforehand. Every time a change is made as a result of refactoring, a testing session has to be run to check that the changes have not affected system behaviour, that is, no defects have been introduced.

These practices (Beck & Cunningham, 1989) can be adapted to the particular features of each system and have been divided in the more recent versions into four classes as indicated in Table 4.2.

CLASS	PRACTICES
Joint Practices	Iterations Common Vocabulary – replaces Metaphors Open Workspace Retrospectives
Programmer Practices	Test-Driven Development Pair Programming Refactoring Collective Ownership Continuous Integration Simple Design
Management Practices	Accepted Responsibility Air Cover for the Team Quarterly Review Mirror – The manager should convey a faithful reflection of the state of affairs Sustainable Pace
Customer Practices	Story Telling Release Planning Acceptance Testing Frequent Releases

Table 4.2. XP practices (Beck & Cunningham, 1989)

The values and practices proposed by XP integrated into the iterative life cycle model define an adaptable development model especially for small developments, where the customer can be totally and continuously integrated into the project from the definition of requirements through to testing. Generally, this type of adaptable model is operational for developing small and non-critical systems, where changes can be addressed as they occur. Management activities are confined to short-term planning activities and mainly development team coordination. This model is illustrated in Figure 4.2, depicting the four XP life cycle phases.

- The purpose of the *exploration phase* is to create enough storycards to gather the information required to undertake the first iteration. The activities defined for this phase are: create prototypes, explore programming technologies and write storycards.

- The purpose of the *planning phase* is to determine the date of the first delivery and what elements storycards will include. The activities for this phase are: plan releases, write storycards.

- The *iterations phase* implements a testing system for the first release and develops the code of what was defined in the preceding phase. This stage includes the following activities: test and program, plan and estimate iteration.

- In the last *production phase*, the operational system is developed and the conditions for the maintenance and following iterations are prepared. The activities defined in this phase are: document code, train and market.

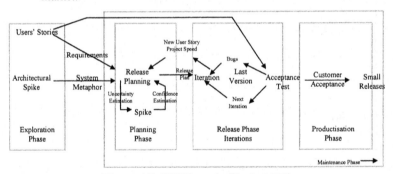

Figure 4.2. XP life cycle (Beck, 1999)

The documentation generated by XP for developing the model is textual and informal. It defines the following input products:

- *Storycard*: this is a handwritten card describing a requirement or a reminder to discuss details with the customer.

- *List of tasks*: during iteration planning, the development team writes on a blackboard or wallchart a list of tasks for all the storycards selected for the iteration. Taking into account that each iteration should be developed within from 10 to 20 days, one alterative is to generate cards for individual tasks.

- *Visible graphics*: the graphics should be simple and understandable for the whole team. XP does not formalise the graphics for documentation, the idea being to put forward, discuss and communicate ideas to the whole team.

Development is code driven in the understanding that the important part of the documentation is source code, and only a minimum and small amount of documentation is required for any given task.

As already mentioned, for XP, the team owns the code. All the code is created by programmers working as pairs and using the same computer. The pairs should switch and rotate frequently to do different tasks. Of the pair of programmers, one should observe and continuously inspect the code, thinking about what it should be coding, and the other member directly writes the code, bearing in mind the tests built previously. Team productivity does not depend on how many people write the code, but on a combination of practices by each programmer pair.

For XP, team communication is guaranteed by rotating programmers around the different development tasks. On the other hand, as mentioned above, code is open to the whole team, and any programmer can modify any part of the code. This practice is enforced by the idea of using coding standards that define a single programming style in the language being implemented in the project so that any programmer can refactor the code at any time.

In this schema of textual and informal communication, minimum documentation and team ownership of code, the capabilities of the people defined by XP become central elements for building the development team. XP defines the need to form workteams with competent, creative professionals who are good communicators, and are highly sociable and adaptable to changes. Such professionals are, for XP, the best at deciding how to direct their own technical work, which takes a lot of self-discipline. Accepting an adaptive process calls for commitment, which calls for the active involvement of the whole team. This is why developers should be able to made the technical decisions, and, in the planning process, only developers can estimate how long it will take them to do a job. Even though XP places sizeable emphasis on the need to build development teams from people with adequate capabilities, it does not go into how to select these people.

The XP model represents the following elements: *agent, activity, artefact, role* and *capability*. This agile model defines the delegational management of projects, where the doers decide how to do the work. This places high knowledge and creativity requirements on people. As regards the process environments covered by the model, the social environment is present, albeit informally, as the model considers the characteristics of creativity and social interaction. The social environment is substituted in XP by the definition of people's and role capabilities generically, although the model does not systematically define the skills, attitudes and aptitudes for applying XP. Additionally, XP addresses both the technological environment, as it prescribes, for example, testing techniques and tools for each development, and the organisational environment, as many of the described XP practices, such as pair programming, 8-hour working day, one team or open workspace, indicate an explicit definition of the organisational behaviour for development using XP.

As mentioned above, the XP model focuses on defining who performs each activity, how the physical space is arranged and where the tasks are performed within the work team. Therefore, this informal model organises information from the organisational perspective only. Accordingly, the representation is incomplete, as it fails to organise information from the functional, behavioural and informational perspectives. As the notation is informal, we do not analyse the criterion of formalised notation.

4.1.4. The Win-Win Spiral Model

The win-win model (Boehm & Ross, 1994) is a modification of the spiral model originally developed by Barry Boehm in 1988 (Boehm, 1988) and very extensively used for developing large-scale systems and software. The original spiral model proposes an evolutionary development model that combines the iterativeness of prototyping with the controlled and systematic aspects of a sequential linear model.

Let us first briefly analyse the spiral model. The spiral model assumes that software evolves (that is, requirements change) as the development process advances and, also, explicitly recognises the risks of this development process. This allows developers and users to better understand and react to these risks at each of the stages of evolution.

These evolutionary stages are represented by prototyping. Therefore, while the model retains the systematic stepwise approach suggested by the classical life cycle to build each prototype, these steps are incorporated into an iterative framework that reflects how software evolves through each successive prototype.

The spiral model suggests that software be developed as a number of incremental releases, each increment conforming a development cycle. Each orbit of the spiral that is constructed represents a software process phase, as shown in Figure 4.3.

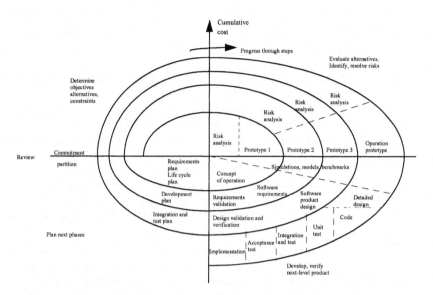

Figure 4.3. Spiral model (Boehm, 1988)

The spiral model is depicted as iterative development cycles in the shape of a spiral, where the inner cycles of the diagram denote analysis and early prototyping, and the outside cycles, the classical model. The radial dimension designates the cumulative costs of development, and the angular dimension the progress made towards completing each spiral development. Risk analysis, which aims to identify situations that can cause the project to fail or go over budget or deadline, is part of each spiral cycle. In each cycle, risk analysis accounts for the same amount of angular movement, whereas the ground covered by the sweeping motion denotes the growth of the effort levels required for risk analysis.

As shown in Figure 4.3, system feasibility is the kernel of the model according to which the subsequent stages of requirements, system design and so on for each development stage are defined. However, each step from one phase to another leads to changes to the project plan, and the cost and schedule should be adjusted depending on the customer's response to the evaluation.

In the spiral model, each organisation should work on a process with generic phases, applicable for all projects, with additional phases added for special projects or when problems are identified during development. There are no fixed phases in the model. The project management should decide how to divide the project into phases.

A set of six fundaments that Boehm terms "invariants" need to be combined to use this development model.

1. Concurrent determination of key issues (operational concepts, requirements plans, design and code).
2. Each cycle has: objectives, constraints, alternatives, risks, reviews and commitments to continue.
3. The effort level is driven by risk considerations.
4. The detail level is driven by risk considerations.
5. The results to be produced during the spiral process become anchor points.
   - Life Cycle Objectives: what should the system do?
   - Life Cycle Architecture: what is the system structure?
   - Initial Operating Capability: first version released
6. The emphasis is placed on the life cycle activities, the system and the products or results.

The win-win spiral model (Boehm & Ross, 1994) emerged as an innovation to this model. The win-win model retains the iterative logic of the original spiral model and also defines a set of negotiation activities at the beginning of each step in the spiral. This means that, apart from the stress that the original model lays on iterative development, the win-win model places special emphasis on the milestones or anchor points that help to establish how complete the cycle around the spiral is and provides milestones for decision making before continuing the software project.

This model suggests that the best negotiations should target a win-win situation, where the customer wins by getting the product or system that satisfies most of his or her needs, at the same time as the developer wins by working to meet realistic budgets and delivery dates.

Therefore, the win-win model aims to solve, quickly and as best meets the needs of each development project, the questions concerning when during development to define the development objectives, constraints and alternatives.

This variation on the spiral model aims to establish and get the customer and development team to agree on the win conditions of each stage of software development, evaluating various alternatives that will enable the agreed plans to be developed and executed. It is not merely an exercise in communication with the customer, but involves the performance of a number of activities defined as part of the process to be enacted by the customer and the developer.

Figure 4.4 shows the win-win model, where the activities added to the original spiral model are highlighted in grey.

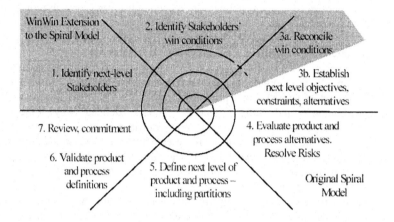

Figure 4.4. Win-win model (Boehm et al., 1998)

The win-win model proposes the following activities for negotiating the win conditions:

    1. Identify next-level stakeholders
    2. Identify stakeholders' win conditions
    3a. Reconcile win conditions

whereas the model retains the following activities from the original spiral model:

    3b. Establish next level objectives, constraints, alternatives
    4. Evaluate product and process alternatives, and resolve risks
    5. Define next level of product and process – including partitions
    6. Validate product and process definitions
    7. Review, commitment.

For the win-win model, each organisation should work to a model with generic phases applicable for all the projects, as well as with phases added for specific projects. The required documents must be produced in each phase. As in the original spiral model, the project management must decide how to divide the process into phases, but there is a lot of participation by users in defining each phase for determining the conditions for negotiation by the customer and the developer.

The definition or characterisation of the development process actors and roles is flexible in this model, although both the customer and the developers must participate in negotiating each stage of the iterative development process. This model describes the following elements: *agents, activities* of the spiral process and *roles.*

This model does not define the technological and organisational process environments, whereas it does define how to generate the social environment in which the customer and the development team closely cooperate in a context of negotiation and environmental flexibility.

The model is automated with a support tool that provides information on the definition of activities and provides graphics for visualising the conditions for negotiation and the generic roles defined by the model (http://sunset.usc.edu/research/WINWIN/winwinspiral.html). Therefore, the quality of the information of the representation is *automated* and the formalised notation is *text* and *graphic*-based. The win-win model addresses the software construction process from the *organisational* and *informational perspectives*.

As mentioned above, the win-win model is a schema that aims to convert the traditional spiral model into a more adaptable and lighter model, allowing the definition of each of the spiral orbits as a feasible, practicable iteration that is clearly decided on the basis of customer needs.

4.2. PRESCRIPTIVE PEOPLE-ORIENTED MODELS

These models are manual or computerised specifications of the software process mainly considering human resources. Their chief purpose is to act as a guide to software process modelling, that is, they are aimed at providing assistance to process agents through the mechanical interpretation of the software process models (Lonchamp, 1994). This model category also includes prescriptions for evaluating and improving the organisation's human resources.

The integration of formalisms for describing both the software process and the members of the process and their relationships, which explicitly include the human parts and the interaction in which they are involved, has been proposed by approaches such as SOCCA, ALF, PMDB+ and the Unified Process. These proposals are based on the fact that *software processes are people driven* (Conradi et al., 1992), and the interactions between humans and between humans and the tools that support their activities (characterised by high variability and unpredictability) should be specified formally. In this manner, the complexity of the resulting software process, which places high demands on technical and organisational management, can be managed better.

The models examined in this section are:

- Process models

    - PMDB+ model (Penedo & Shu, 1991)

  - ALF model (Canals et al., 1994)

  - SOCCA model (Engels & Groenewegen, 1994)

  - Unified Process model (Jacobson et al., 1999)

• Evaluation model

  - People CMM (Curtis et al., 2001).

The first category is composed of formalised automated process models and the second of one manual evaluation model. As explained in Chapter 2, the models in both categories constitute a representative set of people-oriented prescriptive models, as they are an original basis for defining other models in this area (Lonchamp, et al., 1990; Finkelstein et al., 1994; McChesney, 1995; Derniame et al., 1999; Acuña et al., 2001).

4.2.1. Process Models

4.2.1.1. PMDB+ Model

The PMDB (Project Master DataBase) model involves three generations of research on the formalisation, modelling and coding of software life cycle processes. PMDB is sponsored by the company TRW, member of the Arcadia Consortium, a consortium of universities and companies that research innovative technologies for supporting software engineering development environments. The PMDB model (Penedo & Shu, 1991) is an approach for modelling the software process on the basis of an object-based model called PMDB+, which includes the project elements, relationships between these elements and descriptions of the behaviour of the project life-cycle activities.

The PMDB approach for modelling and implementing the software process distinguishes between the different roles that environment users play: software process model designer, manager and developer (environment builders, environment adaptors and project users, according to PMDB terminology) (Penedo & Shu, 1991). Additionally, the PMDB model makes a clear distinction between a process model and its implementation. It provides a generic model, that is, a model that is not bound to specific methodologies and techniques, and which allows extendibility. The views provided by a process model are typically used by the process adaptor roles. Project administrators and managers, for example, can be envisaged in the role of process adaptors. Generally, such project managers are not concerned with implementation details. Therefore, the adaptation process should be easy enough to be performed by non-experts. The process implementation details are of interest to process programmers who play the roles of environment builders.

PMDB+ is an improvement on the original PMDB model (Penedo & Stuckle, 1985; Penedo, 1986). It formalises the entire life cycle using the entity-relationship-attribute approach (where entities are considered as objects), with software process behaviour descriptions modelled in terms of operations associated with these entities.

The original PMDB project investigated and prototyped aspects associated with the database environment (Penedo, 1986). It also investigated entity-relationship models as conceptual representation techniques for modelling the life cycle. On the basis of this research, the entire life cycle model emerged in terms of data and relationships. This model was called Project Master Database (PMDB model). The original PMDB model was composed of 31 entity types (or objects), approximately 200 attributes associated with the different types and 200 relationships between the different types (Penedo & Stuckle, 1985). The original PMDB model did not explicitly include the activities constituting the software process. The descriptions of activities or processes were subsequently included as part of the PMDB+.

As mentioned above, the PMDB+ model (Penedo & Shu, 1991) is an extension of PMDB (Penedo & Stuckle, 1985), which includes process descriptions. These process descriptions are represented either as operations associated with PMDB types or as "active data" associated with the attributes or operations (PMDB types). The types and relationships now included support the entire life cycle process. PMDB+ is composed of the elements described in Table 4.3 (Penedo & Shu, 1991) and represents mainly two process objects (agent and artefact) and their relationships in a hierarchical class structure.

The PMDB+ model represents the following elements: *agent, artefact* and *activity*. This model does not specify the characteristics of the social environment. However, the model does cover the *organisational* and *technological environments*.

This model addresses the software construction process from the *organisational* and *informational perspectives*. The quality of the information of the representation is *automated* as a prototype has been developed (Penedo, 1986; Penedo & Shu, 1991) and the formalised notation is *text*-based.

ELEMENT	DESCRIPTION
Entity/object types	Entity/object types characterise relevant project data (for example, resources, products, schedules, etc.). The PMDB+ model has 32 object types such as Requirement, Problem report, Change item, Test case, Person, etc. They were selected on the basis of their importance and generality as project elements. The object types can be instantiated as objects. For example, there will be as many objects of the type Requirement in a project database as there are requirements for a project or as many objects of the type Person as there are people working on the project. The only type to have been added to the original generic model is Prototype (Penedo & Stuckle, 1985). Specific types, such as COCOMO type, have been added to the base model to support specific methods and techniques, in this case cost estimation.
Attributes	Attributes describe the characteristics of the objects and provide additional information about them. Approximately 230 attributes have been identified for the PMDB+ object types. Some attributes are composite elements and were defined this way for simplicity and clarity. Other attributes have been redefined during the prototyping exercises. A range of attributes has been added to the model since its inception, most of them to support configuration management or specific techniques.
Relationships	Relationships represent associations between object types. For example, the relationship "allocated to" between objects of the type Requirement and Software Component represents the fact that the requirements may be allocated to specific components during software development. Approximately 200 relationships have been identified between objects; they do not include inverse or redundant relationships.
Operations	Operations are associated with object types and represent activities to be performed on objects of this type. For example, the operations associated with the object type "software component" include define a software component, decompose the component, establish the estimated size, build the component and baseline the component. Operations have to be explicitly invoked.
Active data	Active data correspond to events, associated with attributes or operations, that change the data or the execution of these operations, for example, computed attributes, pre- and postconditions, constraint maintainers, triggered functions, etc.

Table 4.3. PMDB+ Model elements

4.2.1.2. ALF Model

The ALF project (1987-1992), financed by the European Commission ESPRIT programmes (Project 1520), was a research project whose aim was to provide computerised facilities to support software development activities (Boveroux et al., 1991; Canals et al., 1994). The ALF model is a framework for building process-centred software engineering environments. This open and adaptable framework supports the representation of the software process models and provides users with intelligent model-based assistance. This model applies knowledge-based systems and advanced information systems techniques to IPSE.

ALF has an associated language called MASP, Model for Assisted Software Process Description Language (Canals et al., 1994). ALF is built on a server structure that provides the underlying model features and is based on a public interface tool, PCTE/PCTE+ (Lonchamp et al., 1990). The MASP (MASP/DL) description language is composed of: a) an object model description language, which is a typed PCTE data definition language; b) a rule model description language, which is influenced by production rules; c) an operator model definition language, which is influenced by abstract data type specifications; and d) operator type ordering model (sequence, simultaneousness, concurrence, grouping, alternative, iteration) (Canals et al., 1994). The ALF project developed an ALF system prototpye, which was satisfactorily demonstrated on the basis of the ISPW6 software process example (Kellner et al., 1991; Canals et al., 1994). This prototype implements most of the PCTE architecture-based MASP/DL language features.

ALF can define and instantiate executable software process models. ALF provides a definition model and an enactment model. The definition model relies on widely recognised concepts (Dowson, 1991; Benali & Derniame, 1992; Conradi et al., 1992; Feiler & Humphrey, 1993; Finkelstein et al., 1994): a process generates products by employing resources and following some policies, with the help of human or computerised agents. The software process model designer, manager and developer roles participate in the model. The software process model designer role designs and improves standard software process models through a MASP (Model for Assisted Software Process). A MASP is a generic model allowing the description of complex software production processes. The software process model manager role instantiates a MASP to provide a production model specific to a project, team or a particular organisation (Legait et al., 1989). This model is called enactment model and is composed essentially of instances and activities (rather than models) and agent or actor initiatives.

The process model developer role (user according to ALF terminology) implements the enactment model. In this model, an agent can be abstracted by the notion of role (set of activities potentially enactable by an agent). Playing a role, an agent can execute its activities, adopting its policies. Agents work in work contexts. In a work context, an agent takes initiatives, applies tools on objects, follows policies in a certain order and follows a set of rules to fulfil an objective. So, fragments of software process models (SPM) are used to model the work contexts. In ALF, a SPM fragment is called a MASP and is a 5-tuple: (Om, OPm, Rm, ORm, C), where:

- Om is the object model, which describes all the data used in the fragment. It is a typed entity-relationship-attribute data model; it is the PTCE model extended with multi-valued attributes.

- OPm is a set of operator types that describes a family of similar tools and pre- and postconditions for tool execution.

- Rm is a set of rules of type event-condition-action, which express how to react to some predefined events. The rules are used to automatically start actions when a specific process state is reached.

- ORm is a set of ordering constraints represented by path expressions. They express how the operator invocations can occur with respect to precedence rules, simultaneity constraints between operators and conditions on object instances.

- C is a "characteristic", that is, an expression that has to be true and is used as an invariant and/or as an objective. First-order logic and events expressions are used.

A MASP allows the modelling of all aspects of a single activity done by a single user within a project, which it supports in an integrated way. This activity runs within a static work context, which is an instance of a MASP (IMASP). Operator typing and the instantiation mechanism allow tools to be encapsulated in this work context (Boveroux et al., 1991). The model allows the expression of prescriptions. They are used for user control (preconditions, orderings, rules), for guidance (pre- and postconditions, with the help of an inference engine), for explanations (pre/post and/or rules), for process observation (rules) and for system initiatives (rules).

The ALF model represents the following elements: *agent, activity, artefact* and *event*. ALF takes a multiparadigm approach to software process model representation. This model covers the characteristics of the *technological* and the *organisational* environments. It does not specify the social environment, as it does not consider the capabilities of the people and the process roles.

The model information is organised from all the perspectives considered: *functional, behavioural, organisational* and *informational*. The representation is *automated* and the formalised notation is *text* based.

4.2.1.3. SOCCA Model

SOCCA (Specifications of Coordinated and Cooperative Activities), developed at the University of Leiden within the framework of the SOCCA project, is a formalism for specifying software process modelling that explicitly includes both the human parts and the interaction in which they are involved (Engels & Groenewegen, 1994). This model specifies the software process from different perspectives: data, process and behaviour. These perspectives are used to formally describe large and complex systems (Rumbaugh et al., 1991) in software engineering. Apart from building on this experience, SOCCA aims to integrate the above-mentioned perspectives into a larger formalism that satisfactorily covers the three perspectives (Morssink, 1993). The data perspective focuses on the static structure of the system, namely, what the system is concerned with, what the system influences and what is influencing the system. The other two perspectives refer to the dynamic behaviour of the system, namely, the things that are taking place within the system or even outside the system but which are connected to it.

SOCCA uses object-oriented class diagrams, based on extended entity-relationship model concepts, to model the data perspective. It models the behaviour perspective and its coordination through state transition diagrams (STD) and PARADIGM. PARADIGM is a specification formalism that was originally developed for and restricted to the specification of parallel processes (van Steen, 1988; Morssink, 1993). Finally, it uses object flow diagrams to model the process perspective. Object flow diagrams are an extended version of data flow diagrams with operations derived from the class diagram specifications. The approach used in SOCCA achieves a better, albeit still incomplete, integration by carefully selecting some elements or aspects of the description according to one formalism to continue the development of the description according to the next formalism. This selection process is described in (Engels & Groenewegen, 1994).

The steps and substeps proposed by SOCCA for modelling the software process are described in Table 4.4.

The elements modelled by SOCCA are: *agent (human), activity, artefact* and *role*. These elements are organised in a class hierarchy and their sequential and parallel behaviours are defined. This application combines, at a high level of abstraction, the best of several formalisms: object-oriented modelling based on extended entity-relationship models, state transition diagrams combined with PARADIGM and object flow diagrams, which are the building blocks of the SOCCA approach. SOCCA addresses the *organisational environment* and *technological environment*. It fails to explicitly account for the creativity, social interaction and flexibility of the people involved. People's capabilities are not represented in this modelling approach either. Therefore, the SOCCA model does not cover the social environment.

DESCRIPTION OF STEPS AND SUBSTEPS

• **PROBLEM FORMULATION**
1. Describe problem by means of global data flow diagram.
• **DATA PERSPECTIVE**
2. Build class diagram:
    2.1. Describe complex structured objects by class hierarchies. These hierarchies consist of class definitions as well as "part-of" and "is-a" relationships.
    2.2. Add missing general relationships. The general relationships are added to connect the different classes from the first step by means other than of the special relationships "part-of" and "is-a".
    2.3. Indicate which of the classes use the operations exported by other classes. A new binary relationship type, called *uses*, explicitly indicates where the various export operations are imported.
• **BEHAVIOUR PERSPECTIVE**
3. Build state transition diagrams. The behaviour of each class is defined, that is, its local and sequential behaviour. This behaviour consists of two different types of behaviour: external and internal.
    3.1. Specify the external behaviour for each class. External behaviour is the behaviour visible from outside, specifying the allowed sequences for calling the exported operations.
    3.2. Indicate for each class which (export) operations it imports from elsewhere.
    3.3. Specify the internal behaviour of each operation for each class. Internal behaviour consists of the actions that the class performs on its own, and of the actions that the class performs on behalf of the calling of imported operations, that is, it specifies the sequences of the calls of operations imported from elsewhere. The "uses" relationship is employed for this specification, outputting a list of imported operations.
4. PARADIGM. Within SOCCA, PARADIGM allows the specification of the overall software process behaviour. This activity determines how the external and internal behaviours are related and coordinated and indicates how the PARADIGM concepts, subprocesses and "traps" are used from within a behaviour to influence the execution of other behaviours. SOCCA distinguishes between two ways of starting the execution of some sequential behaviour from within another sequential behaviour. These two categories of communication are: *type 1* and *type 2*. The first category is the communication taking place between any internal behaviour and some external behaviour of another object. The second category is the communication taking place between any external behaviour and the internal behaviours belonging to the same object. This communication is the immediate result of the actual start of the execution of the operation. *Type 2* communication consists of controlling order, priority and other similar dependencies between all behaviours belonging to one object.
    4.1. Describe the sequential behaviour of each process by a STD.
    4.2. Identify significant subdiagrams (called subprocesses) with respect to coordination with other processes.
    4.3. Identify states (or so-called traps) within each subprocess. "Traps" are situations where an object is ready to switch from one subprocess to another.
    4.4. Describe the transitions and behaviours between subprocesses of all objects. Both are described by a STD or so-called manager process.
• **PROCESS PERSPECTIVE**
5. Build object flow diagrams. This activity connects the class diagram and the PARADIGM description. The class diagram reflects the data perspective of the problem situation, and the PARADIGM description reflects the behaviour perspective. In the class diagram, the communication, or rather the connection between the objects, is modelled using relationships. These relationships express the existence of some, perhaps only temporal, connection between the data descriptions of the related objects. In PARADIGM, the communication between the various behaviours is modelled by means of the subprocesses and traps. They express exactly how the communication influences the behaviour. An integration of both perspectives can be achieved by describing the effect of a transition in terms of insertion, update and deletion of object and relationship instances. This effect on the data, corresponding to the various transitions in the involved STDs, is the starting point for the use of object flow diagrams. These diagrams describe how the objects, being instances of classes or relationships, are created, deleted or transformed and how they flow from transformation to transformation (Wulms, 1995).

Table 4.4. SOCCA modelling procedure

The data, process and behaviour perspectives (following SOCCA terminology) match up with the *organisational* and *informational perspective*, the *functional* perspective and the *behavioural perspective*, respectively, of the information in the software process model representation. The SOCCA model aims to provide a design formalism that unifies the data, behavioural and process perspectives. Additionally, this model, based on experience with the separate formalisms of which SOCCA is composed, expects any particular SOCCA specification to facilitate the implementation of the code for the software process model in question. The information quality of the SOCCA representation is *formalised*, as it has not yet been implemented as a software process enactment environment. The formalised notation is based on a *text* and *graphical* approach.

The SOCCA software process specification explicitly includes the human parts together with the interaction in which they are involved from the data, behaviour and process perspectives. It uses different formalisms and methodological guidance to integrally move from one formalism to another to model these perspectives. But, this integration is not completely and formally defined.

4.2.1.4. Unified Process Model

The Unified Software Development Process or Unified Process (Jacobson et al., 1999) targets people who perform process activities and takes both a technical and organisational view of the management and support of software development, so that it can be tailored to a wide range of projects and organisations. The Unified Process uses the Unified Modelling Language, UML (Booch et al., 1999). UML has become a de facto industry standard, because it was conceived by the authors of the three most commonly used object-oriented methods: Grady Booch, Ivar Jacobson and Jim Rumbaugh. The authors of UML were recruited by the Rational Software Co. to create a unified notation on which to base the construction of its CASE tools. All the models in the Rational Objectory Process used UML. This IPSE was extended, and Rational released a new version of the product, the Rational Unified Process-RUP 2003 (Kroll & Kruchten, 2003), which supports computerised specifications of the Unified Process. Specifically, the Unified Process provides a formalised prescription of the entire software development process, as it specifies all the software process modelling elements through UML.

The Unified Process is associated with an iterative and incremental life cycle model and focuses on the software architecture that guides system development. This architectural design serves as a solid basis on which component-based software development can be planned and managed. The Unified Process activities are characterised by automatically creating and maintaining controlled object-oriented models to minimise the overload associated with generating and maintaining documents and to maximise the relevant information content.

Additionally, development activities under the Unified Process are driven by use cases to give an understanding of how the system will be used when it is delivered. The use cases and scenarios are used to guide the process flow from requirements elicitation to testing and to provide flows that can be reproduced during system development. The Unified Process is adaptable and can be configured for a particular project on the basis of quality control and risk management throughout development.

The Unified Process is composed of the following four phases with their associated objectives:

- Inception: establish project planning and delimit its scope.

- Elaboration: analyse the problem domain, establish a project baseline and architecture.

- Construction: develop the system.

- Transition: deliver the system to its end users.

The inception and elaboration phases include the activities for designing the development process; the construction and transition phases constitute its production. Each of these phases can be decomposed in iterations. An iteration represents a full development cycle, from requirements specification to implementation and testing, which outputs a software product. Each phase and iteration focuses on reducing some risk and concludes with a well-defined milestone that evaluates the extent to which the goals are being achieved and whether the project needs to be restructured in any way to continue.

In turn, each iteration passes through several process workflows, although the emphasis is different in each one, depending on the phase. During the inception phase, interest focuses on analysis and design. During the construction phase, the central activity is implementation, and transition focuses on the installation and use environment. The Unified Process workflows are divided into process workflows and supporting workflows. Workflow activities are performed by roles (workers, according to Unified Process terminology), which develop different artefacts (models according to Unified Process terminology) depending on their workflow profile, as shown in Table 4.5.

The elements modelled by the Unified Process are: *agent (human* and *system), activity, artefact, role* and *event*. These elements are organised in an object-oriented architectural design.

The application of the process specified by this model combines, at a high level of abstraction, the best of the different formalisms based on UML. The Unified

WORKFLOW	DESCRIPTION	WORKERS	OUTPUT MODEL
Process Workflows			
Business modelling	Describes the structure and dynamics of the organisation	Business modellers, Domain analyst	Business Model
Domain modelling	Describes the structure and dynamics of the system context	Domain analyst, System analyst, Use case specifier	Domain Model
Requirements	Describes the use case method for eliciting requirements	System analyst, Use case specifier, User interface designer, Architect	Use Case Model
Analysis	Describes the idea or need for a computerised solution Describes the architectural viewpoint of the use cases	Architect, Use case engineer, Components engineer	Analysis Model
Design	Describes the different architectural views: design, processes, deployment and implementation Covers deliverable system configuration	Architect, Use case engineer, Components engineer	Design Model and Deployment Model (hardware topology on which the system will be run)
Implementation	Takes into account software development, unit and integration testing	Architect, Components engineer, System integrator	Implementation Model
Test	Describes the test cases, procedures and metrics for evaluating defects	Test designer, Components engineer, System tester, Integration tester	Test Model
Supporting Workflows			
Configuration management	Controls the changes and maintains the integrity of the project artefacts	Configuration manager	Software Configuration Management Plan
Project management	Describes several work strategies in an iterative process	Project manager	Software Project Management Plan
Environment	Covers the infrastructure needed to develop a system	Environment manager	System Environment Plan

Table 4.5. Unified Process workflow structure

Process adequately addresses aspects related to the *technological environment* and the *organisational environment*. But it fails to explicitly deal with the creativity, social interaction and flexibility of the people involved. Although it specifies the roles for each workflow, this modelling approach does not represent the capabilities of the people. Therefore, the Unified Process model does not cover the social environment.

The representation of the interrelated process models organises the information from all the perspectives considered: *organisational, informational, functional* and *behavioural*. The model provides a design formalism that unifies all the views of the process models. As regards the information quality of the representation, the Unified Process is *automated*. The formalised notation is both *text-* and *graphics-based*.

4.2.2. Evaluation Model

4.2.2.1. People CMM Model

The People CMM (People Capability Maturity Model) is a guide for implementing work practices that continually promote an organisation's workforce capability. Since an organisation cannot implement the all the best workforce practices, the People CMM introduces these practices in stages. Each progressive level of the People CMM produces a single transformation in the culture of the organisation, providing practices to attract, develop, organise and retain its workforce. So, the People CMM establishes an integrated system of workforce practices that matures through growth according to the organisation's business objectives, performance and changes.

The People CMM was first published in 1995 (Curtis et al., 1995a, Curtis et al., 1995b, Curtis et al., 1995c), and has successfully driven workforce improvement programmes at companies like Boeing, Ericsson, Lockheed Martin, Novo Nordisk IT A/S, and Tata Consulting Services. The People CMM is a method for evaluating software process human resources. Authors like Sommerville and Rodden (1995), Helliwell and Fowler (1994) and Perry et al. (1994), among others, have investigated the influence of human resources on the software development and maintenance process and highlighted the need to analyse, measure and evaluate this type of resources to develop software process improvement strategies that include this decisive factor and not just actions related to activities and technological resources. Nevertheless, there is still only one proposal, updated in 2001, of a method for evaluating these resources: People CMM (Curtis et al, 2001).

The People CMM is a maturity model focused on analysing the human resources of an organisation. This model assumes the same fundaments and reference standard structure as the CMMI, staged representation, analysed earlier. The People CMM's main goal is to promote workforce capability. Workforce capability promotion can be defined at the level of knowledge, capabilities and skills available for performing the organisation's business activities.

To measure and improve workforce capabilities, this workforce should in most organisations be divided according its members' competencies. Each competency represents just one integration of knowledge, capabilities and skills acquired through specialised training or job experience. Strategically, an organisation should design its workforce to cover all the competencies required to perform its basic business activities.

The People CMM's main objective is to apply the maturity principles used in the CMM (Paulk et al., 1993, Paulk et al., 1995) to the company's human resources. Its specific goals are as follows (Curtis et al., 1995a; Curtis et al., 1995c):

- Improve the capability of software organisations by increasing the capability of their human resources.

- Assure that the capability of software production is an attribute of the organisation and does not depend on a small group of human resources.

- Improve the motivation of the human resources to raise their commitment to the organisation and so that they perform their tasks more effectively.

- Retain the most talented human resources.

To achieve these goals, as with the CMM, attention focused, firstly on developing a yardstick for the method (Curtis et al., 1995a) to measure the continual growth of workforce capabilities. The yardstick structure is identical to the CMM method structure. The difference lies in the yardstick content, which is an evolutionary framework for the organisation's people. The philosophy implicit in the People CMM can be summarized in 10 principles.

1. In mature organizations, talent pool capability is directly related to business performance.

2. Talent pool capability is a competitive issue and a source of strategic advantage.

3. Talent capability must be defined in relation to the organization's strategic business objectives.

4. Knowledge-intense work shifts the focus from job elements to people competencies.

5. Capability can be measured and improved at multiple levels, including individuals, workgroups, people competencies, and the organisation.

6. An organisation should invest in improving the capability of those people competencies that are critical to its core competency as a business.

7. Operational management is responsible for the capability of the talent pool.

8. The improvement of talent pool capability can be pursued as a process composed from proven practices and procedures.

9. The organisation is responsible for providing competency and career improvement opportunities, while individuals are responsible for taking advantage of them.

10. Since technologies and organisational forms evolve rapidly, organisations must continually evolve their people practices and develop new people competencies.

The People CMM allows organisations to characterise the maturity of their workforce practices as opposed to policy adopted by other organisations based on individual employee attitudes and satisfaction. These attitudes and satisfaction are usually used as indicators in personnel reorganisation processes rather than reorganising in pursuit of practice improvement. By contrast, People CMM's staged architecture helps organisations to prioritise their improvement actions. Additionally, since the People CMM negotiates workforce development as an organisational process, it has demonstrated that workforce practices are more easily integrated with other improvement activity processes.

The People CMM is built upon the essential practices of one or more domains of the organisational process. The People CMM covers the domain of workforce administration and development. All the CMM models are built upon five maturity levels. In the People CMM, each maturity level is an evolutionary plateau into which one or more domains of the organisational process have been transformed to achieve a new level of organisational capabilities. Each maturity level provides organisations with powerful tools for developing their workforce capabilities.

Figure 4.5 shows the relationship between the concept of maturity level and the behaviour of the organisation and its human resources, that is, what it means for a company to be inserted at a given level of the model. Additionally, it illustrates the process areas (PA) allocated to each maturity level. Each People CMM maturity level, except for the initial level, is composed of three to seven process areas. Each process area identifies a group of related practices, which, if performed together, achieve a set of goals considered important for improving workforce capabilities. Each process area organises a set of practices related to a critical area of workforce administration, such as staffing, compensation or workgroup development. Each area is an important organisational process. The process areas of each maturity level create an interlinking system of processes that transform the organisation's capabilities for managing its people.

Table 4.6 describes the five maturity levels used in the People CMM in some detail (Curtis et al., 2001).

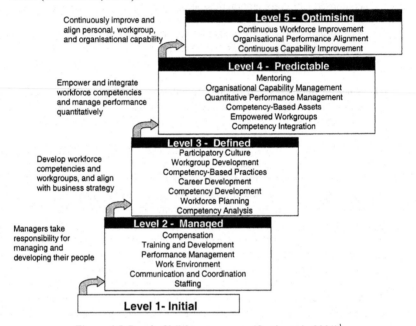

Figure 4.5. People CMM process areas (Curtis et al., 2001)[1]

The People CMM is the only approach that models the capabilities of the organisation's workforce and their associated roles in the software process. However, the representation of the capabilities of the agents is informal, and no modelling procedure has been developed for their inclusion in the software process. The model's informality is a serious handicap, as it can affect its repeatability. There is no guarantee that different people applying the model to the same situation will arrive at similar solutions.

---

[1] Special permission to use People Capability Maturity Model Version 2.0 © 2001 by Carnegie Mellon University, in A Software Process Model Handbook for Incorporating People's Capabilities, is granted by the Software Engineering Institute.

MATURITY LEVEL DESCRIPTION
Level 1. Initial. Workforce practices tend to be inconsistent or ritualistic, but organisations perform processes that are described in the Maturity Level 2 process areas, without, however, achieving the goals.
Level 2. Managed. Main features: Managers perform basic people management practices. The organisation establishes a culture focused at the unit level for ensuring that people are able to meet their work commitments.

Level 2. Managed. Main features: Managers perform basic people management practices. The organisation establishes a culture focused at the unit level for ensuring that people are able to meet their work commitments.

    2.1. Staffing. The purpose of this PA is to establish a process by which committed work is matched to unit resources and qualified individuals are recruited, selected and transitioned into assignments.

    2.2. Communication and Coordination. The purpose of this PA is to establish timely communication across the organisation and to ensure that the workforce has the skills to share information and coordinate their activities efficiently.

    2.3. Work Environment. The purpose of this PA is to establish and maintain working conditions and provide resources that allow individuals to perform their tasks efficiently without unnecessary distractions.

    2.4. Performance Management. The purpose of this PA is to establish objectives related to committed work against which unit and individual performance can be measured, to discuss performance against these objectives and to continuously enhance performance.

    2.5. Training and Development. The purpose of this PA is to ensure that all individuals have the skills required to perform their assignments and are provided relevant development opportunities.

    2.6. Compensation. The purpose of this PA is to provide all individuals with remuneration and benefits based on their contribution and value to the organisation.

Level 3. Defined. Main features: The organisation identifies and develops knowledge, skills and process abilities that constitute the workforce competencies required to perform its business activities.

    3.1. Competency Analysis. The purpose of this PA is to identify the knowledge, skills and process abilities required to perform the organisation's business activities so that they may be developed and used as a basis for workforce practices.

    3.2. Workforce Planning. The purpose of this PA is to coordinate workforce activities with current and future business needs at both the organisational and unit levels.

    3.3. Competency Development. The purpose of this PA is to constantly enhance the capability of the workforce to perform their assigned tasks and responsibilities.

    3.4. Career Development. The purpose of this PA is to ensure that individuals are provided opportunities to develop workforce competencies that enable them to achieve career objectives.

    3.5. Competency-Based Practices. The purpose of this PA is to ensure that all workforce practices are based in part on developing the competencies of the workforce.

    3.6. Workgroup Development. The purpose of this PA is to organise work around competency-based process abilities.

    3.7. Participatory Culture. The purpose of this PA is to ensure a flow of information within the organisation, to incorporate the knowledge of individuals into decision-making processes, and to gain their support for commitments.

Table 4.6. Description of People CMM maturity levels (Curtis et al., 2001)

MATURITY LEVEL DESCRIPTION
Level 4. Predictable. Main features: The organisation quantifies and manages the capability of its workforce and their competency-based processes, in addition to exploiting the opportunities afforded by defined workforce competencies. The organisation creates a culture of measurement and exploits shared experience.
4.1. Competency Integration. The purpose of this PA is to improve the efficiency and agility of interdependent work by integrating the process abilities of difference workforce competencies.
4.2. Empowered Workgroups. The purpose of this PA is to invest workgroups with the responsibility and authority for determining how to conduct their business activities most effectively.
4.3. Competency-Based Assets. The purpose of this PA is to capture the knowledge, experience, and artefacts developed in performing competency-based processes for use in enhancing capability and performance.
4.4. Quantitative Performance Management. The purpose of this PA is to predict and manage the capability of competency-based processes for achieving measurable performance objectives.
4.5. Organisational Capability Management. The purpose of this PA is to quantify and manage the capability of the workforce and of the critical competency-based processes they perform.
4.6. Mentoring. The purpose of this PA is to transfer the lessons of greater experience in a workforce competency to improve the capability of other individuals or workgroups.
Level 5. Optimising. Main features: Everyone in the organisation is focused on continuously improving their capability and the organisation's workforce practices. The organisation creates a culture of product and service excellence. The organisation continuously improves its capability and deploys rapid changes for managing its workforce.
5.1. Continuous Capability Improvement. The purpose of this PA is to provide a foundation for individuals and workgroups to continuously improve their capability for performing competency-based processes.
5.2. Organisational Performance Alignment. The purpose of this PA is to enhance the alignment of performance results across individuals, workgroups, and units with organisational performance and business objectives.
5.3. Continuous Workforce Improvement. The purpose of this PA is to identify and evaluate improved or innovative workforce practices and technologies and implement the most promising ones throughout the organisation.

Table 4.6. Description of People CMM maturity levels (cont'd) (Curtis et al., 2001)

Additionally, the criticisms of the People CMM model can be summarised as follows:

- The software process structure is rigid and static (maturity levels - process area).

- The software process structure is not integrated (it considers people as separate from their activities and technological resources).

- The software process structure is not explicitly defined.

The elements considered by the People CMM are *agents* and *roles* (workforce in People CMM terminology) belonging to the organisation and their associated *capabilities* (although no systematic process is defined to identify and associate these capabilities with specific roles). The People CMM assesses criteria such as personal motivation, competencies, knowledge, experience and performance, workforces, workforce management organisational training and how the organisation promotes individual career development. Therefore, the model covers the *organisational* and *social (creativity, social interaction, flexibility) environments*. On the negative side, however, the People CMM does not address the technological environment. For the software production process descriptions to be really coherent and useful to the organisation, they should model all the elements and characteristics that influence the process together. Separate representations can lead to descriptions, designs and improvements to the processes involved that are inconsistent with each other or are not tailored to the real situation at the company, as well as to inefficiencies in the analysis of the relationships between the elements and modelled aspects. The information perspective of this *informal* model is *organisational.*

Summary of the Overview of Software Process Models

Part I of the book presented an overview of the software process models from the viewpoints of the process model features and properties and the software process representation. Particularly, we highlighted the guidelines that these models provide for outputting the elements and their relationships and the features of the social environment (creativity, social interaction and flexibility) and their incorporation into the software process. This we do to check whether the models examined cover and represent the three environments (organisational, social and technological) that are important for the management of both the activities and the members of a project team.

Table 5.1 presents the features of all the models surveyed in Part I, according to the analysed criteria. If the models cover a feature, the respective cell is marked with an X; otherwise the space is left blank.

Note that the Process Cycle Model is qualitative and orthogonal to existing process models. Although it is extremely informal, this model does address the question of the human agents involved in the software process. With regard to formal models, Madhavji provides a methodological perspective of process cycle evolution, proposes the PRISM methodology for building and adapting generic software process models and provides a process-centred environment for managing changes in the PRISM model. Basili and Rombach formalise the Goal-Question-Metric paradigm for the following tasks: characterisation of the current state of the project environment and planning, construction, analysis, learning and project feedback. Each of these tasks is addressed in the TAME model from the constructive and analytical viewpoint, that is, the model integrates methods and tools to build the products (constructive viewpoint) and methods and tools to analyse the construction processes and products output (analytical viewpoint). On the other hand, STATEMATE covers the four information perspectives, as it integrates three graphical representation languages (state charts, activity charts, module charts) to analyse and predict the behaviour of the process models.

MODEL	Model-Related Criteria — Process elements represented by the model								Process environments covered by the model	Representation-Related Criteria — Information perspectives				Notational characteristics — from the viewpoint of information quality			from the viewpoint of formalised notation	
	agent	activity	artefact	role	capability	event	organisational	social	technological	functional	behavioural	organisational	informational	informal	formalised	automated	text	graphical
TAME	X	X	X				X		X	X	X		X		X		X	
FUNSOFT Nets Based	X	X	X			X			X	X	X	X			X			X
STATEMATE	X	X	X			X	X	X	X	X	X	X	X		X			X
PRISM	X	X	X				X		X	X		X	X			X	X	X
TRIAD	X	X		X					X	X	X		X			X	X	
Marvel	X	X	X						X	X	X					X	X	
IPSE 2.5	X	X	X	X					X			X	X		X		X	
SPADE	X	X	X			X			X	X	X	X			X			X
ISO/IEC 12207		X	X	X			X	X	X	X			X					
IEEE 1074		X	X						X	X			X					
ISO 9001		X					X		X	X			X					
CMMI		X					X		X	X			X					
Systems Dynamics Based	X	X			X		X	X	X		X						X	X
Process Cycle	X	X		X					X	X	X		X					
Win Win	X	X		X				X			X	X				X	X	X
XP	X	X	X	X	X		X	X	X		X			X				
PMDB+	X	X	X				X		X		X	X				X	X	
ALF	X	X	X		X	X		X	X	X	X	X	X			X	X	
SOCCA	X	X	X	X		X		X	X	X	X	X	X		X		X	X
Unified Process	X	X	X	X		X	X		X	X	X	X	X		X	X	X	X
People CMM	X		X	X		X	X					X		X				

Table 5.1. Assessment of Software Process Models

As shown in Table 5.1, the FUNSOFT nets-based model focuses on a formal and graphic notation. It addresses neither organisational issues nor aspects related to the people involved in the process, it merely deals with the technological environment, which is reflected under the column labelled *Process environments covered by the model*. The systems dynamics approach to process modelling is used as a means for simulating proposed processes, predicting dynamic software process behaviour and reporting the administration or management of the right policies and procedures. Abdel-Hamid and Madnick develop a comprehensive automated systems dynamics model of the software development process. This model covers both the organisational environment and people's creativity, but neglects the technological environment. Boehm incorporates negotiating activities into the spiral model. This automated win-win model considers the social environment, as it accounts for the active participation of the customer and the development team in a context of negotiation and environmental flexibility. XP also specifies intensive communication between and participation of the customer and the development team. It is the only descriptive model that includes both the technological and the organisational environment and people's creativity and social interaction, which is reflected under the columns labelled *Process environments covered by the model*.

In relation to the prescriptive models, the software life cycle process standards are informal and consider only the functional perspective of the information in the model, as shown under the columns labelled *Notational characteristics-From the viewpoint of information quality* (informal) and *Information perspectives* (functional). The evaluation models, ISO 9001 and CMMI are also informal. Except for ISO/IEC 12207, they focus exclusively on the activity element of the process and do not cover people's capabilities and the characteristics of the social environment of the process, as shown under the columns labelled *Notational characteristics – From the viewpoint of information quality* (informal), *Process elements represented by the model* (activity) and *Process environments covered by the model* (organisational and technological).

A variety of multi-paradigm software process modelling approaches has been proposed. Most focus on one main paradigm, like rules (Marvel, for example), imperative programs (TRIAD/CML, for example), activity-oriented programs (IPSE 2.5) or Petri nets (SPADE, for example). The integration of formalisms to describe both the software process and the members of the process and their relationships, which explicitly includes the human components and any interaction in which they are involved has been proposed by approaches such as SOCCA, ALF and PMDB+. The complexity of the resulting software, which overstretches both the technical and organisational management, can be better dealt with in this manner. They can be divided into two categories, depending on the guiding criterion selected to address software process modelling: a) activity-oriented models and b) people-oriented models. Activity-oriented models focus on the functions, activities of and information about parts of the management, development and software life cycle supporting processes. These include TRIAD, Marvel, IPSE 2.5 and SPADE, for example. People-oriented models focus on the specifications of the people involved in the software process and their relationships. They include SOCCA, ALF, PMDB+ and the Unified Process. People are the least formalised factor in existing software process models. Their importance, however, is patent: their behaviour is non-deterministic and subjective and has a decisive impact on the results of software production, which is basically an intellectual and social, or people-oriented, activity. Additionally, the non-specification of human resources means that the process does not reflect the actual status of the software process, having the added risk of processes being executed that are not suited to the capability of the organisation's people.

Table 5.1 shows that the representations of prescriptive software process models, except the Unified Process, have focused on three elementary process features: the activity, the artefact and the agent (human and computerised). However, other features, like human and organisational roles, have been empirically proven to have a big impact on the production process (Boehm, 1981; Curtis, 1985; Hastie, 1987; Guindon & Curtis, 1988; Valett & McGarry, 1989; Humphrey, 1995; Sherdil & Madhavji, 1996). Most of the existing software process models deal with roles and related issues that are not formally defined (Lonchamp, 1992; Finkelstein et al., 1994), while the organisation (organisational behaviour, culture and individual abilities) is considered as separate from the characteristics applied for modelling the software process (Min & Bae, 1997) or is ignored (Engels & Groenewegen, 1994). This is because the organisation is the software process environment and is not, therefore, explicitly modelled. Therefore, these software process models are not integral and joint modelling approaches to the technical and organisational characteristics of the software process.

According to Table 5.1, the more complete models are SOCCA and the Unified Process, as the models formally address human resources and the software process interactions in which they are involved. However, the proposed guides do not cover all the desired concepts, elements, characteristics and software process environments.

Owing to the complexity of and the requirements for modelling the software process, the best thing appears to be for each low-level modelling or software process enactment to be derived from a high-level specification step, where all the information perspectives can be modelled: a) separately and b) as integrated components of a full specification. Such a modular specification reduces the complexity of the modelling activity and increases the possibility of software process model change and evolution. SOCCA, ALF and PMDB+ consider these aspects, generally taken into account from the software engineering viewpoint. The Unified Process is iterative, incremental and focuses on the software architecture. This design based on software architecture serves as a solid basis on which to plan and manage the development of component-based software. These are the four most advanced and complete models. They model the software project life cycle process and investigate the use of a process model, in this case SOCCA, ALF, PMDB+ or the Unified Process, as a conceptual and user interaction model and a framework for integrating tools and/or agents and roles. The approach is incremental, as the whole life cycle is long and complex. Special emphasis is placed on process formalisation, large project support, generalisation and extendibility. The Unified Process includes a formal prescription of the process, where all the process elements are specified using the UML. Additionally, as mentioned above, SOCCA and the Unified Process give directions on an aspect that is often neglected in software engineering: the problem of the specification under development having to describe not only the technical but also the human parts of the software process or, better still, people's capabilities, the software process and all classes of interaction between the different non-human and human parts. However, SOCCA and the Unified Process do not deal with social software process modelling issues, missing as well from the other models analysed, as observed under the column *Process environments covered by the model*. Table 5.1 shows that the organisational, social (creativity, social interaction and flexibility) and technological environments are not integrated in the models in question (as shown under the columns of the same name).

The people-oriented software process models considered focus on examining the process agents, attaching less importance to other process elements like roles, for example, which are not formally defined, and human and role capabilities, which are not explicitly modelled. The main drawback of all these models is that, except for XP and the win-win model, they do not consider the social environment of the software process or its integration with the organisational and technological environments, again excepting XP. The win-win model and XP consider the capabilities of creativity, social interaction and flexibility, albeit informally. The People CMM is the only one that models the capabilities of the organisation's human resources and their associated roles in the software process, but the capabilities of the agents are represented informally and no procedures have been developed to incorporate such capabilities into the software process, as observed under the column *Process elements represented by the model* (agent, role, capability), *Notational characteristics – From the information quality viewpoint* (informal). The System Dynamics-based model offers a quantitative and deterministic description of the organisation's human resources from the viewpoint of human resource recruitment, training, inclusion and transfer experience level and not as regards the logic of competencies of the human resources and roles. The models that account for people do not provide a defined set of stages or activities for performing the modelling process. As mentioned, only SOCCA and the Unified Process provide a defined procedure as an aid for modelling, but they do not address all the model components, such as, for example, the social characteristics of the people involved in the software process. These two models, along with ALF, do not consider role capabilities and the

Part

Capabilities-Oriented Software Process Model

The incorporation of people into software development and how they should be organised to work together is a subject that has yet to be decided. This question needs to be settled, as human action and interaction is essential for the success and effectiveness of the software process. Whether or not the software process meets its associated requirements depends on people and what they do or do not do in software development. Assuring that people behave according to the roles they play in the software process is a solid foundation underlying production. This denotes how important it is to settle the subject of incorporating people into the software process. A process model that accounts for people's motivations, values, intuitions, reasoning and capabilities and the work organisation structure provides a better basis for modelling the broad implications of a process.

Part II of the book outlines just such a model. This model addresses some of the above aspects to decide which people should perform which roles in a software process. In particular, we have developed a capabilities-oriented software process model that formalises the capabilities or behavioural competencies of the people who perform development activities. Chapter 6 presents an overview of the model and explains what activities we propose to achieve our objective. These activities address different dimensions of software production: the people dimension, the roles dimension and the production dimension. These dimensions are discussed in detail in Chapters 7, 8 and 9. Chapter 10 presents an application of the capabilities-oriented software process model, and Chapter 11 examines the benefits of applying the proposed method. Finally, Chapter 12 discusses the main conclusions and lessons learned from applying the proposed method.

Adding Capabilities to the Software Process Model

The objective of this book is to provide a software process model that incorporates the capabilities of the people involved in the software process. To this end, our starting point were capabilities validated within the framework of the Assessment Centre Method (ACM), used in the area of human resources selection, which we adapted for software development. The incorporation of human capabilities into a software process involves explicitly performing a range of activities related, on the one hand, to evaluating the capabilities of the organisation's members, and, on the other, to assigning people to roles depending on their capabilities and the capabilities required to play each role. Before describing these activities in depth, we present an overview of the activities, as well as the elements they include, laying the emphasis on the key element: capabilities.

6.1. INCORPORATING CAPABILITIES INTO A SOFTWARE PROCESS MODEL

As mentioned earlier, the objective of this book is to provide a set of activities that allows the incorporation of people's capabilities into the software process. Such activities should be applicable to any development process followed by an organisation. However, to illustrate our proposal, we will use a standard process, namely IEEE STD 1074, to which we will add the activities required to cover the capabilities of the people involved in this process. Figure 6.1 includes two methods (Assignation of People to Roles and People's Capabilities Evaluation). These activities will be detailed later in the book. Note, however, that the Assignation of People to Roles and the People's Capabilities Evaluation methods have been defined to perform these activities systematically. These methods will again be detailed later. The methods are designed to help process engineers to model the people involved in the software process and make use of specific relationships between people's capabilities and software roles, on the one hand, and between people's capabilities and their psychological traits, on the other hand. These relationships as well as the corresponding methods that deal with them have been represented also in Figure 6.1.

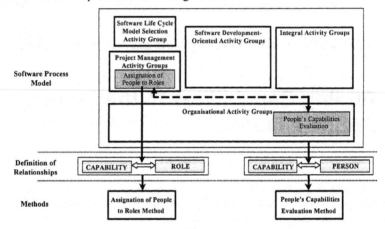

Figure 6.1. Overview of the incorporation of people's capabilities into the software process

Note that capabilities evaluation has been placed in the IEEE 1074 standard within Organisational Activity Groups. These activity groups were inspired by the ISO/IEC 12207 standard Organisational Life Cycle Processes (ISO/IEC, 1995), which apply to organisation- rather than project-related activities. So, the organisational level not the project level is responsible for evaluating the capabilities of the people involved in software development. Capabilities evaluation models the capabilities of the organisation's workforce involved in development and is the basis for incorporating capabilities into a process model. The characteristics of the people ascertained by means of its associated activities are used as part of the Project Management Activity Groups. In particular, people need to be assigned to roles on the basis of their capabilities and the capabilities demanded by each role, which is the function of the Assignation of People to Roles Activities. Assignation includes a structured and planned set of activities to identify, determine and evaluate a group of people whose personal characteristics make them better suited, or more apt or akin to the set of capabilities or behavioural characteristics for effectively and efficiently playing a software process role.

Note that we have used the IEEE STD 1074 process model to illustrate how to incorporate capabilities into the software process. However, this innovation can be added to any other process model. An organisation can incorporate capabilities into its own process model, bearing in mind that people's capabilities evaluation should be built into the organisational view and assignation of people to roles into the management view of the process.

6.2. STRUCTURE OF A CAPABILITIES-ORIENTED SOFTWARE PROCESS

The capabilities-oriented software process model signifies a software process model that prescribes the capabilities of the people who play the role defined for each activity, that is, a software process that represents what to do and who does what. Therefore, as mentioned earlier, two people-oriented methods need to be added to a process model: People's Capabilities Evaluation and Assignation of People to Roles Activities.

Each of these groups of activities needs to define what to do, who does it and how it is done. These activities are characterised in Table 6.1.

ACTIVITIES	OBJECTIVE	VIEW	WHAT	WHO	HOW
People's Capabilities Evaluation	Characterise person	Organisational	Identify and describe the capabilities or behavioural competencies of the people and their improvement strategy	Occupational psychologists Process engineers	People's Capabilities Evaluation Method
Assignation of People to Roles	Characterise person-role	Management	Identify people/role matches and allocate people to software project roles	Process engineer Team leader	Assignation of People to Roles Method

Table 6.1. Characteristics of people-related activities

Organisational and sociocultural characteristics influence all the activity groups. The People's Capabilities Evaluation Activities determine the capabilities of the people who play different project management, development, maintenance and software system support roles. The Assignation of People to Roles Activities allocate the roles according to the capabilities of the people involved and the capabilities required by the roles in question. The aim of this assignation process is for the individuals performing the different activities in software projects to play the roles best suited to their capabilities.

Apart from roles, process models are traditionally described by another four elements, to which we propose here to add capabilities. In other words, the process model will be described by means of the following six elements (Figure 6.2):

- *Activity*. This element defines the activities performed by the actors to develop a product. The activities may be decomposed into other more elementary activities. The activities analysed and synthesised to evaluate capabilities and to assign people to software systems development roles are the focus of this book.

- *Role*. This element defines the responsibilities and capabilities required to perform each activity.

- *Product*. This element defines the products generated by the activities. A product can be decomposed into subproducts.

- *Person*. This element defines the actors who have the capabilities required to play a given role.

- *Capability*. This element defines an individual's behavioural skill or personal attribute that can be considered characteristic of that person's behaviour and, according to which the activity-oriented behaviour can be logically and reliably classified. It is shaded in Figure 6.2 to highlight that it is an original element proposed in this book.

- *Technique*. This element defines the methods and/or techniques used to perform the different activities. The techniques associated with each people-oriented activity (People's Capabilities Evaluation and Assignation of People to Roles), whether imported from occupational psychology or designed especially, will be detailed later in the book. Note that the process elements do not directly include development tools that automate technique application and, therefore, these tools are considered within the technique element.

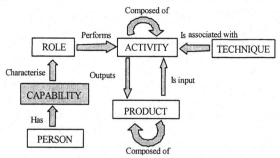

Figure 6.2. Software process elements

These elements and their relationships are illustrated in Figure 6.3 in more detail.

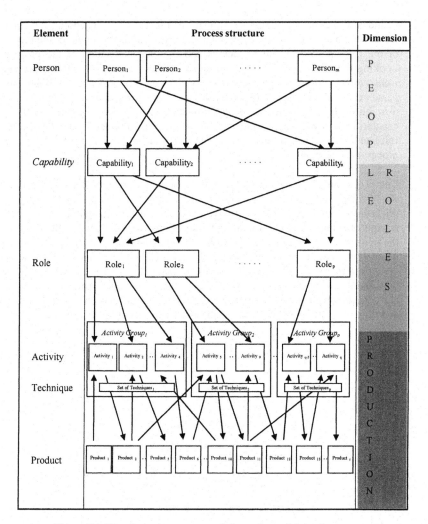

Figure 6.3. Key element, structure and dimensions of the software process

The elements (person, capability, role, activity, technique, product) and their relationships make up the three process dimensions. These dimensions are: *people dimension*, *roles dimension* and *production dimension*. The people dimension deals with the capabilities of the organisation's workforce. The roles dimension considers the capabilities required to perform a given role in the software process. The people and roles dimensions share the capability element. The production dimension deals with the activities that transform the input products into the output products of each process. In that way, each dimension includes different elements, as shown in Figure 6.4. Depending on their dimension, these elements stress human and organisational behaviour, the profile of the roles played by human beings and the characterisation of the process. Looking down at the pyramid from above, we can view the software process from three different perspectives, which are interrelated through the person/capabilities, capabilities/activities and activities/products triangles, and also through the adjacent people/products (who produces the product), capabilities/capabilities (people capable of meeting the requirements of each role) and activities/activities (each role performs activities involved in each process) subtriangles.

The process model is composed of the elements and relationships of the three above-mentioned dimensions. These dimensions allow the elements and relationships involved in the software process to be contextualised, explained, organised, applied and evaluated. The dimensions are segregated exclusively for the purposes of presentation and analysis, but they feed off and feed back to each other. For example, people with given capabilities will be assigned to the set of activities characterised by their required capabilities. These roles will be performed by the assigned people. These people will perform the associated activities to develop the output products. A set of activities corresponds to a role, and this role justifies its required capabilities by means of the assigned activities.

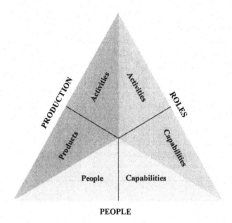

Figure 6.4. Software process model dimension elements

Each dimension is described below:

- *People dimension.* This dimension covers both the developer and the client or user organisation. Organisation refers to the people who perform given processes in a company and form either the actual organisation or a division, department, team or unit. Some characteristics about the people element that will influence development need to be ascertained. Specifically, characteristics like capabilities or behavioural competencies. Chapter 7 details exactly what we need to find out about the people and capabilities elements and how to do this.

- *Roles dimension.* A role is defined for each activity to be enacted, as are the capabilities needed for the role to be able to effectively and efficiently perform its activities. Capabilities are the elements that link the people dimension with the roles dimension, as a method for assigning roles according to people's capabilities and the capabilities required by the roles is specified. Chapter 8 details exactly what we need to find out about the capabilities elements and activities that each role performs and why.

- *Production dimension.* This dimension involves the traditional process elements, such as activities and the products that each one generates or requires. This is the dimension into which the Assignation of People to Roles Activities are incorporated. Chapter 9 details exactly what we need to find out about the activities and products elements for this method.

Of all the elements conforming the above dimensions, capabilities are considered the most relevant from the viewpoint of this book. They are, therefore, referred to as a key modelling element. This key element is addressed in the following section, before continuing with the detailed description of the dimensions involved in a software process.

6.3. CAPABILITIES: A KEY ELEMENT OF THE PROCESS MODEL

The capabilities of people and the capabilities of roles are key elements for developing the software process.

Lists of standard capabilities have been developed in occupational psychology (Boam & Sparrow, 1992; de Ansorena Cao, 1996; Hay Group, 1996; Moses & Byham, 1997). These lists have been refined according to the domain in which the test is applied, for example, banking, industrial processes, etc., identifying the capabilities applicable to each of these domains. In the case of software development, a specific set of capabilities demanded by development activities is required. However, to date, this is an open question, and the community has not accepted a standard set of software development capabilities.

In this book we have considered the list of 50 capabilities developed by de Ansorena Cao (1996), which is accepted within the field of occupational psychology and has been validated within the ACM as a list of independent capabilities for use in job analysis and for analysing the capabilities of candidates in selection processes. From this list (see Appendix A), we have selected and adapted the capabilities pertinent to software development, which have been named and classified, so as to be understandable for software managers and developers. To establish this list of capabilities, we have considered desired software-related job performance for individual situations, one-to-one interpersonal situations and group interpersonal situations. Beforehand, we held structured interviews with managers and practitioners who actually did each software-related job to establish the required capabilities for the job in question. We then held meetings with experts on each set of software process activities and the occupational psychologist Marta Aparicio from the School of Psychology at Madrid's Complutense University to refine and validate the defined list of capabilities.

The final list of capabilities is divided into four categories. This classification is based on the levels of skills acquired by the members (software team members, in this case) of the software development organisation. The categories considered are:

- *Intrapersonal skills*. An individual's underlying, general, elementary behavioural skills or competencies, developed by the processes of basic enculturation and education, which are a preparation for effective and efficient job performance and career development.

- *Organisational skills*. Behavioural skills or competencies related to effective job performance from the viewpoint of both individual, personal performance and the professional's adaptation to the life of a structured organisation with a view to progressing within this organisation.

- *Interpersonal skills*. Behavioural skills or competencies that are related to the successful performance of jobs involving interpersonal contact for correct performance of the process activities. These skills are generally closely related to effectiveness in positions of social contact.

- *Management skills*. Behavioural skills or competencies that are essential for managing other people within the organisation, directing their performance at different levels of supervision and with varying degrees of responsibility.

Table 6.2 describes the capabilities associated with each category that we have considered.

CAPABILITY	DESCRIPTION
Intrapersonal Skills	
Analysis	Identify organisational and/or software problems, recognise significant information, locate and coordinate important data, diagnose possible causes.
Decision-Making	Active decision making, selecting one of several problem-solving alternatives. Commitment to definite opinions, acting in consequence and accepting responsibility for such actions.
Independence	Act on the basis of one's own convictions rather than trying to meet other people's expectations. Uphold the same opinion for as long as possible.
Innovation/ Creativity	Discover new solutions to work-related problems and alternatives to classical solutions, problem-solving methods and approaches.
Judgement	Consider factors and possible courses of action in the light of significant criteria and reach realistic judgements.
Tenacity	Stick to the viewpoint or plan of action until the pursued objective is achieved or until it is no longer reasonable to insist. Keep up the same behaviour for as long as possible.
Stress Tolerance	Act effectively, albeit it under time pressure and in face of disagreement, opposition and adversity.
Organisational Skills	
Self-Organisation	Effectively organise one's own agenda of activities, establishing the necessary priorities and using one's own time as efficiently as possible.
Risk Management	Describe and estimate the likelihood and impact of the software process, project or product development risk as a basis upon which to develop the steps to manage each risk.
Environmental Knowledge	Be aware of the specific conditions of the working environment. Master up-to-date information on the computer systems and software engineering and knowledge engineering environment.
Discipline	Follow organisational policies and procedures. Look for information on changes in the competent authority.
Environmental Orientation	Be aware of social, economic and political developments and other environmental factors that can affect one's job or the organisation, that is, keep up with the broad activity development trends that affect one's own job or business globally with respect to major progress or in general terms.
Interpersonal Skills	
Customer Service	Perceive and be able to reasonably satisfy the needs and demands of the customer with respect to the information system respecting budgetary constraints and organisational resources.
Negotiating Skills	Identify one's own and other people's positions in a negotiation, exchanging concessions and reaching satisfactory agreements on the basis of a "win/win" philosophy.
Empathy	Be aware of and be able to satisfy the present or future needs or demands of a set of potential clients (the abstract client) from any level of the software user or developer organisation. For example, the organisational domain analyst is user-oriented, the systems analyst should have empathy with the knowledge analyst and the requirements specifier, the requirements specifier with the designer, the designer with the implementer, etc.
Sociability	Effortlessly interact with other people. Easily make contacts and engage in social activities.
Teamwork/ Cooperation	Participate actively in achieving a common goal, even when cooperation leads to a goal that is not directly related to one's own interests.
Management Skills	
Co-Worker Evaluation	Be skilful and discerning with regard to the evaluation of the professional aspects of co-worker performance, using the interview, performance assessment, potential development techniques, etc., satisfactorily.
Group Leadership	Guide and direct a team and establish and maintain the team spirit needed to achieve the team's objectives.
Planning and Organisation	Effectively determine goals and priorities, stipulating the actions, deadlines and resources required to achieve them.

Table 6.2. Proposal of capabilities by categories to be used in software development

This list of capabilities can serve as a basis for software organisations that intend to assign people to roles more systematically. They can add or delete capabilities that do not apply to their particular software construction process or even generate their own list of capabilities according to the type of projects they develop. In any case, occupational psychologists will need to participate in the definition of such capabilities. Working with project managers, they have to identify what skills software developers need to have depending on the characteristics of the software projects under development.

The capabilities listed in Table 6.2 are used in the People's Capabilities Evaluation Activities and Assignation of People to Roles Activities, which will be discussed in Chapters 7 and 9, respectively.

People Dimension

The people dimension is where an organisation's workforce is characterised. The changes faced by organisations can be effectively handled if there is a good understanding of human behaviour. The sociocultural environment should be considered in any organisation or problem situation, because it determines how organisations react to change and what changes are perceived as feasible. Culture is the familiar means of thought and action. It refers to characterisations shared by all the levels of an organisation (society, corporation, group, team, people), interpreted as a collectivity of people who have and accept a collaborative and community spirit. The cultural or social perspective not only focuses on technology and organisational structure, but also stresses capabilities, perceptions and values that change people.

The people dimension has traditionally been the most neglected dimension in software development. The originality of incorporating capabilities into the software process is precisely that it considers this dimension and creates a new organisational group of activities that takes into account sociocultural aspects of the workforce with a view to improving the implementation of software projects. These kind of aspects are normally missing from the traditional software process models as we saw in Part I of the book.

The aim, therefore, is to incorporate sociocultural aspects into the process model. As shown in Figure 7.1 (again based on the IEEE 1074 process standard), the people dimension considers People's Capabilities Evaluation Activities and associated roles, and their relationships with the software process. Organisations should discover the capabilities of their members to establish an improvement strategy and take advantage of these capabilities for software development. By performing the People's Capabilities Evaluation Activities a strategic plan can be developed for the members of the organisation involved in software projects.

This plan will be developed considering the roles and production dimensions of the software process model.

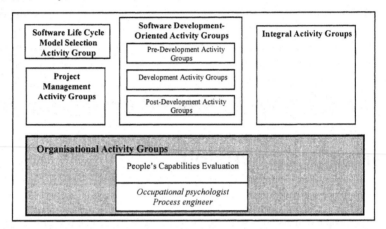

Figure 7.1. Activity groups and roles of the people dimension

People's Capabilities Evaluation Activities are concerned with modelling the people involved in standard organisation-dependent software processes. This kind of activities are located within the Organisational Activity Groups, which, as explained in Chapter 6, have been added to the IEEE 1074 standard for the purpose of incorporating human capabilities-related tasks. The People's Capabilities Evaluation Activities are defined in the following sections. A complete enactment of this process is described in Chapter 10.

The goal of process engineering is to design or improve culturally feasible software process models. This means that process models need to be suited to the capabilities of the organisation's workforce. Standard software process models are the starting point for developing the organisation's software projects. Therefore, it is essential that the process models satisfactorily represent the organisation under analysis. If these models are not adequate, the software process is unlikely to meet the needs of the client organisation, which can be damaging for both the user and the developer organisations. Therefore, the process engineer needs a defined procedure for modelling both the organisational process and the software process.

As we saw in Part I, process models do not account for the incorporation of organisational characteristics and competencies into software development. Organisational characteristics refer here to the determination of the capabilities of the people involved in software projects. Therefore, a People's Capabilities Evaluation method has been designed to perform the People's Capabilities Evaluation Activities. This method details all the steps to be taken by the process engineer to identify the capabilities or behavioural competencies of a person (user or developer) so this person can later be assigned to a particular role.

7.1. PEOPLE'S CAPABILITIES EVALUATION ACTIVITIES

The domain or scope of these activities is the organisation's workforce or the staff involved in each relevant activity defined by the senior management. The activities consist, firstly, of discovering and understanding the behavioural competencies of each person. This involves using appropriate methodological resources (psychometric techniques, focused interviews) to construct conceptual models of the people that reflect the actual competencies of the organisation. The activities start with the software process Workforce Participants document. This input document is used to build the People Model. The capabilities of the people (individual profile) stipulated by the senior management are determined by means of a procedure described later. The people who participate in software projects will be assigned, depending on their capabilities, to the roles (organisational profile) best suited for each activity of the software process (as described in Chapter 9). The People's Capabilities Evaluation Activities are related to other activities, but mainly to the Assignation of People to Roles Activities. The People's Capabilities Evaluation Activities generally have no pre-established sequence or logical dependency.

The activities performed during people's capabilities evaluation to transform the input documents into output documents are detailed in Table 7.1.

INPUT DOCUMENT	ACTIVITIES	OUTPUT DOCUMENTS
Workforce participants	- Determine people's (users' or developers') behavioural competencies	Personality Factors Models
	- Gain a general understanding of the organisation's competencies	People Model *Integrated people's capabilities list. Skills inventory.*

Table 7.1. Activities, and input and output documents for people's capabilities evaluation

A method, composed of phases and stages, is defined to perform the activities listed in Table 7.1.

The activities involved in the evaluation of people's capabilities should be performed by a team of professionals composed of psychologists, human resources managers and organisational process and software process managers (Table 7.2). Depending on their individual viewpoints, these professionals will generate heterogeneous conceptual models and, after a participatory process, design a model that better represents the capabilities of the organisation's workforce.

PRIMARY TEAM	SUPPORTING TEAM
- Occupational psychologists - Process engineers - Human resources managers	- Senior management - Middle management - Sociologists - Team-building specialists

Table 7.2. Primary and supporting teams for people's capabilities evaluation

The primary team role from Table 7.2 that is not common in software engineering is the occupational psychologist. This role is imported from psychology, although its profile is redefined here as follows:

- Uses psychological instruments to express, measure and interpret people and groups.

- Has thorough knowledge of competitor sectors and companies.

- Analyses jobs in the context of the organisation's structure.

- Is familiar with the organisation's culture.

- Correctly assesses people and can develop an adequate and realistic competencies profile with respect to the software process.

Another role defined is the process engineer, which is an essential primary team role and closely liaises with the occupational psychologist. What is a process engineer? A process engineer is a person who:

- Uses generalisation and abstraction instruments for retrospective and prospective modelling.

- Analyses process complexity.

- Symbiotically defines standard models that represent general knowledge on activities, products, roles, people and prescriptions for organisations.

- Has a flexible, all-round training and adapts to change.

- Uses management, development, support and evaluation conceptual tools and techniques.

- Can design alternative, feasible and/or anticipatory process models in face of possible and desirable situations, strategies and attitudes of the members of an organisation and in their meaningful environment.

- Can manage the evolution of standard models and the people who adopt and use them.

They use a method for determining the capabilities of people within an organisation and specifying their competency level. This method, called *People's Capabilities Evaluation Method,* considers the organisational culture: profiles of the organisation's workforce. This method is divided into two phases: quantitative investigation, and analysis and evaluation. The method, its goals and the techniques used are described in Table 7.3. The techniques entered in the last column of Table 7.3 have either been borrowed from other disciplines or were developed especially for the method. Specifically, a) the 16 PF Fifth Edition psychometric test, structured interviews, experts meeting and group techniques are techniques imported from psychology, particularly occupational psychology (Latham et al., 1980; Bentz, 1985; Janz et al., 1986; Bennett et al., 1989; Iles et al., 1989; Woodruffe, 1990; Shackleton & Newell, 1991; Dale & Iles, 1992); and b) the structure of the table of correspondence between the 16 PF personality factors test and people's capabilities, and of the situational test was designed especially for the method.

PHASE	NAME	DESCRIPTION	GOALS	TECHNIQUES
I	QUANTITATIVE INVESTIGATION	Determine the personality factors of the organisation's workforce and/or people involved in the processes defined by the senior management	• Discover the behaviour of the organisation's workforce and/or people involved in relevant processes.	• 16 PF Fifth Edition psychometric test. • Experts meeting.
II	ANALYSIS AND EVALUATION	Conduct an integral analysis of the personality factors and identify people's capabilities or behavioural competencies. Validate the people model output	• Gain an overview of the development level of the organisation's workforce. • Determine the capabilities of the members of the workforce.	• Group techniques. • Experts meeting. • Structured interviews. • Table of correspondence. • Situational test.

Table 7.3. Method for evaluating people's capabilities

7. 2. CAPABILITIES-PERSON RELATIONSHIP

A table of correspondence between each one of the 20 capabilities listed in Table 6.2 and the personality factors of a psychometric test will be used to determine what personality factors or behaviours indicative of personality are associated with the people involved in the software development processes. In particular, we use the projective 16 PF personality test, described by Russell and Karol

(Russell and Karol, 1994; Russell and Karol, 1998). This test evaluates personality structure, identifying its main components, and predicts the behaviour of people in a range of situations and activities. There are other tests, like PRF (Personality Research Form) (Jackson, 1989), CPI (California Psychological Inventory) (Gough, 1987; TEA, 1992) and NEO PI-R (NEO Personality Inventory-Revised) (Costa & McCrae, 1992) for measuring personality traits, which, like the 16 PF test, are adequately validated and correlated with each other. However, the 16 PF test, which should be applied by occupational psychologists, was selected because it is one of the most commonly used and highly reputed instruments for evaluating personality structure. Furthermore, it outrivals the others in terms of wider usage (Russell & Karol, 1994; Russell & Karol, 1998), and is conceptually and experimentally better adapted for psychologists. The 16 PF test measures 16 source personality traits identified by Cattell (Cattell, 1989; Cattell et al., 1993), such us warmth (A), reasoning (B) emotional stability (C), ... which describe primary human behaviours; and five global personality dimensions, such us extroversion (EX), anxiety (ANX) or self-control (SC). This psychometric instrument contains 185 questions or multiple-choice elements, called questionnaire data, aimed at measuring both the 16 primary personality traits and, among others, "impression management" or "social desirability" indexes to correct response biases. These factors and indexes are measured on a standard 10-point scale, referred to as sten scores (Russell & Karol, 1994; Russell & Karol, 1998). After analysing the test scores, these factors are marked with a "+" or "-" sign for each individual, depending on whether the traits of the person in question fall within the high range ("+") or low range ("-"). The weighting rule is as follows:

-    If the sten score is greater than or equal to one and less than or equal to five, the "-" sign is entered.

-    On the other hand, if the sten score is greater than or equal to six and less than or equal to 10, the "+" sign is placed against each factor and dimension of the personal profile.

This test has to be applied by an occupational psychologist, qualified to assess each individual's personality traits. The 16 primary scales are described in Table 7.4 and the five global dimensions in Table 7.5. More detailed concepts and rules for administering Cattell's 16 PF test are described in Appendix B.

The table of correspondence, Table 7.6, between the 16 PF test personality factors and people's capabilities was built to evaluate personality structure by means of suitably validated and correlated factors.

SCALE (NAME)	DESCRIPTION OF THE LOW (-) AND HIGH (+) POLES OF EACH SCALE
Warmth (A)	A-: cool, impersonal and distant A+: warm, outgoing, generous, attentive and communicative person
Reasoning (B)	B-: lower intellectual and reasoning ability B+: higher intellectual ability, shrewd and fast learner
Emotional Stability (C)	C-: reactive, emotionally changeable, affected by feelings and easily upset C+: emotionally stable, adaptive, mature and calm
Dominance (E)	E-: submissive, dependent, conformist, avoids conflict E+: strong, independent, dominant, assertive and competitive
Liveliness (F)	F-: serious, restrained, prudent and sober F+: animated, spontaneous, lively, enthusiastic, talkative and cheerful
Rule Consciousness (G)	G-: non-conforming, aloof, self-indulgent, disregards group moral rules G+: rule-conscious, compliant, reliable, honest and bound by group moral rules
Social Boldness (H)	H-: timid, fearful, repressed and cautious H+: bold, venturesome, impulsive, self-assured and enterprising
Sensitivity (I)	I-: objective, unsentimental, cool, utilitarian and wary I+: sensitive, aesthetic, sentimental, idealist, looks for affection and understanding from others
Vigilance (L)	L-: trusting, conformist, unsuspecting, adaptable and tolerant L+: vigilant, suspicious, sceptical, wary and distrustful
Abstractedness (M)	M-: practical, grounded, realistic and prosaic M+: absent-minded, imaginative, unconventional and absorbed in ideas
Privateness (N)	N-: naïve, forthright, socially awkward and unpretentious N+: private, calculating, discreet and non-disclosing
Apprehension (O)	O-: self-assured, unworried, self-satisfied, serene and confident O+: apprehensive, self-doubting, depressed and worrying
Openness to Change (Q1)	Q1-: traditional, enemy of change and rooted in the past Q1+: open to change, experimenting and analytical
Self-Reliance (Q2)	Q2-: lover of company, joiner and follower, prefers to have consensus and approval before doing anything Q2+: self-reliant, individualistic and solitary
Perfectionism (Q3)	Q3-: flexible, tolerates disorder or faults and careless of social rules Q3+: perfectionistic, organised and self-disciplined
Tension (Q4)	Q4-: relaxed, placid, patient and calm Q4+: tense, high energy, overwrought, impatient and restless

Table 7.4. Description of the primary scales by means of adjectives

DIMENSION (NAME)/ SCALES	DESCRIPTION
Extraversion (EX)/ A+ F+ H+ N- Q2+	EX-: introverted and socially inhibited EX+: extraverted, sociable and participatory
Anxiety (ANX)/ C- L+ O+ Q4+	ANX-: imperturbable, low anxiety ANX+: perturbable, high anxiety
Tough-Mindedness (TM)/ A- I- M- Q1-	TM-: receptive, open-minded and intuitive TM+: tough-minded, firm, inflexible, cool, objective, closed and unempathetic
Independence (IN)/ E+ H+ L+ Q1+	IN-: accommodating, agreeable, subdued IN+: independent, critical, likes controversy
Self-Control (SC)/ F- G+ M- Q3+	SC-: unrestrained, impulsive SC+: self-controlled, inhibitory of impulses

Table 7.5. Description of dimensions by means of adjectives

16 PF Fifth Edition Scales & Dimensions	Poles (-) & (+)	Analysis	Decision-Making	Independence	Innovation/Creativity	Judgement	Tenacity	Stress tolerance	Self-organisation	Risk Management	Environmental Knowledge	Discipline	Environmental Orientation	Customer Service	Negotiating Skills	Empathy	Sociability	Teamwork/Cooperation	Co-worker Evaluation	Group Leadership	Planning and Organisation
														Customer Service	Negotiating Skills	Empathy	Sociability	Teamwork/Cooperation	Co-worker Evaluation	Group Leadership	Planning and Organisation
CAPABILITIES → Intrapersonal Skills (Analysis … Stress tolerance), Organisational Skills (Self-organisation … Environmental Orientation), Interpersonal Skills (Customer Service … Teamwork/Cooperation), Management Skills (Co-worker Evaluation … Planning and Organisation)																					
Warmth	A-																				
	A+													X	X	X	X				
Reasoning	B-																				
	B+	X			X				X												
Emotional Stability	C-																				
	C+						X														
Dominance	E-																				
	E+			X																X	
Liveliness	F-																				
	F+																				
Rule Consciousness	G-																				
	G+											X									
Social Boldness	H-																				
	H+																				
Sensitivity	I-																				
	I+												X	X							
Vigilance	L-																				
	L+									X											
Abstractedness	M-	X				X															
	M+				X																
Privateness	N-																				
	N+														X				X		
Apprehension	O-																			X	
	O+																				
Openness to Change	Q1-																				
	Q1+				X					X											
Self-Reliance	Q2-																				
	Q2+																	X		X	
Perfectionism	Q3-																				
	Q3+					X			X												X
Tension	Q4-							X													
	Q4+																				
Extroversion	EX																				
	EX+																				
Anxiety	ANX-							X													
	ANX+																				
Tough-Mindedness	TM-																				
	TM+		X																		
Independence	IN-																				
	IN+				X																
Self-Control	SC-																				
	SC+																				

Table 7.6. Correspondence between 16 PF personality factors and people's capabilities

Additionally, Table 7.6 provides the process engineer, who conducts this evaluation together with the occupational psychologist, with a friendly interface with the People's Capabilities Evaluation Method through the four categories of capabilities defined here. For the Analysis column, for example, the person's behaviour should be indicative of Reasoning+, that is, the person should be a good thinker, be sharp and a fast learner, and of Abstraction-, that is, a practical-minded, realistic and down-to-earth person. Having identified the primary traits and global dimensions of the individual's personality by means of the 16 PF test, this table of correspondence is used in the People's Capabilities Evaluation Method to integrate these factors and determine the software development-related capabilities, as described in the following section.

Two tasks were performed to define this correspondence:

a)   A two-way analysis of the personality requirements of each capability, as well as the behavioural aspects of each personality factor, and

b)   An assessment, in which occupational psychologists from the Complutense University of Madrid and TEA, Spain, participated. The resulting correspondence is shown in Table 7.6.

The psychological characteristics required for an individual to have or develop a given capability are justified (rationale) in Table 7.7.

CAPABILITY	SCALE/DIMENSION AND POLE (NAME AND POLE)	JUSTIFICATION
Analysis	Reasoning+ (B+) Abstractedness- (M-)	The Reasoning scale measures the ability to abstract relationships depending on how some things are placed with respect to others. High scorers on this scale (B+) are people with higher intellectual ability, who are shrewd and fast learners. Additionally, the Abstractedness scale refers to what subjects and things people focus on. People who score low on this scale (M-) are realistic, practical and down to earth.
Decision-Making	Tough-Mindedness+ (TM+)	This dimension indicates how inclined individuals are to consider reasons or motives other than their own. The high end of Tough-Mindedness (TM+) defines a tough-minded, resolute, inflexible, cool, objective, undisclosing and unempathetic person.
Independence	Dominance+ (E+) Independence+ (IN+)	The concept of dominance evaluated by the Dominance scale is understood as the desire to control others or how controlled people perceive themselves to be. The high range (E+) includes firmer and more independent people. Additionally, the Independence dimension indicates how determined people are about their thoughts and actions. The high pole (IN+) of this dimension defines an independent and critical person.

Table 7.7. Justification (rationale) of the correspondence between the 16 PF personality factors test and people's capabilities

CAPABILITY	SCALE/DIMENSION AND POLE (NAME AND POLE)	JUSTIFICATION
Judgement	Reasoning+ (B+) Abstractedness- (M-)	High scorers on the Reasoning (B+) scale have higher intellectual ability, are shrewd and fast learners. Additionally, the negative end of the Abstractedness (M-) scale denotes people who are realistic, practical and down to earth.
Tenacity	Emotional Stability+ (C+) Perfectionism+ (Q3+)	Emotional Stability evaluated by the 16 PF refers to how adaptable people are to the demands of the environment, routine problems and their challenges. People who score within the high range (C+) are emotionally stable, mature and calm. Additionally, the Perfectionism scale addresses order and perfection. At the high end of this scale (Q3+) are the perfectionists, organised and disciplined people.
Stress Tolerance	Tension- (Q4-) Anxiety- (ANX-)	The Tension scale evaluates people's anxiety level. Lower scores (Q4-) are typical of placid, relaxed and tranquil people. Additionally, the Anxiety dimension indicates how nervous and worried people get about everything they do. A low score on Anxiety (ANX-) defines an imperturbable, low anxiety person.
Self-Organisation	Perfectionism+ (Q3+)	At the high end of this scale (Q3+) are the perfectionists, the organised and disciplined people.
Risk Management	Reasoning+ (B+)	High scorers on this scale (B+) are people with a higher intellectual ability, who are shrewd and fast learners.
Environmental Knowledge	Vigilance+ (L+) Openness to Change+ (Q1+)	The Vigilance scale evaluates how trusting people are of other people's motives and intentions. High scorers on this scale (L+) are wary, suspicious and vigilant people. Additionally, people who score high on the Openness to Change (Q1+) scale shy away from established rules and look to enjoy new experiences outside the more traditional constraints.
Discipline	Rule Consciousness+ (G+)	This scale offers information on the superego of examinees, which is why it is referred to as rule consciousness. Its high pole (G+) characterises the strength of the superego present in staid and moralistic individuals. These are people who are rule conscious, dutiful and conforming.
Environmental Orientation	Sensitivity+ (I+)	This scale analyses the sensitivity of examinees. High scorers on this scale (I+) are generally defined as sensitive. These are idealistic, open people who look for affection and understanding from others.
Customer Service	Warmth+ (A+) Sensitivity+ (I+)	The Warmth scale evaluates the emotional tendency that people generally develop in a situation of social interaction. People at the positive or high pole (A+) would be warm, outgoing, kindly and attentive to others. Additionally, high scorers on the Sensitivity scale (I+) are sensitive, aesthetic, sentimental, idealistic, open people who look for affection and understanding from others.

Table 7.7. Justification (rationale) of the correspondence between the 16 PF personality factors test and people's capabilities (cont'd)

CAPABILITY	SCALE/DIMENSION AND POLE (NAME AND POLE)	JUSTIFICATION
Negotiating Skills	Warmth+ (A+) Privateness+ (N+)	People at the positive or high pole of the Warmth scale (A+) would be warm, outgoing, kindly, attentive to others and communicative. Additionally, the Privateness scale evaluates how open people are to others. High scorers on this scale (N+) are discreet people, who manipulate their expressions to please and generate good feeling with their opposite numbers. These people are private, calculating and non-disclosing.
Empathy	Warmth+ (A+)	People at the positive or high pole of this scale (A+) would be warm, outgoing, kindly and attentive to others.
Sociability	Warmth+ (A+)	People at the positive or high pole of this scale (A+) would be warm, outgoing, kindly, attentive to others and communicative.
Teamwork/ Cooperation	Self-Reliance- (Q2-)	This scale evaluates self-reliance, understood as how dependent people are on others to be able to do things. People who score low on this scale (Q2-) love company, join groups and prefer to have other people's agreement and approval before embarking upon anything.
Co-Worker Evaluation	Privateness+ (N+)	High scorers on this scale (N+) are discreet people, who manipulate their expressions to please and generate good feeling with their opposite numbers.
Group Leadership	Dominance+ (E+) Apprehension- (O-) Self-Reliance- (Q2-)	The high range of the Dominance scale (E+) includes people who are firm and independent, who like to control others. These people are dominant, assertive and competitive. Additionally, the people who score low on Apprehension (O-) are self-assured, secure and confident. Finally, low scorers on the Self-Reliance scale (Q2-) love company, join groups and prefer to have other people's agreement and approval before embarking upon anything.
Planning and Organisation	Perfectionism+ (Q3+)	At the high end of this scale (Q3+) are the perfectionistic, disciplined people who organise others.

Table 7.7. Justification (rationale) of the correspondence between the 16 PF personality factors test and people's capabilities (cont'd)

7. 3. PEOPLE'S CAPABILITIES EVALUATION METHOD

The People's Capabilities Evaluation Method is used to perform the software process model organisational activities related to people's capabilities evaluation. This practical method focuses on *how to identify the capabilities of the people* involved in the software processes. The input for the modelling procedure developed is the Workforce Participants, determined by the organisation's senior management.

The output of the method is formed by two models: the Personality Factors Model and the People Model, which represent an organisational view of the software process.

The People's Capabilities Evaluation Method can be carried out effectively by completing the following phases and stages. For more details on the method, see Chapter 10, where it is applied in practice.

PHASE PCE I. Quantitative Investigation.

    STAGE PCE I.1. Identify Personality Factors.

PHASE PCE II. Analysis and Evaluation.

    STAGE PCE II.1. Determine People's Capabilities.

    STAGE PCE II.2. Validate People Model.

Figure 7.2 illustrates these stages. The directed lines represent the information flows between the stages of the procedure. The fine-lined oval in Figure 7.2 illustrates the Senior Management Process, which is not part of the method. The Senior Management Process determines the people who are to participate in the software development processes for the different software projects. The products generated by the stages illustrated in Figure 7.2 are shown in Figure 7.3.

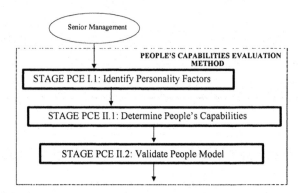

Figure 7.2. People's Capabilities Evaluation Method stages

Stage PCE I.1: Identify Personality Factors, develops the *Personality Factors Model*, which contains a list of the behaviours indicative of the personality of each member involved in the processes or participating in software development projects. This model will be used as input for the second stage.

Stage PCE II.1: Determine People's Capabilities structures the *People Model*, which contains the capabilities or behavioural competencies of the people concerned. Occupational psychologists should carefully check this model for inconsistencies among the competencies. If the process engineer, working with psychologists and managers, detects inconsistencies in the People Model, the psychologists can extend the study by applying psychometric methods (Boyatzis, 1982; Riggio, 1986; Ryan & Sackett, 1987; Boam & Sparrow, 1992) to solve such inconsistencies.

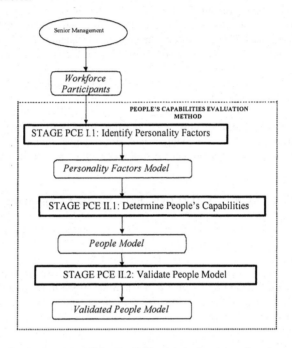

Figure 7.3. People's Capabilities Evaluation Method stages and products

Finally, the People Model is validated in Stage PCE II.2: Validate People Model, to output the *Validated People Model*. As we will see, in this stage, the psychologist uses situational tests to confirm the capabilities of each person identified by the 16 PF test.

Note that this method is not implemented for each project. The idea is that: a) the organisation should have a database containing workforce capabilities, b) this database should be reviewed more or less every two years to check for individual personality variations, and c) this information should be used by project managers when they need to assign people to roles for a particular software project.

Each stage of the procedure is described in the following, detailing the primary techniques used.

7.3.1. STAGE PCE I.1: Identify Personality Factors

In Stage PCE I.1: Identify Personality Factors, the 16 PF test is administered to the selected people. This test can be applied manually. However, there are tools to automate its application, such as, TEA-Plan Version 1.00 16 PF (Russell & Karol, 1994; Russell & Karol, 1998), which is special-purpose software for correcting and later analysing the responses given by each evaluated person. The validity scales (impression management, infrequency and acquiescence), the 16 personality factors and the five global dimensions are described separately, as are the possible strengths and weaknesses of each person's most representative factors. This outputs the *Personality Factors Model*, the format of which is shown in Figure 7.4.

The results output in this stage and the findings of an integrated analysis are interpreted in the following stage. Both stages should be performed in the presence of an occupational psychologist well enough acquainted with the 16 PF test.

7.3.2. STAGE PCE II.1: Determine People's Capabilities

In this stage, the 16 PF test results have to be matched to the capabilities defined in Table 6.2, using the table of correspondence (Table 7.6). This stage organises and structures the personality factors identified in the Personality Factors Model. Additionally, an integrated analysis is conducted of the results of each personality factor and global dimension described in the analytical report on the evaluated person. The result is a *Capabilities Report* for each person. The format of this synthetic report is shown in Figure 7.5. Each capability will be assigned a competency level (high or average). The competency level is determined by applying the following rules to the sten scores for each 16 PF scale and dimension (remember that Chapter 10 illustrates how to apply this procedure):

- For the high pole ("+") of the personality factors:

    o   the competency level will be rated high if the score is greater than or equal to seven and less than or equal to 10;

    o   the competency level will be rated average if the score is equal to six.

- For the low pole ("-") of the personality factors:

Organisation's name	Personality Factors Report
	Person's Name
	Name of activity group performed: ....
	Role played: ....
	Cultural evaluation date: .... Report No.: ....
	Evaluators' names: ....

A. Personal particulars

Age:	Sex:
Nationality: ....,................	☐ Male ☐ Female
Place of birth:	Residence...

Marital status:

☐ Single   ☐ Married   ☐ Separated   ☐ Divorced   ☐ Widowed

B. Graphic profile

	DS	SS
Warmth	A	
Reasoning	B	
Emotional Stability	C	
Dominance	E	
Liveliness	F	
Rule-Consciousness	G	
Social Boldness	H	
Sensitivity	I	
Vigilance	L	
Abstractedness	M	
Privateness	N	
Apprehension	O	
Openness to Change	Q1	
Self-Reliance	Q2	
Perfectionism	Q3	
Tension	Q4	
Impression Management	IM	
Infrequency	INF	
Acquiesence	ACQ	
EXTRAVERSION	EX	
ANXIETY	ANX	
TOUGH-MINDEDNESS	TM	
INDEPENDENCE	IN	
SELF-CONTROL	SC	

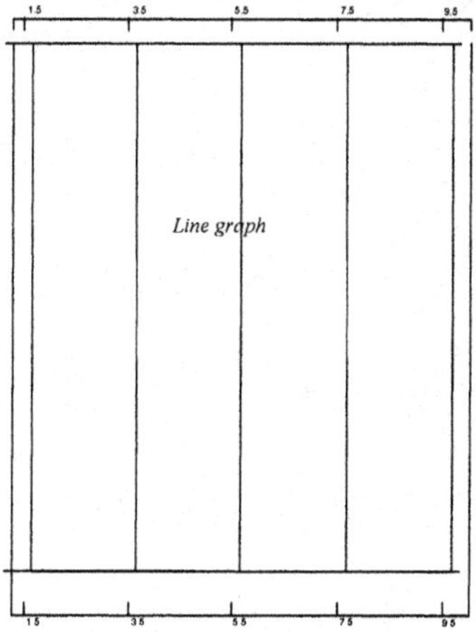

Line graph

DS: Direct scores for the 16 primary scales and three indices

SS: Sten scores for the DS and five dimensions

Observations: ....
....

C. Analytical report

Narrative description detailing appraisals of the evaluated person, following up each 16 PF Fifth Edition personality factor and global dimension, as well as the strengths and weaknesses of detected characteristic factors, written in a language that can be understood by any professional not especially familiar with the methods and terminology of psychological assessment.

Personality-indicative behavioural characteristics:

....
....
....
....
....
....
....

Figure 7.4. Personality Factors Model

	Capabilities Report
Organisation's name	*Person's Name*
	Name of activity group performed: ....
	Role played: ....
	Cultural evaluation date: .... Report No.: ....
	Evaluators' names: ....

A. Personal particulars		

Age: ....   Sex:
Nationality: ....,......... ....   ☐ Male   ☐ Female
Place of birth: ....   Residence............................. . ...

Marital status:
☐ Single   ☐ Married   ☐ Separated   ☐ Divorced   ☐ Widowed

B. Capabilities or behavioural competencies		
No.	Competency	Competency level
1		
2		
3		
4		
5		
6		
7		
8		
9		
10		
11		
12		
13		
14		

Observations: ....
....

C. General summary

Narrative description detailing the appraisals of the evaluated person, following up the detected personality characteristics and skills of the person, and written in a language that can be understood by any professional not especially familiar with the methods and terminology of psychological assessment.

Personality characteristics and skills:
....
....
....
....
....
....
....
....

Figure 7.5. Capabilities Report

o   the competency level will be rated as high if the score is less than or equal to four and greater than or equal to one;

o   the competency level will be rated as average if the score is equal to five.

For each capability, if the number of high ratings within the respective factors is greater than the average rated factors, it is assigned a high competency level; if the number of average ratings within the respective factors is greater than the high rated factors, it is assigned an average competency level; if there is a draw, the highest scoring factors for each pole are analysed and a decision is arbitrated (high or average).

All the lists included in both the Personality Factors Model developed in the preceding stage and the Capabilities Report output after this stage are called the *People Model*. The participation of an occupational psychologist, who works together with the human resources manager and in collaboration with the process engineer, is essential for both constructing the People Model and checking it for inconsistencies.

7.3.3. STAGE PCE II.2: Validate People Model

Finally, a person's capabilities are verified by means of situational tests. Focused interviews are one such test that can be applied for this purpose. This focused interview is a projective test involving a series of questions designed to provoke flashbacks (de Ansorena Cao, 1996). The goal of the interview is to precisely and thoroughly test the capabilities of the person to later assign or reassign the person to a given role. The questions envisaged for this interview are shown in Table 7.8. These interviews aim to analyse the behaviour of each individual under given circumstances to check or refine the identified capabilities. The *Validated People Model* is output after analysing the checks run by the occupational psychologist and the human resources manager in collaboration with the process engineer. This model will be equivalent to the input model, except that it will include a report on the validation conducted.

7.4. COLLATERAL USES OF CAPABILITIES

The models output by the People's Capabilities Evaluation Method can be used in other processes within the organisation, such as:

* *Job design.* The specification of the activities and roles to be played by the organisation's workforce include job design. These job design aspects can be further developed and expanded, by identifying, on the one hand, the

capabilities required by the new roles established in the organisational models
and evaluating candidates to play the role.

CAPABILITY	DONE	RESULT
Stress Tolerance		
Do you recall any situation in which you have had to endure high and long-term pressure?		
Have you had serious personal and/or family problems at any time of your life that you have had to solve without giving up your regular employment?		
Can you remember the tensest situation that you have had to face in your life?		
When you are under extraordinary pressure at work and the problems mount up, what do you do to solve them?		
Independence		
Have you ever had to change your mind about something important in your life?		
Courses of action that worked well in a particular situation, sometimes no longer do so. Has this ever happened to you?		
When you meet people who hold very different opinions to yours, what do you usually do? Can you remember any such situation?		
Do you remember ever having been completely mistaken about something that you thought was right?		
Analysis		
What is the most complicated problem you have faced in your professional career?		
Can you think of a problem situation you had to solve recently? What happened?		
When you have to deal with a system failure, what do you do? Can you remember the last time it happened?		
Co-Worker Evaluation		
Can you remember the last time you had to assess anyone? What happened?		
When did you last have to give your opinion about someone in writing or officially? How did you do this?		
What steps do you take to form an opinion about someone's behaviour?		
Judgement		
When was the last time you had to make a decision? What were the reasons for your decision?		
What most influences your personal decisions? Can you remember a recent example?		
Decision-Making		
Can you remember ever having to make a decision without having time to think about it?		
One sometimes has to act without being able to weigh up the situation, can you remember any such situations that have happened to you?		
When in doubt about how to act in an emergency, what are you guided by? Can you give an example from your own experience?		
Discipline		
One sometimes has to act against one's own beliefs to comply with the instructions of a superior, can you remember this ever happening to you?		
Do you remember ever having to convince someone about something in which you did not believe in compliance with instructions from a superior of yours?		
Can you remember any situation in which you had to do something against your will or your convictions in compliance with the rules or code of conduct?		

Table 7.8. Determining people's capabilities: detail of a focused interview

The selected people should perform the activities of each subprocess and/or process defined in the organisation according to their capabilities and the capabilities required by the role. In this activity, the results provided by the People Model can be applied to the new roles that emerge in the organisation. Moreover, the status of the people involved in each role can be determined to implement integrated management of the organisation's workforce by ascertaining each person's needs in terms of capabilities and specifying the respective participation and training programmes.

- *Organisation reengineering.* This process involves three Rs: Rethink, Redesign and Reequip and their relationships. The first activity calls for an examination of the goals and current baseline assumptions of the organisation to determine how well they reflect a commitment to customer satisfaction. The second activity involves analysing how the organisation produces goods or services (how workflows are structured, who performs what tasks and what results they get) and determining what elements should be redesigned to increase job satisfaction and focus on customer service. The third activity calls for an evaluation of the use of advanced technologies, particularly computer equipment to identify opportunities for change that improve the service and product quality and customer satisfaction. The models output in the People's Capabilities Evaluation Method can be used to define culturally feasible processes by identifying the attitudinal, structural and procedural changes for each process and defining the organisational requirements.

The above-mentioned utilities are beyond the scope of this book, but would help to identify the processes that the organisation should implement to assure adequate technology, methodology and educational transfer.

Let's see in the following chapters, the roles and production dimensions of the proposed process model.

Chapter

8

Roles Dimension

The roles dimension is where *the capabilities or behavioural competencies demanded by a role are identified*, the capability requirement levels are specified and the *performance required of the people who play each role* is characterised. It is a key dimension for allocating roles within each software project, as it specifies an activity in the production dimension for assigning people to roles according to their capabilities and the capabilities required by the role.

As we have seen in Chapter 7, capabilities are the element that integrates the people dimension (which deals with the profile of each person) and the roles dimension (which deals with the profile of each role). It is impossible to predict how people will behave and assign them to a role with any chances of success, even if we know what their capabilities are, unless we know what behavioural competencies the role requires.

8.1. IDENTIFYING SOFTWARE ROLES

To address the roles dimension of a software process, the critical capabilities required and the requirement level for each role considered need to be incorporated into the process model. Again taking up the idea applied in earlier chapters of using IEEE STD 1074 (IEEE, 1997) to illustrate the proposed approach, we have analysed the activities to be performed in this standard and, particularly, the competencies profile. The activities performed by and the products used and produced are described in detail in the IEEE 1074 process model (IEEE, 1995; IEEE, 1997). For each activity group of the IEEE software process, we have defined a role, as shown in Figure 8.1. Apart from the activity groups prescribed by IEEE STD 1074-1997, we have also considered the software life cycle model selection and the software quality management activities from IEEE STD 1074-1995. Although the revised IEEE STD 1074-

1997 does not include these activities, this should not be taken to mean that they do not need to be performed. In actual fact, the IEEE process refers to individual SLCM activities and specific quality management standards for its application. Therefore, these activities are performed in software development and call for specific SLCM selection and software process quality management capabilities. Process engineers should select the defined role profiles required to develop their software projects. Note that different roles can really be assumed by one and the same person or even be decomposed into more specific roles. For example, requirements engineer could be divided into requirements elicitor, requirements modeller and requirements specifier. However, this all depends on the size and type of projects of the software organisation that is applying the method.

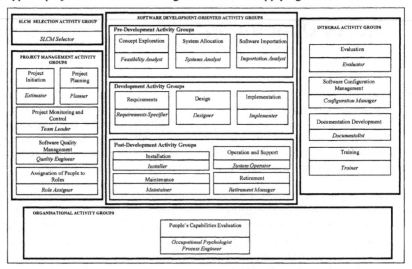

Figure 8.1. Integral software activities and roles

8.2. CAPABILITIES-ROLE RELATIONSHIP

We propose to assign capabilities to roles as shown in Table 8.1. For each role of the IEEE software process, we have defined the capabilities required to successfully achieve the associated activities. The proposed capabilities are compulsory for each role. Nevertheless, the person could have other desirable capabilities. Each of these capabilities is weighted at two levels: high (H) and average (A). The weighting indicates that a high or average level of the capability is required. The level low (L) is not considered, because people cannot be assigned to a role because they have a low level of a capability: a person is not required to have a low level of a capability or not to have a capability. For example (Table 8.1), the intrapersonal skills of an estimator are analysis (high), decision-making (high), independence and innovation/creativity (average) and judgement and stress tolerance (high). An estimator's organisational skills are self-organisation and environmental orientation (average) and risk management (high). Interpersonal skills are negotiating capability and cooperation (high) and empathy (average), and management skills are co-worker evaluation (average), group leadership (high) and planning and organisation (high).

Table 8.1 is prescriptive and generic. Therefore, each organisation should implement the respective tailoring process. This table was put together by analysing the behavioural competencies required to effectively play each role. It is justified in the following sections.

ACTIVITY GROUPS	ROLES	Intrapersonal Skills							Organisational Skills				Interpersonal Skills					Management Skills			
		Analysis	Decision-Making	Independence	Innovation/Creativity	Judgement	Tenacity	Stress Tolerance	Self-Organisation	Risk Management	Environmental Knowledge	Discipline	Environmental Orientation	Customer Service	Negotiating Skills	Empathy	Sociability	Teamwork/Cooperation	Co-worker Evaluation	Group Leadership	Planning and Organisation
SLCM SELECTION ACTIVITY GROUP	SLCM Selector	H	H	A	A			A	A			A	A	A			A			A	
PROJECT MANAGEMENT ACTIVITY GROUPS																					
Project Initiation	Estimator	H	H	A	A	H			H	A	H		A		H	A		H	A	H	H
Project Planning	Planner	H	H	A	A	H			H	A	H		A		H	A		H	A	H	H
Project Monitoring and Control	Team Leader	H	H		A			H	A	H	A		A	A	H	H	H	H	H	H	H
Software Quality Management	Quality Engineer	H	H	A	A			A	A			A		A		H	A	H	H	H	
Assignation of People to Roles	Role Assigner	H	H	A	A			A	A			A		A		H	A	H	H	H	
SW DEVELOPMENT-ORIENTED ACTIVITY GROUPS																					
PRE-DEVELOPMENT ACTIVITY GROUPS																					
Concept Exploration	Feasibility Analyst	H	A	A	H	A		A		H			A	A	A	H					
System Allocation	Systems Analyst	H				H		A				A	H	A	A	H					
Software Importation	Importation Analyst	H	A	A	H	A		A		H			A	A	A	H					
DEVELOPMENT ACTIVITY GROUPS																					
Requirements	Requirements Specifier	H				H		A				A	H	A	A	H					
Design	Designer	H	H	A				A	A	H		A		A		A		A			
Implementation	Implementer	H	H	A				A	A	A		A		A		A		A			
POST-DEVELOPMENT ACTIVITY GROUPS																					
Installation	Installer					H	H	H		A	A	H		H	A						
Operation and Support	System Operator					H	H	H		A	A	H		H	A						
Maintenance	Maintainer					H	H	H		A	A	H		H	A						
Retirement	Retirement Manager					H	H	H		A	A	H		H	A						
INTEGRAL ACTIVITY GROUPS																					
Evaluation	Evaluator		A		A		A	H		H	A		A		H						
Software Configuration Management	Configuration Manager		A		A		A	H		H	A		A		H						
Documentation Development	Documentalist					A				A	H		H		H						
Training Activities	Trainer					A				A	H		H		H						

Table 8.1. Role/capabilities table

The table designed was refined and validated by means of the experts meeting technique, used in the area of human resources management to describe newly created jobs. These meetings were held as follows. One experts meetings was held for the activities of each activity group. The experts were well acquainted with the goals of each activity group, the stages to be performed to achieve these goals and the capabilities that were to be discussed for allocation to each role. The capabilities required by each role of a set of activities, for example, the capabilities for estimator, planner, team leader, quality engineer and role assigner for the Project Management Activity Groups, were determined at each meeting. Experts in estimation, planning, monitoring and control, quality and people management and at least one expert on the primary activity groups that consumed the products generated by the set of roles in question and supplied input products to this group participated in this meeting. The same procedure was used to determine the capabilities of the other roles for the different activity groups at their respective meetings. For this purpose, all the participants in each meeting engaged in a process of deliberation that involved several analyses:

a) Analysis of the activities performed by each role,

b) Analysis of the critical situations for successful performance of each role, classified according to the four categories of capabilities described above, considering individual, organisational, group or management situations, and

c) Analysis of the 20 proposed behavioural competencies, identifying the competencies that are required to achieve a positive outcome in each of the critical situations.

Remember that we are dealing with critical situations where the desired outcome will not or is unlikely to be achieved unless they are properly resolved. Note, also, that the required behavioural competencies refer to capabilities that are absolutely essential (and not merely desirable or just important). These are behavioural competencies that the person who performs the role must have. A person without these capabilities will be unable to entirely and satisfactorily deal with the critical situation, and the objective of the respective activity will not be achieved. The result was reflected in tables similar to Table 8.1 for each critical situation and role.

Finally, the list of behavioural competencies was systematically and fully reviewed in participatory sessions, indicating which capabilities are necessary for successfully resolving each of the critical situations and the relevance or importance (high or average) of each one. These were again experts meetings between people playing the role under analysis, people playing roles that supply input products to this role, people consuming the products generated by the role in question, and an occupational psychologist, who was responsible for reviewing the capabilities agreed upon for each set of roles per activity group and for the overall validation of the agreed upon matrix. A total of ten experts meetings were held for validation purposes.

These meetings led to the Role/Capabilities Table (Table 8.1). The capabilities required to satisfactorily perform each role considered, as specified in Table 8.1, are justified in the following. The competencies profiles are discussed for each set of roles classed by activity groups.

8.2.1. Software Life Cycle Model Selection Role

The SLCM Selection Activity Group is enacted by the *SLCM selector* role. The selector's main job is to identify the important process characteristics of the software project and product and organise and order the individual activities to be performed during the project. This role chooses a model for each project and defends this selection.

As they have to choose and justify a model, the *decision-making* capability of the people who play the SLCM selector role should be within the high range. People without this capability would find it difficult to opt for one model or another, and the project would be held up while they made a decision.

Their *analytical* capability should also be within the high range, as they identify responsibilities and have to be able to recognise significant information within the process. They will use this information to make their choice between one model and another. People without the capability to analyse and solve problems would not fit this role, because they would not analyse the information to be used to make a decision properly.

An average level of *independence* is recommended for this position, as it is envisaged that this role will have to make decisions individually. The people who analyse the models have to be able to cut themselves off from outside influences. This independence will allow the people playing this role to be objective and correctly identify the line to be followed in the project.

An average level of *stress tolerance* is important in almost any software development-related role. This also applies to SLCM selectors. SLCM selectors will be under time pressure to finalise the selection and define the life cycle. This is because management and development needs to be initiated at the least possible cost for the organisation. People with low stress tolerance would find that their anxiety would escalate in complex situations. This would hold up their work and project initiation.

An adequate *knowledge of the environment* is a fundamental characteristic for this job, because the people performing this role have to be knowledgeable enough to be able to develop and choose the best possible approach and order of phases. People who do not have knowledge of the environment should at least to be able to quickly learn new models and technologies to make up for their shortcomings.

Although this role is not expected to create new life cycle models, SLCM selectors do need to know how to adequately and precisely combine them. Therefore, *creative* people will find it easier to identify the phases required for the model.

The importance of satisfactorily finalising the directive programme or project plan means that people playing this role need to be *tenacious and capable of pursuing their objectives without succumbing to adversity*. People who fall apart in face of any negative incident and fail to pursue their objectives through to the end would continually have to initiate and reformulate objectives and methods, which would be neither profitable nor effective. As mentioned above, software project initiation depends on SLCM selection.

An adequate level of *discipline* will allow SLCM selectors to straightforwardly select a specific approach for the project following organisational procedures. They have *to be aware of work-related aspects* to be able to correctly identify the best factors for defining the software life cycle.

As they select a software life cycle model for the entire project, SLCM selectors have to be aware of the needs of the other team members, especially of the person playing the role of project estimator. However, their work does not strictly depend on this capability, which means that only an average level of *empathy* is required. As participatory sessions are likely to be held to discuss the justifications of the selected SLCM, selectors should have an average level of *teamwork* capability.

8.2.2. Project Management Roles

The roles involved in the Project Management Activity Groups are *estimator* (Project Initiation), *planner* (Project Planning), *team leader* (Project Monitoring and Control), *quality engineer* (Software Quality Management) and *role assigner* (Assignation of People to Roles). These roles establish the project infrastructure and assure the right level of project management throughout the whole software life cycle. Their activities involve project initiation, planning, resource estimation, monitoring, control, quality management and role specification. Although the IEEE model does not directly specify the team leader role, this task is implicit in project management. Therefore, the scope of the team leader role is extended. This role should also improve communication and understanding among customers, users, specialists, developers, and organise and consolidate work teams. The purpose of this role is to achieve the following objectives: better understand customer requirements to produce systems that efficiently satisfy the real needs of the organisation; gather the information needed to adequately evaluate the impact of risks and prepare more efficient contingency plans; easily determine the most important system functions without going into unnecessary detail; detect problems in the work team in time and reduce their impact.

To estimate resources, plan and manage the software life cycle as well as smooth over character incompatibilities among team members, the people who play these roles have to locate and coordinate important data and recognise significant information. Therefore, their *analytical* capability needs to be within the high range. People who are unable to analyse problems would find it difficult to find solutions to possible problems and to select a suitable project management infrastructure. Additionally, people without this capability would cause havoc both as regards gathering information and building shared views in the organisation. This would interfere with the exchange of information and communication between developers, and between developers and users.

These are the people who really decide which path will be taken during the development of the software life cycle, which means that they should have a high *decision-making* capability. They have to make decisions quickly and be committed to and accept responsibility for their decisions. If they are unable make or accept responsibility for their decisions, they will have to seek authorisation and find someone to take the responsibility. This will slow down the project. Also they will require constant support for their decisions.

The level of *independence* of this group of workers, except for team leader, has to be high enough (average) for them to be able to do their job without having to ask for authorisation, although their teamwork possibilities would be held back if they were too independent. The independence level for this set of roles should be within the average range. Additionally, these people should be capable of *self-organisation*, because they should be able to organise themselves effectively to be able to coordinate and organise the project management and quality plan and other people's work.

Stress tolerance should be sufficient to assure that they do not succumb to regular adversities and opposition. A high level is required for the Project Initiation, Project Planning and Project Monitoring and Control Activities, because it is key factor in the type of work both the estimator, planner and team leader do.

The level of *innovation* or *creativity* required of the five project management activity group roles should be sufficient for them to be able to find satisfactory solutions to any incidents. However, their work is not characterised by a high level of innovation, as their job will mostly involve coordination and planning, whereas the development of new creative projects is up to other roles. The process engineer involved in the Organisational Activity Groups will generally propose such projects.

The team leader should be able to foresee and suitably manage risks, estimating their impact to prevent a project development breakdown. Therefore, *risk management* capability within the high range is required for this profile, as are *risk management* and *judgement* for the estimator and planner with respect to resource estimation and all planning for the software project. These estimates and schedules should be based on realistic judgements. Additionally, the ability to *negotiate* possible solutions for each identified and defined risk and each project rescheduling with the senior management and the work team members is also important for the roles of estimator, planner and team leader.

The estimator, planner, team leader, quality engineer and role assigner should have average levels of *environmental orientation,* because they need to be aware of all the work-related aspects. As the team leader is responsible for project and people administration, this role has to be able to capture any possible or necessary developments (*environmental knowledge*) in the respective activity that could improve project management and implementation.

As they develop and manage a project requested by a customer, these roles also need to be aware of and adapt to the needs raised by customers and team members, although their job does not directly depend on this capability. Therefore, they require only an average level of *empathy*. Team leaders, however, require a high level of empathy, as, of course, monitoring and control process workers should be able to attend to customers cordially and be *customer-oriented*. They need to be sensitive to customer needs and requests to be able to effectively carry out, and monitor and control the communication between the developer and the user organisations and mainly between the work team members. Team leaders also require a high level of sociability, primarily to deal with work team members.

Even if the project management roles are played by only one person, this individual needs to have a high *teamwork* capability, as this is the person who has to bring the project to the people who will effectively develop it. Therefore, all five roles have to be capable of actively participating in the achievement of a common goal and be capable of adapting to other people's proposals to assure that the project goes ahead.

As these roles are responsible for quality planning and management, and also have to be able to specify the people who will perform a given role and control the activities carried out by each role in the other activity groups, they need to be capable of *evaluating the performance of their co-workers*, although co-worker evaluation is not actually their job. However, a high level of this capability is required for the team leader role. Additionally, the *leadership* capability needs to be within the high range for all five roles, because the people who play these roles have to direct their co-workers towards the achievement of the objectives set out in the project. Furthermore, the team leader role should also motivate developers and customers (users) to achieve objectives that satisfy both parties. This is the key to monitoring and controlling all the activity groups, because the final success of the software project largely depends on this. Defective leadership can impede the achievement of objectives and increase the scheduled execution times, because the planned and organised actions are carried out without the right direction. Establishing order and assuring that the project goes ahead are the very grounds of success for these activity groups. Therefore, the capability of *planning and organisation* is essential for all five Project Management Activity Groups.

8.2.3. Pre-Development Roles

The Pre-Development Activity Groups includes the roles of *feasibility analyst* (Concept Exploration), *systems analyst* (System Allocation) and *importation analyst* (Software Importation). These roles examine, analyse and diagnose situations that allow the problem to be identified and appropriately formulated, the idea or need for a computerised solution to be delimited and precisely defined, the feasibility of the system under development to be determined and the software importation methods to be defined.

The people who play the Concept Exploration and Software Importation roles should have a high capability for *analysing problems*, as they have to identify problems and coordinate important data. This is the essence of their job, and it is therefore essential for them to be able to understand what situations customers and developers face.

Their *decision-making* level should be average, because they do not actually make decisions, but determine the feasibility of a system under development. This average level is required, above all, to assure that they give the evaluated aspects the importance they merit from the viewpoint of both customers and developers.

They should have an average level of *independence*, as they should be able to stick to their viewpoint that could be contested by two parties (customers and developers). Nevertheless, it should not be high, because they have to take into account other people's opinions. If the people playing the roles of feasibility analyst and/or importation analyst are too dependent, they are likely to be influenced either by the customer or the developer, depending on the circumstances, and unlikely to use their own judgement.

An average level of *judgement* is required for this set of roles, because they should be able to consider the positions of customers and developers in their fair measure. Otherwise, as explained under decision making, they will not be able to analyse the situation realistically and objectively. They need a large measure of *knowledge of the organisation's environment* and of the developments of competitor organisations. This will offer up-to-date criteria for analysing and judging the different alternatives and potential solutions to be defined.

They should have an adequate level of *stress tolerance*, because they will work under a lot of pressure and should be able to control their anxiety in the event of adverse situations. High anxiety levels are prejudicial in any job situation, and especially in ones where there is contact with customers, who usually demand speed, effectiveness and precision, which can put a lot of pressure on a worker.

These two roles, feasibility analyst and importation analyst, are expected to come up with new ideas and alternative solutions and/or locate and combine ideas and alternatives. *Creativity and innovation* are, therefore, essential for effortlessly analysing the components of the solutions for the idea or need of the software system under development and the requirements of the imported software.

Average *negotiating skills* are required for this set of roles, because they act to some extent as mediators between customers and developers. If they are unable to negotiate decisions, the mediation will be defective and these decisions will be a long time coming.

These roles have to deal with customers and they need to be sensitive to the needs they raise. For this same reason, they should be customer oriented, as this is the capability that allows them to interact with other people fluently. People without these two capabilities, *empathy and sociability*, would be unable to adequately deal with the everyday social situations that would be part of their work, and their ability to convince customers would be much lower. *Teamwork and cooperation* is a highly demanded capability for these roles, as they should be able to coordinate people (customer and developer) to achieve a common goal: an adequate and feasible project.

With respect to the System Allocation, its specific activities are performed by the *systems analyst*, whose job is to define the system and understand the relevant relationships between the information and objects and the problem-solving processes through analysis and conceptual modelling. This role describes how the system functionality and structure and the relationships between relevant elements are viewed.

Because of the job type in question, the people who play this role should necessarily be able to *analyse problems*, as, while they are not involved in problem solving, they should have a clear view of the situation in which the software is going to be developed to be able to foresee possible incidents. People who do not have this capability of analysis would be unable to clearly understand the relationships between the information and knowledge of the problem solver (user, specialist) and would hold up the work of colleagues, software engineers and users.

These people do not need to be independent, because, while they do have to stand by their position, they are first and foremost team workers, and an independent person would find it difficult to adequately fit in with a team. The activities of this pre-development process are iterative and depend on each other for successful achievement.

On the other hand, these people do need to have good *judgement,* as they have to consider all the relevant factors and situations to reach realistic judgements. This is the principal function of this type of process, and judgement within the high range is required for this role.

As anxiety needs to be controlled in all situations, *stress tolerance*, in this case within the average range, is included for this role.

People who hold this position should also be sensitive to the organisational situation, as it is their job to be able to understand system and product operation. If they are unable to *understand the environmental relationships*, they will not be able to understand the needs of either the company or the user.

As in the other pre-development processes, they should be able to perceive user needs and customer expectations effectively to be able to conceptualise the system and the final product, for which purpose they will require an average level of *empathy*. But, above all, they should be able to adequately satisfy needs and expectations by activating a high level of *customer service*. If they were not sensitive to customer needs, customers would find it much more difficult to make themselves understood, which could discourage them from working on the project.

The people who play this set of roles should also be *sociable*, because, as mentioned above, they have to interact with analysts, specifiers, specialists and users. This capability will help them to maintain a flowing relationship with their opposite numbers. People who are unable to communicate with others would not be able to reach satisfactory agreements.

Finally, *teamwork and cooperation* are essential in this type of activity group, as the set of associated roles should be oriented to the achievement of a goal that is common to the user, developers, the organisation, colleagues and themselves.

8.2.4. Development Roles

The roles involved in the Development Activity Groups are *requirements specifier* (Requirements), *designer* (Design) and *implementer* (Implementation). Their function is to represent the elements handled in the Pre-Development Activity Groups, as well as to analyse and model the software requirements, or design the formalised and computerised model to represent the requirements specified beforehand. Their goal is to produce a model or representation of the conceptual model and translate this representation to a programming language implementation.

On the one hand, the requirements specifier role shares the capabilities of the systems analyst role (System Allocation), although, in this case, it defines and develops the software requirements, defines the interface requirements and prioritises and integrates the software requirements.

On the other hand, the designer and implementer should be able to analyse design and implementation models in detail and combine different design and programming approaches, respectively, to arrive at an efficient model, selecting one of several formalised problem-solving alternatives. Therefore, these roles require a high level of *analysis* and *decision-making* capability to successfully perform their associated activities.

Additionally, intuition and experience in model design and development principles are needed to play these roles. The *stress tolerance* level of the people who play the roles associated with the Development Activity Groups should be average. This also applies to *independence* and *tenacity* for designers and implementers, as these people should be able to initiate and try to successfully complete a design or software implementation to prevent designs or different versions being reinitiated out of lack of perseverance or judgement and/or because of action taken under pressure.

Self-organisation is very important in these processes, because designers and implementers have to order their information and organise their time properly to formalise quality models on time.

Discipline is an advantageous capability, because they need to respect organisational procedures, although they should be independent enough so as not to be continually hanging on to the orders of superiors. *Environmental orientation* is also needed, because they have to be aware of factors that affect the work they do on the project for the organisation. Otherwise, they would not be able to formalise the project usefully for the company.

The levels of customer orientedness, *teamwork and cooperation* should be within the average range. *Empathy* is needed because the project is directed at customers, and people working on these processes should be sensitive enough to capture their performance and security requirements and also be able to put themselves in the place of the people who receive their formalised and computerised models. Teamwork and cooperation are needed, because they have to piece together information from the Pre-Development Activity Groups, as is an ability to adapt to and organise themselves to work with a lot of people (systems analyst, requirements specifier, user). These activity groups encourage participatory design.

8.2.5. Post-Development Roles

The roles that perform these activities are *installer* (Installation), *system operator* (Operation and Support), *maintainer* (Maintenance) and *retirement manager* (Retirement). These roles should fulfil the functions of installing, operating, supporting, maintaining and retiring a software product. The roles pass from the construction of the formalised models, which ends in software, to the construction of use models, that is, from activities that produce software to activities that allow its use. In these activity groups, the software is installed and evaluated in the user environment, making any modifications required until final customer acceptance. User technical assistance is an ongoing task of the software supplier. When the software is delivered to users, the engineer's activity focuses on error correction, environment adaptation and function improvement within the full software configuration.

The people working on the Post-Development Activity Groups need to be *stress tolerant*, as they will receive countless remarks, suggestions and criticisms from users on products. They, therefore, have to be imperturbable in face of difficulties. Generally, if any software has errors, users start to worry and even get angry with the person who is trying to help them, which means that these people have to be able to put themselves in the place of the users and control their anxiety in response to their anger. They have to persevere, performing and repeating their activities until the user gets acquainted with and finally accepts the new or modified software system. Therefore, a high level of *tenacity* is required for these roles.

A higher level of *self-organisation* is needed in this set of roles than in any other role. Additionally, they should be *disciplined*, because, as mentioned above, they have to be attentive to users (customers) and satisfy their expectations. *Environmental orientation* is also a must, as they have to find out the needs and developments of the user organisation, as this is where the implemented projects are used.

The people who play the Post-Development Activity Groups roles should be continually at the service of the customer. Therefore, two very important capabilities for these activity groups, of which a high level is required, are *customer service* and *empathy*. The people who play these roles, as mentioned above, need to be sensitive to and perceive the needs raised by both customers and users to be able to intervene and improve or retire the software adequately.

Finally, they should be able to *work in a team and cooperate*, because they coordinate the information and the software system that reaches the customer with the work of the developers.

8.2.6. Integral Roles

The activities under the Integral Activity Groups deal with two areas: quality protection and technology transfer. The quality protection activity groups address two basic activities: evaluation, including software verification and validation, and software configuration management. The principal function is to uncover defects in the product or processes that are used to develop the product. This includes review and auditing activities, traceability analysis, test preparation and execution, and the reporting of results of all evaluation activities. Formalised change management is also carried out. The roles associated with these activities are *evaluator* (Evaluation) and *configuration manager* (Software Configuration Management).

The people who play either of these roles should have an average level of *stress tolerance*, as they evaluate the quality of the tasks performed by colleagues, which will continually generate ill feeling, especially when tasks performed by others need to be modified. These attitudes should not affect their opinion of the work performed, that is, they should take an *independent stance* with regard to the errors or defects detected and who made them. They should abstract from the people involved in task performance and guarantee *objectivity in the judgements* they issue.

As mentioned for the Development and Post-Development Roles, *self-organisation* is an essential capability when people have to organise their time to perform their activities, as they will then be able to establish priorities for getting their work done. A high level of this capability is also required for the evaluator and configuration manager roles, because it better assures the quality of the product that finally reaches the customers.

The quality protection activity groups workers have an organisational responsibility. They should therefore have a high level of *discipline* to be able to ascertain, respect and adapt to the organisation's policies and procedures. Another requirement for the roles involved in these activity groups is *environmental orientation*, as they should keep track of any social and organisational developments that affect their work. These are the last set of work activity groups, and the software products should be thoroughly evaluated before they become project baselines or are extracted for formal change.

As the product will reach the customer (understood as the developers who are to correct the error detected or the actual user) after passing through their hands, these workers should have an average level of *empathy* to capture customer needs and demands and achieve an appropriate satisfaction level.

As in almost all the activities, *teamwork and cooperation* is very important, as the roles involved have to coordinate their work with the other activities of the software process to complete the project on time.

The aim of the set of technology transfer activity groups is to deliver the product by providing adequate system documentation and user training. The associated roles are *documentalist* (Documentation Development) and *trainer* (Training). The activity of these roles mainly involves providing guides for software use. Another central activity is to develop, validate and implement developer technical support personnel and user training courses and prepare adequate training materials.

Environmental orientation is essential for these two roles, as they have to be familiar with the work done by their colleagues in other activity groups, apart from with the organisational policies on the transmission of the information that should and needs to be communicated and the type of training required.

Discipline and *stress tolerance* are two capabilities that are required, as in any other process dependent on organisational policies and self-control, respectively, without either standing out for any particular reason.

Customer awareness or *empathy* is also essential, as, in the final analysis, it is the product consumers who are going to interpret the guides and ask for information from the technical support workers. The job of the documentalist and trainer roles is mainly customer oriented. Therefore, people playing these roles should be able to understand and satisfy the customers' demands. Empathy will assure that the technological material and training is appropriate and satisfies the customers' needs.

Again, *teamwork* is important, because the two roles associated with the technology transfer activities need to be in contact with other software process roles or with groups of people being trained to do their work. People without this capability will find it difficult to perform effectively, as they will obstruct the relationships between the people they are training and between the organisational roles. Additionally, they will tend to solve problems off their own back, without consulting other people, which would slow down their own and their colleagues' work.

Production Dimension

The production dimension is where the *software is produced and developed.* This dimension denotes what to develop and how to develop it. It involves the group of activities that transform the input documents into output documents for software construction, as well as the software development methods and techniques they use, including personality behavioural evaluation techniques. This is the dimension on which most research has focused in the past.

In previous chapters, we have determined a role for each activity in the software process and we have defined the capabilities or behavioural competencies required for successful role performance. The next step is related to assigning specific people to individual roles. For this purpose, we have defined the Assignation of People to Roles activities. These activities can be used to assign people on the basis of their capabilities (determined through the People's Capabilities Evaluation Method described in Chapter 7) to a role in the software development process (identified in Chapter 8) that they can perform satisfactorily.

9.1. ASSIGNATION OF PEOPLE TO ROLES

Based on the activities of the traditional software engineering activity groups, prescribed, for example, by IEEE STD 1074 (IEEE 1995; IEEE 1997), Figure 9.1 shows the new activities that address the question of assigning people to roles according to capabilities.

Assignation of People to Roles activities are described in the following section, explaining its purpose and function, determining the input and output documents, as well as the capabilities of the actual role required to perform the activities involved and associated techniques. We then show how people can be assigned to software project roles using the Assignation of People to Roles Method.

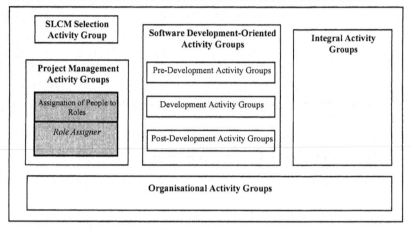

Figure 9.1 Software process model

9.1.1. Assignation of People to Roles Activities

This activity covers the stages of project team building. It involves a method of the same name that proposes a way of assigning people to roles in software projects. This activity applies the results provided by the People Model (capabilities of the people involved in the relevant organisational processes or of workforce participants) to the Role/Capabilities Table (Table 8.1) of the roles dimension, described in section 8.2.

As we have already seen, two tables have been put together and are used as input for the Assignation of People to Roles activities:

1) Role/Capabilities Table. This model, presented in Table 8.1, is a model of roles and capabilities or skills, which constitutes a profile for each integral software process role according to the capabilities and skills categories presented and defined in Table 6.2.

2) Table of Correspondence. This model, presented in Table 7.6, and described in section 7.2, specifies the correspondence between the capabilities of Table 6.2 and the 16 PF personality test factors used to determine personal capabilities.

Both tables are integrated in Table 9.1, Role/Capabilities Profile. This table aims to ease decision making on which person to assign to which role and is also the input for the Assignation of People to Roles activities. Finally, these activities are fed by the People Model generated in the People's Capabilities Evaluation Method, which determines the profiles of each person involved.

The structure of the Assignation of People to Roles activities is shown in Figure 9.2.

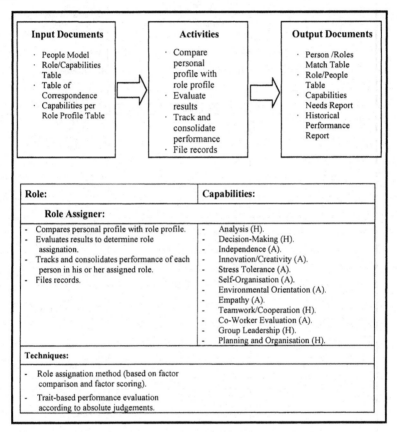

Figure 9.2. Assignation of People to Roles activities structure

9.1.2. Assignation of People to Roles Method

The Assignation of People to Roles Method can be used to assign people to play roles, that is, to perform each activity in the software process depending on the capabilities these people have and the capabilities required by the roles. To achieve this objective, this procedure divides profile structuring into four activities:

CAPABILITY REQUIRED (HIGH RANGE)	CAPABILITY REQUIRED (AVERAGE RANGE)	16 PF PERSONALITY FACTOR+/-
SLCM Selector		
Analysis Decision making		Reasoning+ Abstractedness- Tough-Mindedness+
	Independence Innovation/creativity Tenacity Stress tolerance Environmental knowledge Discipline Environmental orientation Empathy Teamwork/cooperation	Dominance+ Independence+ Openness to Change+ Emotional Stability+ Perfectionism+ Tension- Anxiety- Vigilance+ Rule-Consciousness+ Sensitivity+ Warmth+ Self-Reliance-
Estimator, Planner, Quality Engineer and Role Assigner		
Analysis Decision making Teamwork/cooperation Group leadership Planning and organisation Judgement Stress tolerance Risk Management Negotiating skills		Reasoning+ Abstractedness- Tough-Mindedness+ Self-Reliance- Dominance+ Apprehension- Perfectionism+ Tension- Anxiety- Warmth+ Privateness+
	Independence Innovation/creativity Self-organisation Environmental orientation Empathy Co-worker evaluation	Independence+ Openness to Change+ Sensitivity+
Team Leader		
Analysis Decision making Stress tolerance Risk management Negotiating skills Empathy Sociability Teamwork/cooperation Co-worker evaluation Group leadership Planning and organisation		Reasoning+ Abstractedness- Tough-Mindedness+ Tension- Anxiety- Warmth+ Privateness+ Self-Reliance- Dominance+ Apprehension- Perfectionism+
	Innovation/creativity Self-organisation Environmental knowledge Environmental orientation Customer service	Openness to Change+ Vigilance+ Sensitivity+
Feasibility and Importation Analyst		
Analysis Innovation/creativity Environmental knowledge Teamwork/cooperation		Reasoning+ Abstractedness- Openness to Change+ Vigilance+ Self-Reliance-
	Decision making Independence Judgement Stress tolerance Negotiating skills Empathy Sociability	Tough-Mindedness+ Dominance+ Independence+ Tension- Anxiety- Warmth+ Privateness+

Table 9.1. Capabilities/Role profile

CAPABILITY REQUIRED (HIGH RANGE)	CAPABILITY REQUIRED (AVERAGE RANGE)	16 PF PERSONALITY FACTOR+/-
Systems Analyst and Requirements Specifier		
Analysis Judgement Customer service Teamwork/cooperation		Reasoning+ Abstractedness- Sensitivity+ Warmth+ Self-Reliance-
	Stress tolerance Environmental orientation Empathy Sociability	Tension- Anxiety-
Designer and Implementer		
Analysis Decision making Self-organisation		Reasoning+ Abstractedness- Tough-Mindedness+ Perfectionism+
	Independence Tenacity Stress tolerance Discipline Environmental orientation Empathy Teamwork/cooperation	Dominance+ Independence+ Emotional Stability+ Tension- Anxiety- Rule-Consciousness+ Sensitivity+ Warmth+ Self-Reliance-
Installer, System Operator, Maintainer and Retirement Manager		
Tenacity Stress tolerance Self-organisation Customer service Empathy		Emotional Stability+ Perfectionism+ Tension- Anxiety- Sensitivity+ Warmth+
	Discipline Environmental orientation Teamwork/cooperation	Rule-Consciousness+ Self-Reliance-
Evaluator and Configuration Manager		
Self-organisation Discipline Teamwork/cooperation		Perfectionism+ Rule-Consciousness+ Self-Reliance-
	Independence Judgement Stress tolerance Environmental orientation Empathy	Dominance+ Independence+ Reasoning+ Abstractedness- Tension- Anxiety- Sensitivity+ Warmth+
Documentalist and Trainer		
Environmental orientation Empathy Teamwork/cooperation		Sensitivity+ Warmth+ Self-Reliance-
	Stress tolerance Discipline	Tension- Anxiety- Rule-Consciousness+

Table 9.1. Capabilities/Role profile (cont'd)

a) Comparison,

b) Evaluation,

c)   Monitoring and consolidation, and

d)   Documentation.

These activities, their tasks and associated input and output documents are
detailed in Figure 9.3 (an application of this method to a particular case is
illustrated in Chapter 10). The input and output documents are organised
differently to represent different viewpoints.

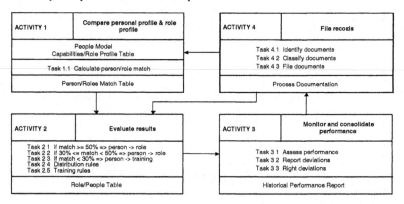

Figure 9.3. Assignation of People to Roles Method

The Compare personal profile/role profile activity analyses each person's profile
against each role profile, looking for the closest match between the personal
profile and the role profile. The inputs for this activity are the People Model
generated in the People's Capabilities Evaluation Method and Capabilities/Role
Profile (Table 9.1). A ratio between the number of individual personality factors
that match the factors required by the role and the total number of factors
required by the role is established on the basis of these two inputs. Note that the
discipline of psychology deals with people, which means that we have to use
probability rather than static percentages to express the match (agreement). So,
the aim is to predict as accurately as possible how a person is likely to behave in
a given role, depending on the responses this person gives to the 16 PF
personality factor questionnaire. Thus, the output of this activity is the
Person/Roles Match Table (the format of this table is shown in Table 9.2). This
table is the input for the Evaluate results activity.

In the Evaluate results activity, a decision is made on whether or not the person
should be assigned to a role according to the following rules of assignation. If the
match between the person and the role is greater than or equal to 50%, then the
person is assigned to the role for respective participation in the project; that is,
this person should satisfy at least 50% of the factors required by each role. The
Person/Roles Match Table will show such results. If there were a similar match

with two roles, the person would be assigned to one of the two depending on a higher number of personality factors classified at the high level. The Role/Capabilities Table (Table 8.1), the Capabilities/Role Profile (Table 9.1) and the Table of Correspondence (Table 7.6) are used for this purpose. If the match between the personal profile and the role profile is lower than 50% and greater than or equal to 30%, the likelihood of a good match between the person and the role is much lower, which means that the only thing to do is to look for a role whose profile is better suited to the person in question.

ACTIVITY GROUPS	ROLES	PERSONALITY FACTORS RATIO	PERCENTAGE
SLCM Selection Activity Group	SLCM Selector		
Project Management Activity Groups	Estimator Planner Team Leader Quality Engineer Role Assigner		
Pre-Development Activity Groups	Feasibility Analyst Systems Analyst Importation Analyst		
Development Activity Groups	Requirements Specifier Designer Implementer		
Post-Development Activity Groups	Installer System Operator Maintainer Retirement Manager		
Integral Activity Groups	Evaluator Configuration Manager Documentalist Trainer		

Table 9.2. Format of Person/Roles Match Table for a specific person

Otherwise, if the match is less than 30%, the person should directly participate in training programmes implemented through Training activities and then be assigned to the range between 30% and 50%, participate in the respective role and continue training until the person has a probability of over 50% of matching a software process role. People who play a role with a match of 30% or more will join training programmes after participation to achieve a better match with the role or be assigned to another role, depending on performance and the endurance of the training effect. The output of the Evaluate results activity is the *Role/People Table*, shown in Table 9.3, which indicates which people participate in which roles and establishes whether the people who match the role require capability development, that is, training, or capability stimulation, that is, participation. These suggestions are added under a Status column where the possible values are: training or participation. This is how the Role/People Table, called Capabilities Needs Report, is put together. This report feeds the Training activities within the Integral Activity Groups.

ACTIVITY GROUPS	ROLES	PERSON	STATUS
SLCM Selection Activity Group	SLCM Selector		
Project Management Activity Groups	Estimator Planner Team Leader Quality Engineer Role Assigner		
Pre-Development Activity Groups	Feasibility Analyst Systems Analyst Importation Analyst		
Development Activity Groups	Requirements Specifier Designer Implementer		
Post-Development Activity Groups	Installer System Operator Maintainer Retirement Manager		
Integral Activity Groups	Evaluator Configuration Manager Documentalist Trainer		

Table 9.3. Format of Role/People Table

It is worth mentioning that the metric of considering a match equal to or greater than 50% or greater than or equal to 30% and less than 50% between the personal profile and the role profile has been determined and validated by means of judges agreement using the experts meeting technique, consulting experts in the field of occupational psychology and by means of empirical validations at developer organisations. However, this metric could be modified depending on the characteristics of the project to which people are assigned and the characteristics of the other people to be assigned to the project. So, for example, in a particular project, where there is an absence of people with better matches to the roles demanded by the project in question, the percentages of all the people considered are compared for the roles involved, and the people with the highest percentage and better suited synthetic reports for the role profile are selected.

The Role/People Table is an input for the Performance Monitoring and Consolidation Activity, which assures that the role/person match effect endures, assessing whether the personalised assignation has managed to improve performance, reporting deviations and assuring that this effect does not fall by applying tested techniques that support and sustain the assignation made. This outputs the *Historical Performance Report*, which is appropriately documented in the File records activity to become part of the *Process Documentation*. This documentation should be taken into account in later role assignations that are performed using this procedure.

To summarise, the main parts of this Assignation of People to Roles Method can be shown in Figure 9.4. As mentioned earlier, Chapter 10 shows an application of this method for a particular case.

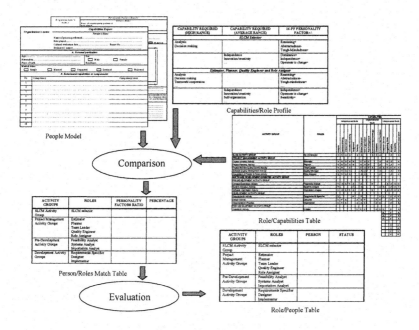

Figure 9.4. Main components of the Assignation of People to Roles Method

The Capabilities-Based Assignation Method in Action

The People's Capabilities Evaluation Method and the Assignation of People to Roles Method, described in Chapter 7 and Chapter 9 respectively, were applied at several organisations for refinement and to analyse their applicability. In this chapter, we illustrate the case of an Argentine software company to give an understanding of how the proposed process can be applied at a particular organisation. For reasons of confidentiality, we will refer in the book to this organisation as Company. Company is a service provider for several Argentine provinces.

First we illustrate the People's Capabilities Evaluation Method was applied to the people who were to participate in Company's development projects. Then, we describe how the Assignation of People to Roles Method was applied to allocate some developers from Company to roles according to their capabilities and the capabilities required by each role. The data on the capabilities and roles of these developers are real and were collected by applying the capabilities-based assignation method. However, the names of the individuals have been changed, again for reasons of confidentiality.

10.1. PEOPLE'S CAPABILITIES EVALUATION METHOD IN ACTION

The People's Capabilities Evaluation Method was applied at Company. The senior management of this organisation provided the Workforce Participants (the candidate software project members) whose capabilities or behavioural competencies were to be identified through the stages of the method. These people, forming a group totalling 26 participants, are developers at Company.

The results of each stage of the People's Capabilities Evaluation Method are described in the following.

10.1.1. STAGE PCE I.1: Identify Personality Factors

The personality traits of each developer need to be identified to be able to examine the best assignation of people to roles. As explained before, we use the 16 PF test to evaluate personality structure and identify its main components, and to predict how people will behave under different circumstances. The 16 PF questionnaires (an extract of the questionnaire is shown in Appendix B) were completed by the people on the list of Workforce Participants supplied by Company's senior management. We used TEA-Plan Version 1.00 16 PF-5 and TEA System 2000 software to process the 16 PF questionnaires. This software outputs the direct scores (DS) and sten scores (SS), that is, the transformation of the direct scores on a standard ten-point scale, for each primary scale, and also determines the sten scores for the five 16 PF global dimensions. The scores are then used to prepare the Graphic Profile and Analytical Report. This profile and report make up the Personality Factors Model, which is the output of this stage. An example of the graphic profile is shown in Figure 10.1 and an extract of the respective analytical report is shown in Table 10.1. The Personality Factor Models of all the Company people involved in the process are attached in Appendix C. It should be noted that this stage was performed in the presence of the licensed occupational psychologist Marta Evelia Aparicio García, of the Complutense University of Madrid, and psychologists from TEA Madrid, Spain.

10.1.2. STAGE PCE II.1: Determine People's Capabilities

The ultimate objective of a systematic assignation of people to roles is to identify the roles best suited to each individual depending on their psychological characteristics. But the psychological tests were developed with a view to analysing personality rather than for the purpose of job allocation. As such, they are related to people's personality traits and not a priori to their occupations. Therefore, we need to ascertain what personality traits are required to perform a given job, that is, to identify what psychological characteristics a given individual needs to have to possess certain job-related capabilities. In Chapter 6, we enumerate the set of capabilities that we have selected from a standard list, after several interviews with project leaders. Table 7.6 in Chapter 7 identifies the relationship between these 20 capabilities and the psychological traits identified by the 16 PF test.

The capabilities of each person and their competency level (average or high) are determined on the basis of the table of correspondence between the 16 PF personality test factors and people's capabilities (Table 7.6) using the method defined in Chapter 7.

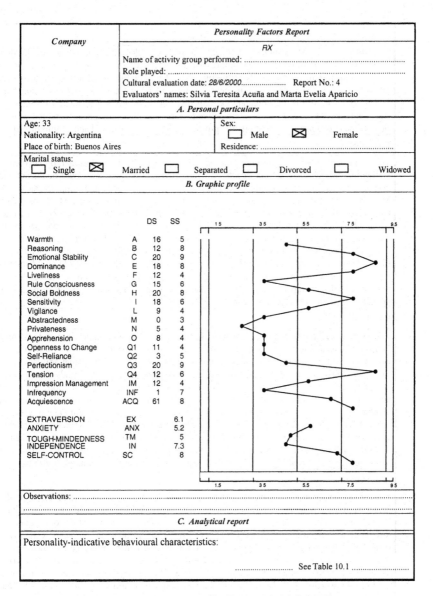

Company	Personality Factors Report

RX

Name of activity group performed: ....

Role played: ....

Cultural evaluation date: *28/6/2000*.................... Report No.: 4

Evaluators' names: Silvia Teresita Acuña and Marta Evelia Aparicio

A. Personal particulars

Age: 33

Nationality: Argentina

Place of birth: Buenos Aires

Sex:
☐ Male ☒ Female

Residence: ....

Marital status:
☐ Single ☒ Married ☐ Separated ☐ Divorced ☐ Widowed

B. Graphic profile

		DS	SS
Warmth	A	16	5
Reasoning	B	12	8
Emotional Stability	C	20	9
Dominance	E	18	8
Liveliness	F	12	4
Rule Consciousness	G	15	6
Social Boldness	H	20	8
Sensitivity	I	18	6
Vigilance	L	9	4
Abstractedness	M	0	3
Privateness	N	5	4
Apprehension	O	8	4
Openness to Change	Q1	11	4
Self-Reliance	Q2	3	5
Perfectionism	Q3	20	9
Tension	Q4	12	6
Impression Management	IM	12	4
Infrequency	INF	1	7
Acquiescence	ACQ	61	8
EXTRAVERSION	EX		6.1
ANXIETY	ANX		5.2
TOUGH-MINDEDNESS	TM		5
INDEPENDENCE	IN		7.3
SELF-CONTROL	SC		8

Observations: ....

C. Analytical report

Personality-indicative behavioural characteristics:

.... See Table 10.1 ....

Figure 10.1. Personality Factors Model # 4 (RX)

RESPONSE STYLE INDICES: IM, INF AND ACQ
The three response style indices of the 16 PF aim to disclose the significance of the data supplied by the questionnaire. IM (impression management) exposes test-taker attempts to put over a distorted self-image; INF (infrequency) is based on the rate of infrequent responses given by the examinee; ACQ (acquiescence) reports a test-taker's tendency to systematically assent to most of the questionnaire statements. Although RX's responses to some test statements are designed to convey a positive picture, this does not appear to be the general flow of the questionnaire. Therefore, the profile can be considered valid and be interpreted.
FACTOR A
This scale, called Warmth, evaluates the emotional tendency that people generally develop in a situation of social interaction. People at the negative end of the scale would be distant and even disobedient, whereas people at the positive end would be kindly and communicative. RX has scored near average for her norm group on this scale. This indicates that she finds it easy to get on with people, but also knows how to make the most of the time she spends alone. Although she does not dislike being with other people, she prefers to alternate company with moments of solitude. From the professional viewpoint, she will easily get used to jobs that do not involve isolation from interpersonal contact. Her score may denote some social skill, especially for building relationships with customers. Although she can be cold and distant at times, she will know how to give her best when the occasion so requires. She has a very positive profile for supervisory or middle management jobs. She is also likely to be a very proficient mediator or arbitrator.
FACTOR B
This scale (Reasoning) measures the ability to abstract relationships depending on how some things are placed with respect to others. Low scorers on this scale would be people with a low intellectual and reasoning ability; high scorers would have a higher intellectual ability, and be shrewd and fast learners. RX stands out on rationality and astuteness. She finds it easier than others to understand and establish relationships, and grasp ideas. She is concretely and abstractly creative, intuitive and speculative. Professionally, she is likely to excel in jobs that involve thinking and reasoning. Being rational, she is likely to be very proficient at creative or teaching jobs or occupations that place high demands on intellectual resources (any related to sciences or research). Other scales of the questionnaire should be analysed to see whether there is any relevant factor that could block these aptitudes. Her intellectual ability may lead her to be arrogant and breed conceit that will detract from her interpersonal relationships.
FACTOR C
The Emotional Stability evaluated by 16 PF refers to how adaptable people are to the demands of the environment, routine problems and their challenges. People who score within the high range are emotionally stable, mature and calm people; people who score within the low range are affected by feelings and easily upset. The questionnaire defines RX as a very stable and balanced person, secure and imperturbable. She is not dominated by emotional or affective states, nor is she prone to brusque changes of mood. She is not bewildered or carried along by her feelings when judging people or things. She is objective, pacific, placid and is not upset by worries. A person with such strong emotional control would do well in jobs that involve urgency and composure at the same time: fire fighters, pilots, flight assistants, judges, surgeons or public transport drivers. Her personal relationships with colleagues will be good and, as a member of a work team, she will act as a good antidote against stress and other work-related pressures. As she also scores high on the Q3 scale, she appears to have a profile typical of someone who is very self-controlled and has a lot of willpower.

Table 10.1. Extract of the Personality Factors Model (Analytical Report)

A general summary of the person is prepared from the participatory analysis of the Personality Factors Model. The result is the Capabilities Report. This synthetic report for RX (the same person as evaluated in the example illustrated in Figure 10.1) is shown in Figure 10.2. For example, the Analysis capability has been rated High, because, according to Table 7.6, it requires Reasoning (B) "+" and Abstractedness (M) "−". These values are calculated from Figure 10.1, applying the method described in 7.2, according to which Reasoning (B) is scored "+" because the sten score is 8. Applying the same procedure to the Abstractedness (M), it is rated "−" because her sten score is 3. Then, applying the procedure described in section 7.3.2, the Analysis capability is assigned a High value for Reasoning (B), as it has a positive pole and its score is greater than or equal to seven; and a High value for Abstractedness (M), as it has a negative pole and its score is less than or equal to four. So, the Analysis capability has a higher number of High values, and RX is assigned a High competency level for this capability. We proceeded similarly for the other capabilities illustrated in Table 7.6.

The Capabilities Reports of the other 25 people involved in the study are detailed in Appendix C. These reports (Personality Factors Model and Capabilities Report) are what make up the People Model of the Company software developer organisation. Note that, as in the previous stage, the licensed occupational psychologist Marta Evelia Aparicio García also participated in this stage.

10.1.3. STAGE PCE II.2: Validate People Model

An occupational psychologist should validate the list of capabilities resulting from the Capabilities Report of each individual by means of focused interviews. In this case, the occupational psychologist Aparicio García and the process engineer held focused interviews to check the capabilities determined for each person. The result of this stage is the Validated People Model, which, in this case, is the same as the output of the last stage.

Company	Capabilities Report
	RX
	Name of activity group performed: ....
	Role played: ....
	Cultural evaluation date: *28/7/2000*......................... Report No.: 4
	Evaluators' names: Silvia Teresita Acuña and Marta Evelia Aparicio

A. Personal particulars

Age: 33	Sex:
Nationality: Argentina	☐ Male ☒ Female
Place of birth: Buenos Aires	Residence: ....

Marital status:
☐ Single   ☒ Married   ☐ Separated   ☐ Divorced   ☐ Widowed

B. Capabilities or behavioural competencies

No.	Competency	Competency level
1	Analysis	High
2	Independence	High
3	Judgement	High
4	Tenacity	High
5	Self-Organisation	High
6	Risk Management	High
7	Discipline	Average
8	Environmental Orientation	Average
9	Teamwork/Cooperation	Average
10	Group Leadership	Average
11	Planning and Organisation	High

Observations: ....

C. General summary

Personality characteristics and skills

RX stands out on rationality and astuteness. She is likely to excel in jobs that involve thinking and reasoning. Being rational, she is likely to be very proficient at creative or teaching jobs or occupations that place high demands on intellectual resources. She is tenacious, dominant, aggressive, energetic and will persistently argue her ideas and viewpoints. However, this will not necessarily lead her into insurmountable conflicts with colleagues. She is not a person who blindly fights to get her ideas through, although she will defend them tactfully. She is likely to be a good salesperson and will struggle to get customers to sign a contract.
She is likely to be highly regarded by her superiors, as she will conscientiously accept any rule they enforce. Jobs involving thought and reflection, such as the scientific and technical professions, would be ideal positions for her.
She will take risks that others turn away from. She is firm in the face of difficulties and usually accepts responsibility for her acts. She contributes to creating an agreeable and pleasant working environment. However, she is easily manipulated and deceived, and is, therefore, not recommended for jobs that require strength and decisiveness, like supervisory positions.
RX is objective and realistic, looking for immediate benefits and acting on practical grounds only. She is not very creative or original, which may be a limitation. She will focus well on her work, especially if it involves mechanical behaviour with little room for decision making. She tends to be thorough, and is unlikely to leave a job unfinished
She is frank and sincere, which may put her at odds with other colleagues or customers. In more complicated situations, however, she will know just how far to go. She should not work dealing with claims or in direct sales. She would be better suited for help or assistance jobs.
At work she will show herself to have a headstrong character, quick to pass judgement on others but far from willing to accept criticism herself. She may appear to be sure of her decisions. If anything goes wrong, however, she will want to have nothing to do with the matter. She is likely to be a loyal employee, who, faced with the uncertain prospects of a change, prefers to stay in the same place for a long time. She is very much a perfectionist, which leads her demand a lot of herself and never to be satisfied with her actions. In her interpersonal behaviour, she will be constantly watchful of the impression she causes, analysing her every word or action. Being a person inclined to perfectionism and thoroughness, she may often to fall prey to impractical obsessions that slow down her work and affect her performance. Her job should ideally not include risk taking.

Figure 10.2. Capabilities Report # 4

10.2. ASSIGNATION OF PEOPLE TO ROLES METHOD IN ACTION

Once the individuals of an organisation have been characterised by analysing their personality traits and capabilities, it is possible to determine how to assign these individuals to each of the roles. For this purpose, the roles involved in a software process need to have been examined beforehand to decide on the best capabilities for performing the role in question, as clarified in Chapter 8.

As explained in Chapter 9, the capabilities-based assignation method uses the ratio between the personality factors satisfied by each individual and the personality factors required by each role. The greater this ratio is for a given individual and role, the better the match of this individual to the role will be. The specific value of the ratio to be used to determine when to assign an individual to a particular role depends on the characteristics of each organisation, and the number of available and required resources. As we have seen in Chapter 9, we suggest that the capabilities satisfied/capabilities required ratio should not be under 50% for an individual to be assigned to a particular role. If this ratio were from 30% to 50% and there were no individuals better suited for the role in question, the person might then be assigned to this role, but would also need to participate in training programmes to develop the required capabilities. Otherwise, if the match were less than 30%, the person should be directly sent on training programmes.

In the following, we describe an example of this assignation procedure for RX. Table 10.2 shows the result of the ratios calculated for her along with the respective percentages. They have been calculated from Figure 10.1, where RX's personality factors have been identified and compared against the personality factors required for each role according to Table 9.1. This process is illustrated in Figure 10.3 showing the personality factors for the analysed person (RX) and the personality factors required by each of the analysed roles. The personality factors of each role scored High are highlighted in bold type and the factors scoring within the Average range appear in normal type, as described in Table 9.1. RX's personality factors are highlighted in bold type and the factors scoring within the Average range appear in normal type, according to the procedure described in section 7.3.2.

According to Table 10.2, RX could do well in any of the identified roles. Nevertheless, she would be best suited for two areas of work. The first one is quality protection, where the percentage match between the characteristics of the set of roles and personality traits for the Evaluation and Configuration Management Activity Groups is 82%. The other area where RX would fit in best would be the Design and Implementation Activity Groups, where the percentage match between the characteristics of this set of roles and RX's personality characteristics is 77%. The particular role to which this person will be assigned in a work team will depend on the characteristics of the other candidates and how well they can address the different project roles. Note that another variable to be taken into account at this point would be what experience the candidate has with the software technologies to be used by the different project members to play each of the roles. Accordingly, there will need to be trade-off between several factors: individual capabilities, experience in software technologies, personal preferences, personal relationships with other team members, etc. In this case, and taking into account these characteristics, the role assigned to RX at Company was Designer/Implementer (this has been highlighted in Table 10.2 by writing this role in capital letters). Note, therefore, that the final assignation of people to roles in a software organisation is a very complex process that covers several variables. This book focuses on one such variable that we consider to be key factor, namely, the analysis of the individual capabilities of each team member.

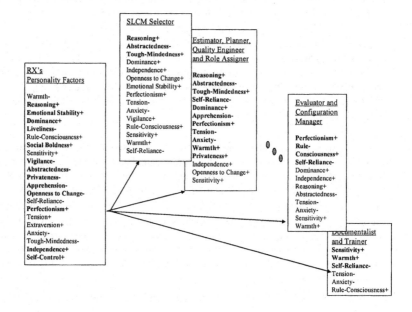

Figure 10.3. Identification of roles that can be satisfied by RX

ACTIVITY GROUPS	ROLES	PERSONALITY FACTORS RATIO	PERCENTAGE
SLCM Selection Activity Group	SLCM Selector	10/15	67%
Project Management Activity Groups	Estimator	9/14	64%
	Planner	9/14	64%
	Quality Engineer	9/14	64%
	Role Assigner	9/14	64%
	Team Leader	8/14	57%
Pre-Development Activity Groups	Feasibility Analyst	6/12	50%
	Importation Analyst	6/12	50%
	Systems Analyst	5/7	71%
Development Activity Groups	Requirements Specifier	5/7	71%
	DESIGNER	10/13	77%
	IMPLEMENTER	10/13	77%
Post-Development Activity Groups	Installer	6/8	75%
	System Operator	6/8	75%
	Maintainer	6/8	75%
	Retirement Manager	6/8	75%
Integral Activity Groups	Evaluator	9/11	82%
	Configuration Manager	9/11	82%
	Documentalist	4/6	67%
	Trainer	4/6	67%

Table 10.2. Assignation of RX to Roles

A similar process was enacted for the other 15 people that Company management appointed to develop four different software projects (their personality factors and capabilities are described in Appendix C). Because of the size of the software projects, the Company software managers decided to work with only four roles: Planner, Requirements Specifier, Designer/Implementer, and Evaluator.

Tables 10.3 to 10.17 show the ratios and percentages of the profile match for each set of roles, and the assignation of all the people who are to participate in the projects to their particular role (capitalised letter in the table). Note that, due to the project characteristics, one person will play just one role in this case, but this does not necessarily always apply.

Figure 10.4 illustrates the match between personality factors and roles for GR (her personality factors have been identified from her Personality Factors Model shown in Appendix C, Figure C.5). She could be suited for three areas of work. According to Table 10.3 GR could work as a Planner, Designer/Implementer or Evaluator as their percentages range from 62% to 64%. Her scores for Requirements Specifier (43%) mean that she is not a suitable candidate for this role. As regards the planner role, we can see from Figure 10.4 how she has scores that do not match the profile for this area on Abstractedness, Tough-Mindedness, Self-Reliance, Tension and Warmth, which should be taken into account with respect to her adaptation to the job if she were ultimately assigned to the planner role. Additionally, GR prefers to work alone and occupy a position in areas involving creativity and a variety of tasks. Bearing all these factors in mind, she has been assigned to the role of Evaluator in this case.

ACTIVITY GROUPS	ROLES	PERSONALITY FACTORS RATIO	PERCENTAGE
Project Management Activity Groups	Planner	9/14	64%
Development Activity Groups	Requirements Specifier	3/7	43%
	Designer/Implementer	8/13	62%
Integral Process Activity Groups	EVALUATOR	7/11	64%

Table 10.3. Assignation of GR to Roles

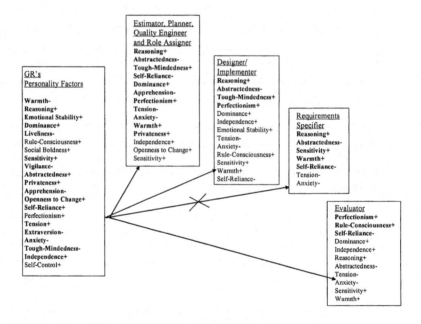

Figure 10.4. Identification of roles that GR can play

The other Company members where analysed similarly. Below we show the resultant personality factor ratios and percentages.

In relation to the role assigned from Table 10.4, FR could fit the profile for Evaluator and Designer/Implementer roles, as his profile matches this set of roles on the high scores (+ sign), such us Rule Consciousness, Dominance, Independence, Reasoning, Sensitivity or Warmth (see his Personality Factors Model in Figure C.8). The match of his profile with this set of roles is about 55%. The final role assigned to FR was Evaluator, as the Designer roles had been filled by other Company members.

ACTIVITY GROUPS	ROLES	PERSONALITY FACTORS RATIO	PERCENTAGE
Project Management Activity Groups	Planner	5/14	36%
Development Activity Groups	Requirements Specifier Designer/Implementer	3/7 7/13	43% 54%
Integral Activity Groups	EVALUATOR	6/11	55%

Table 10.4. Assignation of FR to Roles

With respect to the role assigned in Table 10.5, CA could fit the Evaluation Activities role, because she has a 55% match with the role profile. She scores high on the scales of Perfectionism, Rule Consciousness, Dominance, Independence, Reasoning and Sensitivity (see her Personality Factors Model in Figure C.10). This role was the one finally assigned to her.

ACTIVITY GROUPS	ROLES	PERSONALITY FACTORS RATIO	PERCENTAGE
Project Management Activity Groups	Planner	6/14	43%
Development Activity Groups	Requirements Specifier Designer/Implementer	2/7 6/13	29% 46%
Integral Activity Groups	EVALUATOR	6/11	55%

Table 10.5. Assignation of CA to Roles

Considering the role assigned in Table 10.6, the role that best matches CS's profile is the Evaluator role. She scores high on Perfectionism, Rule Consciousness, Dominance, Reasoning and Sensitivity and low, as required, on Self-Reliance (see her Personality Factors Model in Figure C.12). Therefore, the role assigned to CS in this case was Evaluator.

ACTIVITY GROUPS	ROLES	PERSONALITY FACTORS RATIO	PERCENTAGE
Project Management Activity Groups	Planner	5/14	36%
Development Activity Groups	Requirements Specifier Designer/Implementer	3/7 6/13	43% 46%
Integral Activity Groups	EVALUATOR	6/11	55%

Table 10.6. Assignation of CS to Roles

With respect to the role assigned in Table 10.7, the area best suited to MA's profile would be design and implementation, as her profile includes high scores on Reasoning, Tough-Mindedness, Dominance, Perfectionism and Rule Consciousness and low scores, as also required, on Abstractedness (see her Personality Factors Model in Figure C.3). However, her profile reveals very low levels of Sensitivity, whereas Sensitivity is a requirement for this area. Her supervisors would, therefore, have to take this into account. Although the percentage match between the role characteristics (Designer/Implementer) and personality characteristics is 46%, this is the role that this person could play best. She was, therefore, finally assigned to this role. However, the team leader was notified of her weakness as regards the Sensitivity factor. If she were to play this role in the company for any length of time, MA should ideally be sent on training to improve the sensitivity factor.

ACTIVITY GROUPS	ROLES	PERSONALITY FACTORS RATIO	PERCENTAGE
Project Management Activity Groups	Planner	6/14	43%
Development Activity Groups	Requirements Specifier DESIGNER/IMPLEMENTER	2/7 6/13	29% 46%
Integral Activity Groups	Evaluator	4/11	36%

Table 10.7. Assignation of MA to Roles

With respect to the role assigned from Table 10.8, the position in which EL would be best able to develop her potential is within the Design and Implementation Activity Groups, as she has high scores on Reasoning, Tough-Mindedness, Emotional Stability, Perfectionism and Rule Consciousness and low scores on Abstractedness and Self-Reliance (see her Personality Factors Model in Figure C.23), constituting a 54% match. Therefore, the role assigned to EL in this case was Designer/Implementer.

ACTIVITY GROUPS	ROLES	PERSONALITY FACTORS RATIO	PERCENTAGE
Project Management Activity Groups	Planner	6/14	43%
Development Activity Groups	Requirements Specifier DESIGNER/IMPLEMENTER	2/7 7/13	29% 54%
Integral Activity Groups	Evaluator	5/11	45%

Table 10.8. Assignation of EL to Roles

Looking at Table 10.9, the profile of AD (see the Personality Factors Model in Figure C.22) could fit several roles, but the best match would be for the Requirements Specifier role, where the match is 86%. She has scores that match the profile on Reasoning, Abstractedness and Warmth (high scores) and Self-Reliance, Tension and Anxiety (low scores). The other set of roles where AD would fit in best is Design and Implementation, where she matches on the scales of Reasoning, Abstractedness, Dominance, Independence, Emotional Stability, Perfectionism, Tension, Anxiety, Warmth and Self-Reliance. The percentage match between the characteristics of this set of roles and AD's personality characteristics is 77%. Additionally, she has an 82% match for the Evaluator role. The Role assigned to AD in this case was Designer/Implementer bearing in mind her technical experience and that other people were able to play the other roles.

ACTIVITY GROUPS	ROLES	PERSONALITY FACTORS RATIO	PERCENTAGE
Project Management Activity Groups	Planner	10/14	71%
Development Activity Groups	Requirements Specifier DESIGNER/IMPLEMENTER	6/7 10/13	86% 77%
Integral Activity Groups	Evaluator	9/11	82%

Table 10.9. Assignation of AD to Roles

In relation to the role assigned in Table 10.10, we believe that the area where PB could best develop his potential would be Requirements Specifier, as he scores high on Reasoning, Sensitivity and Warmth (see his Personality Factors Model in Figure C.21). However, it should be taken into account that he also has a tendency to score high on Abstractedness and Self-Reliance, which could detract from his work somewhat. The percentage match between roles and personality characteristics is 57%. Therefore, in spite of the above point and bearing in mind the other people analysed, the role assigned to PB in this case was Requirements Specifier.

ACTIVITY GROUPS	ROLES	PERSONALITY FACTORS RATIO	PERCENTAGE
Project Management Activity Groups	Planner	4/14	29%
Development Activity Groups	REQUIREMENTS SPECIFIER Designer/Implementer	4/7 3/13	57% 23%
Integral Activity Groups	Evaluator	3/11	27%

Table 10.10. Assignation of PB to Roles

With respect to the role assigned from Table 10.11 (see the Personality Factors Model in Figure C.9), PR could play all four roles. However, the best option according to his capabilities would be to assign him to the Requirements Specifier role, where, according to his scores on Reasoning, Sensitivity, Self-Reliance, Tension and Anxiety, he has a 71% match. Therefore, bearing in mind the characteristics of the other people evaluated, the role assigned to PR in this case was Requirements Specifier. Table 10.12 illustrates a similar situation, where AL (see the Personality Factors Model in Figure C.17) is best qualified for the Requirements Specifier role. He matches on the scales of Reasoning, Abstractedness, Sensitivity, Warmth and Self-Reliance, adding up to a percentage of 71%. So, again the role assigned to AL in this case was also Requirements Specifier.

ACTIVITY GROUPS	ROLES	PERSONALITY FACTORS RATIO	PERCENTAGE
Project Management Activity Groups	Planner	8/14	57%
Development Activity Groups	REQUIREMENTS SPECIFIER Designer/Implementer	5/7 8/13	71% 62%
Integral Activity Groups	Evaluator	7/11	64%

Table 10.11. Assignation of PR to Roles

ACTIVITY GROUPS	ROLES	PERSONALITY FACTORS RATIO	PERCENTAGE
Project Management Activity Groups	Planner	7/14	50%
Development Activity Groups	REQUIREMENTS SPECIFIER Designer/Implementer	5/7 7/13	71% 54%
Integral Activity Groups	Evaluator	6/11	55%

Table 10.12. Assignation of AL to Roles

With respect to the role assigned in Table 10.13, ER (see the Personality Factors Model in Figure C.18) could play the roles of Planner, Requirements Specifier or Evaluator. However, the best match for him would be with Requirements

Specifier, as his profile match is 57% for this role. He matches on the scales of Reasoning, Abstractedness, Sensitivity and Self-Reliance. The role assigned to ER in this case is Requirements Specifier, because other people were able to play the other roles.

ACTIVITY GROUPS	ROLES	PERSONALITY FACTORS RATIO	PERCENTAGE
Project Management Activity Groups	Planner	7/14	50%
Development Activity Groups	REQUIREMENTS SPECIFIER Designer/Implementer	4/7 6/13	57% 46%
Integral Activity Groups	Evaluator	6/11	55%

Table 10.13. Assignation of ER to Roles

In relation to the role assigned in Table 10.14, FM does not achieve the minimum 50% match for any role (see his Personality Factors Model in Figure C.11). The closest match would be for the Planner role, as this is his highest percentage match (43% of the required capabilities). In particular, for this role he matches on the traits of Reasoning, Abstractedness, Apprehension, Anxiety, Privateness and Openness to Change. However, he does not match on eight traits: Tough-Mindedness, Self-Reliance, Dominance, Perfectionism, Tension, Warmth, Independence and Sensitivity. He could also fit the Requirements Specifier role, because he also has a match of 43% and scores high on Reasoning and low on Abstractedness, Tension and Anxiety. However, he does not match on Sensitivity, Warmth and Self-Reliance. Bearing in mind that FM does not achieve the minimum for any role, but has to be assigned to some role in the project, the role assigned to FM in this case was Planner. However, as in previous cases the team leader was advised of FM's weaknesses as regards this role. Additionally, his training needs were defined accordingly.

ACTIVITY GROUPS	ROLES	PERSONALITY FACTORS RATIO	PERCENTAGE
Project Management Activity Groups	PLANNER	6/14	43%
Development Activity Groups	Requirements Specifier Designer/Implementer	3/7 4/13	43% 31%
Integral Activity Groups	Evaluator	4/11	36%

Table 10.14. Assignation of FM to Roles

In relation to the role assigned in Table 10.15, MB could be assigned to any of the four analysed roles (see her Personality Factors Model in Figure C.4), where her highest percentage match is for Requirements Specifier (71%). She could also fit the Project Management Activity Groups roles, as she has low scores on Abstractedness, Self-Reliance, Apprehension, Tension, Anxiety and high scores on Privateness, Openness to Change and Sensitivity, although she does not respond to the profile on scales such as Reasoning, Tough-Mindedness, Dominance, Perfectionism, Warmth and Independence. The percentage similarity with the role is 57%. The role finally assigned to MB in this case was Planner, in spite of the fact that the percentage was not the optimum. In this case, we took into account the other people involved and her preferences, and Planner was the final decision.

ACTIVITY GROUPS	ROLES	PERSONALITY FACTORS RATIO	PERCENTAGE
Project Management Activity Groups	PLANNER	8/14	57%
Development Activity Groups	Requirements Specifier Designer/Implementer	5/7 7/13	71% 54%
Integral Activity Groups	Evaluator	6/11	55%

Table 10.15. Assignation of MB to Roles

Considering the role assigned in Table 10.16, DN could adapt to work in several areas. She could fit the Project Management Activity Groups roles, as she scores low on Apprehension, Tension, Anxiety and high on Reasoning, Privateness, Openness to Change and Sensitivity, although she does not respond to the role profile on scales such as Abstractedness, Tough-Mindedness, Self-Reliance, Dominance, Perfectionism, Warmth and Independence (see her Personality Factors Model in Figure C.24). The percentage match with this profile is 50%. She could also play a role as Requirements Specifier with a percentage match of 57%. However, the role finally assigned to DN in this case was Planner, as there were enough Requirements Specifier with higher or equal percentages, and she was experienced in planning activities and techniques.

ACTIVITY GROUPS	ROLES	PERSONALITY FACTORS RATIO	PERCENTAGE
Project Management Activity Groups	PLANNER	7/14	50%
Development Activity Groups	Requirements Specifier Designer/Implementer	4/7 6/13	57% 46%
Integral Activity Groups	Evaluator	4/11	36%

Table 10.16. Assignation of DN to Roles

Finally, with respect to the role assigned in Table 10.17, CL could fit the Project Management Activity Groups roles, as she has low scores on Abstractedness, Apprehension, Tension, Anxiety and high scores on Tough-Mindedness, Perfectionism, Privateness and Sensitivity, although she does not match the role profile on scales such as Reasoning, Self-Reliance, Dominance, Warmth, Independence and Openness to Change (see her Personality Factors Model in

Figure C.15). The percentage match with the profile is 57%. She could also play a role as Designer/Implementer with a percentage match of 54%. The role finally assigned to CL in this case was Planner, bearing in mind the other people involved in the process and her personal preferences.

ACTIVITY GROUPS	ROLES	PERSONALITY FACTORS RATIO	PERCENTAGE
Project Management Activity Groups	PLANNER	8/14	57%
Development Activity Groups	Requirements Specifier	3/7	43%
	Designer/Implementer	7/13	54%
Integral Activity Groups	Evaluator	5/11	45%

Table 10.17. Assignation of CL to roles

Finally, Table 10.18 shows the Role/People Table derived from applying the method. The status column indicates the final recommendation on whether to assign the person directly to a project or to place this person on a training programme. In this particular case, the status of all the people was defined as "participation", although "training" was added for the people who did not meet 50% of the required capabilities for their role. This was because, at the time of assignation, it was not feasible to define training programmes and the software projects needed to be completed as soon as possible. Nevertheless, this indication assures that their limitations will be taken into account both during the ongoing project and in the future, when training programmes targeting these capabilities can be designed.

ROLE	PERSON	STATUS
Evaluator	GR	Participation
	FR	Participation
	CA	Participation
	CS	Participation
Designer/Implementer	RX	Participation
	MA	Participation/Training
	EL	Participation
	AD	Participation
Requirements Specifier	PB	Participation
	PR	Participation
	AL	Participation
	ER	Participation
Planner	FM	Participation/Training
	MB	Participation
	DN	Participation
	CL	Participation

Table 10.18. Role/People Table

Benefits of Incorporating People's Capabilities into the Software Process

This chapter describes a study including several groups of developers working on software projects at a medium-sized organisation. We have compared some projects in which people are assigned to roles based on their capabilities (that is, using the approach described in this book) against projects in which no such approach is employed.

Taking into account the assignation of people to roles for Company, described in Chapter 10, we analysed this organisation to find out whether there was any improvement by assigning people to roles according to their capabilities as opposed to using the traditional assignation method, which depends on the team leader's opinion. This chapter describes the empirical validation of the person/capabilities/role relationship implemented at this organisation. Although, as we will see, the study we present is incomplete, it did serve to provide some preliminary results indicating that we can be sure about the benefits of using the capabilities model presented in this book. Specifically, the results generated by this study confirm the hypothesis that assigning people to roles according to their capabilities and the capabilities required by the role improves various aspects of software development.

11.1. DESIGN OF THE EXPERIMENT ON THE ASSIGNATION OF PEOPLE TO ROLES

The hypothesis to be tested in this experiment is as follows: *the allocation of roles according to people's capabilities and the capabilities required by the role influences the effectiveness and efficiency of software development.* To test this hypothesis, we have used two response variables measuring the deviation between the estimated and real development time and the number of defects detected in formal reviews of the software requirements specifications. The aim is to check whether both the deviation in time and the number of defects in the specification are statistically lower when the people who play the roles of planner, requirements specifier, designer and evaluator are assigned taking into account the set of critical capabilities that the person who plays the role should have according to the proposed capabilities-oriented model. Additionally, performance is evaluated to determine how well matched these people are to the role assigned on the basis of their personality traits. Therefore, we will use another response variable that will measure the performance of the person in the role played.

The study was conducted on eight software projects. The capabilities-based assignation method described throughout this book was applied to four project (the four projects for which the roles were assigned according to capabilities in Chapter 10) and another four projects that had already been developed by Company, where people had been assigned to roles informally by the team leader. In the first four projects, the treatment involved assigning people rated according to their capabilities as being best suited for the roles of planner, requirements specifier, designer/implementer and evaluator. In the projects in which the roles were allocated according to the team leader's preferences, the teams were composed of just a few members (at most 6), who, apart from the four above-mentioned roles, played the roles of systems analyst and configuration manager. Table 11.1 shows the application scope of each project, classified by project type, and its complexity, characterised by function points.

All the projects were developed following the corporate methodology, which is based on the structured paradigm.

Both the measurements of the projects listed in Table 11.1 and the personality traits of the individuals who play the four above-mentioned roles were evaluated. The response variables examined in this experiment are as follows:

1. *Performance of the person in the role.* The performance of each person in his/her role was measured by evaluating specific personality traits. The personality traits considered were: leadership, motivation, creativity, initiative, responsibility and commitment. These traits were pairwise

evaluated using personality trait measurement-based evaluation following the absolute judgement method (Moses & Byham, 1997; Morales Gutiérrez et al., 1990). The technique of absolute judgement-based paired evaluation employs a questionnaire to assess personality characteristics or traits quantitatively on a Likert-type scale (from 1 to 5). Such traits where evaluated for each of the roles identified in the projects (planner, requirements specifier, designer/implementer and evaluator).

PROJECT	TEAM SIZE	DOMAIN	NO. ADJUSTED FUNCTION POINTS
Roles assigned according to capabilities	4	Management of a private dentistry institute.	522.24
	4	Management of quality of life (noise measurements, environmental pollution and citizens' claims) in the city of Santiago de Estero, Argentina.	1205.00
	4	Administration of educational self-assessment at the National University of Santiago del Estero, Argentina.	487.50
	4	Management of drainage systems.	130.00
Roles assigned according to team leader's preferences	6	Administration and control of teaching and research at the National University of Santiago del Estero, Argentina.	1043.10
	5	Mutual benefit society credit control.	226.71
	4	Management of materials and inputs purchase and works certification for a construction company.	215.74
	3	Generation of diets on demand for 3- to 5-year-old children with malnutrition in North Western Argentina.	87.15

Table 11.1. Project characterisation

2. *Development Time.* Percentage deviation from the estimated time for the whole project and for the particular tasks of planning, requirements, design and evaluation. We should point out that all the projects considered in the study were estimated by the same person who is experienced in software project estimation.

3. *Defects in Formal Reviews.* Percentage of defects in the software requirements specification checklists. The defects in the formal inspection of the software requirements specification were measured and the ratios of defects to function points for each project and of defects to number of requirements for each project were calculated.

As we are dealing with different projects, relative measurements are used with respect to development time and defects for the purposes of comparison. The measurements of the performance characteristics are not biased by project type, because performance is evaluated between pairs from the same team. Each person's role performance was measured and assessed by people from each team who were blind to the experimental conditions and hypothesis. The Wilcoxon rank sum test statistical technique (Devore, 1998; Juristo & Moreno, 2001) was used to analyse the data output, as the data were taken from independent samples that were not normally distributed.

11.2. RESULTS OF THE EXPERIMENT

The results of the Wilcoxon rank sum test applied to the performance of the person in the role criterion are shown in Table 11.2, where m is the number of teams applying the treatment (roles assigned according to capabilities) and n is the number of teams without treatment (roles assigned based on team leader's opinion), W is the value calculated for the Wilcoxon test used and p is the probability of the null hypothesis (the performance of the teams without treatment is the same as the performance of teams where the Assignation of People to Roles Method was applied) being rejected when it is actually true. The significance level is 95%. The difference in sample sizes is due to missing data, as the samples were originally composed of four teams each. The symbol "*" at the side of the W value indicates that there is evidence of statistically significant differences and the probability p is specified in these cases. For example, $p=0.014$ means that the null hypothesis is rejected with an error of less than 5% and with a confidence level of 95%, which is highly significant. The symbol "-" indicates that there is no evidence of statistically significant differences.

From the results of the performance evaluation for all the roles and the personality traits considered according to the null hypothesis, we find that the teams with treatment do manifest statistically significant performance differences as compared with the untreated teams for the leadership capability in the roles of planner, requirements specifier and designer. The performance evaluation for the creativity trait is better for the roles of planner and requirements specifier. The evaluation of initiative is better for the roles of evaluator and designer. The match for people assigned according to capabilities to the role of planner evidences more effective responsibility and commitment as compared with people assigned casually to the same role.

ROLE	TRAIT	PAIRED EVALUATION			
		m	n	W	p is less than or equal to
Planner	Leadership	4	4	24 *	0.047
	Motivation	4	4	22.5	-
	Creativity	4	4	26 *	0.014
	Initiative	4	4	23.5	-
	Responsibility	4	4	26 *	0.014
	Commitment	4	4	26 *	0.014
Evaluator	Leadership	4	4	23	-
	Motivation	4	4	22	-
	Creativity	4	4	23	-
	Initiative	4	4	24 *	0.047
	Responsibility	4	4	22	-
	Commitment	4	4	23	-
Requirements specifier	Leadership	4	3	21 *	0.029
	Motivation	4	3	10	-
	Creativity	4	3	20.5 *	0.029
	Initiative	4	3	15.5	-
	Responsibility	4	3	13.5	-
	Commitment	4	3	13	-
Designer	Leadership	3	4	17.5 *	0.047
	Motivation	3	4	13.5	-
	Creativity	3	4	16.5	-
	Initiative	3	4	17 *	0.047
	Responsibility	3	4	15	-
	Commitment	3	4	16	-

Table 11.2. Results for the performance of people in roles criterion

The results for the development time criterion are shown in Table 11.3. The null hypothesis established is that there is no difference in the deviations from the estimated time between the projects with treatment and the projects without treatment. The results of Table 11.3 are statistically significant. Accordingly, it can be said that the deviation of real from estimated project development time for the projects with treatment was lower than for the projects without treatment in all the cases, both with respect to the duration of the whole project and for each identified activity group.

ACTIVITY GROUP	m	n	W	p is less than or equal to
Project Planning	4	4	10.5 *	0.029
Evaluation	4	4	10 *	0.014
Requirements	4	4	10 *	0.014
Design	4	4	10.5 *	0.029
Project	4	4	10*	0.014

Table 11.3. Results for the development time criterion for each activity group and the project

As regards the defects in formal reviews of the software requirements specification criterion, where we considered number of defects/number of requirements by 100, we got $w=10$ ($m=4$, $n=4$, $p<=0.014$) and for the number of defects/adjusted function points by 100, we got $w=12$ ($m=4$, $n=4$, $p<=0.047$). Our results mean that the groups with treatment can be said to have a lower percentage of defects than the groups without treatment, in both cases.

Therefore, the formulated hypothesis that assigning people to roles according to their capabilities and the capabilities required by the role improves the software development process is accepted. Specifically, the assignation of people to roles by matching people's capabilities to the capabilities required by roles raises the efficiency with which people perform a development activity (that is, it takes less time to do a task) and improves people's reliability (they make fewer defects when performing the allocated activities). Additionally, depending on the roles, it improves some personality traits.

Conclusions

Of the different aspects related to the management of the members of an organisation, we have focused on the process of assigning people to roles. This process is usually performed unsystematically in the field of software development, which does not contribute to effectively building software development teams. Indeed, it prevents organisations from benefiting from the advantages provided by the application of systematic occupational psychology techniques, which have been applied in other industrial organisations for some time.

The approach presented in this book is one of the very few aiming to connect occupational psychology and software production. People influence the results of software development and their capabilities should be included in the software process to assign people to roles according to their capabilities and the capabilities required by the role. The approach that we take is to use the capabilities or behavioural competencies of people, according to psychology, and the capabilities or behavioural competencies required by the roles, according to occupational psychology and integrated people management.

In particular, our capabilities-oriented approach provides:

1. *People Dimension.* We propose a procedure for taking this dimension into account within the software process. The People's Capabilities Evaluation Method determines people's capabilities for later assigning and/or reallocating them to roles in the software projects to be undertaken by the developer organisation. The People's Capabilities Evaluation Method is one of the People's Capabilities Evaluation Activities, which are classed in the Organisational Activity Groups. We have applied this procedure to real

cases to test the feasibility of incorporating people's capabilities, which are normally missing from the traditional software process models, into the software process.

2. *Production Dimension.* We propose a procedure for enhancing this dimension within the software process. The Assignation of People to Roles Method provides a method for allocating roles according to people's capabilities and the capabilities required by the roles. This method is one of the Assignation of People to Roles Activities, which are classed in the Project Management Activity Groups of the software process. This assignation method defines the intersection between the Organisational Activity Groups and software development-related activities. We have applied this method to real cases to test the feasibility of incorporating the role capabilities, also usually missing from the traditional software process models, into the capabilities-oriented software process. This and the People's Capabilities Evaluation Method overcome one of the limitations of existing software process models that we mentioned in Part I: the shortage of guidelines for identifying, defining and formalising people's capabilities and the roles involved in the software development process. Capabilities modelling is a task to be taken into account in any development process and should, therefore, be considered explicitly.

3. *Roles Dimension.* We have determined the capabilities of the roles for each software process activity group, so that the person who plays the respective role can effectively and efficiently perform his or her activities. We have defined the Capabilities/Role Table for each activity, specifying 20 general capabilities considered critical in software development and classified as intrapersonal skills, organisational skills, interpersonal skills and management skills.

4. *Formalised Software Process Model.* This capabilities-oriented software process model has been formalised in UML (Acuña, 2002). We have implemented this process model as a computerised tool, which incorporates the results of the People's Capabilities Evaluation Method and performs the Assignation of People to Roles Method. This tool is available at http://www.ls.fi.upm.es/spt/. Although this tool provides support for the People's Capabilities Evaluation Method, this method requires significant input on the part of the people concerned, as well as the process engineer and occupational psychologist.

On the basis of the results of the empirical study run (and presented in Chapter 11), it can be said that the assignation of people to roles based on their capabilities improves some aspects of software development. We found that both the deviation from the estimated time and the errors detected in the formal review of the software requirements specification were lower when the people who perform the roles of planner, requirements specifier, designer/implementer and evaluator are assigned taking into account the set of critical capabilities that the person performing the role should have. Also, from the performance evaluation, the match between the person and the assigned role can be said to be satisfactory, especially for the planner role.

The People's Capabilities Evaluation Method and the Assignation of People to Roles Method can be applied to help incorporate the capabilities of the people involved in the software process, making it easier to manage human resources. Our approach is especially useful in medium- and large-sized organisations where there are personnel enough to rotate from one project to another. The human resources departments of these organisations should have a database of their technical staff, specifying their defined behavioural competencies. Then, before assigning people to roles, each team leader should consult this database and apply the Assignation of People to Roles Method to match people to roles. This database should be updated every two years according to role performance and participation in training programmes. Apart from assigning individuals to roles, the procedures proposed here could be used to indicate possible training needs for an organisation's resources. These needs are detected mainly where there are low people's capabilities/role capabilities ratios. Improvement programmes for the people involved in the software process can be established based on the results achieved in the People's Capabilities Evaluation Activities and the Assignation of People to Roles Activities. The follow-on process from a cultural evaluation is the implementation of an improvement programme. Its main objective is to implement all the recommendations included in the results of the personal profile evaluation. A combination of the methods for determining capabilities, assigning people to roles and evaluating performance, and the implementation of an improvement programme is the best means for software organisations to systematically evolve towards an improvement of their human resources.

In small organisations, all staff tend to work on all projects, and projects are developed sequentially, which means that people are not usually assigned to roles, because they all participate in all roles. Nevertheless, the procedures described in this book can be useful for analysing what behavioural competencies are missing in their teams, that is, what capabilities are not covered. This can identify what employee training is required or what new people should be selected purposely to cover these missing behavioural competencies.

Despite the benefits of capabilities-based human resources management, organisations may encounter problems related to the cost of the associated training programmes, the availability (and willingness) of staff to undergo training, staff flexibility (to move from one role to another), how to address existing management/union agreements and individual and group cultural resistance to the use of these methods.

Furthermore, capabilities are not the be all and end all of human resources management. Other aspects need to be taken into account to adequately manage human resources in software development. Our capabilities-based approach is complementary to other approaches employing traditional strategies to assign people to roles, such as approaches focused on domain familiarity, and knowledge and know-how. Moreover, a decision on role assignation takes many other parameters into account, like interpersonal problems between team members or compensation by a close colleague for a person's weaknesses (complementary capability). Indeed, organising work teams involves considering personal and interpersonal capabilities to achieve harmonious teamwork, a resonance in interpersonal communication and effective and efficient team behaviour. Our approach can be combined with the MBTI (Myers Briggs Type Indicator) (Briggs-Myers, 1995; Hammer et al., 1998; Hirsch & Kummerow, 1997; Hirsch & Kummerow, 1998), which describes the preferences of work team members, allowing people to comprehend themselves and their behaviour and understand others. Thus, they will be able to make the most of individual differences and accept that putting forward different viewpoints on the same problems can be beneficial and effective for the organisation. More specifically, MBTI can be used to improve communication between the integral software process enacters, specialists, users and customers to solve personal problems, to get better results from the team members, to assess the inputs of team members, to resolve conflicts and to improve teamwork. Another important aspect is team member commitment and motivation, ranging from how committed (keen to staunchly accomplish their activities) and motivated developers initially are to undertaking the planned project activities to how the team leader can get commitment from and motivate people through to the end of the software projects.

References

T. K. Abdel-Hamid, "The dynamics of software project staffing: A system dynamics based simulation approach". *IEEE Transactions on Software Engineering* **15**, 2 (February 1989) 109-119.

T. K. Abdel-Hamid and S. E. Madnick, "Lessons learned from modelling the dynamics of software development". *Communications of the ACM* **32**, 12 (December 1989) 1426-1438.

T. K. Abdel-Hamid and S. E. Madnick, *Software Project Dynamics: An Integrated Approach.* (Prentice Hall, 1991).

S. T. Acuña, *Capabilities-Oriented Integral Software Process Model.* Ph.D. thesis, Universidad Politécnica de Madrid, Madrid. (2002).

S. T. Acuña, A. De Antonio, X. Ferré, L. Maté and M. López, "The software process: Modeling, evaluation and improvement". In: S.-K. Chang (Ed.), *Handbook of Software Engineering & Knowledge Engineering. Fundamentals.* Vol. 1. (World Scientific, 2001) 193-237.

S. T. Acuña and N. Juristo, "Assigning people to roles in software projects". *Software: Practice & Experience* **34**, 7 (2004) 675-696.

S. T. Acuña, M. López, N. Juristo and A. Moreno, "A process model applicable to software engineering and knowledge engineering". *International Journal of Software Engineering and Knowledge Engineering* **9**, 5 (1999) 663-687.

B. Adelson and E. Soloway, "The role of domain experience in software design". *IEEE Transactions on Software Engineering* **11**, 11 (November 1985) 1351-1360.

L. Alexander and A. Davis, "Criteria for selecting software process models". *Proceedings of COMPSAC'91* (1991) 521-528.

V. Ambriola, R. Conradi and A. Fuggetta, "Assessing process-centered software engineering environments". *ACM Transactions on Software Engineering and Methodology* **6**, 3 (1997) 283-328.

V. Ambriola and M. L. Jaccheri, "Definition and enactment of OIKOS software process entities". *Proceedings of the First European Workshop on Software Process Modeling* (May 1991).

S. Arbaoui and F. Oquendo, "PEACE: Goal-oriented logic-based formalism for process modelling". In: A. Finkelstein, J. Kramer and B. Nuseibeh (Eds.), *Software Process Modelling and Technology*. Chap. 10. (Research Studies Press, 1994) 249-278.

P. Armenise, S. Bandinelli, C. Ghezzi and A. Morzenti, "Software process representation languages: Survey and assessment". *Proceedings of the Fourth International Conference on Software Engineering and Knowledge Engineering* (June 1992) 455-462.

P. Armenise, S. Bandinelli, C. Ghezzi and A. Morzenti, "A survey and assessment of software process representation formalisms". *International Journal of Software Engineering and Knowledge Engineering* **3**, 3 (1993) 401-426.

M. Baldi, S. Gai, M. L. Jaccheri and P. Lago, "E^3: Object-oriented software process model design". In: A. Finkelstein, J. Kramer and B. Nuseibeh (Eds.), *Software Process Modelling and Technology*. Chap. 11. (Research Studies Press, 1994) 279-292.

J. Bamberger, "Essence of the Capability Maturity Model". *IEEE Computer* **30**, 6 (June 1997) 112-114.

S. C. Bandinelli and A. Fuggetta, "Computational reflection in software process modeling: The SLANG approach". *Proceedings of the 15th International Conference on Software Engineering* (May 1993) 144-154.

S. C. Bandinelli, A. Fuggetta and C. Ghezzi, "Software process model evolution in the SPADE environment". *IEEE Transactions on Software Engineering* **19**, 12 (December 1993) 1128-1144.

S. C. Bandinelli, A. Fuggetta, C. Ghezzi and S. Grigolli, "Process enactment in SPADE". *Proceedings of the Second European Workshop on Software Process Technology* (September 1992) 67-83.

S. C. Bandinelli, A. Fuggetta, C. Ghezzi and L. Lavazza, "SPADE: An environment for software process analysis, design, and enactment". In: A. Finkelstein, J. Kramer and B. Nuseibeh (Eds.), *Software Process Modelling and Technology*. Chap. 9. (Research Studies Press, 1994) 223-247.

S. C. Bandinelli, A. Fuggetta, L. Lavazza, M. Loi and G. Picco, "Modeling and improving an industrial software process". *IEEE Transactions on Software Engineering* **21**, 5 (1995) 440-454.

L. Baresi, F. Casati, S. Castano, M. G. Fugini, I. Mirbel and B. Pernici, "WIDE workflow development methodology". *Software Engineering Notes in Work Activities Coordination and Collaboration: Proceedings of the International Joint Conference* **24**, 2 (ACM Press, 1999) 19-28.

N. S. Barghouti, D. S. Rosenblum, D. G. Belanger and C. Alliegro, "Two case studies in modeling real, corporate processes". *Software Process Improvement and Practice* **1**, Pilot Issue (August 1995) 17-32.

V. R. Basili, "Can we measure software technology: Lessons learned from 8 years of trying". *Proceedings of the Tenth Annual Software Engineering Workshop*, NASA Goddard Space Flight Center (December 1985).

V. R. Basili and H. D. Rombach, "TAME: Tailoring an Ada measurement environment". *Proceedings of the Joint Ada Conference* (March 1987a) 318-325.

V. R. Basili and H. D. Rombach, "TAME: Integrating measurement into software environments". University of Maryland, College Park, Department of Computer Science. *Technical Report TR-1764. TAME-TR-1-1987.* (June 1987b).

V. R. Basili and H. D. Rombach, "The TAME project: Towards improvement-oriented software environments". *IEEE Transactions on Software Engineering* **14**, 6 (June 1988) 758-773.

J. Baugh, "Rewarding competencies in flatter organizations". *Competency: The Journal of Performance through People* **4**, 3 (1997).

K. Beck, *Extreme Programming Explained: Embrace Change.* (Addison Wesley, 1999).

K. Beck, M. Beedle, A. Cockburn, W. Cunningham, M. Fowler et al., *Agile Manifesto.* (2001).
http://agilemanifesto.org.

K. Beck and W. Cunningham, "A laboratory for teaching object-oriented thinking". *OOPSLA '89 Proceedings of SIGPLAN Notices* 24, 10 (October 1989).

N. Belkhatir, J. Estublier and W. L. Melo, "Software process model and work space control in the Adele system". *Proceedings of the Second International Conference on Software Process* (February 1993) 2-11.

Bell, *Trillium. Model for Telecom Product Development and Support Process Capability. Version 3.0.* (Bell Canada, 1994).

K. Benali and J. C. Derniame, "Software processes modeling: What, who, and when". *Proceedings of the Second European Workshop on Software Process Technology* (September 1992) 21-25.

G. K. Bennett, H. G. Seashore and A. G. Wesman, *Differential Aptitude Tests for Personnel and Career Assessment: Directions for Administration and Scoring.* (Psychological Corporation, 1989).

V. J. Bentz, "Research findings from personality assessment of executives". In: H. J. Bernardin and D. A. Bownans (Eds.), *Personality Assessment in Organisations.* (Praeger, 1985) 84-144.

J. Bleger, *Psicología de la Conducta.* (Paidós, 1974).

B. I. Blum, *Software Engineering: A Holistic View.* (Oxford University Press, 1992).

R. Boam and P. Sparrow, *Designing and Achieving Competency: A Competency-based Approach to Developing People and Organization.* (McGraw Hill, 1992).

B. W. Boehm, *Software Engineering Economics.* (Prentice Hall, 1981).

B. W. Boehm, "A spiral model of software development and enhancement". *IEEE Computer* **21**, 5 (May 1988) 61-72.

B. W. Boehm, C. Abts, A. W. Brown, S. Chulani, B. Clark, E. Horiwitz, R. Madachy, D. Reifer and B. Steece, *Software Cost Estimation with COCOMO II.* (Prentice Hall, 2000).

B. W. Boehm, A. Egyed, D. Port and A. Shah, "A stakeholder Win-Win approach to software engineering education". *Software Engineering Education* 6 (1998).

B. W. Boehm and R. Ross, "A collaborative spiral software process model based on Theory W". *Proceedings of the ICSP3* (October 1994).

T. B. Bollinger and C. McGowan, "A critical look at software capability evaluations". *IEEE Software* **8**, 4 (July 1991) 25-41.

G. Booch, J. Rumbaugh and I. Jacobson, *The Unified Modeling Language. User Guide.* (Addison Wesley, 1999).

Ph. Boveroux, G. Canals, C. Godart, Ph. Jamart and J. Lonchamp, "Software process modelling in the ALF system: An example". *Proceedings of the First European Workshop on Software Process Modelling* (May 1991).

R. E. Boyatzis, *The Competent Manager: A Model of Effective Performance.* (John Wiley & Sons, 1982).

L. Briand, W. Melo, C. Seaman and V. Basili, "Characterizing and assessing a large-scale software maintenance organization". *Proceedings of the 17th International Conference on Software Engineering* (1995).

I. Briggs-Myers, *MBTI. Inventario Tipológico Forma G.* 2nd edn. (TEA Ediciones, 1995).

R. F. Bruynooghe, R. M. Greenwood, I. Robertson, J. Sa and B. C. Warboys, "PADM: Towards a total process modelling system". In: A. Finkelstein, J. Kramer and B. Nuseibeh (Eds.), *Software Process Modelling and Technology.* Chap. 12. (Research Studies Press, 1994) 293-334.

BSI, *The TickIT Guide. A Guide to Software Quality Management System Construction and Certification to ISO 9001.* (British Standards Institution, 1995).

B. G. Cain and J. O. Coplien, "A role-based empirical process modeling environment". *Proceedings of the Second International Conference on Software Process* (February 1993) 125-133.

G. Canals, N. Boudjlida, J. C. Derniame, C. Godart and J. Lonchamp, "ALF: A framework for building process-centred software engineering environments". In: A. Finkelstein, J. Kramer and B. Nuseibeh (Eds.), *Software Process Modelling and Technology*. Chap. 7. (Research Studies Press, 1994) 153-185.

R. Charette, "The decision is in: Agile versus heavy methodologies". *Cutter Consortium, Executive Update* **2**, 19 (Cutter Consortium web site, 2004). http://www.cutter.com/freestuff/apmupdate.html.

F. Cattaneo, A. Fuggetta and L. Lavazza, "An experience in process assessment". *Proceedings of the 17th International Conference on Software Engineering* (1995) 115-121.

H. B. Cattell, *The 16PF: Personality in Depth.* (Institute for Personality and Ability Testing, 1989).

R. B. Cattell, A. K. Cattell and H. E. P. Cattell, *Sixteen Personality Factor Questionnaire.* 5th edn. (Institute for Personality and Ability Testing, 1993).

P. Checkland and S. Holwell, *Information, Systems and Information Systems: Making Sense of the Field.* (John Wiley, 1998).

P. Checkland and J. Scholes, *Soft Systems Methodology in Action.* (Wiley, 1999).

A. Cockburn and J. Highsmith, "Agile software development: The business of innovation". *Computer* (September 2001a) 120-122.

A. Cockburn and J. Highsmith, "Agile software development: The people factor". *Computer* (November 2001b) 131-133.

D. Cohen, M. Lindvall and P. Costa, *Agile Software Development. A DACS State-of-the-Art Report.* University of Maryland. DACS Report. (2003).

E. Comer, "Alternative software life cycle models". In: R. H. Thayer and M. C. Tensen (Eds.), *Software Engineering.* Vol. 2. (IEEE Computer Society Press, 1997).

R. Conradi, C. Fernström and A. Fuggetta, "Concepts for evolving software processes". In: A. Finkelstein, J. Kramer and B. Nuseibeh (Eds.), *Software Process Modelling and Technology.* Chap. 2. (Research Studies Press, 1994a) 9-31.

R. Conradi, C. Fernström, A. Fuggetta and R. Snowdon, "Towards a reference framework for process concepts". *Proceedings of the Second European Workshop on Software Process Technology* (September 1992) 3-17.

R. Conradi, M. Hagaseth, J.-O. Larsen, M. N. Nguyen, B. P. Munch, P. H. Westby, W. Zhu, M. L. Jaccheri and C. Liu, "EPOS: Object-oriented cooperative process modelling". In: A. Finkelstein, J. Kramer and B. Nuseibeh (Eds.), *Software Process Modelling and Technology.* Chap. 3. (Research Studies Press, 1994b) 33-70.

R. Conradi, C. Liu and M. L. Jaccheri, "Process modelling paradigms: An evaluation". *Proceedings of the Seventh International Software Process Workshop* (1991a) 51-53.

R. Conradi, E. Osjord, P. H. Westby and C. Liu, "Initial software process management in EPOS". *Software Engineering Journal* (Special Issue on Software Process and its Support) **6**, 5 (September 1991b) 275-284.

L. Constantine, *Peopleware Papers: The Notes on the Human Side of Software.* (Prentice Hall, 2001).

P. T. Costa Jr. and R. R. McCrae, *NEO Personality Inventory, Revised.* (Psychological Assessment Resources, 1992).

J. D. Cougar and R. A. Zawacky, *Motivating and Managing Computer Personnel.* (Wiley, 1980).

A. Crabtree, "Talking work: Language-games, organisations and computer supported cooperative work". *Computer Supported Cooperative Work* 9 (2000) 215-237.

B. Curtis, *Human Factors in Software Development*. (IEEE Computer Society Press, 1985).

B. Curtis, "Three problems overcome with behavioral models of the software development process". *Proceedings of the 11th International Conference on Software Engineering* (May 1989) 398-399.

B. Curtis, W. E. Hefley and S. A. Miller, "Overview of the People Capability Maturity Model® (P-CMM®)". Carnegie Mellon University, Software Engineering Institute. *Maturity Model CMU/SEI-95-MM-001*. (1995a).

B. Curtis, W. E. Hefley and S. A. Miller, "People Capability Maturity Model® (P-CMM®)". Carnegie Mellon University, Software Engineering Institute. *Maturity Model CMU/SEI-95-MM-002*. (1995b).

B. Curtis, W. E. Hefley and S. A. Miller, "People Capability Maturity Model® (P-CMM®). Version 2.0". Carnegie Mellon University, Software Engineering Institute. *Maturity Model CMU/SEI-2001-MM-001*. (2001).

B. Curtis, W. E. Hefley, S. A. Miller and M. Konrad, "The People-CMM". *Software Process Newsletter* 4 (Fall 1995c) 7-10.

B. Curtis, M. Kellner and J. Over, "Process modeling". *Communications of the ACM* **35**, 9 (September 1992) 75-90.

B. Curtis, H. Krasner and N. Iscoe, "A field study of the software design process for large systems". *Communications of the ACM* **31**, 11 (November 1988) 1268-1287.

M. Dale and P. A. Iles, *Assessing Management Skills*. (Kogan Page, 1992).

A. M. Davis, *Software Requirements: Objects, Functions and States*. (Prentice Hall, 1993).

A. M. Davis, E. Bersoff and E. Comer, "A strategy for comparing alternative software development life cycle models". *IEEE Transactions on Software Engineering* **14**, 10 (1988) 1453-1461.

N. Davis and J. McHale, "Relating the Team Software Process[SM] (TSP[SM]) to the Capability Maturity Model® for Software (SW-CMM®)". Carnegie Mellon University, Software Engineering Institute. *Technical Report CMU/SEI-2002-TR-008*. (2002).

A. de Ansorena Cao, *Quince Pasos para la Selección de Personal con Éxito*. 3rd edn. (Paidós, 1996).

F. De Cindio, C. Simone, R. Vassalo and A. Zanaboni, "CHAOS: A knowledge-based system for conversing within offices". In: N. Lamersdorf (Ed.), *Office Knowledge: Representation, Management, and Utilization*. (Elsevier, 1988) 257-276.

T. DeMarco and T. Lister, *Peopleware: Productive Projects and Teams*. 2nd edn. (Dorset House, 1999).

F. M. de Vasconcelos Jr. and C. M. L. Werner, "Software development process reuse based on patterns". *Proceedings of the Ninth International Conference on Software Engineering and Knowledge Engineering* (June 1997) 97-104.

W. Deiters and V. Gruhn, "Managing software processes in the environment MELMAC". *ACM SIGSOFT Software Engineering Notes* **15**, 6 (December 1990) 193-205.

W. Deiters and V. Gruhn, "Software process analysis based on FUNSOFT nets". *Systems Analysis Modelling Simulation* **8**, 4-5 (1991) 315-325.

W. Deiters, V. Gruhn and W. Schäfer, "Systematic development of formal software process models". *Lecture Notes in Computer Science, Proceedings of the Second European Software Engineering Conference* 387 (Springer-Verlag, 1989) 100-117.

J. C. Derniame, B. A. Kaba and D. Wastell (Eds.), *Software Process: Principles, Methodology and Technology*. Lecture Notes in Computer Science 1500 (Springer-Verlag, 1999).

J. L. Devore, *Probability and Statistics for Engineering and the Sciences*. 4th edn. (Brooks/Cole Publishing Company, 1998).

DoD Military Standard Defense System Software Development, DoD-STD-2167A (February 1988).

DoD Military Standard Software Development and Documentation, MIL STA 498 (1995).

M. Dowson (Ed.), *Proceedings of the First International Conference on Software Process*. (IEEE Computer Society Press, October 1991).

M. Dowson, B. A. Nejmeh and W. E. Riddle, "Concepts for process definition and support". *Proceedings of the Fifth International Software Process Workshop*, IEEE Computer Society (1990) 87-90.

M. Dowson, B. Nejmeh and W. Riddle, "Fundamental software process concepts". *Proceedings of the First European Workshop on Software Process Modeling* (May 1991) 16-37.

L. Druffel, "Professionalism and the software business". *IEEE Software* **11**, 4 (July 1994) 6.

E. Ellmer, "Extending process-centered environments with organizational competence". *Lecture Notes in Computer Science, Software Process Technology: Proceedings of the Fifth European Workshop* 1149 (Springer-Verlag, 1996) 271-275.

G. Engels and L. Groenewegen, "SOCCA: Specifications of coordinated and cooperative activities". In: A. Finkelstein, J. Kramer and B. Nuseibeh (Eds.), *Software Process Modelling and Technology*. Chap. 4. (Research Studies Press, 1994) 71-102.

P. H. Feiler and W. S. Humphrey, "Software process development and enactment: Concepts and definitions". *Proceedings of the Second International Conference on Software Process* (February 1993) 28-40.

P. Ferrer, J. M. Sanz, E. Gallo, M. Vergara and G. Satriani, "Business improvement guide: BIG-CMM – Part A; User Manual". European Software Institute. *Technical Report ESI-1999-TR-007.* (February 1999).

A. Finkelstein, J. Kramer and B. Nuseibeh (Eds.), *Software Process Modelling and Technology.* (Research Studies Press, 1994).

R. Flood and M. Jackson, *Creative Problem Solving: Total Systems Intervention.* (John Wiley & Sons, 1991).

J. W. Forrester, *Industrial Dynamics.* (MIT Press, 1961).

M. Fowler, "Is design dead?". *Proceedings XP2000* (2001). http://www.martinfowler.com/articles/designDead.html. http://www.refactoring.com/

M. Fowler, K. Beck, J. Brant, W. Opdyke and D. Roberts, *Refactoring: Improving the Design of Existing Code.* (Addison Wesley, 1999).

C. Fox and W. Frakes, "The quality approach: Is it delivering?". *Communications of the ACM* **40**, 6 (June 1997) 25-29.

D. Frailey, "Defining a corporate-wide software process". *Proceedings of the First International Conference on Software Process* (1991) 113-121.

A. Fuggetta, "Software process: A roadmap". In: A. Finkelstein (Ed.), *The Future of Software Engineering.* (ACM Press, 2000) 27-34.

A. Fuggetta and A. Wolf (Eds.), *Software Process.* (John Wiley & Sons, 1996).

H. J. Genrich, "Predicate/Transition nets". *Lecture Notes on Computer Science* 254 (Springer-Verlag, 1986).

H. J. Genrich and K. Lautenbach, "System modeling with high-level Petri nets". *Theoretical Computer Science* 13 (1981) 109-136.

C. Ghezzi, M. Jazayeri and D. Mandrioli, *Fundamentals of Software Engineering.* (Prentice Hall, 1991).

T. Gilb, "10 Evolutionary Project Management (Evo) Principles". (2002) http://www.xs4all.nl/nrm/EvoPrinc/EvoPrinciples.pdf.

R. Glass, "Agile versus traditional: Make love, not war". *Cutter IT Journal* 14 (December 2001).

H. Gomaa, "The impact of rapid prototyping on specifying user requirements". *ACM Software Engineering Notes* **8**, 2 (1983) 17-28.

H. G. Gough, *California Psychological Inventory Administrator's Guide.* (Consulting Psychologists Press, 1987).

R. B. Grady, "Measuring and managing software maintenance". *IEEE Software* **4**, 5 (September 1987) 35-45.

I. Graham, B. Henderson-Sellers and H. Younessi, *The OPEN Process Specification.* (Addison Wesley, 1997).

V. Gruhn, *Validation and Verification of Software Process.* Ph.D. thesis, University of Dortmund, Dortmund. (1991).

V. Gruhn, "Software processes are social processes". University of Dortmund. *Technical Report.* (February 1992).

R. Guindon and B. Curtis, "Control of cognitive processes during design: What tools would support software designers?". *Proceedings of the CHI'88, Human Factors in Computing Systems*, ACM (1988) 263-268.

G. Hamel and C. K. Prahalad, *Competing for the Future.* (Harvard Business School Press, 1994).

A. L. Hammer, M. H. McCaulley, I. Briggs-Myers and N. L. Quenk, *MBTI® Manual (A). A Guide to the Development and Use of the Myers-Briggs Type Indicator®*. 3rd edn. (Consulting Psychologists Press, 1998).

D. Harel, H. Lachover, A. Naamad, A. Pnueli, M. Politi, R. Sherman, A. Shtull-Trauring and M. Trakhtenbrot, "STATEMATE: A working environment for the development of complex reactive systems". *IEEE Transactions on Software Engineering* **16**, 4 (April 1990) 403-414.

D. Harel and M. Politi, *Modeling Reactive Systems with Statecharts: The Statemate Approach.* (McGraw-Hill, 1998).

M. Harzallah, M. Leclère and F. Trichet, "CommOnCV: Modelling the competencies underlying a curriculum vitae". *Proceedings of the 14th International Conference on Software Engineering and Knowledge Engineering,* ACM (2002) 65-71.

M. Harzallah and F. Vernadat, "IT-based competency modeling and management: From theory to practice in enterprise engineering and operations". *Computers in Industry* **48**, 2 (2002) 157-179.

A. Hass, "Handbuch Qualifizierungsmodell". Fraunhofer Institut Experimentelles Software Engineering (Fraunhofer- IESE). *Internal Report.* (2001). http://www.iese.fhg.de/ESF-Baukasten/BSK/Quali_Modell.

R. Hastie, "Experimental evidence on group accuracy". In: G. Owen and B. Grofman (Eds.), *Information Processing and Group Decision-Making.* (JAI Press, 1987) 129-157.

Hay Group, *Las Competencias: Clave para una Gestión Integrada de los Recursos Humanos.* 2nd edn. Coordinadores: M. M. Dalziel, J. C. Cubeiro and G. Fernández. (Ediciones Deusto, 1996).

J. Helliwell and A. Fowler, "Introducing IT into a mature production related work environment: The human resource factor". *Journal of Information Technology* 9 (1994) 39-50.

D. Hellriegel, J. W. Slocum Jr. and R. W. Woodman, *Organizational Behavior.* (South Western College Publishing, 1998).

D. S. Hinley, "Software evolution management: A process-oriented perspective". *Information and Software Technology* **38**, 11 (November 1996) 723-730.

E. Hirsch, "Evolutionary acquisition of command and control systems". *Program Manager* (November/December 1985) 18-22.

S. K. Hirsch and J. M. Kummerow, *Introduction to Type® in Organizations (A)*. 3rd edn. (Consulting Psychologists Press, 1997).

S. K. Hirsch and J. M. Kummerow, *Los Tipos MBTI en las Organizaciones.* 3rd edn. (TEA Ediciones, 1998).

C. Hollenbach and W. Frakes, "Software process reuse in an industrial setting". *Proceedings of the Fourth International Conference on Software Reuse*, IEEE Computer Society (April 1996).

K. E. Huff and V. R. Lesser, "A plan-based intelligent assistant that supports the software development process". *ACM SIGSOFT Software Engineering Notes* **13**, 5 (November 1988) 97-106.

K. E. Huff, "Software process modeling". In: A. Fuggetta and A. Wolf (Eds.), *Software Process*. (John Wiley & Sons, 1996).

W. S. Humphrey, *Managing the Software Process*. (Addison Wesley, 1989).

W. S. Humphrey, *A Discipline for Software Engineering*. (Addison Wesley, 1995).

W. S. Humphrey, *Introduction to the Personal Software Process*. SEI Series in Software Engineering. (Addison Wesley, 1997).

W. S. Humphrey, "Three dimensions of process improvement. Part III: The team software process". *Crosstalk The Journal of Defense Software Engineering* **11**, 2 (April 1998a) 14-17.

W. S. Humphrey, *Managing Technical People: Innovation, Teamwork and the Software Process*. (Addison Wesley, 1998b).

W. S. Humphrey and M. I. Kellner, "Software process modeling: Principles of entity process models". *Proceedings of the 11th International Conference on Software Engineering* (May 1989).

IEEE Standard for Developing Software Life Cycle Processes, IEEE Standard 1074-1991.

IEEE Standard for Developing Software Life Cycle Processes, IEEE Standard 1074-1995.

IEEE Standard for Developing Software Life Cycle Processes, IEEE Standard 1074-1997.

H. Iida, K. Mimura, K. Inoue and K. Torii, "Hakoniwa: Monitor and navigation system for cooperative development based on activity sequence model". *Proceedings of the Second International Conference on Software Process* (February 1993) 64-74.

P. A. Iles, I. T. Robertson and U. Rout, "Assessment based development centres". *Journal of Managerial Psychology* **4**, 3 (1989) 11-16.

ISO/IEC 15504, Information Technology – Software Process Assessment. International Organization for Standardization, International Electrotechnical Commission. (1998). http://isospice.com/standard/tr15504.htm.

ISO, ISO 9004-4:1993, Quality Management and Quality System Elements (Part 2) – Guidelines for Quality Improvement. International Organization for Standardization. (ISO, 1993).

ISO, ISO 9001:1994, Quality Systems – Model for Quality Assurance in Design, Development, Production, Installation and Servicing. International Organization for Standardization. (ISO, 1994).

ISO 9002:1994, Quality Systems – Model for Quality Assurance in Production, Installation and Servicing. International Organization for Standardization. (ISO, 1994).

ISO 9003:1994, Quality Systems – Model for Quality Assurance in Final Inspection and Test. International Organization for Standardization. (ISO, 1994).

ISO, ISO 9000-3:1997, Quality Management and Quality Assurance Standards – Part 3: Guidelines for the Application of ISO 9001: 1994 to the Development, Supply, Installation and Maintenance of Computer Software. International Organisation for Standardization. (ISO, 1997).

ISO 9001:2000, Quality Management Systems – Requirements. International Organization for Standardization. (ISO, 2000).

ISO/IEC International Standard: Information Technology. Software Life Cycle Processes, ISO/IEC Standard 12207-1995.

ISO/IEC International Standard: Information Technology. Software Life Cycle Processes, Amendment 1, ISO/IEC Standard 12207-1995/Amd. 1-2002.

L. Jaccheri, J.-O. Larsen and R. Conradi, "Software process modeling and evolution in EPOS". *Proceedings of the Fourth International Conference on Software Engineering and Knowledge Engineering* (June 1992) 574-581.

I. Jacobson, G. Booch and J. Rumbaugh, *The Unified Software Development Process.* (Addison Wesley, 1999).

D. N. Jackson, *Personality Research Form Manual.* (Sigma Assessment Systems, 1989).

T. Janz, L. Hellervik and D. C. Gilmore, *Behavior Description Interviewing: New, Accurate, Cost Effective.* (Prentice Hall, 1986).

G. Junkermann, B. Peuschel, W. Schäfer and S. Wolf, "MERLIN: Supporting cooperation in software development through a knowledge-based environment". In: A. Finkelstein, J. Kramer and B. Nuseibeh (Eds.), *Software Process Modelling and Technology.* Chap. 5. (Research Studies Press, 1994) 103-129.

N. Juristo and A. M. Moreno, *Basics of Software Engineering Experimentation.* (Kluwer Academic Publishers, 2001).

G. E. Kaiser, "Intelligent assistance for software development and maintenance". *IEEE Software* (May 1988a) 40-49.

G. E. Kaiser, "Rule-based modeling of the software development process". *Proceedings of the Fourth International Software Process Workshop* (1988b) 36-38.

G. E. Kaiser and P. H. Feiler, "An architecture for intelligent assistance in software development". *Proceedings of the Ninth International Conference on Software Engineering* (April 1987) 180-188.

G. E. Kaiser, P. H. Feiler and S. S. Popovich, "Intelligent assistance for software development and maintenance". *IEEE Software* (May 1988) 40-49.

S. M. Kaplan, W. J. Tolone, A. M. Carroll, D. P. Bogia and C. Bignoli, "Supporting collaborative software development with Conversation-Builder". *Proceedings of the Fifth Symposium Software Development Environments, ACM SIGSOFT Software Engineering Notes* 17, 5 (December 1992) 11-20.

T. Katayama, "A hierarchical and functional software process description and its enaction". *Proceedings of the 11th International Conference on Software Engineering* (May 1989) 343-352.

P. Kawalek and D. G. Wastell, "Organisational design for software development: A cybernetic perspective". *Lecture Notes in Computer Science, Software Process Technology: Proceedings of the Fifth European Workshop* 1149 (Springer-Verlag, 1996) 258-270.

M. I. Kellner, "Software process modeling: Value and experience". Carnegie-Mellon University, Software Engineering Institute. *SEI Technical Review.* (1989) 23-54.

M. I. Kellner, "Software process modeling example". *Proceedings of the Fifth International Software Process Workshop*, IEEE Computer Society (1990) 163-166.

M. I. Kellner, "Software process modelling support for management planning and control". *Proceedings of the First International Conference on Software Process* (October 1991) 8-28.

M. I. Kellner, P. H. Feiler, A. Finkelstein, T. Katayama, L. J. Osterweil, M. H. Penedo and H. D. Rombach, "ISPW-6 software process example". *Proceedings of the First International Conference on Software Process* (October 1991) 176-186.

M. I. Kellner and G. A. Hansen, "Software process modeling". Carnegie-Mellon University, Software Engineering Institute. *Technical Report CMU/SEI-88-TR-9.* (1988).

M. I. Kellner and G. A. Hansen, "Software process modeling: A case study". *Proceedings of the 22nd Hawaii International Conference on System Sciences,* Vol. II, IEEE Computer Society (1989) 175-188.

C. F. Kemerer, "An empirical validation of software cost estimation models". *Communications of the ACM* **30**, 5 (May 1987) 416-428.

H. Koontz and C. O'Donnell, *Principles of Management: An Analysis of Managerial Functions.* 5th edn. (McGraw-Hill, 1972).

P. Kroll and P. Kruchten, *The Rational Unified Process Made Easy. A Practitioner's Guide to the RUP.* (Addison Wesley, 2003).

P. Kuvaja, J. Similä, L. Krzanik, A. Bicego, G. Koch and S. Saukkonen, *Software Process Assessment and Improvement. The BOOTSTRAP Approach.* (Blackwell Publishers, 1994).

C. Larman, *Agile & Iterative Development. A Manager's Guide.* (Addison Wesley, 2004).

G. Latham, L. M. Saari, E. D. Pursell and M. A. Campion, "The situational interview". *Journal of Applied Psychology* 65 (1980) 422-427.

G. Le Boterf, *De la Compétence à la Navigation Professionnelle.* (Les Editions d'Organisation, 1997).

A. Legait, D. Oldfield and F. Oquendo, "MASP: A model for assisted software environments". *ADA-Europe International Workshop on Environments* (September 1989).

M. M. Lehman, "Software engineering, the software process and their support". *Software Engineering Journal* **6**, 5 (September 1991) 243-258.

N. G. Leveson, "Intent specifications: An approach to building human-centered specifications". *IEEE Transactions on Software Engineering* **26**, 1 (January 2000) 15-35.

C. Levy-Leboyer, La Gestion des Compétences. (Les Editions d'Organisation, 1996).

J. Lonchamp, "Supporting social interaction activities of software processes". *Proceedings of the Second European Workshop on Software Process Technology* (September 1992) 34-54.

J. Lonchamp, "A structured conceptual and terminological framework for software process engineering". *Proceedings of the Second International Conference on Software Process* (February 1993) 41-53.

J. Lonchamp, "An assessment exercise". In: A. Finkelstein, J. Kramer and B. Nuseibeh (Eds.), *Software Process Modelling and Technology*. Chap. 13. (Research Studies Press, 1994) 335-356.

J. Lonchamp, K. Benali, C. Godart and J. C. Derniame, "Modeling and enacting software processes: An analysis". *Proceedings of the 14th Annual International Computer Software and Applications Conference* (October/November 1990) 727-736.

M. López Fernández, *Formal Integral Software Process Evaluation Model*. Ph.D. thesis, Universidad Politécnica de Madrid, Madrid. (1998).

N. H. Madhavji, "The process cycle". *Software Engineering Journal* **6**, 5 (September 1991) 234-242.

N. H. Madhavji, "Environment evolution: The Prism model of changes". *IEEE Transactions on Software Engineering* **18**, 5 (May 1992) 380-392.

N. H. Madhavji and W. Schäfer, "Prism – Methodology and process-oriented environment". *IEEE Transactions on Software Engineering* **17**, 12 (December 1991) 1270-1283.

I. R. McChesney, "Toward a classification scheme for software process modelling approaches". *Information and Software Technology* **37**, 7 (1995) 363-374.

D. McCracken and M. Jackson, "Life cycle concept considered harmful". *ACM SIGSOFT Software Engineering Notes* **7**, 2 (April 1982) 29-32.

M. A. McDowell, "From crisis to quality: Managing the software development process". *American Programmer* **7**, 9 (September 1994) 44-49.

B. McFeeley, *IDEAL: A User's Guide for Software Process Improvement.* Handbook CMU/SEI-96-HB-001. (Carnegie Mellon University, Software Engineering Institute, 1996).

C. McGowan and S. Bohner, "Model based process assessments". *Proceedings of the 15th International Conference on Software Engineering* (1993) 202-211.

P. Mi and W. Scacchi, "A knowledge-based environment for modelling and simulating software engineering processes". *IEEE Transactions on Knowledge and Data Engineering* **2**, 3 (September 1990) 283-294.

P. Mi and W. Scacchi, "Modeling articulation work in software engineering processes". *Proceedings of the First International Conference on Software Process* (October 1991) 188-210.

S.-Y. Min and D.-H. Bae, "MAM nets: A Petri-net based approach to software process modeling, analysis and management". *Proceedings of the Ninth International Conference on Software Engineering and Knowledge Engineering* (June 1997) 78-86.

N. H. Minsky and D. Rozenshtein, "Configuration management by consensus. An application of law-governed systems". *Proceedings of the Fourth Symposium Practical Software Development Environments*, ACM SIGSOFT (December 1990).

A. Mitrani, M. Dalziel and D. Fitt, *Competency-based Human Resource Management: Value-driven Strategies for Recruitment, Development and Reward.* (Kogan Page, 1992).

R. T. Mittermeir and R. A. Schlemmer, "Stepwise improvement of the software-process in a multidimensional framework". *Annual Review of Automatic Programming* 16 (1992) 63-70.

J. Mogilensky and B. L. Deimel, "Where do people fit in the CMM?". *American Programmer* 7, 9 (September 1994) 36-43.

E. Molleman and M. Broekhuis, "Sociotechnical systems: Towards an organizational learning approach". *Journal of Engineering and Technology Management* 18 (2001) 271-294.

A. C. Morales Gutiérrez, J. A. Ariza Montes and E. Morales Fernández, *Gestión Integrada de Personas. Una Perspectiva de Organización.* (Desclée De Brouwer, 1999).

P. J. A. Morssink, *Behaviour Modelling in Information Systems Design: Application of the PARADIGM Formalism.* Ph.D. thesis. University of Leiden, Leiden. (1993).

J. L. Moses and W. C. Byham, *Applying the Assessment Center Method.* (Pergamon, 1997).

M. N. Nguyen and R. Conradi, "Towards a rigoroues approach for managing process evolution". *Lecture Notes in Computer Science, Software Process Technology: Proceedings of the Fifth European Workshop* 1149 (Springer-Verlag, 1996) 18-35.

L. J. Osterweil, "Software processes are software too". *Proceedings of the Ninth International Conference on Software Engineering* (1987) 2-13.

E. Ostolaza, E. Gallo, M. L. Escalante and G. Benguria, "Business improvement guide: BIG-TTM Version 1.0". European Software Institute. *Technical Report ESI-1999-TR-012.* (February 1999).

M. A. Ould and C. Roberts, "Defining formal models of the software development process". In: P. Brereton (Ed.), *Software Engineering Environments.* (Ellis Horwood, 1988) 13-26.

D. Pan, D. Zhu and K. Johnson, "Requirements engineering techniques". (1997) 1-17. *Internet Report*:
http://www.cpsc.ucalgary.ca/~johnsonk/SENG/SENG611/Project/report.htm

M. C. Paulk, "Extreme Programming from a CMM perspective*". IEEE Software* (2001) 19-26.

M. C. Paulk, B. Curtis, M. B. Chrissis and C. V. Weber, "Capability Maturity Model for Software, Version 1.1". Carnegie Mellon University, Software Engineering Institute. *Technical Report CMU/SEI-93-TR-24*. (1993).

M. C. Paulk, C. V. Weber and M. B. Chrissis, *The Capability Maturity Model: Guidelines for Improving the Software Process.* (Addison Wesley, 1995).

M. H. Penedo, "Prototyping a project master database for software engineering environments". *Proceedings of the Second ACM Software Engineering Symposium on Practical SDEs* (December 1986).

M. H. Penedo and C. Shu, "Acquiring experiences with the modelling and implementation of the project life-cycle process: The PMDB work". *Software Engineering Journal* **6**, 5 (September 1991) 259-274.

M. H. Penedo and E. D. Stuckle, "PMDB – A project master database for software engineering environments". *Proceedings of the Eighth International Conference on Software Engineering* (August 1985).

S. Pereda and F. Berrocal, *Gestión de Recursos Humanos.* (Centro de Estudios Ramón Areces, 1999).

D. E. Perry, N. A. Staudenmayer and L. G. Votta, "People, organizations and process improvement". *IEEE Software* **11**, 4 (July 1994) 36-45.

D. Pfahl and G. Ruhe, "System dynamics as an enabling technology for learning in software organization". *Proceedings of the 13th International Conference on Software Engineering and Knowledge Engineering* (2001) 355-362.

S.-L. Pfleeger, *Software Engineering: Theory and Practice.* (Prentice Hall, 1998).

R. Pressman, *Software Engineering: A Practitioner's Approach.* 4th edn. (McGraw-Hill, 1997).

D. Raffo and M. Kellner, "Modeling software processes quantitatively and evaluating the performance of process alternatives". In: K. El Emam and N. Madhavji (Eds.), *Elements of Software Process Assessment and Improvement.* (IEEE Computer Society Press, 1999).

J. Ramanathan and S. Sarkar, "Providing customized assistance for software lifecycle approaches". *IEEE Transactions on Software Engineering* **14**, 6 (June 1988) 749-757.

G. Rhue and F. Bomarius (Eds.), *Learning Software Organization – Methodology and Applications.* Lecture Notes in Computer Science 1756 (Springer-Verlag, 2000).

D. Riehle, *A comparison of the value systems of Adaptive Software Development and Extreme Programming: How methodologies may learn from each other.* (2000).
http://www.riehle.org/computer-science/research/2000/xp-2000.

R. E. Riggio, "Assessment of basic social skills". *Journal of Personality and Social Psychology.* 51 (1986) 649-660.

H. D. Rombach and V. R. Basili, "A quantitative assessment of software maintenance: An industrial case study". *Proceedings of the Conference on Software Maintenance* (September 1987) 134-144.

H. D. Rombach and M. Verlage, "How to assess a software process modeling formalism from a project member's point of view". *Proceedings of the Second International Conference on Software Process* (February 1993) 147-158.

J. Rumbaugh, M. Blaha, W. Premerlani, F. Eddy and W. Lorensen, *Object-Oriented Modeling and Design.* (Prentice Hall, 1991).

M. T. Russell and D. L. Karol, *16PF Fifth Edition Administrator's Manual.* (Institute for Personality and Ability Testing, 1994).

M. T. Russell and D. L. Karol, *16 PF-5 Manual.* (TEA Ediciones, 1998).

A. M. Ryan and P. R. Sackett, "A survey of individual assessment practices by I/O psychologists". *Personnel Psychology* 40 (1987) 489-504.

J. Sanders and E. Curran, *Software Quality. A Framework for Success in Software Development and Support.* (Addison Wesley, 1994).

G. Satriani, A. Andrés, M. L. Escalante and L. Marcaida, "Business improvement guide: SPICE – ISO9001 Version 1.0". European Software Institute. *Technical Report ESI-1998-TR-007.* (May 1998).

W. Scacchi, "Models of software evolution: Life cycle and process". Carnegie Mellon University, Software Engineering Institute. *SEI Curriculum Modules SEI-CM-10-1.0.* (1987).

C. H. Schmauch, *ISO 9000 for Software Developers.* (ASQC Quality Press, 1995).

K. Schwaber, "The Scrum development process". *OOPSLA '95* (1995).

C. B. Seaman and V. R. Basili, "OPT: An approach to organizational and process improvement". *Proceedings of AAAI Symposium on Computational Organizational Design* (March 1994) 168-174.

SEI, "CMMI[SM] for Systems Engineering/Software Engineering, Version 1.1. Staged Representation. (CMMI-SE/SW, V1.1, Staged)". Carnegie Mellon University, Software Engineering Institute. *Technical Report CMU/SEI-2002-TR-002.* (2002a).

SEI, "CMMI[SM] for Systems Engineering/Software Engineering, Version 1.1. Continuous Representation. (CMMI-SE/SW, V1.1, Continuous)". Carnegie Mellon University, Software Engineering Institute. *Technical Report CMU/SEI-2002-TR-001.* (2002b).

SEI, "CMMI[SM] for Software Engineering, Version 1.1. Staged Representation. (CMMI-SW, V1.1, Staged)". Carnegie Mellon University, Software Engineering Institute. *Technical Report CMU/SEI-2002-TR-029.* (2002c).

SEI, "CMMI[SM] for Software Engineering, Version 1.1. Continuous Representation. (CMMI-SW, V1.1, Continuous)". Carnegie Mellon University,

Software Engineering Institute. *Technical Report CMU/SEI-2002-TR-028.* (2002d).

SEI, "CMMI[SM] for Systems Engineering/Software Engineering/Integrated Product and Process Development/Supplier Sourcing, Version 1.1, Staged Representation. (CMMI-SE/SW/IPPD/SS, V1.1, Staged)". Carnegie Mellon University, Software Engineering Institute. *Technical Report CMU/SEI-2002-TR-012.* (2002e).

SEI, "CMMI[SM] for Systems Engineering/Software Engineering/Integrated Product and Process Development/Supplier Sourcing, Version 1.1. Continuous Representation. (CMMI-SE/SW/IPPD/SS, V1.1, Continuous)". Carnegie Mellon University, Software Engineering Institute. *Technical Report CMU/SEI-2002-TR-011.* (2002f).

R. W. Selby, V. R. Basili and T. Baker, "CLEANROOM software development: An empirical evaluation". *IEEE Transactions on Software Engineering* **13**, 9 (September 1987) 1027-1037.

R. W. Selby, A. A. Porter, D. C. Schmidt and J. Berney, "Metric-driven analysis and feedback systems for enabling empirically guided software development". *Proceedings of the 13th International Conference on Software Engineering* (May 1991) 288-298.

V. Shackleton and S. Newell, "Management selection: A comparative survey of methods used in top British and French companies". *Journal of Occupational Psychology* **64**, 1 (1991) 23-37.

K. Sherdil and N. H. Madhavji, "Human-oriented improvement in the software process". *Lecture Notes in Computer Science, Software Process Technology: Proceedings of the Fifth European Workshop* 1149 (Springer-Verlag, 1996) 145-166.

L. M. Spencer Jr., D. C. McClelland and S. M. Spencer, *Competency Assessment Methods: History and State of the Art.* (Hay/McBer, 1992).

J. Slomp and E. Molleman, "Cross-training policies and team performance". *International Journal of Production Research* 40 (2002) 1193-1219.

I. Sommerville and T. Rodden, "Human, social and organisational influences on the software process". Lancaster University, Computing Department, Cooperative Systems Engineering Group. *Technical Report CSEG/2/1995.* (1995) 1-21.

SPICE, SPICE project web site. (2003). http://www-sqi.cit.gu.edu.au/spice.

F. Stallinger and P. Grünbacher, "System dynamics modelling and simulation of collaborative requirements engineering". *The Journal of Systems and Software* 59 (2001) 311-321.

J. Stapleton, *Dynamic Systems Development Method – The Method in Practice.* (Addison Wesley, 1997).

I. D. Steiner, *Group Process and Productivity.* (Academic Press, 1972).

S. M. Sutton Jr., D. Heimbigner and L. J. Osterweil, "Language constructs for managing change in process-centred environments". *Proceedings of the Fourth Symposium on Software Development Environments*, ACM SIGSOFT (December 1990).

TEA, *Inventario Psicológico de California. CPI Manual.* (TEA Ediciones, 1992).

C. J. Tully, "Representing and enacting the software process". *Proceedings of the Fourth International Software Process Workshop, ACM SIGSOFT Software Engineering Notes* **14**, 4 (June 1989) 159-162.

J. D. Valett and F. E. McGarry, "A summnary of software measurement experiences in the software engineering laboratory". *Journal of Systems and Software* **9**, 2 (1989) 137-148.

M. R. van Steen, *Modelling Dynamic Systems by Parallel Decision Processes.* Ph.D. thesis, University of Leiden, Leiden. (1988).

L. Walley and M. Smith, *Deception in Selection.* (Wiley, 1998).

B. Warboys, "The IPSE 2.5 project: Process modelling as the basis for a support environment". *Proceedings of the First International Conference on System Development Environments and Factories* (May 1989).

M. Weske, T. Goesmann, R. Holten and R. Striemer, "A reference model for workflow application development processes". *Software Engineering Notes in Work Activities Coordination and Collaboration: Proceedings of the International Joint Conference* **24**, 2 (ACM Press, 1999) 1-10.

D. West, *Towards a Subjective Knowledge Elicitation Methodology for the Development of Expert Systems*. Ph.D. thesis, Univesity of Portsmouth, Portsmouth. (1991).

K. Whitaker, *Managing Software Maniacs*. (John Wiley & Sons, 1994).

L. Wolf and D. S. Rosenblum, "A study in software process data capture and analysis". *Proceedings of the Second International Conference on Software Process* (February 1993) 115-124.

R. W. Woodman, "Organization development". In: N. Nicholson (Ed.), *Blackwell Encyclopedic Dictionary of Organizational Behavior*. (Blackwell, 1995) 359-361.

C. Woodruff, *Competent by Any Other Name*. (People Management Journal, 1991).

C. Woodruffe, *Assessment Centres: Identifying and Developing Competencies*. (IPM, 1990).

A. Wulms, "*Adaptive software process modelling with SOCCA and PARADIGM*". University of Leiden. Department of Computer Science. Supervisado por: Dr. L. P. J. Groenewegen. (April 1995) 1-80.

K. Yasumoto, T. Higashino and K. Taniguchi, "Software process description using LOTOS and its enaction". *Proceedings of the 16th International Conference on Software Engineering* (May 1994) 169-178.

R. T. Yeh, D. A. Naumann, R. T. Mittermeir, R. A. Schlemmer, W. S. Gilmore, G. E. Sumrall and J. T. LeBaron, "A commonsense management model". *IEEE Software* **8**, 6 (1991) 23-33.

E. S. K. Yu, "Modelling organizations for information systems requirements engineering". *Proceedings of the First Symposium on Requirements Engineering*, IEEE Computer Society (January 1993) 34-41.

E. S. K. Yu and J. Mylopoulos, "Understanding "why" in software process modelling, analysis, and design". *Proceedings of the 16th International Conference on Software Engineering*, IEEE Computer Society (May 1994) 1-10.

H. Zhuge and X. Shi, "Communication cost of cognitive co-operation for distributed team development". *The Journal of Systems and Software* 57 (2001) 227-233.

People's Capabilities

The descriptions of people's capabilities or behavioural competencies can be as varied and dissimilar as the organisations that go about analysing and classifying behaviour. Behaviour is the set of physiological, motor, verbal and mental operations by means of which an organism reduces its tensions and achieves its potential in a situation. *Capability is understood as above average behaviour* in a given intellectual, motor area, etc.; *a capability is formed* (Bleger, 1974).

Behaviour can be viewed from multiple viewpoints and defined with fine distinctions. This means that some concrete aspects of how particular professional behaviours are achieved are included in a definition of one specific capability or another. These different ways of looking at the more sophisticated facets of behaviour lead to diverse "lists of capabilities" and, consequently, different ways of analysing jobs and the capabilities of job candidates in selection processes.

On the one hand, following de Ansorena Cao (1996), 50 general capabilities have been defined and classified, and validated within the framework of Assessment Centre Method (ACM). These skills are divided into five categories: *meta skills, beta skills, operational skills, interpersonal skills and management skills*. The behavioural competencies classed according to above-mentioned categories are listed in Table A.1 (de Ansorena Cao, 1996).

On the other hand, the Hay Group (1996) has found that there are a number of competencies that are frequently repeated in different jobs. Specifically, this multinational group determines some 20 generic competencies that appear to be the origin of some aspects that lead to higher performance in a number of business, technical, professional, service, sales and management roles. These generic competencies are divided into six main categories, as shown in Table A.2.

CATEGORY	BEHAVIOURAL SKILLS
Meta skills	Adaptability, Problem analysis, Learning, Decision making, Energy, Flexibility, Independence, Integrity, Judgement, Resoluteness, Interpersonal sensitivity, Stress tolerance
Beta Skills	Professional ambition, Knowledge of the environment, Extensive range of interests, Innovation/creativity, Impact, Success drive, Tenacity, Risk taking
Operational Skills	Numerical analysis, Attention to detail, Self-organisation, Oral communication, Written communication, Discipline, Mastery of non-verbal communication, Further/participate in meetings, Environmental orientation, Sense of urgency
Interpersonal skills	Customer service, Negotiating skill, Active listening, Mastery of audiovisual media, Customer orientation, Persuasion, Presentation, Sociability, Teamwork/cooperation
Management Skills	Management control, Delegation, Co-worker development/ support, Enterprising spirit, Co-worker evaluation, Management identification, Group leadership, People leadership, Planning and organisation, Organisational sensitivity, Vision

Table A.1. Classification of behavioural competencies by categories according to de Ansorena Cao

CATEGORY	BEHAVIOURAL SKILLS
Achievement and action capabilities	Motivation to achieve, Concern for order and quality, Initiative, Search for information
Help and service capabilities	Interpersonal sensitivity, Customer service orientation
Capabilities of Persuasion	Impact and influence, Organisational knowledge, Building relationships
Management capabilities	People development, People management, Teamwork and cooperation, Leadership
Cognitive capabilities	Analytical thinking, Conceptual thinking, Knowledge and experience
Personal effectiveness capabilities	Self-control, Self-confidence, Reaction to failure, Commitment to the organisation

Table A.2. Classification of behavioural competencies by categories according to the Hay Group

The two specified lists of competencies meet the essential condition of being independent, that is, the presence of one behavioural competency in a person does not necessarily imply the presence of the others. If this were not the case, it would be difficult to identify and discriminate one competency from another in the process of job or profile analysis and the evaluation of the people concerned.

It is difficult to demonstrate empirically and statistically that each of the behavioural competencies for new lists created *ad hoc* for an organisation are independent, and this research process tends to be costly and time consuming (de Ansorena Cao, 1996). In most cases, therefore, organisations opt to use lists of descriptions of behavioural competencies that have been previously prepared and researched by specialists. The most applicable behavioural competencies for the use of a specific organisation are selected from these lists. Occasionally, distinctions or particular constraints are added to these standard definitions so that they, ultimately, better reflect the *personality of the organisation* in which they are to be implemented (de Ansorena Cao, 1996; Hay Group, 1996).

Therefore, if a list is operativised for a particular organisation, the characteristics of the corporate culture that the senior management aims to encourage are vividly highlighted, and the aspects related to values and characteristic behavioural conducts that the organisation would like to see in its members are clearly defined.

16 PF Fifth Edition Personality Factor Questionnaire

B.1. DESCRIPTION OF THE 16 PF FIFTH EDITION

For forty years, Raymond B. Cattell's 16 PF personality factor questionnaire has been one of the most widely used and highly reputed instruments for evaluating personality structure all over the world. Its source is IPAT, Institute for Personality and Ability Testing, Champaign, Illinois. This psychometric instrument has been adapted (forms A, B, C and D) up to the fifth edition (Russell & Karol, 1994; Russell & Karol, 1998). The fifth edition includes the revised and updated wording of the elements, improved reliability and validity of its primary scales, the development of new response style indices (attitudinal approaches to the instrument) and the replacement of the former secondary factors by five global dimensions that bear a notable parallelism with the famous Big Five personality factors. These dimensions are output factorially from the 16 PF Fifth Edition.

The 16 PF Fifth Edition, as a broad-spectrum measure of personality, is useful for predicting people's behaviour in wide-ranging situations and activities. These include: industrial applications, "human potential" surveys, personnel selection and classification in human resources departments and experimental applications in the field of psychology. This instrument is composed of a questionnaire containing 185 elements (questions) aimed at measuring: a) 16 primary scales or traits; b) five global personality dimensions; and c) three response style indices (impression management, infrequency and acquiescence). The primary scales contain from 10 to 15 elements. They are labelled with letters A, B, C, Q ... and are identified with a descriptive name (for example, C is Emotional Stability). Additionally, each factor has a negative range or low pole (represented by the minus sign "-") and a positive range or high pole (represented by the plus sign "+"). For example, C- describes a reactive and emotionally changeable person and C+ an emotionally stable, calm and mature person. The 16 primary scales are detailed in Table B.1.

SCALE (NAME)	DESCRIPTION
Warmth (A)	This scale evaluates the emotional tendency that people generally develop in a situation of social interaction. People at the negative end of the scale (A-) would be distant and even disobedient, whereas people at the positive end (A+) would be kindly and communicative.
Reasoning (B)	This scale measures the ability to abstract relationships depending on how some things are placed with respect to others. Low scorers on this scale (B-) would be people with a low intellectual and reasoning ability; high scorers (B+) would have a higher intellectual ability, be shrewd and fast learners.
Emotional Stability (C)	The emotional stability evaluated by 16 PF Fifth Edition refers to how adaptable people are to the demands of the environment, routine problems and their challenges. People who score within the high range (C+) are emotionally stable, mature and calm people; people who score within the low range (C-) are affected by feelings and easily upset.
Dominance (E)	The concept of dominance evaluated by this scale is understood as the desire to control others or how controlled people perceive themselves to be. At its low end (E-) are the submissive, dependent or conformist people, whereas its high range (E+) contains firmer and more independent people.
Liveliness (F)	This scale is understood as a person's impulsiveness. It describes attitudes that range from enthusiasm, talkativeness and joviality (positive pole, F+) to seriousness and soberness (negative pole, F-).
Rule Consciousness (G)	This scale offers information on the superego of examinees, which is why it is referred to as rule consciousness. It compares the concepts of low superego strength (negative pole, G-), typical of individuals who are reluctant to accept group moral rules, and high superego strength (positive pole, G+), present in staid and moralistic individuals.
Social Boldness (H)	This scale indicates people's tendency to take risks as opposed to analysing and weighing up things before taking action. High scorers on this scale (H+) are more audacious, venturesome and impulsive people, whereas low scorers (H-) are timid, repressed and wary people.
Sensitivity (I)	This scale analyses the sensitivity of the examinee. High scorers on this scale (I+) are generally defined as sensitive. These are idealistic, open people who seek affection and understanding from others. On the other hand, low scorers (I-) are cold, unsentimental and distrustful people.
Vigilance (L)	This scale evaluates how trusting people are of other people's motives and intentions. It has been called vigilance and very much conditions interpersonal relationships. High scorers (L+) are wary, suspicious and distrustful people. The opposite pole (L-) includes more trusting, conforming and tolerant people.

Table B.1. Description of the 16 PF Fifth Edition primary scales

SCALE (NAME)	DESCRIPTION
Abstractedness (M)	This scale refers to what subjects and things people focus on. People who score high (M+) are imaginative, unconventional and extravagant. People who score low (M-) are more realistic, practical and down to earth.
Privateness (N)	This scale evaluates how open people are to others. In particular, high scorers on this scale (N+) are discreet people, who manipulate their expressions to please. At the other end of the scale (N-) are naive, socially awkward people, who are not at pains to prompt good feeling with their opposite numbers.
Apprehension (O)	This scale offers a view of how people see themselves, that is, their self-apprehension. It indicates the level of self-esteem and self-acceptance. High scorers (O+) are apprehensive, insecure and depressed people. These people are oversensitive and concerned about what they have done, what they should have said and did not say, are hurt if they are not accepted by others, etc. Low scorers (O-) are self-assured, serene and confident people.
Openness to Change (Q1)	This scale indicates how inclined people are towards the new and unconventional. Individuals at the positive pole (Q1+) shy away from established rules and look to enjoy new experiences outside the more traditional constraints. On the other hand, low-scoring individuals (Q1-) will make a show of a more conservative behaviour pattern, typical of people who are enemies of change and rooted in the past.
Self-Reliance (Q2)	This scale evaluates self-reliance, understood as how dependent people are on others to be able to do things. It distinguishes between two types of people: high-scoring individuals (Q2+) tend to be solitary and enjoy doing things without anyone else's help and the low-scoring individuals (Q2-) enjoy company more, join groups and prefer to have consent and approval from others before embarking upon anything.
Perfectionism (Q3)	This scale addresses order and perfection. At the high end of this scale (Q3+) are the perfectionistic, organised and disciplined people. The negative pole (Q3-) includes flexible and fault tolerant, weak individuals who are indifferent to social norms.
Tension (Q4)	This scale evaluates people's anxiety level. This scale places more emphasis on anxiety as a trait than as a state, and is, therefore, sometimes called "floating anxiety". Tense, irritable and overexcited people have the highest scores (Q4+), whereas as the lowest scores (Q4-) are typical of tranquil, relaxed and serene people.

Table B.1. Description of the 16 PF Fifth Edition primary scales (cont'd)

As mentioned above, apart from the primary scales (A to Q4), the 16 PF Fifth Edition provides five groupings of these scales to output global personality dimensions. These dimensions have been referred to as "second-order factors" in the literature, because they are calculated by means of factor analysis. Table B.2 describes these global dimensions. Finally, there are three control scales or indices to measure response biases, aiming to indicate the relevance of the data collected using the questionnaire. The IM (impression management) index reveals an examinee's attempt to offer a distorted picture. The INF (Infrequency) index is based on the rate of infrequent responses given by the test-taker. The ACQ (Acquiescence) index reports the examinee's tendency to systematically agree to most of the questionnaire sentences.

DIMENSIONS	DESCRIPTION
Extraversion	This dimension positions people on the introversion-extraversion continuum. It is calculated from the primary scales A, F, H, N and Q2. For example, the low pole of the Extraversion scale (-) defines an introverted, socially inhibited person, whereas the high pole (+) defines an extraverted, sociable and participatory individual.
Anxiety	This dimension indicates how nervous and worried people are about everything they do. It is calculated from the scores on the primary scales C, O, Q4 and L. For example, the low pole on the Anxiety scale (-) defines an imperturbable, low anxiety person, whereas the high pole (+) defines a perturbable, high anxiety person.
Tough-Mindedness	This dimension, known as tough-mindedness, indicates how inclined people are to consider reasons or motives other than their own. It is calculated from the scores on A, I, M and Q1. For example, the low pole on the Tough-Mindedness scale (-) defines a receptive, open-minded and intuitive person, whereas the high pole (+) defines a tough-minded, firm, inflexible, cool, objective, closed and unempathetic person.
Independence	This dimension indicates how determined people are in their thoughts and actions. It is calculated from the primary scales Q1, E, H and L. For example, the low pole on the Independence scale (-) defines an accommodating, agreeable person who is quick to yield, whereas the high pole (+) defines an independent, critical person who likes controversy.
Self-Control	This dimension evaluates how self-controlled people are in their social relationships. The scale is calculated from the scores on G, M, Q3 and F. As the scores increase, so does people's control over their actions. For example, the low pole on the Self-Control scale (-) defines an unrestrained, impulsive person, whereas the high pole (+) defines a self-controlled person who inhibits impulses.

Table B.2. Description of the 16 PF Fifth Edition global dimensions

B.2. 16 PF FIFTH EDITION TEST ADMINISTRATION ELEMENTS

The 16 PF identifies the primary scales of behaviour, described in Table B.1, by means of factor analysis of the total set of personality descriptors. The interrelationship of the primary scales determines the five global factors, specified in Table B.2, examining personality from a broader perspective than is specified by the primary factors. The 16 PF Fifth Edition test is designed to be administered to adults individually or collectively in less than an hour. Some specimen questions completed by examinees are illustrated in Figure B.1. Except for scale B ("reasoning"), the questions include three alternative responses, where the middle alternative is always a question mark ("?"). The 15 reasoning elements are placed at the end of the questionnaire, after the personality elements. This presentation assures the continuity of the personality responses, which are separated from the intellectual measure, as is advantageous in some settings.

1. In a business, it would be more interesting to be responsible for:
   A. machines or records
   B. ?
   C. interviewing and speaking to people

2. I usually go to bed feeling satisfied about how my day has gone
   A. True
   B. ?
   C. False

3. If I notice someone else's line of reasoning is incorrect, I usually:
   A. tell the person
   B. ?
   C. forget about it

4. I really enjoy having guests and making sure they have a good time:
   A. True
   B. ?
   C. False

5. When I make a decision I always think carefully about whether it is correct and fair.
   A. True
   B. ?
   C. False

6. I would rather spend an afternoon on a quiet task than attend a lively meeting
   A. True
   B. ?
   C. False

7. I have more admiration for:
   A. a person with average ability, but strict morals
   B. ?
   C. a talented, albeit occasionally irresponsible person

8. It would be more interesting to be:
   A. a civil engineer
   B. ?
   C. a play writer

9. I usually take the first step to make new friends.
   A. True
   B. ?
   C. False

10. I love good novels and plays or films.
    A. True
    B. ?
    C. False

11. When authoritative people try to dominate me, I do just the opposite to what they want.
    A. True
    B. ?
    C. False

12. I sometimes do not get on with other people because my ideas are unconventional and original.
    A. True
    B. ?
    C. False

13. A lot of people would "stab you in the back" to get on themselves.
    A. True
    B. ?
    C. False

14. I get into trouble because I sometimes go ahead with my ideas without discussing them with any other people involved.
    A. True
    B. ?
    C. False

15. I talk about my feelings:.
    A. readily if people seem to be interested
    B. ?
    C. only if I have no choice

16. I take advantage of people.
    A. Sometimes
    B. ?
    C. Never

CONTINUES ON THE NEXT PAGE

● ● ● ● ● ●

Figure B.1. Specimen 16 PF Fifth Edition Questions

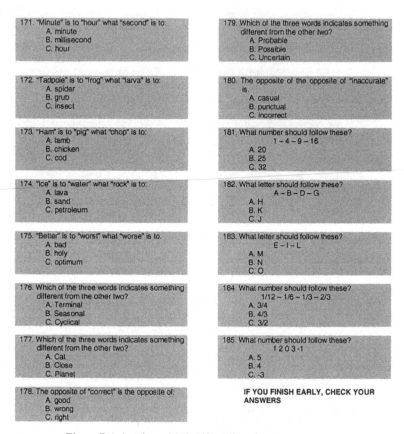

171. "Minute" is to "hour" what "second" is to:
    A. minute
    B. millisecond
    C. hour

172. "Tadpole" is to "frog" what "larva" is to:
    A. spider
    B. grub
    C. insect

173. "Ham" is to "pig" what "chop" is to:
    A. lamb
    B. chicken
    C. cod

174. "Ice" is to "water" what "rock" is to:
    A. lava
    B. sand
    C. petroleum

175. "Better" is to "worst" what "worse" is to:
    A. bad
    B. holy
    C. optimum

176. Which of the three words indicates something
    different from the other two?
    A. Terminal
    B. Seasonal
    C. Cyclical

177. Which of the three words indicates something
    different from the other two?
    A. Cat
    B. Close
    C. Planet

178. The opposite of "correct" is the opposite of:
    A. good
    B. wrong
    C. right

179. Which of the three words indicates something
    different from the other two?
    A. Probable
    B. Possible
    C. Uncertain

180. The opposite of the opposite of "inaccurate"
    is:
    A. casual
    B. punctual
    C. incorrect

181. What number should follow these?
    1 – 4 – 9 – 16
    A. 20
    B. 25
    C. 32

182. What letter should follow these?
    A – B – D – G
    A. H
    B. K
    C. J

183. What letter should follow these?
    E – I – L
    A. M
    B. N
    C. O

184. What number should follow these?
    1/12 – 1/6 – 1/3 – 2/3
    A. 3/4
    B. 4/3
    C. 3/2

185. What number should follow these?
    1 2 0 3 -1
    A. 5
    B. 4
    C. -3

IF YOU FINISH EARLY, CHECK YOUR
ANSWERS

Figure B.1. Specimen 16 PF Fifth Edition Questions (cont'd)

Examinees should answer the test questions naturally and not spend a lot of time
thinking about the content of a sentence. After administering the questionnaire,
the steps taken are as follows (Russell & Karol, 1994; Russell & Karol, 1998):
correction and scoring of the test, calculation of sten scores (the direct 16 PF
scores are transformed on a standard ten-point scale) and global dimensions,
plotting of a graphic profile and later analysis. The documents used during these
steps are shown in Figures B.2 and B.3. Only qualified psychologists with
sufficient knowledge of test administration should interpret the responses given
by the examinees and the resultant findings.

16 PF FIFTH EDITION PROFILE SHEET

Calculating global dimensions

Enter the direct scores of the 16 primary scales in the DS column and the three indices in the boxes on the right (IM, INF, ACQ) Then consult the scales in the manual to calculate the sten scores for the DS and enter them in the primary scales SS column

Then, and for each of the five dimensions, multiply the sten score value by the weights printed horizontally along the same row and enter the results in the small boxes Add up the values of the positive columns (+) and the negative columns (-), including the constants, if any, and enter the results in the Sums boxes at the bottom

Finally, for each dimension, calculate the difference between the results of the above two columns, and the datum, with a decimal comma in front of the last digit, is the sten score for the dimension The decimal comma has already been entered in the bottom box

PRIMARY SCALES	DS	SS	EXTRAVERSION +	EXTRAVERSION −	ANXIETY +	ANXIETY −	TOUGH-MINDEDNESS +	TOUGH-MINDEDNESS −	INDEPENDENCE +	INDEPENDENCE −	SELF-CONTROL +	SELF-CONTROL −
A Warmth	18	7	[5]35		[2]14		[2]14			7	[3]21	
B Reasoning	10	6	[1]6		[2]12		[1]6		[1]6			
C Emotional Stability	14	4		[1]4		[3]12	[1]4		4			[1]4
E Dominance	15	5			5		[1]5		[7]35		[1]5	
F Liveliness	14	5	[3]15		[1]5		[3]15		[3]15			[3]15
G Rule Consciousness	17	6	[1]6		[1]6					6	[5]30	
H Social Boldness	18	6	[1]6			[2]12	[2]12		[3]12			[1]6
I Sensitivity	17	9	[2]18		[1]9		[3]27			[2]18	[1]9	
L Vigilance	17	9			[3]27		[2]18		[3]27			
M Abstractedness	8	7					[3]21					[1]7
N Privateness	8	5		[3]15	[1]5		5		[2]10			
O Apprehension	17	8	[2]16		[5]40		8				[3]24	
Q1 Openness to Change	21	9		[2]18		[4]36		[8]72	[1]9			
Q2 Self-Reliance	5	7		[4]28	[2]14		[3]21					
Q3 Perfectionism	17	6	[1]6		[3]18		[1]6		[1]6		[7]42	
Q4 Tension	8	6	[1]6		[4]24		[3]18		[2]12			
Constants			16		16		138		50		22	
Sums			130	65	165	90	202	188	136	81	131	54
Sten scores on dimension			6.5		7.5		1.4		5.5		7.7	

RESPONSE STYLES

IM
DS = 18
Pc = 79

INF
DS = 1
Pc = 81

ACQ
DS = 41
Pc = 20

Note: The results of these operations may differ (sometimes by almost a whole sten score) from the results output by means of a process of mechanisation (because this process uses all the weights and constants in hundredths)

Figure B.2. Calculating global dimensions

PROFILE OF PRIMARY SCALES AND GLOBAL DIMENSIONS

Fill in the small circuit underneath the sten score (1 to 10) for each scale (A to Q4). Then join these dots with straight lines to produce the primary scales profile. The dots outside the central area (sten scores 4-7) indicate significant deviations. The adjectives entered in the high or low poles are more likely to apply in these cases.

Repeat the process for the sten scores of the global dimensions (trying to specify the decimal values), and the result will be the profile for these higher-order dimensions. The extent to which the examinee has used the IM "response style" in responses to the 16 PF Fifth Edition can be entered at the bottom.

Surname and name ___ Illustrative case
Age ___ 25 ___ Sex ___ M ___ Date 14/3/95

Scale	SS	The low pole defines a person who is	1	2	3	4	5	6	7	8	9	10	The high pole defines a person who is	Scale
A Warmth	7	Cool, impersonal, distant							•				Warm, outgoing, generous, attentive to others	A
B Reasoning	6	Concrete-thinking											Abstract-thinking	B
C Emotional Stability	4	Reactive, emotionally changeable			•								Emotionally stable, adaptive, mature	C
E Dominance	5	Deferential, cooperative, avoids conflicts					•						Dominant, assertive, competitive	E
F Liveliness	5	Serious, restrained, prudent					•						Lively, spontaneous, animated, enthusiastic	F
G Rule Consciousness	5	Nonconforming, disregards rules, self-indulgent					•						Rule conscious, dutiful, conscientious	G
H Social Boldness	6	Timid, hesitant, intimidated						•					Enterprising, venturesome, socially bold	H
I Sensitivity	9	Objective, unsentimental, utilitarian									•		Sensitive, aesthetic, sentimental	I
L Vigilance	9	Trusting, unsuspecting, easy									•		Vigilant, suspicious, sceptical, wary	L
M Abstractedness	7	Practical, grounded, realistic							•				Abstracted, imaginative, idealistic	M
N Privateness	5	Forthright, genuine, artless, open			•								Private, calculating, discrete, non-disclosing	N
O Apprehension	8	Self-assured, unworried, self-satisfied							•				Apprehensive, insecure, worrying	O
Q1 Openness to Change	9	Traditional, attached to familiar									•		Open to change, experimenting, analytical	Q1
Q2 Self-Reliance	7	Follower, affiliative						•					Self-reliant, individualistic, solitary	Q2
Q3 Perfectionism	6	Flexible, tolerates disorder or errors				•							Perfectionist, organised, self-disciplined	Q3
Q4 Tension	6	Relaxed, placid, patient				•							Tense, high energy, impatient, intranquil	Q4

Global Dimensions			1	2	3	4	5	6	7	8	9	10		
EXT Extraversion	6.5	Introverted, socially inhibited						•					Extraverted, social participant	EXT
ANX Anxiety	7.5	Imperturbable, low anxiety							•				Perturbable, high anxiety	ANX
TM Tough-Mindedness	1.4	Receptive, open-minded, intuitive	•										Tough-minded, resolute, inflexible, cool, objective	TM
IN Independence	5.5	Accommodating, agreeable, selfless					•						Independent, critical, likes controversy, analytical	IN
SC Self Control	7.7	Unrestrained, impulsive							•				Self-controlled, inhibitory of impulses	SC
IM Impression Mgmt.		Desirous to give a bad impression							x				Desirous to give good impression	IM

Figure B.3. Primary scales and global dimensions profile

People Models

This appendix contains the Personality Factors Models and the Capabilities Reports. These reports make up the People Models and are the documents output by the People's Capabilities Evaluation Method. These are the reports for the 25 people from the software developer organisation, Company, Argentina, who took the test, apart from the person already discussed in Chapter 10.

Figures C.1 to C.26 illustrate the Personality Factors Models of the 26 people. Table C.1 shows the full Analytical Report for the person already discussed in Chapter 10. Figures C.27 to C.52 are the Capabilities Reports of same 26 people.

Company	*Personality Factors Report*
	RX
	Name of activity group performed: ....
	Role played: ....
	Cultural evaluation date: *28/6/2000*..................... Report No.: 4
	Evaluators' names: Silvia Teresita Acuña and Marta Evelia Aparicio

A. Personal particulars

Age: 33	Sex:
Nationality: Argentina	☐ Male ☒ Female
Place of birth: Buenos Aires	Residence: ....

Marital status:

☐ Single   ☒ Married   ☐ Separated   ☐ Divorced   ☐ Widowed

B. Graphic profile

		DS	SS
Warmth	A	16	5
Reasoning	B	12	8
Emotional Stability	C	20	9
Dominance	E	18	8
Liveliness	F	12	4
Rule Consciousness	G	15	6
Social Boldness	H	20	8
Sensitivity	I	18	6
Vigilance	L	9	4
Abstractedness	M	0	3
Privateness	N	5	4
Apprehension	O	8	4
Openness to Change	Q1	11	4
Self-Reliance	Q2	3	5
Perfectionism	Q3	20	9
Tension	Q4	12	6
Impression Management	IM	12	4
Infrequency	INF	1	7
Acquiescence	ACQ	61	8
EXTRAVERSION	EX		6.1
ANXIETY	ANX		5.2
TOUGH-MINDEDNESS	TM		5
INDEPENDENCE	IN		7.3
SELF-CONTROL	SC		8

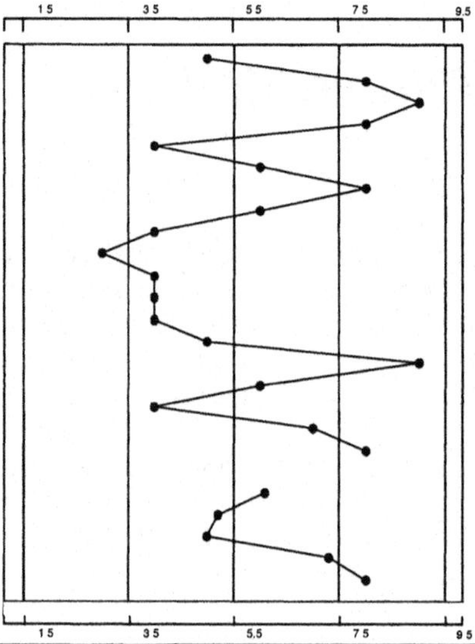

Observations: ....
....

C. Analytical report

Personality-indicative behavioural characteristics:

.... See following report ....

Figure C.1. Personality Factors Model # 4

RESPONSE STYLE INDICES: IM, INF AND ACQ
The three response style indices of the 16 PF aim to disclose the significance of the data supplied by the questionnaire. IM (impression management) exposes test-taker attempts to put over a distorted self-image; INF (infrequency) is based on the rate of infrequent responses given by the examinee; ACQ (acquiescence) reports a test-taker's tendency to systematically assent to most of the questionnaire statements. Although RX's responses to some test statements are designed to convey a positive picture, this does not appear to be the general flow of the questionnaire. Therefore, the profile can be considered valid and be interpreted.
FACTOR A
This scale, called Warmth, evaluates the emotional tendency that people generally develop in a situation of social interaction. People at the negative end of the scale would be distant and even disobedient, whereas people at the positive end would be kindly and communicative. RX has scored near average for her norm group on this scale. This indicates that she finds it easy to get on with people, but also knows how to make the most of the time she spends alone. Although she does not dislike being with other people, she prefers to alternate company with moments of solitude. From the professional viewpoint, she will easily get used to jobs that do not involve isolation from interpersonal contact. Her score may denote some social skill, especially for building relationships with customers. Although she can be cold and distant at times, she will know how to give her best when the occasion so requires. She has a very positive profile for supervisory or middle management jobs. She is also likely to be a very proficient mediator or arbitrator.
FACTOR B
This scale (Reasoning) measures the ability to abstract relationships depending on how some things are placed with respect to others. Low scorers on this scale would be people with a low intellectual and reasoning ability; high scorers would have a higher intellectual ability, and be shrewd and fast learners. RX stands out on rationality and astuteness. She finds it easier than others to understand and establish relationships, and grasp ideas. She is concretely and abstractly creative, intuitive and speculative. Professionally, she is likely to excel in jobs that involve thinking and reasoning. Being rational, she is likely to be very proficient at creative or teaching jobs or occupations that place high demands on intellectual resources (any related to sciences or research). Other scales of the questionnaire should be analysed to see whether there is any relevant factor that could block these aptitudes. Her intellectual ability may lead her to be arrogant and breed conceit that will detract from her interpersonal relationships.
FACTOR C
The Emotional Stability evaluated by 16 PF refers to how adaptable people are to the demands of the environment, routine problems and their challenges. People who score within the high range are emotionally stable, mature and calm people; people who score within the low range are affected by feelings and easily upset. The questionnaire defines RX as a very stable and balanced person, secure and imperturbable. She is not dominated by emotional or affective states, nor is she prone to brusque changes of mood. She is not bewildered or carried along by her feelings when judging people or things. She is objective, pacific, placid and is not upset by worries. A person with such strong emotional control would do well in jobs that involve urgency and composure at the same time: fire-fighters, pilots, flight assistants, judges, surgeons or public transport drivers. Her personal relationships with colleagues will be good and, as a member of a work team, she will act as a good antidote against stress and other work-related pressures. As she also scores high on the Q3 scale, she appears to have a profile typical of someone who is very self-controlled and has a lot of willpower.

Table C.1. Analytical Report Section of the Personality Factors Model

FACTOR E
The concept of Dominance evaluated by this scale is understood as the desire to control others or how controlled people perceive themselves to be. At its low end are the submissive, dependent or conformist people, whereas its high range includes firmer and independent people. Scoring high on scale E, RX can be defined as tenacious, somewhat dominant, aggressive, energetic and will persistently argue her ideas and viewpoints. She may be intolerant of opposing viewpoints, which would affect her interpersonal relationships. While she scores high on the E scale, her score is not high enough to cause insurmountable conflicts with her work colleagues. She does not appear to be a person who blindly fights to get her ideas through, although she will defend them tactfully. She is likely to be a good salesperson and will struggle to get customers to sign a contract. Other professions in which assertiveness can be beneficial are: athletes, judges, clinical psychologists, scientists or management positions. She gets a high score on the H scale, which, taken together with her assertiveness, is indicative of an intrepid, uninhibited and bold person.

FACTOR F
Liveliness is understood as a person's impulsiveness. It describes attitudes that range from enthusiasm, talkativeness and joviality (positive pole) to seriousness and soberness (negative pole). RX tends to be sober, serious and cautious. She may find it difficult to make risky decisions, as she fears making mistakes. She is not an articulate thinker and checks and refutes each idea before moving on to the next to rule out mistakes. Professionally, she is likely to be highly regarded by her superiors, as she will conscientiously accept any rule they enforce. However, her colleagues will see her as a boring and distant person. Jobs involving thought and reflection, such as the scientific and technical professions (physicist, biologist, geologist, programmer, etc.), are ideal positions for her.

FACTOR G
This scale offers information on the superego of examinees, which is why it is referred to as Rule Consciousness. It compares the concepts of low superego strength (negative pole), typical of individuals who are reluctant to accept group moral rules, and high superego strength (positive pole), present in staid and moralistic individuals. On this scale, RX has demonstrated that she has a similar superego strength to most people. In some cases, she can be critical of the rules, but she knows how to be responsible and disciplined. She may encounter difficulties in overdemanding and thorough environments. However, she has the inclination to be responsible with respect to her everyday obligations.

FACTOR H
The Social Boldness scale indicates people's tendency to take risks as opposed to analysing and weighing up things before taking action. High scorers on this scale are more audacious, venturesome and impulsive people, whereas low scorers are timid, repressed and wary people. RX is an active person who finds risk appealing. Her impulsiveness in uncertain situations may lead to setbacks, as she is unlikely to assess all the possible consequences. She may tend to make happy-go-lucky decisions and ignore other people's advice. On the job front, she will assume risks that others turn away from. She will be firm in face of difficulties and will usually accept responsibility for her acts. She is not discouraged by adversity. Such people are well suited for jobs where success is founded on taking risks and accepting responsibilities: sales, financial advisor, teacher and publicist, among others.

FACTOR I
The I scale analyses the Sensitivity of the examinee. High scorers on this scale are generally defined as sensitive. These are idealistic, open people who look for affection and understanding of others. On the other hand, low scorers are cold, unsentimental and distrustful people. RX scores similarly to most people on sensitivity. She is a very emotionally stable person, who may have temperamental outbursts, which will, however, always be for justified reasons. She will not get overinvolved in the other people's problems and will know how to keep the right affective distance so as not to be moved. Her emotional sensitivity does not appear to be an impediment for any job. This is a balanced person who will take criticism in its just measure and, above all, will know how to control herself in unpleasant situations.

Table C.1. Analytical Report Section of the Personality Factors Model (cont'd)

FACTOR L
The L scale evaluates how trusting people are of other people's motives and intentions. It has been called Vigilance and very much conditions interpersonal relationships. High scorers are wary, suspicious and distrustful people. The opposite pole includes more trusting, conforming and tolerant people. RX is defined as conformist. She tolerates frustration and is trusting of others. She is likely to be easily deceived. She is cordial and adapts well to new situations. Not only is she not a conflictive person, but also she contributes to creating an agreeable and pleasant working environment. However, she is easily manipulated and deceived, and is, therefore, not recommended for jobs that demand strength and decisiveness, like any management position. Additionally, she may be less efficient if success depends on acting in very competitive environments, such as sales. The strength of her ego, high on C, makes her an emotionally stable and very mature person.

FACTOR M
The M Scale, Abstractedness, refers to the what subjects and things people focus on. People who score high are imaginative, unconventional and extravagant. People who score low are more realistic, practical and down to earth. RX is objective and realistic. She looks for immediate benefits and acts on practical grounds only. She is calm and composed and does not let her moods affect her. She is not very creative or original, which may be a limitation. Resistant to changes and innovation, she will act on the basis of well-tested methods and procedures. She will focus well on her work, especially if this involves very mechanical actions and has little room for decision making. She tends to be very thorough and is unlikely to leave a task unfinished. Accordingly, the best suited jobs for this type of profile are office work, accounting, assembly lines, etc.

FACTOR N
The Privateness scale evaluates how open people are to others. In particular, high scorers on this scale are discreet people, who manipulate their expressions to please. At the other end of the scale are naïve, socially awkward people, who are not at pains to prompt good feeling with their opposite numbers. RX's score on this scale is typical of someone who prefers sincerity, although this can get her into trouble with other people. She is somewhat naïve and not very reserved, as she likes to say what she thinks. Her frankness and sincerity may put her at odds with other colleagues or customers. In more complicated situations, however, she will know just how far to go. It is inadvisable that she should be employed to deal with claims or work in direct sales, as she will find it difficult to sell the excellences of the product in question. This score is more typical of assistance and help jobs, requiring sincerity on both parts (psychologist, social worker, nursing, etc.), than of jobs where tact and artificial diplomacy play a fundamental role. As she has a high score on E, her behaviour may be overassertive, sometimes bordering on aggressiveness.

FACTOR O
The O scale offers a view of how people see themselves, that is, their self-apprehension. It indicates the level of self-esteem and self-acceptance. High scorers are apprehensive, insecure and depressed people. Low scorers are self-assured, composed and confident people. RX is self-confident, lively and vigorous. She does not let tensions get her down and tries to rationalise any appraisable fear. Her high self-esteem leads her to blame others for her mistakes. She will occasionally find it difficult to accept responsibility for her mistakes even in face of evidence that they are hers. She may find it difficult to understand others and will be perceived as a cool and distant person. At work she will show herself to have a headstrong character, quick to pass judgement on others but far from willing to accept criticism herself. She may appear to be sure of her decisions. If anything goes wrong, however, she will want to have nothing to do with the matter. As is to be expected, this person also scores high on C, which indicates emotional stability and conveys a picture of a calm person.

Table C.1. Analytical Report Section of the Personality Factors Model (cont'd)

FACTOR Q1
The Q1 scale, Openness to change, indicates how inclined people are towards the new and unconventional. Individuals at the positive pole shy away from established rules and look to enjoy new experiences outside the more traditional constraints. On the other hand, low-scoring individuals will make a show of a more conservative behaviour pattern, typical of people who are enemies of change and rooted in the past. RX is a person who is prepared to accept uncomfortable situations. She resists changes and adheres to the popular phrase "better the devil we know...". She tends to accept things that have already been tried out, even in the knowledge that there may be something better. She may be perceived as boring and insubstantial. She is not very conflictive, hardly ever disagrees, is understanding, acts calmly and is unruffled. She will tolerate some of the most routine and frustrating jobs without complaint. She is likely to be a loyal employee, who, faced with the uncertain prospects of a change, prefers to stay in the same place for a long time. This profile is typical of highly disciplined professions: police and other areas of security, military, supervision and machine maintenance, air traffic control, etc. Scoring low on M, this person focuses on the here and now, accepts things as they are and does not analyse other potentially more appealing possibilities.
FACTOR Q2
The Q2 scale evaluates Self-reliance, understood as how dependent people are on others to be able to do things. It distinguishes between two types of people: high-scoring individuals tend to be solitary and enjoy doing things without anyone else's help and the low-scoring individuals enjoy company more, join groups and prefer to have other people's consent and approval before embarking upon anything. The central position of RX on this scale, similar to most of her norm group, is indicative that her actions are somewhat ambivalent; that is, this person will tend to follow her own mind provided she is sure of success. However, she will be open to other people's suggestions if she perceives that the results are uncertain. She may be very useful as a member of a work team, as she will input inventiveness and originality, whereas she will not find it difficult to take up the concept of team. She will know how to strike a balance between what she inputs to the group and where she should back down.
FACTOR Q3
The Q3 scale addresses order and perfection. At the high end of this scale are the perfectionistic, organised and disciplined people. The negative pole includes flexible and fault tolerant, weak individuals who are indifferent to social norms. RX is a person who aspires to fit how she sees herself to what she would like to be. She is very perfectionistic, which leads her to ask a lot and never be satisfied with her actions. In her interpersonal behaviour, she will be constantly mindful of what impression she causes, analysing her every word or action Having such a strong inclination towards perfectionism and thoroughness, she is often likely to fall prey to impractical obsessions that slow down her work and affect her performance. Her work should not include risk taking, nor is she recommended for professions such as pilot, air traffic controller, surgeon, etc. Additionally, and according to her score on C, she tolerates frustration well and is emotionally very mature.
FACTOR Q4
The Q4 scale, Tension, evaluates people's anxiety level. This scale places more emphasis on anxiety as a trait than as a state, and is, therefore, sometimes called "floating anxiety". Tense, irritable and overexcited people have the highest scores, whereas as the lowest scores are typical of tranquil, relaxed and composed people. RX has a similar anxiety level to most other people. Therefore, she is not given to nervousness, although this does not mean that she, like most people, will not be wound up by or lose her cool for important reasons. Anxiety does not appear to be a key element for finding out what this person is like in the professional world. However, her average score on this anxiety scale indicates that she is neither unproductively laid-back nor abnormally tense.

Table C.1. Analytical Report Section of the Personality Factors Model (cont'd)

EXTRAVERSION DIMENSION
This dimension positions people on the introversion-extraversion continuum. It is calculated from the primary scales A, F, H, N and Q2. RX finds it easy to enter into relationships with others. She likes people and also has the ability to forge bonds with others. At work, she will sow friendship and propagate good relationships between her colleagues. She may find it difficult to get used to solitary and isolated jobs, but, on the other hand, she will be enthusiastic about and motivated by teamwork.
ANXIETY DIMENSION
This dimension indicates how nervous and worried people are about everything they do. It is calculated from the scores on the primary scales C, O, Q4 and L. RX appears to have a similar anxiety level to most people. She is a person who will know how to measure out her anxiety according to the demands of the environment. At work, she will not be identified as a nervous person and will know how to take the heat out of situations where necessary.
TOUGH-MINDEDNESS DIMENSION
This dimension, known as tough-mindedness, indicates how inclined people are to consider reasons or motives other than their own. At the negative pole are the more receptive, intuitive and open-minded people, whereas at the positive pole they appear to be cool, closed and unempathetic. The scale is calculated from the scores on A, I, M and Q1. RX is a rather discreet and reserved person. She is not extremely sensitive, but, functionally, successfully relates to others. RX will input more imagination than ability to the job and will not be very receptive to other people's opinions.
INDEPENDENCE DIMENSION
This dimension indicates how determined people are in their thoughts and actions. It is calculated from the primary scales Q1, E, H and L. The questionnaire defines RX as having some measure of suspiciousness, independence, daring and initiative. She does not like to adhere to conventional models of behaviour. She is assertive and sure of herself. She will like to find out new things and will always be ready to learn, especially anything that sets her apart from others. However, she may sometimes give the impression of going it alone and may find herself out on a limb. She may participate with others in group activities or teamwork, but she will not encourage this.
SELF-CONTROL DIMENSION
This dimension evaluates how self-controlled people are in their social relationships. As the scores increases, so does people's control over their actions. The scale is calculated from the scores on G, M, Q3 and F. RX is responsible and organised. She likes to make a good impression on people. She is astute and shrewd. She shows herself to be assured and does not find it easy to take criticism. Her confidence and responsibility will ease the work of her colleagues and managers. She will be committed to obligations and make an effort to achieve goals and meet deadlines. She is unlikely to overlook details because of overconfidence.

Table C.1. Analytical Report Section of the Personality Factors Model (cont'd)

POSSIBLE STRENGTHS AND WEAKNESSES		
FACTOR	POSSIBLE POSITIVE POINTS	POSSIBLE NEGATIVE POINTS
B+	She grasps ideas and reasoning quickly and accurately She is creative, intuitive and intellectually inquisitive	She inputs very individual working methods She forms an opinion about and judges the instructions of her superiors
C+	She is very assured and balanced She does not have brusque changes of mood She unconcernedly takes action	She does not get emotionally involved in the job She can be arrogant and haughty She tends to be self-reliant
E+	She is able to consolidate her judgements She exercises authority, makes decisions and is accepted She perseveres until she achieves an objective	She intimidates and enslaves others She is hostile and violent towards others She is so stubborn and cannot be made to see reason She views her job as if it were a competition with her colleagues
H+	She is socially bold and takes risks She is resolute against adversity, determined She finds variety and novelty appealing	She is venturesome and daring, unwary She is impulsive and overlooks details She is very talkative and not very reserved
M-	She is practical and realistic, down to earth She is operational and functional She analyses the facts before making a decision	She is not very imaginative and creative She does not input novel and original solutions She is not satisfied by the recognition of her worth She is superficial and does not go into things in enough depth
Q3+	She is controlled, has self-mastery and is measured She respects rules She is wary and methodical She dictates her moods	She is overdisciplined and too thorough She gets bogged down by petty concerns and trivialities She is rigid and uncreative

Table C.1. Analytical Report Section of the Personality Factors Model (cont'd)

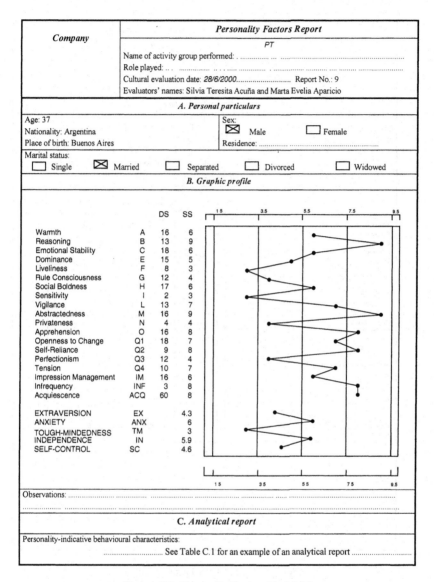

Figure C.2. Personality Factors Model # 9

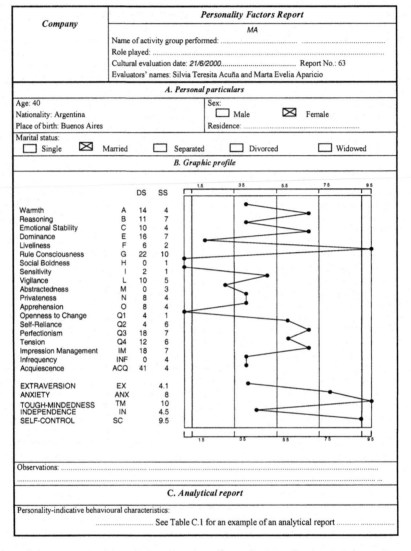

Figure C.3. Personality Factors Model # 63

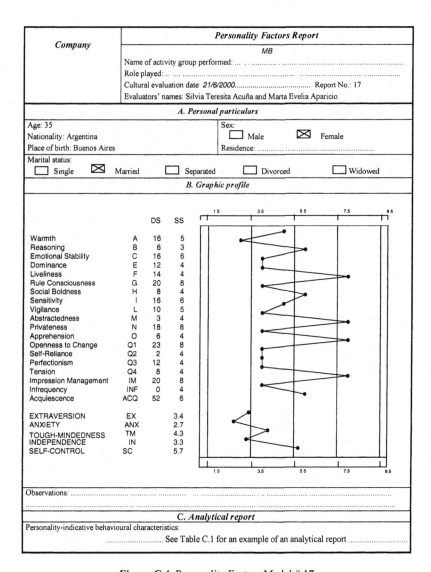

Figure C.4. Personality Factors Model # 17

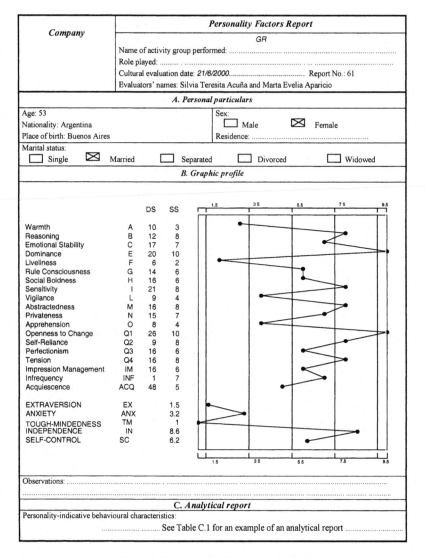

Company	Personality Factors Report

GR

Name of activity group performed: ....

Role played: ....

Cultural evaluation date: *21/6/2000*.................................... Report No.: 61

Evaluators' names: Silvia Teresita Acuña and Marta Evelia Aparicio

A. Personal particulars

Age: 53
Nationality: Argentina
Place of birth: Buenos Aires

Sex:
☐ Male   ☒ Female
Residence: ....

Marital status:
☐ Single   ☒ Married   ☐ Separated   ☐ Divorced   ☐ Widowed

B. Graphic profile

		DS	SS
Warmth	A	10	3
Reasoning	B	12	8
Emotional Stability	C	17	7
Dominance	E	20	10
Liveliness	F	6	2
Rule Consciousness	G	14	6
Social Boldness	H	16	6
Sensitivity	I	21	8
Vigilance	L	9	4
Abstractedness	M	16	8
Privateness	N	15	7
Apprehension	O	8	4
Openness to Change	Q1	26	10
Self-Reliance	Q2	9	8
Perfectionism	Q3	16	6
Tension	Q4	16	8
Impression Management	IM	16	6
Infrequency	INF	1	7
Acquiescence	ACQ	48	5
EXTRAVERSION	EX		1.5
ANXIETY	ANX		3.2
TOUGH-MINDEDNESS	TM		1
INDEPENDENCE	IN		8.6
SELF-CONTROL	SC		6.2

Observations: ....
....

C. Analytical report

Personality-indicative behavioural characteristics:
.... See Table C.1 for an example of an analytical report ....

Figure C.5. Personality Factors Model # 61

Company	Personality Factors Report
	GR'
	Name of activity group performed: ....
	Role played: . ...
	Cultural evaluation date: *21/6/2000*..................................... Report No.: 64
	Evaluators' names: Silvia Teresita Acuña and Marta Evelia Aparicio

A. Personal particulars

Age: 40	Sex:
Nationality: Argentina	☐ Male ⊠ Female
Place of birth: Buenos Aires	Residence: . .. .

Marital status:
☐ Single   ☐ Married   ☐ Separated   ☐ Divorced   ⊠ Widowed

B. Graphic profile

		DS	SS
Warmth	A	14	4
Reasoning	B	7	3
Emotional Stability	C	8	4
Dominance	E	10	4
Liveliness	F	14	4
Rule Consciousness	G	19	8
Social Boldness	H	14	6
Sensitivity	I	15	5
Vigilance	L	10	5
Abstractedness	M	0	3
Privateness	N	8	4
Apprehension	O	16	6
Openness to Change	Q1	4	1
Self-Reliance	Q2	0	3
Perfectionism	Q3	14	5
Tension	Q4	14	7
Impression Management	IM	7	3
Infrequency	INF	1	7
Acquiescence	ACQ	44	4
EXTRAVERSION	EX		6.9
ANXIETY	ANX		7.7
TOUGH-MINDEDNESS	TM		10
INDEPENDENCE	IN		3
SELF-CONTROL	SC		6.7

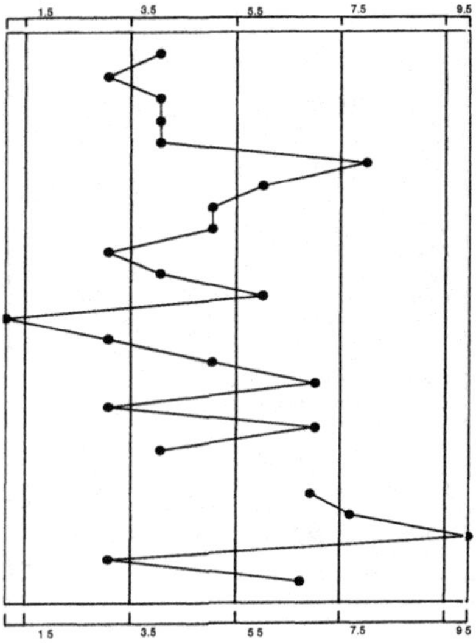

Observations: ....
....

C. Analytical report

Personality-indicative behavioural characteristics:
.... See Table C.1 for an example of an analytical report ....

Figure C.6. Personality Factors Model # 64

Company	**Personality Factors Report**
	RD
	Name of activity group performed: ....
	Role played: ....
	Cultural evaluation date: *21/6/2000*......................... Report No.: 7
	Evaluators' names: Silvia Teresita Acuña and Marta Evelia Aparicio

A. Personal particulars

Age: 47

Nationality: Argentina

Place of birth: Buenos Aires

Sex: ☒ Male ☐ Female

Residence: ....

Marital status:

☐ Single ☒ Married ☐ Separated ☐ Divorced ☐ Widowed

B. Graphic profile

		DS	SS
Warmth	A	14	5
Reasoning	B	8	4
Emotional Stability	C	12	4
Dominance	E	7	2
Liveliness	F	9	3
Rule Consciousness	G	21	8
Social Boldness	H	8	4
Sensitivity	I	13	8
Vigilance	L	6	4
Abstractedness	M	8	7
Privateness	N	8	5
Apprehension	O	8	6
Openness to Change	Q1	18	7
Self-Reliance	Q2	6	7
Perfectionism	Q3	8	3
Tension	Q4	6	6
Impression Management	IM	17	6
Infrequency	INF	0	7
Acquiescence	ACQ	45	4
EXTRAVERSION	EX		4.2
ANXIETY	ANX		4.1
TOUGH-MINDEDNESS	TM		3.1
INDEPENDENCE	IN		1
SELF-CONTROL	SC		5.8

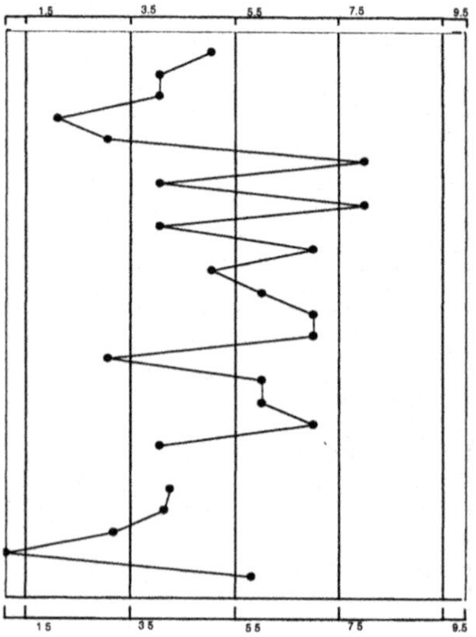

Observations: ....

....

C. Analytical report

Personality-indicative behavioural characteristics:

.... See Table C.1 for an example of an analytical report ....

Figure C.7. Personality Factors Model # 7

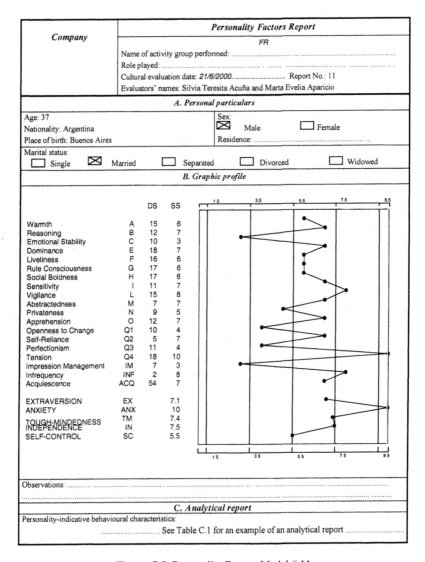

Figure C.8. Personality Factors Model # 11

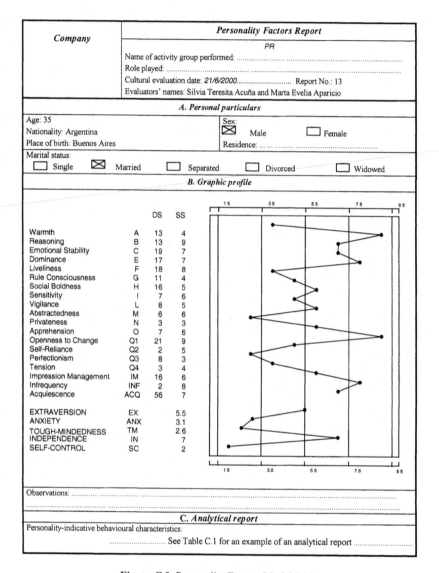

		DS	SS
Warmth	A	13	4
Reasoning	B	13	9
Emotional Stability	C	19	7
Dominance	E	17	7
Liveliness	F	18	8
Rule Consciousness	G	11	4
Social Boldness	H	16	5
Sensitivity	I	7	6
Vigilance	L	8	5
Abstractedness	M	6	6
Privateness	N	3	3
Apprehension	O	7	6
Openness to Change	Q1	21	9
Self-Reliance	Q2	2	5
Perfectionism	Q3	8	3
Tension	Q4	3	4
Impression Management	IM	16	6
Infrequency	INF	2	8
Acquiescence	ACQ	56	7
EXTRAVERSION	EX		5.5
ANXIETY	ANX		3.1
TOUGH-MINDEDNESS	TM		2.6
INDEPENDENCE	IN		7
SELF-CONTROL	SC		2

Figure C.9. Personality Factors Model # 13

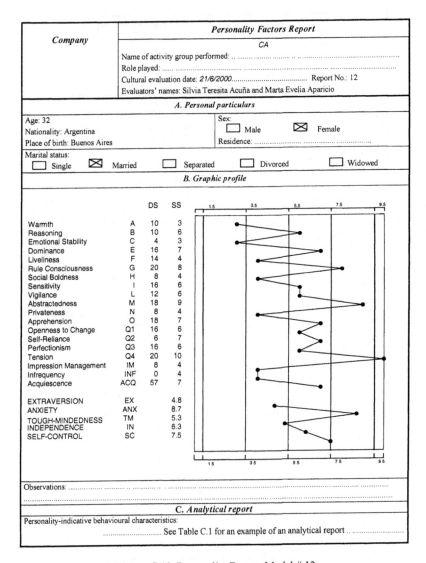

Figure C.10. Personality Factors Model # 12

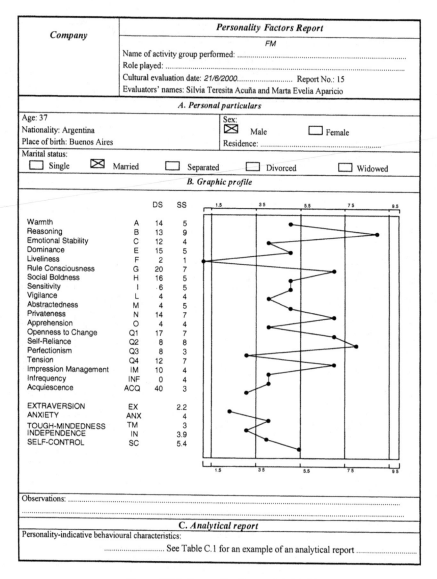

| Company | **Personality Factors Report** |
| | FM |

Name of activity group performed: ....
Role played: ....
Cultural evaluation date: *21/6/2000*.......................... Report No.: 15
Evaluators' names: Silvia Teresita Acuña and Marta Evelia Aparicio

A. Personal particulars

Age: 37
Nationality: Argentina
Place of birth: Buenos Aires

Sex:
☒ Male   ☐ Female
Residence: ....

Marital status:
☐ Single   ☒ Married   ☐ Separated   ☐ Divorced   ☐ Widowed

B. Graphic profile

		DS	SS
Warmth	A	14	5
Reasoning	B	13	9
Emotional Stability	C	12	4
Dominance	E	15	5
Liveliness	F	2	1
Rule Consciousness	G	20	7
Social Boldness	H	16	5
Sensitivity	I	6	5
Vigilance	L	4	4
Abstractedness	M	4	5
Privateness	N	14	7
Apprehension	O	4	4
Openness to Change	Q1	17	7
Self-Reliance	Q2	8	8
Perfectionism	Q3	8	3
Tension	Q4	12	7
Impression Management	IM	10	4
Infrequency	INF	0	4
Acquiescence	ACQ	40	3
EXTRAVERSION	EX		2.2
ANXIETY	ANX		4
TOUGH-MINDEDNESS	TM		3
INDEPENDENCE	IN		3.9
SELF-CONTROL	SC		5.4

Observations: ....
....

C. Analytical report

Personality-indicative behavioural characteristics:
.... See Table C.1 for an example of an analytical report ....

Figure C.11. Personality Factors Model # 15

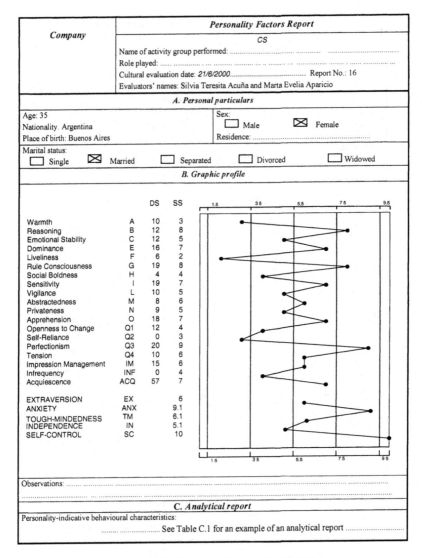

Company	**Personality Factors Report**
	CS
	Name of activity group performed: ....
	Role played: ....
	Cultural evaluation date: *21/6/2000*.................................... Report No.: 16
	Evaluators' names: Silvia Teresita Acuña and Marta Evelia Aparicio

A. Personal particulars

Age: 35
Nationality. Argentina
Place of birth: Buenos Aires

Sex:
☐ Male   ☒ Female
Residence: ....

Marital status:
☐ Single   ☒ Married   ☐ Separated   ☐ Divorced   ☐ Widowed

B. Graphic profile

		DS	SS
Warmth	A	10	3
Reasoning	B	12	8
Emotional Stability	C	12	5
Dominance	E	16	7
Liveliness	F	6	2
Rule Consciousness	G	19	8
Social Boldness	H	4	4
Sensitivity	I	19	7
Vigilance	L	10	5
Abstractedness	M	8	6
Privateness	N	9	5
Apprehension	O	18	7
Openness to Change	Q1	12	4
Self-Reliance	Q2	0	3
Perfectionism	Q3	20	9
Tension	Q4	10	6
Impression Management	IM	15	6
Infrequency	INF	0	4
Acquiescence	ACQ	57	7
EXTRAVERSION	EX		6
ANXIETY	ANX		9.1
TOUGH-MINDEDNESS	TM		6.1
INDEPENDENCE	IN		5.1
SELF-CONTROL	SC		10

Observations: ....
....

C. Analytical report

Personality-indicative behavioural characteristics:
.... See Table C.1 for an example of an analytical report ....

Figure C.12. Personality Factors Model # 16

Company	Personality Factors Report
	CR

Name of activity group performed: ....
Role played: ....
Cultural evaluation date: *21/6/2000*.......................... Report No.: 40
Evaluators' names: Silvia Teresita Acuña and Marta Evelia Aparicio

A. Personal particulars

Age: 45

Nationality: Argentina

Place of birth: Buenos Aires

Sex:
☒ Male   ☐ Female

Residence: ....

Marital status:
☐ Single   ☒ Married   ☐ Separated   ☐ Divorced   ☐ Widowed

B. Graphic profile

		DS	SS
Warmth	A	2	1
Reasoning	B	13	9
Emotional Stability	C	15	4
Dominance	E	15	5
Liveliness	F	8	3
Rule Consciousness	G	15	5
Social Boldness	H	10	4
Sensitivity	I	5	4
Vigilance	L	14	7
Abstractedness	M	8	7
Privateness	N	11	6
Apprehension	O	14	7
Openness to Change	Q1	14	6
Self-Reliance	Q2	11	8
Perfectionism	Q3	7	3
Tension	Q4	14	8
Impression Management	IM	6	3
Infrequency	INF	3	8
Acquiescence	ACQ	64	9
EXTRAVERSION	EX		1.5
ANXIETY	ANX		6.4
TOUGH-MINDEDNESS	TM		6.2
INDEPENDENCE	IN		5.9
SELF-CONTROL	SC		3.3

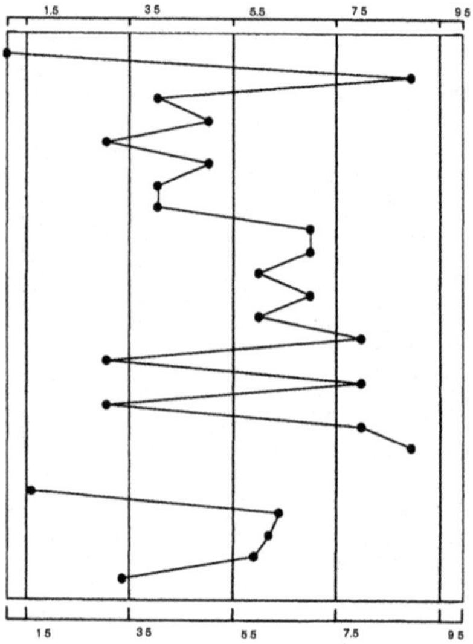

Observations: ....
....

C. Analytical report

Personality-indicative behavioural characteristics:
.... See Table C.1 for an example of an analytical report ....

Figure C.13. Personality Factors Model # 40

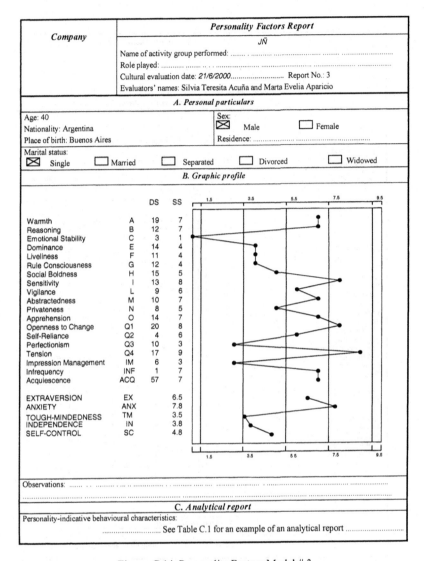

Figure C.14. Personality Factors Model # 3

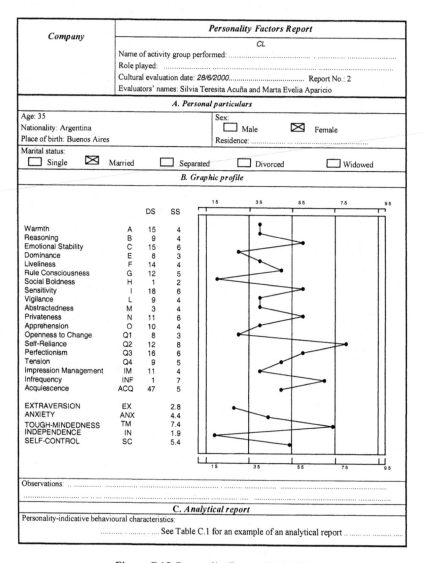

		DS	SS
Warmth	A	15	4
Reasoning	B	9	4
Emotional Stability	C	15	6
Dominance	E	8	3
Liveliness	F	14	4
Rule Consciousness	G	12	5
Social Boldness	H	1	2
Sensitivity	I	18	6
Vigilance	L	9	4
Abstractedness	M	3	4
Privateness	N	11	6
Apprehension	O	10	4
Openness to Change	Q1	8	3
Self-Reliance	Q2	12	8
Perfectionism	Q3	16	6
Tension	Q4	9	5
Impression Management	IM	11	4
Infrequency	INF	1	7
Acquiescence	ACQ	47	5
EXTRAVERSION	EX		2.8
ANXIETY	ANX		4.4
TOUGH-MINDEDNESS	TM		7.4
INDEPENDENCE	IN		1.9
SELF-CONTROL	SC		5.4

Personality Factors Report — CL

Name of activity group performed: ....

Role played: ....

Cultural evaluation date: *28/6/2000*...................................... Report No.: 2

Evaluators' names: Silvia Teresita Acuña and Marta Evelia Aparicio

A. Personal particulars

Age: 35
Nationality: Argentina
Place of birth: Buenos Aires

Sex: ☐ Male ☒ Female
Residence: ....

Marital status:
☐ Single ☒ Married ☐ Separated ☐ Divorced ☐ Widowed

B. Graphic profile

Observations: ....

C. Analytical report

Personality-indicative behavioural characteristics:

.... See Table C.1 for an example of an analytical report ....

Figure C.15. Personality Factors Model # 2

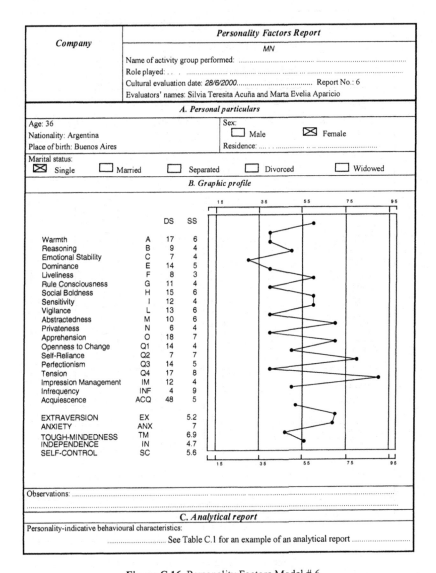

			Personality Factors Report			
Company			MN			

A. Personal particulars

Age: 36
Nationality: Argentina
Place of birth: Buenos Aires

Sex:
☐ Male   ☒ Female
Residence: ....

Marital status:
☒ Single   ☐ Married   ☐ Separated   ☐ Divorced   ☐ Widowed

B. Graphic profile

		DS	SS
Warmth	A	17	6
Reasoning	B	9	4
Emotional Stability	C	7	4
Dominance	E	14	5
Liveliness	F	8	3
Rule Consciousness	G	11	4
Social Boldness	H	15	6
Sensitivity	I	12	4
Vigilance	L	13	6
Abstractedness	M	10	6
Privateness	N	6	4
Apprehension	O	18	7
Openness to Change	Q1	14	4
Self-Reliance	Q2	7	7
Perfectionism	Q3	14	5
Tension	Q4	17	8
Impression Management	IM	12	4
Infrequency	INF	4	9
Acquiescence	ACQ	48	5
EXTRAVERSION	EX		5.2
ANXIETY	ANX		7
TOUGH-MINDEDNESS	TM		6.9
INDEPENDENCE	IN		4.7
SELF-CONTROL	SC		5.6

Observations: ....

C. Analytical report

Personality-indicative behavioural characteristics:
.... See Table C.1 for an example of an analytical report ....

Figure C.16. Personality Factors Model # 6

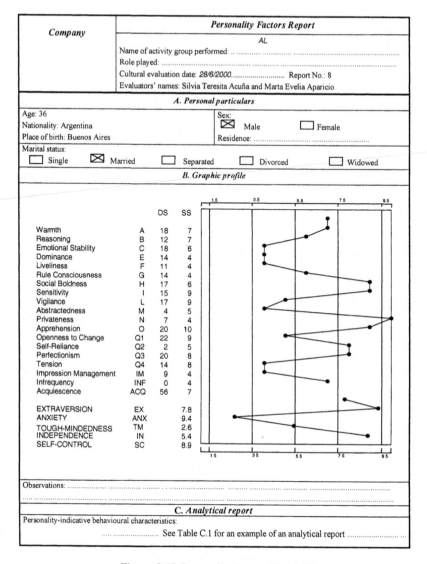

Figure C.17. Personality Factors Model # 8

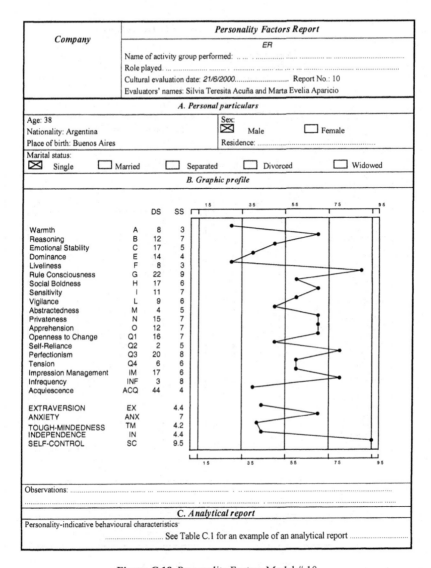

Figure C.18. Personality Factors Model # 10

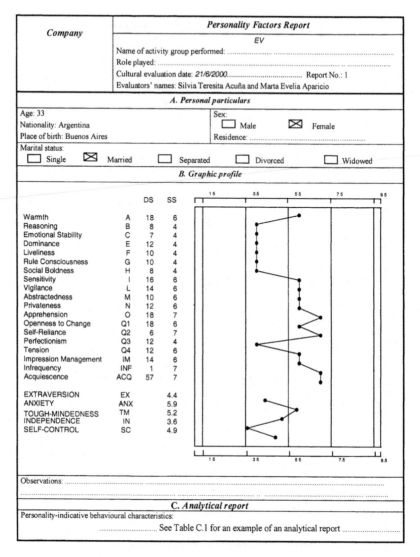

Figure C.19. Personality Factors Model # 1

Company	**Personality Factors Report**
	AF
	Name of activity group performed: ....
	Role played: ....
	Cultural evaluation date. *21/6/2000*........................... Report No.: 14
	Evaluators' names: Silvia Teresita Acuña and Marta Evelia Aparicio

A. Personal particulars

Age: 35
Nationality: Argentina
Place of birth: Buenos Aires

Sex:
☒ Male   ☐ Female
Residence: ....

Marital status:
☐ Single   ☒ Married   ☐ Separated   ☐ Divorced   ☐ Widowed

B. Graphic profile

		DS	SS
Warmth	A	6	2
Reasoning	B	5	2
Emotional Stability	C	4	2
Dominance	E	12	4
Liveliness	F	4	2
Rule Consciousness	G	17	6
Social Boldness	H	4	3
Sensitivity	I	11	7
Vigilance	L	8	5
Abstractedness	M	9	7
Privateness	N	16	8
Apprehension	O	12	7
Openness to Change	Q1	20	8
Self-Reliance	Q2	12	9
Perfectionism	Q3	16	5
Tension	Q4	2	4
Impression Management	IM	16	6
Infrequency	INF	0	4
Acquiescence	ACQ	44	4
EXTRAVERSION	EX		1
ANXIETY	ANX		3.8
TOUGH-MINDEDNESS	TM		2.5
INDEPENDENCE	IN		2.4
SELF-CONTROL	SC		6.3

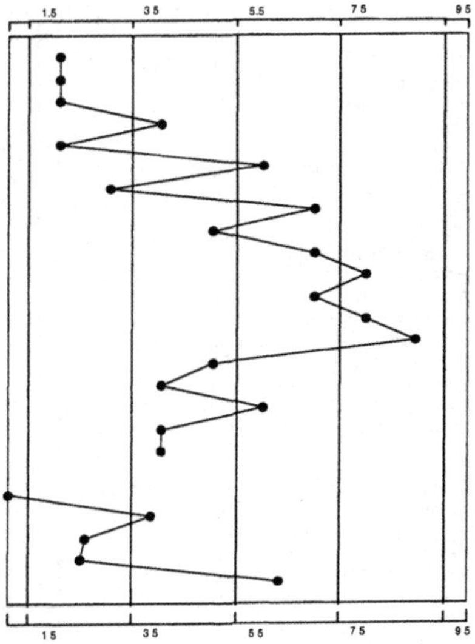

Observations ....
....

C. Analytical report

Personality-indicative behavioural characteristics:
.... See Table C.1 for an example of an analytical report ....

Figure C.20. Personality Factors Model # 14

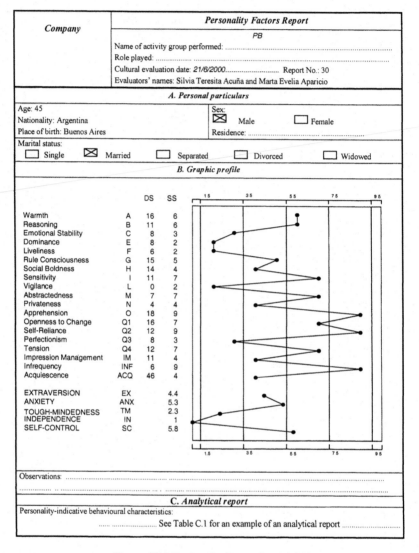

Figure C.21. Personality Factors Model # 30

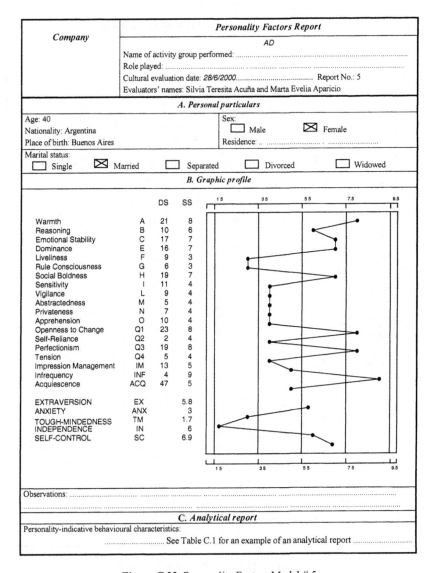

Company	*Personality Factors Report*		
	AD		
	Name of activity group performed:		
	Role played:		
	Cultural evaluation date: *28/6/2000*.................................... Report No.: 5		
	Evaluators' names: Silvia Teresita Acuña and Marta Evelia Aparicio		

A. Personal particulars

Age: 40
Nationality: Argentina
Place of birth: Buenos Aires

Sex:
☐ Male   ☒ Female
Residence: .. ..

Marital status:
☐ Single   ☒ Married   ☐ Separated   ☐ Divorced   ☐ Widowed

B. Graphic profile

		DS	SS
Warmth	A	21	8
Reasoning	B	10	6
Emotional Stability	C	17	7
Dominance	E	16	7
Liveliness	F	9	3
Rule Consciousness	G	6	3
Social Boldness	H	19	7
Sensitivity	I	11	4
Vigilance	L	9	4
Abstractedness	M	5	4
Privateness	N	7	4
Apprehension	O	10	4
Openness to Change	Q1	23	8
Self-Reliance	Q2	2	4
Perfectionism	Q3	19	8
Tension	Q4	5	4
Impression Management	IM	13	5
Infrequency	INF	4	9
Acquiescence	ACQ	47	5
EXTRAVERSION	EX		5.8
ANXIETY	ANX		3
TOUGH-MINDEDNESS	TM		1.7
INDEPENDENCE	IN		6
SELF-CONTROL	SC		6.9

Observations: ....
....

C. Analytical report

Personality-indicative behavioural characteristics:
.... See Table C.1 for an example of an analytical report ....

Figure C.22. Personality Factors Model # 5

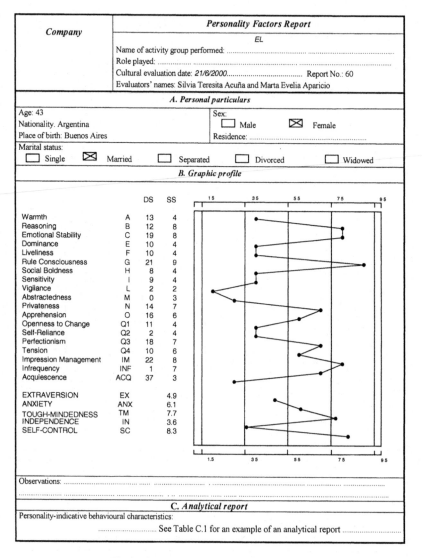

		DS	SS	
Warmth	A	13	4	
Reasoning	B	12	8	
Emotional Stability	C	19	8	
Dominance	E	10	4	
Liveliness	F	10	4	
Rule Consciousness	G	21	9	
Social Boldness	H	8	4	
Sensitivity	I	9	4	
Vigilance	L	2	2	
Abstractedness	M	0	3	
Privateness	N	14	7	
Apprehension	O	16	6	
Openness to Change	Q1	11	4	
Self-Reliance	Q2	2	4	
Perfectionism	Q3	18	7	
Tension	Q4	10	6	
Impression Management	IM	22	8	
Infrequency	INF	1	7	
Acquiescence	ACQ	37	3	
EXTRAVERSION	EX		4.9	
ANXIETY	ANX		6.1	
TOUGH-MINDEDNESS	TM		7.7	
INDEPENDENCE	IN		3.6	
SELF-CONTROL	SC		8.3	

Figure C.23. Personality Factors Model # 60

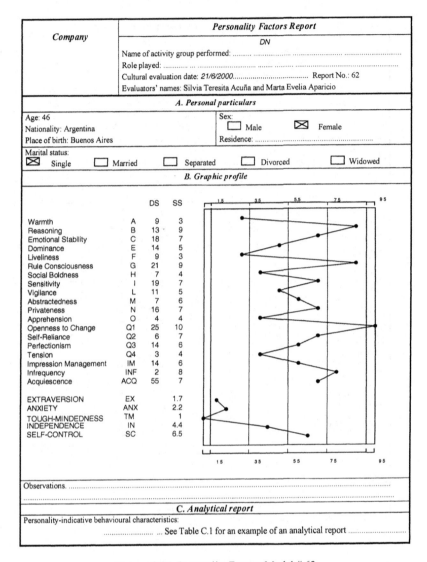

Figure C.24. Personality Factors Model # 62

Company	Personality Factors Report
	SL

Name of activity group performed: ....
Role played: ....
Cultural evaluation date: *28/6/2000*................................... Report No · 100
Evaluators' names: Silvia Teresita Acuña and Marta Evelia Aparicio

A. Personal particulars

Age: 35
Nationality: Argentina
Place of birth: Buenos Aires

Sex:
☐ Male   ☒ Female
Residence: ....

Marital status:
☒ Single   ☐ Married   ☐ Separated   ☐ Divorced   ☐ Widowed

B. Graphic profile

		DS	SS
Warmth	A	16	5
Reasoning	B	10	6
Emotional Stability	C	12	5
Dominance	E	11	4
Liveliness	F	11	4
Rule Consciousness	G	12	5
Social Boldness	H	6	4
Sensitivity	I	20	8
Vigilance	L	11	5
Abstractedness	M	18	9
Privateness	N	8	4
Apprehension	O	10	4
Openness to Change	Q1	20	7
Self-Reliance	Q2	9	8
Perfectionism	Q3	16	6
Tension	Q4	4	4
Impression Management	IM	16	6
Infrequency	INF	0	4
Acquiescence	ACQ	62	8
EXTRAVERSION	EX		3.9
ANXIETY	ANX		3.3
TOUGH-MINDEDNESS	TM		1
INDEPENDENCE	IN		2.7
SELF-CONTROL	SC		5.4

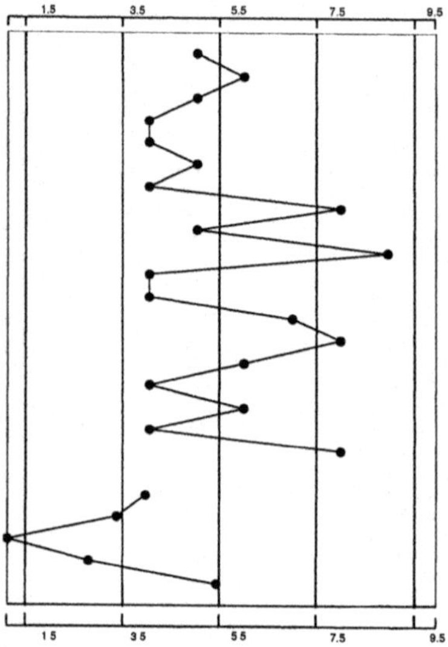

Observations: ....
....

C. Analytical report

Personality-indicative behavioural characteristics:
.... See Table C.1 for an example of an analytical report ....

Figure C.25. Personality Factors Model # 100

Company	**Personality Factors Report**
	AK
	Name of activity group performed: ... .
	Role played: .. ..
	Cultural evaluation date: *21/6/2000*.......................... Report No.: 18
	Evaluators' names: Silvia Teresita Acuña and Marta Evelia Aparicio

A. Personal particulars

Age: 35
Nationality: Argentina
Place of birth: Buenos Aires

Sex:
☒ Male   ☐ Female
Residence: ....

Marital status:
☐ Single   ☒ Married   ☐ Separated   ☐ Divorced   ☐ Widowed

B. Graphic profile

		DS	SS
Warmth	A	14	5
Reasoning	B	13	9
Emotional Stability	C	18	6
Dominance	E	12	7
Liveliness	F	22	4
Rule- Consciousness	G	19	9
Social Boldness	H	6	7
Sensitivity	I	11	5
Vigilance	L	7	6
Abstractedness	M	8	7
Privateness	N	8	5
Apprehension	O	16	6
Openness to Change	Q1	1	7
Self-Reliance	Q2	16	4
Perfectionism	Q3	1	5
Tension	Q4	16	7
Impression Management	IM	9	7
Infrequency	IN	18	10
Acquiescence	ACQ	50	6
EXTRAVERSION	EX		6.1
ANXIETY	ANX		6.5
TOUGH-MINDEDNESS	TM		3.9
INDEPENDENCE	IN		7
SELF-CONTROL	SC		7.1

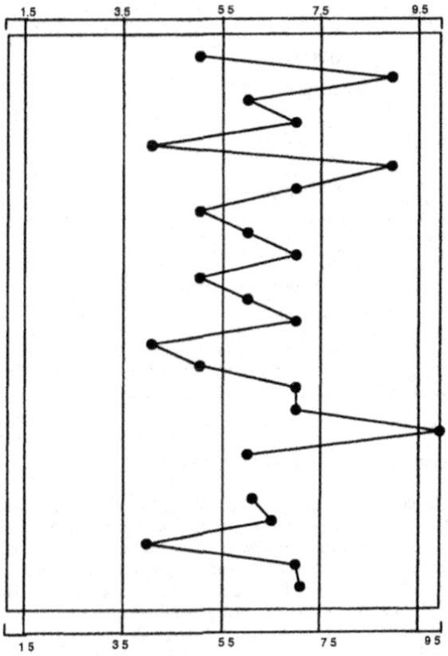

Observations: ....
....

C. Analytical report

Personality-indicative behavioural characteristics:
.... See Table C.1 for an example of an analytical report ....

Figure C.26. Personality Factors Model # 18

Company	Capabilities Report
	RX
	Name of activity group performed: ....
	Role played: ....
	Cultural evaluation date: 28/7/2000.......................... Report No.: 4
	Evaluators' names: Silvia Teresita Acuña and Marta Evelia Aparicio

A. Personal particulars

Age: 33	Sex:
Nationality: Argentina	☐ Male ☒ Female
Place of birth: Buenos Aires	Residence: ....

Marital status:

☐ Single   ☒ Married   ☐ Separated   ☐ Divorced   ☐ Widowed

B. Capabilities or behavioural competencies

No.	Competency	Competency level
1	Analysis	High
2	Independence	High
3	Judgement	High
4	Tenacity	High
5	Self-Organisation	High
6	Risk Management	High
7	Discipline	Average
8	Environmental Orientation	Average
9	Teamwork/Cooperation	Average
10	Group Leadership	Average
11	Planning and Organisation	High

Observations: ....

C. General summary

Personality characteristics and skills:

RX stands out on rationality and astuteness. She is likely to excel in jobs that involve thinking and reasoning. Being rational, she is likely to be very proficient at creative or teaching jobs or occupations that place high demands on intellectual resources. She is tenacious, dominant, aggressive, energetic and will persistently argue her ideas and viewpoints. However, this will not necessarily lead her into insurmountable conflicts with colleagues. She is not a person who blindly fights to get her ideas through, although she will defend them tactfully. She is likely to be a good salesperson and will struggle to get customers to sign a contract.
She is likely to be highly regarded by her superiors, as she will conscientiously accept any rule they enforce. Jobs involving thought and reflection, such as the scientific and technical professions, would be ideal positions for her.
She will take risks that others turn away from. She is firm in the face of difficulties and usually accepts responsibility for her acts. She contributes to creating an agreeable and pleasant working environment. However, she is easily manipulated and deceived, and is, therefore, not recommended for jobs that require strength and decisiveness, like supervisory positions.
RX is objective and realistic, looking for immediate benefits and acting on practical grounds only. She is not very creative or original, which may be a limitation. She will focus well on her work, especially if it involves mechanical behaviour with little room for decision making. She tends to be thorough, and is unlikely to leave a job unfinished.
She is frank and sincere, which may put her at odds with other colleagues or customers. In more complicated situations, however, she will know just how far to go. She should not work dealing with claims or in direct sales. She would be better suited for help or assistance jobs.
At work she will show herself to have a headstrong character, quick to pass judgement on others but far from willing to accept criticism herself. She may appear to be sure of her decisions. If anything goes wrong, however, she will want to have nothing to do with the matter. She is likely to be a loyal employee, who, faced with the uncertain prospects of a change, prefers to stay in the same place for a long time. She is very much a perfectionist, which leads her demand a lot of herself and never to be satisfied with her actions. In her interpersonal behaviour, she will be constantly watchful of the impression she causes, analysing her every word or action. Being a person inclined to perfectionism and thoroughness, she may often to fall prey to impractical obsessions that slow down her work and affect her performance. Her job should ideally not include risk taking.

Figure C.27. Capabilities Report # 4

Company	**Capabilities Report**	
	PTT	
	Name of activity group performed:	
	Role played:	
	Cultural evaluation date: *28/7/2000*.......................... List No.: 9	
	Evaluators' names: Silvia Teresita Acuña and Marta Evelia Aparicio	

A. Personal particulars

Age: 37	Sex:
Nationality: Argentina	☒ Male ☐ Female
Place of birth: Buenos Aires	Residence: ....

Marital status:
☐ Single   ☒ Married   ☐ Separated   ☐ Divorced   ☐ Widowed

B. Capabilities or behavioural competencies

No.	Competency	Competency level
1	Innovation/creativity	High
2	Risk management	High
3	Environmental knowledge	High

Observations: ....
....

C. General summary

Personality characteristics and skills:

PT is an intelligent and astute person, capable of understanding and establishing relationships, and grasping ideas. He is likely to perform well in jobs that involve thinking and reasoning. Being rational, he is likely to be very proficient in creative or teaching jobs or occupations that place high demands on intellectual resources.

He is likely to be highly regarded by his superiors, as he will conscientiously accept any rule they enforce. Jobs involving thought and reflection, such as the scientific and technical professions, would be ideal positions for him.

He may be unconcerned about, or neglectful and careless of obligations. He has little perseverance. His carelessness may cause conflicts within work teams.

He is a rational and logical person. He will analyse problems focusing on the facts only, rejecting any trace of subjectivity. Jobs requiring fast and clear-cut action, where cool-headedness is a priority, are his strongest suit. This could be a good profile for performing supervisory or management jobs in organisations with clearly delimited hierarchical levels, where he is unlikely to have much contact with subordinates.

He tends to be obstinate and takes pains to put his viewpoints over. He is somewhat distrustful, as he thinks people are talking behind his back. He likes to unearth and air other people's mistakes. His interpersonal tendencies could cloud the working environment. He would get on well in highly competitive jobs.

He is very creative and imaginative. He will input great ideas to his work, although he may sometimes disregard risks. He may appear to be detached from his work and will find it hard to concentrate on monotonous and repetitive tasks. His divergent thinking is a great ally for succeeding in jobs the involve inventiveness and creativeness.

His frankness and sincerity may put him at odds with other colleagues or clients. In more complicated situations, however, he will know just how far to go. It is inadvisable that he should be employed to deal with claims or work in direct sales, as he will find it difficult to sell the excellences of the product in question. His profile is more typical of assistance and help occupations.

He suffers more than normal when his work is criticised. He is likely to be emotionally affected by any rebuke, which he will find discouraging.

He may cause conflicts at work, because he likes to bend the rules and tends to disregard instructions from his superiors with which he does not agree. Jobs that afford some independence and involve a wide variety of tasks would be the best positions for him.

He is self-confident and prefers to do things his own way, and, therefore, is likely to find it difficult to get used to teamwork. He is very analytical and will espouse extremely impartial positions in any negotiation. The technical and research occupations would be his strongest suit, especially if they have a supervisory or management status.

He is led by his own opinion and is sometimes tactless. He may be disorganised and careless, and he does not find it easy to adhere to systematic methods. It is not advisable that he be given major responsibilities, nor would he get on well in rigid and inflexible environments.

He is a tense person, who is likely to transmit his edginess to other people that he has dealings with. He is overconcerned about less important matters. His anxiety may have an effect on his skills of analysis and observation, and he may appear to be forgetful or neglectful.

Figure C.28. Capabilities Report # 9

Company	Capabilities Report
	MA

Name of activity group performed: ....
Role played: ....
Cultural evaluation date: *28/7/2000*... List No.: 63
Evaluators' names: Silvia Teresita Acuña and Marta Evelia Aparicio

A. Personal particulars

Age: 40
Nationality: Argentina
Place of birth: Buenos Aires

Sex:
☐ Male   ☒ Female
Residence: ....

Marital status:
☐ Single   ☒ Married   ☐ Separated   ☐ Divorced   ☐ Widowed

B. Capabilities or behavioural competencies

No.	Competency	Competency level
1	Analysis	High
2	Decision making	High
3	Judgement	High
4	Self-organisation	High
5	Risk management	High
6	Discipline	High
7	Planning and organisation	High

Observations: ....
....

C. General summary

Personality characteristics and skills:

MA is not likely to be proficient at tasks that involve interpersonal contact.
Professionally, she is likely to excel in jobs that involve thinking and reasoning. Being rational, she is likely to be very proficient in creative or teaching jobs or occupations that place high demands on intellectual resources.
She has the qualities of a good salesperson in the sense that she will fight to get customers to sign a contract and assure that the pre-established terms are complied with.
Jobs involving thought and reflection, as well as self-discipline and conscientiousness, would be ideal positions for her. Being rational and logical, she can analyse problems focusing on the facts only, and is, therefore, well qualified to perform jobs requiring fast and clear-cut actions.
Closely supervised jobs are ideal positions for her. She will be highly stressed by changes to her job and will distrust any enforced working method.
She is a person who may be checked by her disinterest in change and innovation, and will act based on tried and tested methods and procedures.
She is a sincere person, which may put her at odds with colleagues and customers. Therefore, it is inadvisable that she be employed to deal with claims or work in direct sales.
She has a profile that tolerates routine jobs, and she is likely to be a loyal employee who will withstand highly disciplined professions.
She is useful as a member of a work team, as she will input inventiveness and originality, whereas she will not find it difficult to take up the concept of team.
MA's profile is somewhat confusing, because, in some areas, she appears to manage well working on tasks where a measure of creativity comes into play, whereas, on other points, changes do not appear to be very in line with her personality.
Therefore, we think that she could excel in areas where she has to provide input, but where she is not in continuous contact with customers, or in work teams.

Figure C.29. Capabilities Report # 63

Company	Capabilities Report
	MB
	Name of activity group performed: ....
	Role played: . .. .
	Cultural evaluation date: 28/7/2000....................................... List No.: 17
	Evaluators' names: Silvia Teresita Acuña and Marta Evelia Aparicio

A. Personal particulars

Age: 35	Sex:
Nationality: Argentina	☐ Male ☒ Female
Place of birth: Buenos Aires	Residence: ....

Marital status:
  ☐ Single   ☒ Married   ☐ Separated   ☐ Divorced   ☐ Widowed

B. Capabilities or behavioural competencies

No.	Competency	Competency level
1	Stress tolerance	High
2	Discipline	High
3	Environmental orientation	Average
4	Teamwork/cooperation	High
5	Coworker evaluation	High

Observations: ....

C. General summary

Personality characteristics and skills:

MB will easily get used to tasks that are not totally devoid of interpersonal contact, as she has some social skill, especially for relating to customers.
She will get on confidently in jobs where she has all the information she needs to perform her routine tasks.
She will conscientiously respect rules, and jobs involving thought and reflection are ideal positions for her. She also has a strong sense of responsibility and of established rules.
She is an emotionally stable person, and will, therefore, be able to take criticism, controlling herself in disagreeable situations. Professionally, she will prefer jobs where emotional control is not a requirement against the job in question.
She is objective and realistic, looking for immediate benefits and acting on practical grounds only. She is not very creative or original, which may be a limitation, as she is not open to change and innovation and always acts according to tried and tested methods and procedures. In this respect, she will focus well on her work, especially if it involves mechanical behaviour, albeit with some room for decision making.
She is a calculating person, and her pains to impress others may be interpreted by her colleagues as falseness. She is ambitious and socially assured. She will get on well in environments that require extreme diplomacy, where success largely depends on selling oneself.
She is self-confident, lively and vigorous. She does not let tensions get her down and tries to rationalise any appraisable fear. She will occasionally find it difficult to accept responsibility for her mistakes even in face of evidence that they are hers. She may find it difficult to understand others and will be perceived as a cool and distant person.
Professionally, she prefers to be given some independence and jobs that involve a variety of tasks. She will be cooperative and participatory, she prefers to work in the company of others and follows instructions without questioning or contravening them. She is motivated by other people's appreciation and enjoys praise of her work. She could encounter difficulties in management jobs, but might, on the other hand, be a loyal and disciplined subordinate.

Figure C.30. Capabilities Report # 17

Company	Capabilities Report
	GR
	Name of activity group performed: ....
	Role played: ....
	Cultural evaluation date: *28/7/2000*.................................... List No.: 61
	Evaluators' names: Silvia Teresita Acuña and Marta Evelia Aparicio

A. Personal particulars

Age: 53	Sex:
Nationality: Argentina	☐ Male ☒ Female
Place of birth: Buenos Aires	Residence: .. ..

Marital status:
☐ Single   ☒ Married   ☐ Separated   ☐ Divorced   ☐ Widowed

B. Capabilities or behavioural competencies

No.	Competency	Competency level
1	Independence	High
2	Innovation/creativity	High
3	Self-organisation	Average
4	Risk management	High
5	Discipline	Average
6	Environmental orientation	High
7	Coworker evaluation	High
8	Planning and organisation	Average

Observations: ....
....

C. General summary

Personality characteristics and skills:

GR has excellent powers of analysis and concentration. Professionally, she is likely to excel in jobs that involve thinking and reasoning. Being rational, she is likely to be very proficient in creative or teaching jobs or occupations that place high demands on intellectual resources.
She is not contented by teamwork, and is indifferent to others. The working environment may be obscured where individuals with this same profile compete. Working in the sales field, however, her tenacity and constancy will lead her on to great success.
Professionally, she will find it difficult to make unclear decisions, although she will not hesitate to act where the prospect of success is certain.
She will not be at home performing tasks that require fast and clear-cut action.
She is the type of person that contributes to creating an agreeable and pleasant working environment. Being gullible, however, she is not recommended for jobs that require strength and decisiveness, like supervisory positions.
She will input good ideas to her work, as she is divergent thinker, which is a great ally for succeeding in jobs the involve inventiveness and creativeness.
She is suited for jobs where a measure of diplomacy comes into play and she will need to sell herself, as she is guaranteed to manage very well.
At work, she prefers to do things her own way, and she may find it difficult to get used to teamwork. Graciela prefers to work on her own and will perform well in areas that involve a variety of creative tasks

Figure C.31. Capabilities Report # 61

Company	Capabilities Report
	GR'
	Name of activity group performed: .... Role played: .... Cultural evaluation date: 28/7/2000.. List No.: 64 Evaluators' names: Silvia Teresita Acuña and Marta Evelia Aparicio

A. Personal particulars

Age: 40 Nationality: Argentina Place of birth: Buenos Aires	Sex: ☐ Male ☒ Female Residence: ....

Marital status:

☐ Single   ☐ Married   ☐ Separated   ☐ Divorced   ☒ Widowed

B. Capabilities or behavioural competencies

No.	Competency	Competency level
1	Decision making	High
2	Discipline	High
3	Empathy	High
4	Sociability	High
5	Teamwork/cooperation	High

Observations: ....
....

C. General summary

Personality characteristics and skills:

From her profile, GR' would be suited for jobs involving interpersonal contact. She finds it easy to get on with others, she likes people and has the ability to forge bonds with others.

She is emotionally unstable, which means that she will manage well in jobs where she does not have to deal with emergencies or unexpected demands. She will also get on well in jobs that do not involve directing others and where there are dominant people to supervise and organise her work

She has a strong sense of responsibility and duty and will, therefore, be suited for occupations that require self-discipline and conscientiousness.

Creativity and originality are her noteworthy weaknesses. She will focus well on her work, especially if it involves mechanical behaviour with little room for decision making.

She is a very inflexible person who refuses to accept other people's viewpoints and will obstinately and blindly entrench herself in her own convictions. She is, therefore, very decided, and always tends to look for prompt solutions, based, however, on her own personal opinions.

GR' will best realise her potential in engineering, transfer or maintenance jobs, that is, in operational rather than management positions, provided that they do not involve directing others and where she does not have to make important decisions or create new products.

Figure C.32. Capabilities Report # 64

Company	Capabilities Report
	RD
	Name of activity group performed:
	....
	Role played: ....
	Cultural evaluation date: *28/7/2000* .... List No.: 7
	Evaluators' names: Silvia Teresita Acuña and Marta Evelia Aparicio

A. Personal particulars

Age: 47	Sex:
Nationality: Argentina	☒ Male ☐ Female
Place of birth: Buenos Aires	Residence: ....

Marital status:

☐ Single   ☒ Married   ☐ Separated   ☐ Divorced   ☐ Widowed

B. Capabilities or behavioural competencies

No.	Competency	Competency level
1	Innovation/creativity	High
2	Discipline	High
3	Environmental orientation	High

Observations: ....
....

C. General summary

Personality characteristics and skills:

RD adjusts to situations according to internal rather than environmental demands. He may be very submissive, driven by a strong desire to avoid conflicts and by an attempt to please and gain approbation. He needs to be surrounded by dominant people who supervise and organise his work. Otherwise, he is likely to get discouraged and frustrated, because he is hesitant about accepting responsibility

He tends to be sober, serious and wary. He finds it difficult to make decisions for fear of making mistakes. Professionally, he is likely to be highly regarded by his superiors, as he will conscientiously accept any rule they enforce. He has a strong sense of responsibility, duty and of established rules.

He is instinctive and emotive, which may influence his logical reasoning. Criticism will affect him more than normal to the point of lowering his performance. He might not be at home performing tasks that require fast and clear-cut action, and would get better results in job situations that require empathy.

He contributes to creating an agreeable and pleasant working environment. However, he is easy to manipulate and deceive and is, therefore, not recommended for jobs that require strength and decisiveness, like supervisory positions.

He is a creative and imaginative person. He is intellectually very active, which leads him to very often come up with new ideas and thoughts. He will input good ideas to the job. His divergent thinking is a great ally for succeeding in jobs the involve inventiveness and creativeness.

He may cause the odd dispute at work, as he likes to bend the rules and tends to disregard instructions from his superiors, provided he is clear about what he wants. He is likely to slow down meetings or teamwork and drive his colleagues to despair because he is inclined to be against everything. He may sometimes be tactless. He may appear to be disorganised and careless, and he does not find it easy to adhere to systematic methods.

He is self-confident and prefers to do things his own way. He is likely to find it difficult to get used to teamwork.

Figure C.33. Capabilities Report # 7

Company	Capabilities Report	
	FR	

Name of activity group performed: ....
Role played: ....
Cultural evaluation date: 28/7/2000.......................... List No.: 11
Evaluators' names: Silvia Teresita Acuña and Marta Evelia Aparicio

A. Personal particulars

Age: 37
Nationality: Argentina
Place of birth: Buenos Aires

Sex: ☒ Male ☐ Female
Residence: ....

Marital status:
☐ Single ☒ Married ☐ Separated ☐ Divorced ☐ Widowed

B. Capabilities or behavioural competencies

No.	Competency	Competency level
1	Decision making	High
2	Independence	High
3	Risk management	High
4	Discipline	Average
5	Environmental orientation	High
6	Customer service	Average
7	Empathy	Average
8	Sociability	Average

Observations. ....

C. General summary

Personality characteristics and skills:

FR has the profile of someone who is somewhat easily upset, unstable, insecure, impressionable and with changeable moods. Because of the difficulties he has in controlling his emotions, he should be apt for routine tasks, where he does not have to deal with emergencies or unexpected demands.

FR is tenacious, dominant, aggressive, energetic and will persistently argue his ideas and viewpoints. He is not so dominant as to cause insurmountable conflicts with colleagues. He does not appear to be a person who blindly fights to get his ideas through, although he will defend them tactfully. He is likely to be a good salesperson and will struggle to get customers to sign a contract.

He is a sensitive person, and may occasionally be more impressionable and softer than normal. He might not be at home performing tasks that require fast and concise action, and would getter better results in jobs where success depends on empathy (where he has to put himself in someone else's place).

FR tends to be obstinate and takes pains to put his viewpoints over. He likes to unearth and air other people's mistakes, which could cloud the working environment. He may be distrustful of other people, who he may regard as having ulterior motives. He would get on well in highly competitive jobs.

He is creative and imaginative. He will input good ideas to his job. However, he suffers more than normal when his work is criticised. Fearful of failure, he will be constantly alert keeping his behaviour in check and guarding against mistakes. He does not like change, and agrees to things that have already been tested. He tolerates the more routine and frustrating jobs without complaint. He is likely to be a loyal employee, who, faced with the uncertain prospects of a change, prefers to stay in the same place for a long time. This is a profile typical of highly disciplined professions.

He is characteristically self-confident. He prefers to work alone and do things without anyone else's help. This self-assuredness leads him to act, think and decide for himself.

He may be conflictive at work, as he is led by his own opinions and may, occasionally, be tactless. He may be disorganised and careless, and he does not find it easy to adhere to systematic methods. It is not advisable that he be given major responsibilities, nor would he get on well in rigid and inflexible environments.

He has a very high anxiety level that may generate a tense and edgy atmosphere that may put other colleagues ill at ease.

Figure C.34. Capabilities Report # 11

Company	Capabilities Report	
	PR	
	Name of activity group performed.	
	Role played·	
	Cultural evaluation date: *28/7/2000*........................ List No.: 13	
	Evaluators' names: Silvia Teresita Acuña and Marta Evelia Aparicio	

A. Personal particulars

Age: 35	Sex·
Nationality: Argentina	☒ Male ☐ Female
Place of birth: Buenos Aires	Residence: ....

Marital status:

☐ Single   ☒ Married   ☐ Separated   ☐ Divorced   ☐ Widowed

B. Capabilities or behavioural competencies

No.	Competency	Competency level
1	Independence	High
2	Innovation/creativity	Average
3	Stress tolerance	High
4	Risk management	High
5	Discipline	High
6	Environmental orientation	Average
7	Teamwork/cooperation	Average

Observations: ....
....

C. General summary

Personality characteristics and skills:

PR is not a person who feels at home in interpersonal situations. Professionally, he is not likely to be proficient at tasks that involve interpersonal contact. Technical (analyst, programmer) and systems maintenance occupations would match this profile. He is likely to excel in jobs that involve thinking and reasoning. Being rational, he is likely to be very proficient in creative or teaching jobs or occupations that place high demands on intellectual resources.

He is emotionally stable, and could perform well in jobs that require urgency and serenity at the same time. His personal relationships with colleagues will be good and, as a member of a work team, he will act as a good antidote to stress and other work pressures.

He can be defined as tenacious, dominant, aggressive, energetic and will persistently argue his ideas and viewpoints. He may be intolerant of opposing viewpoints, which would affect his interpersonal relationships. However, this will not necessarily lead him into disputes with colleagues. He is likely to be a good salesperson and will struggle to get customers to sign a contract.

He finds it easy to forge interpersonal relationships, but they are unlikely to last long because of his inconstancy. He is resourceful and quick thinking. He finds it difficult to complete long-term projects, even though he starts off with resolve He needs to be stimulated by new things.

He may be unconcerned about, or neglectful and careless of obligations. He has little perseverance. Professionally, he may cause disputes in work teams. He is negligent, impulsive and indifferent to social norms. He also has no interest in respecting rules and established procedures.

He prefers sincerity, although this can get him into trouble with other people. He is somewhat naïve and not very reserved, and he tends to say what he thinks. His frankness and sincerity may put him at odds with other colleagues or customers. He should be employed in assistance and help occupations rather than to deal with claims or work in direct sales.

He is a calm, serene, low anxiety person. He is likely to transmit his calmness and indifference to other colleagues, and will be easy to work with under some circumstances.

Figure C.35. Capabilities Report # 13

Company	Capabilities Report	
	CA	
	Name of activity group performed:	
	Role played:	
	Cultural evaluation date: *28/7/2000*.................................... List No.: 12	
	Evaluators' names: Silvia Teresita Acuña and Marta Evelia Aparicio	

A. Personal particulars		
Age: 32	Sex:	
Nationality: Argentina	☐ Male ☒ Female	
Place of birth: Buenos Aires	Residence:	

Marital status:
☐ Single ☒ Married ☐ Separated ☐ Divorced ☐ Widowed

B. Capabilities or behavioural competencies

No.	Competency	Competency level
1	Independence	Average
2	Innovation/creativity	High
3	Self-organisation	Average
4	Risk management	Average
5	Environmental knowledge	Average
6	Discipline	High
7	Environmental orientation	Average
8	Planning and organisation	Average

Observations: ....

C. General summary

Personality characteristics and skills:

CA does not feel at home in interpersonal situations. She may be critical of others and distrustful of people with whom she does not have a solid relationship. Professionally, she is not likely to be proficient at tasks that involve interpersonal contact. Occupations matching this profile would be technical and systems maintenance jobs, as well as programmer or researcher. She is somewhat easily upset, unstable, insecure, impressionable and has changeable moods. Because of the difficulties she has in controlling her emotions, she should be apt for routine tasks, where he does not have to deal with emergencies or unexpected demands.

She is tenacious, dominant, aggressive, energetic and will persistently argue her ideas and viewpoints. She is likely to be a good salesperson and will struggle to get customers to sign a contract.

She is likely to be highly regarded by her superiors, as she will conscientiously accept any rule they enforce. Jobs involving thought and reflection, such as the scientific and technical professions, would be ideal positions for her.

She has a strong sense of responsibility, duty and established rules. She may perform positively in occupations that require self-discipline and conscientiousness. She is wary and conservative, she fears making mistakes at work. She will act with utmost discretion to rule out negative appraisals of her behaviour. She does not find it easy to get to know new people, which means that she would be more at home working on static tasks that others find boring.

She is very creative and imaginative. She is constantly analysing and conceiving new thoughts. She will input great ideas to her work, although she may sometimes disregard risks. She may tend to be inattentive and, therefore, needs supervision.

She prefers sincerity, which may put her at odds with colleagues or customers. It is inadvisable that she should be employed to deal with claims or work in direct sales, as she will find it difficult to sell the excellences of the product in question. She would be better suited for help or assistance jobs.

She suffers more than normal when here work is criticised. She is likely to be emotionally affected by any rebuke, which she will find discouraging. She should not be given management responsibilities and she should always be supervised and encouraged by a superior.

She is self-confident and prefers to work alone. She may find it difficult to get used to teamwork.

She is a very tense and anxious person, which may generate a tense and edgy atmosphere that may put other colleagues ill at ease.

Figure C.36. Capabilities Report # 12

Company	Capabilities Report
	FM
	Name of activity group performed: ....
	Role played: ....
	Cultural evaluation date: *28/7/2000*........................... List No.: 15
	Evaluators' names: Silvia Teresita Acuña and Marta Evelia Aparicio

A. Personal particulars

Age: 37	Sex.
Nationality: Argentina	☒ Male ☐ Female
Place of birth: Buenos Aires	Residence: ....

Marital status:

☐ Single   ☒ Married   ☐ Separated   ☐ Divorced   ☐ Widowed

B. Capabilities or behavioural competencies

No.	Competency	Competency level
1	Analysis	Average
2	Judgement	Average
3	Risk management	High
4	Discipline	High
5	Coworker evaluation	High
6	Planning and organisation	High

Observations: ....
....

C. General summary

Personality characteristics and skills:

FM is an intelligent and astute person, capable of understanding and establishing relationships and grasping ideas. He is concretely and abstractly creative, instinctive and speculative. He is likely to perform well in jobs that involve thinking and reasoning. Being rational, he is likely to be very proficient in creative or teaching jobs or occupations that place high demands on intellectual resources. He is a very serious, highly meditative and pensive person who is sure of his decisions. He is very sensitive to errors, which will affect his decision-making fluency, although he is tolerant of frustration. He is likely to be highly regarded by his superiors, as he will conscientiously accept any rule they enforce. At other times, his overconfidence in his actions may be counterproductive for business interests Jobs involving thought and reflection, such as the scientific and technical professions, would be ideal positions for him. He is self-reliant and prefers to make his own decisions, even if it takes longer

He has a strong sense of responsibility, duty and established rules. He may perform positively in occupations that require self-discipline and conscientiousness.

He defines himself as conforming and is trustful of others. He is pleasant and adapts to new situations. Not only is he not a conflictive person, but he also contributes to creating an agreeable and pleasant working environment. He is easily manipulated and deceived and is, therefore, not recommended for jobs that require strength and decisiveness, such as supervisory positions.

He is a calculating person, who likes to analyse things before taking action. He takes pains to cause a good impression on people. His relationships at work will be good, but only from a functional viewpoint. He is ambitious and socially assured. He will get on well in environments that require extreme diplomacy, where success largely depends on selling oneself.

He is self-confident, lively and vigorous. He has a headstrong character, quick to pass judgement on others but far from willing to accept criticism himself. He may appear to be sure of his decisions. If anything goes wrong, however, he will want to have nothing to do with the matter.

He may cause conflicts at work, because he likes to bend the rules and tends to disregard instructions from his superiors with which he does not agree. He is usually led by his own opinions and can sometimes be tactless. He may be disorganised and careless, and he does not find it easy to adhere to systematic methods. It is not advisable that he be given major responsibilities, nor would he get on well in rigid and inflexible environments.

He is the model of an independent person who prefers to work alone. He may have difficulties in direct dealings with customers. However, if his work calls for care and thoroughness, his introvertedness is likely to play in his favour.

Figure C.37. Capabilities Report # 15

Company	Capabilities Report
	CS

Name of activity group performed: ....

Role played: ....

Cultural evaluation date: 28/7/2000... List No.: 16

Evaluators' names. Silvia Teresita Acuña and Marta Evelia Aparicio

A. Personal particulars

Age: 35
Nationality: Argentina
Place of birth: Buenos Aires

Sex:
☐ Male   ☒ Female
Residence: ....

Marital status:
☐ Single   ☒ Married   ☐ Separated   ☐ Divorced   ☐ Widowed

B. Capabilities or behavioural competencies

No.	Competency	Competency level
1	Decision making	Average
2	Self-organisation	High
3	Risk management	High
4	Discipline	High
5	Environmental orientation	High
6	Teamwork/cooperation	High
7	Planning and organisation	High

Observations. ....
....

C. General summary

Personality characteristics and skills:

CS is unlikely to be proficient at tasks that involve interpersonal contact. Suitable occupations would be technical or systems maintenance jobs

She is a highly rational and shrewd person. She finds it easier than others to understand and establish relationships, and grasp ideas She is concretely and abstractly creative, intuitive and speculative. She is likely to excel in jobs that involve thinking and reasoning.

She is a very serious, highly meditative and pensive person who is sure of her decisions. She is very sensitive to errors, which will affect her decision-making fluency. She is likely to be highly regarded by her superiors, as she will conscientiously accept any rule they enforce.

She has a strong sense of responsibility, duty and of established rules. She may perform well in occupations that require self-discipline and conscientiousness. She has a lot of willpower, she is controlled and socially very proper.

She is instinctive and emotive, which may negatively influence her logical reasoning. Criticism will affect her more than normal to the point of possibly lowering her performance She might not be at home performing tasks that require fast and clear-cut actions, and will perform better in jobs that involve a good measure of empathy (where she has to put herself in someone else's place). As mentioned above, she suffers more than normal when her work is criticised. She is likely to be emotionally affected by any rebuke, which she will find discouraging. She finds it difficult to undertake actions for fear of the possible result. She should not be given management responsibilities, and should always be supervised and encouraged by a superior.

At work, she will be cooperative and participatory, she prefers to work in the company of others and follows instructions without questioning or contravening them. She is motivated by other people's appreciation and enjoys praise of her work. She is disciplined, although she may be submissive. She could encounter difficulties in management positions, but might, on the other hand, be a loyal and disciplined subordinate.

Figure C.38. Capabilities Report # 16

Company	Capabilities Report
	CR

	Name of activity group performed: ....
	Role played: ....
	Cultural evaluation date. *28/7/2000*.......................... List No.: 40
	Evaluators' names· Silvia Teresita Acuña and Marta Evelia Aparicio

A. Personal particulars

Age: 45
Nationality: Argentina
Place of birth. Buenos Aires

Sex:
☒ Male   ☐ Female
Residence: ....

Marital status:
☐ Single   ☒ Married   ☐ Separated   ☐ Divorced   ☐ Widowed

B. Capabilities or behavioural competencies

No.	Competency	Competency level
1	Decision making	Average
2	Innovation/creativity	Average
3	Risk management	High
4	Environmental knowledge	Average
5	Coworker evaluation	Average

Observations: ....
.... ·· ....

C. General summary

Personality characteristics and skills:

CR has a very low score on Warmth, which defines him as a person who does not care for interpersonal situations. He will be critical of others and distrustful of people with whom he does not have a solid relationship. Therefore, at work, he is unlikely to be motivated by or proficient at tasks that involve interpersonal contact.

He is an intelligent and astute person, capable of understanding and establishing relationships, and grasping ideas He is concretely and abstractly creative, intuitive and speculative.

He tends to be sober, serious and wary. He finds it difficult to make risky decisions because he fears making mistakes. Professionally, he is likely to be highly regarded by his superiors, as he will conscientiously accept any rule they enforce. Jobs that involve thought and reflection are ideal positions for him. He will analyse problems focusing on the facts only, rejecting any trace of subjectivity.

He takes pains to put his viewpoints over, tending to be obstinate. His interpersonal tendency could cloud the working environment. Highly competitive jobs might be his strongest suit.

He should not be given major responsibilities, nor will he get on well in rigid and inflexible environments. He could excel in informal jobs where there are no written rules, such as some creative fields, as, otherwise, he will need to be pressed and supervised to be successful.

He scores high on anxiety, which may generate a tense and edgy atmosphere that may put other colleagues ill at ease. His anxiety may affect his skills of analysis and observation, and he may appear to be forgetful or neglectful. His anxiety level may be counterproductive, although it may sometimes help to raise his commitment to and involvement in his work.

Figure C.39. Capabilities Report # 40

Company	*Capabilities Report*
	JÑ
	Name of activity group performed: ....
	Role played: ....
	Cultural evaluation date: *28/7/2000*........................... List No.: 3
	Evaluators' names: Silvia Teresita Acuña and Marta Evelia Aparicio

A. Personal particulars

Age: 40	Sex:
Nationality: Argentina	☒ Male ☐ Female
Place of birth: Buenos Aires	Residence: ....

Marital status:
☒ Single   ☐ Married   ☐ Separated   ☐ Divorced   ☐ Widowed

B. Capabilities or behavioural competencies

No	Competency	Competency level
1	Innovation/creativity	High
2	Risk management	High
3	Environmental knowledge	Average
4	Environmental orientation	High
5	Customer service	High

Observations: ....
....

C. General summary

Personality characteristics and skills:

JÑ is a warm person who is easy to get along with. He does not appear to find it difficult to forge relationships and knows how to keep them up. Professionally, he will be motivated by and decided if undertaking tasks that involve social contact. He could be defined as a good member of any work team, easily relating to other members and not being very critical of others.

He stands out on rationality and astuteness. He is likely to excel in jobs that involve thinking and reasoning. Being rational, he is likely to be very proficient in creative or teaching jobs or occupations that place high demands on intellectual resources.

He is defined as somewhat easily upset, unstable, insecure and impressionable. Because of the difficulties he has in controlling his emotions, he should be apt for routine tasks, where he does not have to deal with emergencies or unexpected demands. He often shirks his responsibilities and is very apprehensive, which may put him at odds with colleagues who find this unfair.

He adapts his conduct according to internal rather than environmental demands. He will be more at home working alongside dominant people who supervise and organise his work. Otherwise, he is likely to get discouraged and frustrated, because he is hesitant about accepting responsibility.

He is a person who tends to be sober, serious and wary. He may find it difficult to make risky decisions, as he fears making mistakes. Professionally, he is likely to be highly regarded by his superiors, as he will conscientiously accept any rule they enforce.

He may be unconcerned about, or neglectful and careless of obligations. He is negligent, impulsive and indifferent to social norms. He has little interest in respecting rules and established procedures.

He is instinctive and emotive, which may negatively influence his logical reasoning. Criticism will affect him more than normal to the point of possible lowering his performance. He might not be at home performing tasks that require fast and clear-cut action.

He has high anxiety levels, and is edgy and overemotional. He may generate a tense and edgy atmosphere that may put other colleagues ill at ease. As a direct consequence of his anxiety, he finds it difficult to analyse and observe detail, and he may tend to be forgetful and careless.

Figure C.40. Capabilities Report # 3

Company	Capabilities Report
	CL
	Name of activity group performed: ....
	Role played: ....
	Cultural evaluation date: *28/7/2000*................................... List No.. 2
	Evaluators' names: Silvia Teresita Acuña and Marta Evelia Aparicio

A. Personal particulars

Age: 35	Sex:
Nationality: Argentina	☐ Male ☒ Female
Place of birth: Buenos Aires	Residence: ....

Marital status:
☐ Single   ☒ Married   ☐ Separated   ☐ Divorced   ☐ Widowed

B. Capabilities or behavioural competencies

No.	Competency	Competency level
1	Decision making	High
2	Tenacity	Average
3	Stress tolerance	Average
4	Self-organisation	High
5	Environmental orientation	Average
6	Coworker evaluation	Average
7	Planning and organisation	Average

Observations: ....
....

C. General summary

Personality characteristics and skills:

CL would fit in better in technical and systems maintenance jobs. She adapts her conduct according to internal rather than environmental demands. She is driven by a strong desire to avoid conflicts and by an attempt to please and gain approbation. She will be more at home working alongside dominant people who supervise and organise her work. Otherwise, she is likely to get discouraged and frustrated, because she is hesitant about accepting responsibility. She will manage confidently in jobs where she has all the information she needs to get on with her routine tasks. She is a reserved, timid and conservative person, who is rooted in traditional ideas.

She is defined as conforming. She tolerates frustration and is trustful of others. Not only is she not a conflictive person, she will also contribute to creating an agreeable and pleasant working environment.

She is not open to change and innovation and always acts according to tried and tested methods and procedures. She will focus on her work, especially if this involves very mechanical behaviour, with little room for decision making. She tends to be painstaking, and is unlikely to leave a job unfinished.

At work she will show herself to have a headstrong character, quick to pass judgement on others but far from willing to accept criticism herself. She may appear to be sure of her decisions. If anything goes wrong, however, she will want to have nothing to do with the matter.

She is self-confident. She prefers to work alone and do things without anyone else's help. This self-assuredness leads her to act, think and decide for herself. She prefers to do things her own way. She may find it difficult to get used to work teams. She is very analytical and will espouse extremely impartial positions in any negotiation. The jobs that are best suited for her are the technical and research occupations, especially if they have a supervisory or management status.

Figure C.41. Capabilities Report # 2

Company	Capabilities Report
	MN
	Name of activity group performed: ....
	Role played: ....
	Cultural evaluation date: 28/7/2000.................................... List No.: 6
	Evaluators' names: Silvia Teresita Acuña and Marta Evelia Aparicio

A. Personal particulars

Age: 36	Sex.
Nationality. Argentina	☐ Male ⊠ Female
Place of birth: Buenos Aires	Residence: . . ..

Marital status:
⊠ Single   ☐ Married   ☐ Separated   ☐ Divorced   ☐ Widowed

B. Capabilities or behavioural competencies

No.	Competency	Competency level
1	Decision making	High
2	Empathy	Average
3	Sociability	Average

Observations: ....
....

C. General summary

Personality characteristics and skills:

MN's is the profile of someone who is somewhat easily upset, unstable, insecure, impressionable and has changeable moods. Because of the difficulties she has in controlling her emotions, she should be apt for routine tasks, where she does not have to deal with emergencies or unexpected demands.

She tends to be sober and serious. She is likely to be highly regarded by her superiors, as she will conscientiously accept any rule they enforce.

She is a firm, perseverant, self-possessed person. She will analyse problems focusing on the facts only, rejecting any trace of subjectivity. She would fit in well in jobs that require fast and clear-cut action.

MN is a sincere person, which may put her at odds with other colleagues or customers. In more complicated situations, however, she will know just how far to go. She should not work dealing with claims or in direct sales.

She tends to blame herself for everything, even for things that are beyond her control. She suffers more than normal when her work is criticised. She is likely to be emotionally affected by any rebuke, which she will find discouraging. She should not be given management responsibilities, and she should always be supervised and encouraged by a superior.

She tolerates the more routine and frustrating tasks without complaint. She is likely to be a loyal employee, who, faced with the uncertain prospects of a change, prefers to stay in the same place for a long time.

She is self-confident and prefers to do things her own way. She is likely to find it difficult to get used to teamwork. The jobs that are best suited for her are the technical and research occupations, especially if they have a supervisory or management status.

She is an anxious and nervous person People with such high anxiety levels tend to generate a tense and edgy atmosphere that may put other colleagues ill at ease. Her anxiety may have an effect on her skills of analysis and observation, and she may appear to be forgetful or neglectful.

Figure C.42. Capabilities Report # 6

Company	Capabilities Report
	AL
	Name of activity group performed: ....
	Role played: ....
	Cultural evaluation date: 28/7/2000.......................... List No.: 8
	Evaluators' names: Silvia Teresita Acuña and Marta Evelia Aparicio

A. Personal particulars

Age: 36	Sex:
Nationality: Argentina	☒ Male ☐ Female
Place of birth: Buenos Aires	Residence: ....

Marital status:

☐ Single   ☒ Married   ☐ Separated   ☐ Divorced   ☐ Widowed

B. Capabilities or behavioural competencies

No.	Competency	Competency level
1	Analysis	Average
2	Judgement	Average
3	Tenacity	Average
4	Self-organisation	High
5	Risk management	High
6	Environmental knowledge	High
7	Environmental orientation	High
8	Customer service	High
9	Empathy	High
10	Sociability	High
11	Teamwork/cooperation	Average
12	Planning and organisation	High

Observations: ....

C. General summary

Personality characteristics and skills:

AL is a warm person who is easy to get along with. Professionally, he will be motivated by and decided if undertaking tasks that involve social contact. He stands out on rationality and astuteness. He is likely to excel in jobs that involve thinking and reasoning. Being rational, he is likely to be very proficient in creative or teaching jobs or occupations that place high demands on intellectual resources.

He adapts his conduct according to internal rather than environmental demands. He will be more at home working alongside dominant people who supervise and organise his work. He may find it difficult to make risky decisions, as he fears making mistakes, and will, therefore, accept his supervisors' rules. He may be unconcerned about, or neglectful and careless of obligations. He has little perseverance. This may cause conflicts within work teams.

He is a very sensitive person. He will, therefore, often be weighed down by his feelings, which may cause him more suffering than they do other people. He is very instinctive and emotive, which may detract from his logical reasoning. Any criticism he receives about his work is likely to affect him a great deal to the point of noticeably lowering his performance.

He is very obstinate and takes great pains to put his viewpoints over. His inclinations tend to cloud the working environment. He is distrustful, thinks that everyone is trying to pull one over on him and regards others as having ulterior motives. He would get on well in highly competitive jobs. His frankness and sincerity may put him at odds with other colleagues or clients. He should not work dealing with claims or in direct sales. He tends to blame himself for everything, and any criticism or reproach may depress him and make him fail. He cannot be given management responsibilities and he should always be supervised and encouraged by a superior. Although he is not a rebel, he finds it difficult to acknowledge authority and accept enforced rules.

He tends to be thorough and a perfectionist, which may lead him to often fall prey to impractical obsessions that slow down his work and affect his performance.

Figure C.43. Capabilities Report # 8

Company	Capabilities Report
	ER

Name of activity group performed: ....
Role played: ....
Cultural evaluation date: 28/7/2000.......................... List No.: 10
Evaluators' names: Silvia Teresita Acuña and Marta Evelia Aparicio

A. Personal particulars

Age: 38	Sex:
Nationality: Argentina	☒ Male ☐ Female
Place of birth. Buenos Aires	Residence. ....

Marital status:
☒ Single   ☐ Married   ☐ Separated   ☐ Divorced   ☐ Widowed

B. Capabilities or behavioural competencies

No.	Competency	Competency level
1	Analysis	Average
2	Judgement	Average
3	Self-organisation	High
4	Risk management	High
5	Environmental knowledge	Average
6	Discipline	High
7	Environmental orientation	High
8	Teamwork/cooperation	Average
9	Coworker evaluation	High
10	Planning and organisation	High

Observations: ....

C. General summary

Personality characteristics and skills:

ER does not usually feel at home in interpersonal situations. He is not likely to be proficient at tasks that involve interpersonal contact. Jobs suited to this profile would be technical and systems maintenance occupations, as well as programmer or researcher. He stands out on rationality and astuteness. He is likely to excel in jobs that involve thinking and reasoning. Being rational, he is likely to be very proficient in creative or teaching jobs or occupations that place high demands on intellectual resources.

He adapts his conduct according to internal rather than environmental demands. He will be more at home working alongside dominant people who supervise and organise his work. Otherwise, he is likely to get discouraged and frustrated, because he is hesitant about accepting responsibility. He tends to be sober, serious and wary. He is likely to be highly regarded by his superiors, as he will conscientiously accept any rule they enforce.

He stands out on conscientiousness and is incapable of contravening ethical provisions. He is likely to be highly successful in occupations that require self-discipline and thoroughness. He is instinctive and emotive, which may negatively affect his logical reasoning. Criticism will affect him more than normal to the point of possibly lowering his performance. He might not be at ease performing tasks that require fast and clear-cut action.

He likes to analyse things before taking action. He is at pains to make a good impression on people. His efforts to impress others may be interpreted by his colleagues as falseness. His relationships at work will be good, but only from a functional viewpoint. He will get on better in areas that require extreme diplomacy, where selling oneself accounts for a large slice of success. He suffers more than normal when his work is criticised. He is likely to be emotionally affected by any rebuke, which he will find discouraging.

He may cause conflicts, because he likes to bend the rules and tends to disregard instructions from his superiors with which he does not agree. He is likely to slow down meetings or teamwork and drive his colleagues to despair because he is inclined to be against everything. Being a person inclined to perfectionism and thoroughness, he may often to fall prey to impractical obsessions that slow down his work and affect his performance. His job should ideally not include risk taking.

Figure C.44. Capabilities Report # 10

Company	Capabilities Report	
	EV	
	Name of activity group performed:	
	Role played:	
	Cultural evaluation date. *28/7/2000*.................................... List No.: 1	
	Evaluators' names: Silvia Teresita Acuña and Marta Evelia Aparicio	

A. Personal particulars

Age. 33	Sex:
Nationality: Argentina	☐ Male ☒ Female
Place of birth: Buenos Aires	Residence: ....

Marital status:

☐ Single ☒ Married ☐ Separated ☐ Divorced ☐ Widowed

B. Capabilities or behavioural competencies

No.	Competency	Competency level
1	Decision making	Average
2	Innovation/creativity	Average
3	Environmental knowledge	Average
4	Environmental orientation	Average
5	Customer service	Average
6	Capacidad de negociación	Average
7	Empathy	Average
8	Sociability	Average
9	Coworker evaluation	Average

Observations: ....
....

C. General summary

Personality characteristics and skills:

EV's profile denotes social skill for forging relationships with other people, as well as for performing supervisory or middle management jobs. Because she tends to be indecisive, however, she would not be suited for working in positions involving directing others.
She is emotionally unstable, which means that she will manage well in jobs where she does not have to deal with emergencies or unexpected demands.
Professionally, EV is likely to be highly regarded by her superiors, as she will conscientiously accept any rule they enforce.
She has little perseverance for seeing a matter through to the end. She will work better on her own than as a member of a group.
Jobs that are strictly supervised and whose procedures are clearly stipulated are ideal positions for her.
She suffers more than normal when her work is criticised. She should not be given management responsibilities, and she should always be supervised and encouraged by a superior.
Therefore, EV would fit in well in a job that does not entail much responsibility, where she does not have to depend too much on teamwork and where she needs to put her imagination and interpersonal skills to work.

Figure C.45. Capabilities Report # 1

Company	Capabilities Report	
	AF	
	Name of activity group performed:	
	Role played:	
	Cultural evaluation date: 28/7/2000........................... List No.: 14	
	Evaluators' names: Silvia Teresita Acuña and Marta Evelia Aparicio	

A. Personal particulars

Age: 35 Nationality: Argentina Place of birth: Buenos Aires	Sex: ☒ Male ☐ Female Residence: ....

Marital status:
☐ Single ☒ Married ☐ Separated ☐ Divorced ☐ Widowed

B. Capabilities or behavioural competencies

No.	Competency	Competency level
1	Innovation/creativity	High
2	Stress tolerance	High
3	Discipline	Average
4	Environmental orientation	High
5	Coworker evaluation	High

Observations: ....
....

C. General summary

Personality characteristics and skills.

AF is a person who does not like to find himself in interpersonal situations He may be critical of others and distrustful of people with whom he does not have a solid relationship. Professionally, he is unlikely to be motivated by or very proficient at tasks that involve interpersonal contact. Occupations suited for this profile are technical and systems maintenance jobs, as well as programmer or researcher.

He is emotionally unstable, and has little control over his emotions. Therefore, jobs where he does not have to deal with emergencies or unexpected demands would suit him.

He will be more at home working alongside dominant people who supervise and organise his work. Therefore, he will get on confidently in jobs that do not involve directing others and where he has all the information he needs to get on with his routine tasks.

Judging by his profile, he may find it difficult to get on in overdemanding and methodical environments. He fears making mistakes at work. He will act with utmost discretion to rule out negative appraisals of his behaviour. He will prefer to work on static tasks that others find boring.

He can be defined as a highly sensitive person, and may be both weak and indulgent, and not very objective, in the defence of his opinions. He could be ill at ease performing jobs that require fast and clear-cut action and would get on better in professions where success depends on empathy (where he has to put himself in someone else's place).

He is a creative and imaginative person. He will input good ideas to his work. His divergent thinking is a great ally for succeeding in jobs the involve inventiveness and creativeness.

He suffers more than normal when his work is criticised. He is likely to be emotionally affected by any rebuke, which he will find discouraging. He would be unable to cope with management responsibilities and should always be supervised and encouraged by a superior

Figure C.46. Capabilities Report # 14

Company	Capabilities Report
	PB
	Name of activity group performed: ....
	Role played: ....
	Cultural evaluation date: *28/7/2000*........................... List No.: 30
	Evaluators' names: Silvia Teresita Acuña and Marta Evelia Aparicio

A. Personal particulars

Age: 45
Nationality: Argentina
Place of birth: Buenos Aires

Sex
☒ Male   ☐ Female
Residence: .. ..

Marital status:
☐ Single   ☒ Married   ☐ Separated   ☐ Divorced   ☐ Widowed

B. Capabilities or behavioural competencies

No.	Competency	Competency level
1	Innovation/creativity	High
2	Risk management	Average
3	Environmental orientation	High
4	Customer service	Average
5	Empathy	Average
6	Sociability	Average

Observations: ....

C. General summary

Personality characteristics and skills:

PB will easily get used to jobs that involve social skill for forging relationships with customers.

He is an emotionally unstable person, and his interests will tend to change. He is also indecisive and finds it difficult to accept rules. Because of his indecisiveness, he will manage well in jobs that do not involve directing others and where he has all the information he needs to get on with his routine tasks.

Jobs involving thought and reflection, such as the scientific and technical professions, would be ideal positions for him. He could be ill at ease performing jobs that require fast and clear-cut action.

He contributes to creating an agreeable and pleasant working environment. He is not suited for jobs that require strength and decisiveness, such as supervisory positions Therefore, he should not work in positions of responsibility at management level and should always be supervised and encouraged by a superior

He should not be employed to deal with claims or directly with the public, as he is easily upset. His profile is better suited for assistance and help jobs.

Neither is he suited for teamwork, as he is likely to slow down meetings or teamwork and drive his colleagues to despair because he is inclined to be against everything He will fit in better in jobs that afford a measure of independence and involve a wide variety of tasks.

He could excel in informal jobs where there are no written rules, such as some creative fields, as, otherwise, he will need to be pressed and supervised to be successful.

In sum, PB will fit in better in jobs where he can input ideas and where he is supervised by others, but where not a lot of teamwork is involved.

Figure C.47. Capabilities Report # 30

Company	Capabilities Report
	AD
	Name of activity group performed: ....
	Role played: ....
	Cultural evaluation date: 28/7/2000.................................... List No.: 5
	Evaluators' names: Silvia Teresita Acuña and Marta Evelia Aparicio

A. Personal particulars

Age: 40	Sex:
Nationality: Argentina	☐ Male ☒ Female
Place of birth: Buenos Aires	Residence: ....

Marital status:
☐ Single   ☒ Married   ☐ Separated   ☐ Divorced   ☐ Widowed

B. Capabilities or behavioural competencies

No.	Competency	Competency level
1	Analysis	Average
2	Independence	Average
3	Judgement	Average
4	Tenacity	High
5	Self-organisation	High
6	Risk management	Average
7	Empathy	High
8	Sociability	High
9	Teamwork/cooperation	High
10	Team leadership	High
11	Planning and organisation	High

Observations: ....

C. General summary

Personality characteristics and skills:

AD is a pleasant and warm person. She will be motivated by and decided when undertaking jobs that involve social contact. However, she is unlikely to be the most creative member of the group.

She is able to control her emotions and would, therefore, perform well in jobs that demand urgency and serenity at the same time. Her relationships with colleagues will be good and, as a member of a work team, she will act as a good antidote against stress and other work pressures. She is defined as tenacious, dominant, aggressive, energetic and will persistently argue her ideas and viewpoints. She is likely to be a good salesperson and will struggle to get customers to sign a contract.

Professionally, she is likely to be highly regarded by her superiors, as she will conscientiously accept any rule they enforce. Jobs involving thought and reflection, such as the scientific and technical professions, would be ideal positions for her.

She may be unconcerned and over calm. She has little perseverance. These characteristics may cause conflicts in work teams. She is an active person, who enjoys risk. Professionally, she will take risks that others turn away from. She is firm in the face of difficulties and usually accepts responsibility for her acts. Jobs where success is based on taking risks and accepting responsibilities are ideal positions for her.

She will analyse problems focusing on the facts only, rejecting any trace of subjectivity. Her colleagues may see her as distant and cool. Jobs requiring fast and clear-cut action, where cool-headedness is a priority, are her strongest suit. Hers could be a good profile for performing supervisory or management jobs in organisations with clearly delimited hierarchical levels, where she is unlikely to have much contact with subordinates. She is well-disposed towards people, will seek out company and will avoid being alone. She tolerates frustration and is trusting of others. She contributes to generating a good working environment. She is objective and realistic, looking for immediate benefits and acting on practical grounds only. She is a person who may be checked by her lack of interest in change and innovation, and will act based on tried and tested methods and procedures. She tends to be thorough, and is unlikely to leave a job unfinished.

Her frankness and sincerity may put her at odds with other colleagues or clients. She should not be employed to deal with claims or in direct sales. She has a headstrong character, always quick to pass judgment on others but far from willing to accept criticism. She is self-confident and may appear to be sure of her decisions. If anything goes wrong, however, she will want to have nothing to do with the matter. She may cause conflicts at work, because she likes to bend the rules and tends to disregard instructions from her superiors with which she does not agree. At work she will be cooperative and participatory, she prefers to work in other people's company. Being a person inclined to perfectionism and thoroughness, she may often fall prey to impractical obsessions that slow down her work and affect her performance. Finally, she is a calm and tranquil person, who is low on anxiety, which will help her to analyse problems from other angles without them getting her down.

Figure C.48. Capabilities Report # 5

Company	Capabilities Report
	EL
	Name of activity group performed: ....
	Role played: ....
	Cultural evaluation date: 28/7/2000.................................... List No.: 60
	Evaluators' names: Silvia Teresita Acuña and Marta Evelia Aparicio

A. Personal particulars

Age: 43	Sex:
Nationality: Argentina	☐ Male ☒ Female
Place of birth: Buenos Aires	Residence: . ...

Marital status:
☐ Single   ☒ Married   ☐ Separated   ☐ Divorced   ☐ Widowed

B. Capabilities or behavioural competencies

No.	Competency	Competency level
1	Analysis	High
2	Decision making	High
3	Judgement	High
4	Tenacity	High
5	Self-organisation	High
6	Risk management	High
7	Discipline	High
8	Teamwork/cooperation	High
9	Coworker evaluation	High
10	Planning and organisation	High

Observations: ....
....

C. General summary

Personality characteristics and skills:

EL may encounter difficulties in jobs that involve interpersonal contact, and, therefore, occupations that would suit her are technical and systems maintenance jobs, as well as programmer or researcher.

Professionally, she is likely to excel in jobs that involve thought and reasoning, as well as creative or teaching occupations or jobs that place high demands on intellectual resources.

She will be more at home working alongside dominant people who supervise and organise her work. Otherwise, she is likely to get discouraged and frustrated, because she is hesitant about accepting responsibility. Similarly, she is very capable of accepting rules enforced by her superiors and is likely to get on well in jobs that require self-discipline and thoroughness.

Her profile could be suited for performing supervisory and management jobs in organisations whose hierarchical levels are clearly delimited and there is not much contact with subordinates: she is not a born leader.

She is a thorough person who is suited for jobs that require care.

She may get on successfully in situations requiring the diplomacy to deal with others, as well as where she needs to sell herself.

She is organised and a perfectionist, but her perfectionism may sometimes slow down her work.

Figure C.49. Capabilities Report # 60

Company	*Capabilities Report*
	DN
	Name of activity group performed: ....
	Role played: ....
	Cultural evaluation date: *28/7/2000*..................................... List No. 62
	Evaluators' names Silvia Teresita Acuña and Marta Evelia Aparicio

A. Personal particulars

Age: 46	Sex:
Nationality: Argentina	☐ Male ☒ Female
Place of birth: Buenos Aires	Residence: ....

Marital status:
☒ Single   ☐ Married   ☐ Separated   ☐ Divorced   ☐ Widowed

B. Capabilities or behavioural competencies

No.	Competency	Competency level
1	Innovation/creativity	Average
2	Stress tolerance	High
3	Risk management	High
4	Discipline	High
5	Environmental orientation	High
6	Coworker evaluation	High

Observations: ....
....

C. General summary

Personality characteristics and skills:

DN has excellent powers of analysis and concentration, but she does not enjoy teamwork and is not likely to be proficient at jobs that involve interpersonal contact. Professionally, she is likely to perform well in jobs that involve thought and reasoning, like creative and teaching occupations or jobs that place high demands on intellectual resources.

Being emotionally stable, she is likely to perform well in jobs that require urgency and serenity at the same time. She prefers, however, to work under close supervision from her superiors.

She will conscientiously accept any rule enforced by her superiors, and will fit in better in an occupation that involves thought and reflection, like the scientific and technical professions, as well as jobs that require self-discipline and thoroughness.

She will perform very well in jobs that require extreme diplomacy and where it is important that she sell herself. However, she will not perform well as a member of a team, as she tends to oppose others.

Figure C.50. Capabilities Report # 62

Company	Capabilities Report
	SL
	Name of activity group performed: ....
	Role played: .. ..
	Cultural evaluation date: *28/7/2000*...................................... List No.: 100
	Evaluators' names: Silvia Teresita Acuña and Marta Evelia Aparicio

A. Personal particulars

Age: 46	Sex.
Nationality. Argentina	☐ Male ⊠ Female
Place of birth: Buenos Aires	Residence: ....

Marital status:

⊠ Single   ☐ Married   ☐ Separated   ☐ Divorced   ☐ Widowed

B. Capabilities or behavioural competencies		
No.	Competency	Competency level
1	Innovation/creativity	High
2	Stress tolerance	High
3	Self-organisation	Average
4	Risk management	Average
5	Environmental orientation	High
6	Planning and organisation	Average

Observations: ....

C. General summary

Personality characteristics and skills:

SL is a person who adapts her conduct according to internal rather than environmental demands. She will be more at home working alongside dominant people who supervise and organise her work. Otherwise, she is likely to get discouraged and frustrated, because she is hesitant about accepting responsibility. She is wary and conservative, she will steer clear of stimuli that are likely to be stressful. She does not like being drawn into unfamiliar situations, or dealing with people who she does not know. Jobs that are closely supervised and have clearly stipulated procedures are ideal positions for her.

She is highly empathic (very good at putting herself in someone else's place) Her feelings and perception of the world may get her down and may sometimes cause her suffering. She may be weak and indulgent, and not very objective, in the defence of her opinions. She could be ill at ease performing jobs that require fast and clear-cut actions, and would get better results in jobs where success is founded on good empathy

She is very creative and imaginative. She is constantly analysing and developing new thoughts. Her isolation from the world may make her egocentric and very independent. She will input good ideas, although she may sometimes disregard risks. She may appear to be detached from her work and will find it hard to concentrate on monotonous and repetitive tasks. Her divergent thinking is a great ally for succeeding in jobs that involve inventiveness and creativeness. She may be very inattentive and needs someone at hand to supervise her. She scores high on emotional sensitivity, and she is likely to share her own findings with other people and get involved in other people's problems.

Her frankness and sincerity may put her at odds with other colleagues or clients. In more complicated situations, however, she will know just how far to go. It is inadvisable that she should be employed to deal with claims or work in direct sales, as she will find it difficult to sell the excellences of the product in question This score is more typical of assistance and help jobs, requiring sincerity on both parts.

She may sometimes appear to be rebellious. She may find it difficult to acknowledge authority and accept compulsory rules when she is sure of what she is doing. She enjoys trying new things and likes to the get to the bottom of everything. Professionally, she may cause conflict, as she likes to bend the rules and tends to disregard instructions from her superiors with which she does not agree. She is likely to slow down meetings or teamwork and drive her colleagues to despair because he is inclined to be against everything. Jobs that afford some independence and involve a wide variety of tasks would be the best positions for her.

She is self-reliant and self-confident. She prefers to do things in her own way. She is likely to find it difficult to get used to teamwork. She may sometimes be very stubborn and arrogant. The jobs that are best suited for her are the technical and research occupations, especially if they have a supervisory or management status. SL is very calm, serene, and has little anxiety. She is likely to transmit her calmness and indifference to other colleagues, and will be easy to work with under some circumstances. This may help her to analyse problems from other angles, with her resources more intact and without being influenced by limitative apprehension or tension. The best occupations for people like SL are jobs that do not require a large measure of activity and involve a lot of static work.

Figure C.51. Capabilities Report # 100

Company	Capabilities Report
	AK
	Name of activity group performed: ....
	Role played: ... .
	Cultural evaluation date: 28/7/2000.......................... List No.: 18
	Evaluators' names: Silvia Teresita Acuña and Marta Evelia Aparicio

A. Personal particulars

Age: 35	Sex:
Nationality: Argentina	☒ Male ☐ Female
Place of birth: Buenos Aires	Residence: ....

Marital status:
☐ Single   ☒ Married   ☐ Separated   ☐ Divorced   ☐ Widowed

B. Capabilities or behavioural competencies

No.	Competency	Competency level
1	Independence	High
2	Innovation/creativity	High
3	Risk management	High
4	Environmental knowledge	Average
5	Discipline	High

Observations: ....
....

C. General summary

Personality characteristics and skills:

AK is an intelligent and astute person, capable of understanding and establishing relationships, and grasping ideas. He is concretely and abstractly creative, instinctive and speculative. Professionally, he is likely to perform well in jobs that involve thought and reflection. Being rational, he is likely to be very proficient in creative or teaching jobs or occupations that place high demands on intellectual resources.

His high score on Dominance defines him as a tenacious, dominant, aggressive, energetic person who will persistently argue his ideas and viewpoints. He may be intolerant of opposing viewpoints, which would affect his interpersonal relationships. He is likely to be a good salesperson and will struggle to get customers to sign a contract. He is likely to be a good director.

Professionally, AK is likely to be highly successful in occupations that require self-discipline and thoroughness. He will be capable of taking risks that others turn away from. He is firm in face of difficulties and usually accepts responsibility for his acts.

At work, he will be cooperative and participatory. He prefers to work in the company of others and follows instructions without questioning or contravening them.

He is open and considerate to others. He likes people and likes to find out what makes them tick. He is always open to change and will disregard his own views in face of advice or instructions from someone he respects. At work, he will be imaginative and easy to get on with. He is inclined to try out and experiment with new ways to doing things.

He is responsible and organised. He likes to make a good impression on people. He is astute and shrewd. He is self-assured, confident and secure.

Figure C.52. Capabilities Report # 18

Index

A

Activity,
definition, 31, 140
groups, 140
integral, 140, 180
organisational, 140, 173
project management, 140, 172
software development-oriented 140
pre-development 140, 175
development 140, 177
post-development 140, 179
software life cycle model selection 140, 170
Actor, 31
Agent, 31
Agile methods, 29, 30, **98**, 130
Analysis, 145, 178
Analytical report, 196, 263-268
Artefact, 32
Assignation of people to roles, 183-191, 199-209
activities, 183-191
comparison, 188
documentation, 190
evaluation, 188
monitoring & consolidation, 190
method, 185-191, 199-209

C

Capability, 31
definition, 140, 249
Capabilities, 143
Assessment Centre Method, 16, 249
categories, 144
interpersonal skills, 144
intrapersonal skills, 144
management skills, 144
organisational skills, 144
lists, 143, 249
modelling, 134, 143, 218
Capabilities needs report, 185, 189
Capabilities-oriented software process, 139
dimensions, 141
people, 147, 217
production, 183, 218
roles, 167, 218
experiment, 212
absolute judgements, 213
effectiveness, 212
efficiency, 212, 216
hypothesis, 212
pairwise evaluation, 212
response variables, 212
defects, 213
development time, 213
performance, 212
relationships,
capabilities-person, 151
capabilities-role, 168

tool, 23
Capabilities report, 162
Capabilities/role profile, 186-187
Competencies, 12
behavioural, 15
categories, 13
definition, 12, 13
hard, 13
soft, 14
Configuration manager, 168, 180
Co-worker evaluation, 145, 169, 174
Customer service, 145, 177, 179

D

Decision making, 145, 168, 171, 173, 175, 178
Designer, 168, 177, 178
Discipline, 145, 172, 178, 179, 180, 181
Documentalist, 168, 181

E

Empathy,
145, 169, 172, 174, 176, 177, 179, 180, 181
Environmental knowledge, 145, 174
Environmental orientation,
145, 169, 174, 178, 179, 180, 181
Estimator, 169, 172, 173, 174
Evaluation methods, 5, 85, 137
Evaluator, 168, 180
Event, 32
eXtreme Programming, 99

F

Feasibility analyst, 168, 175, 176
Focused interview, 164, 197

G

Graphic profile, 194, 258
Group leadership, 145, 174

H

Historical performance report, 185
Human capital, 9-10

I

Implementer, 168, 177, 178
Importation analyst, 168, 175, 176
Independence, 145, 171, 173, 175, 178
Innovation/creativity, 145, 173, 176
Installer, 168, 179
Integrated people management, 12, 22-23

J

Job design, 163
Judgement, 145, 173, 175, 176, 177

M

Maintainer, 168, 179

N

Needs,
  participation, 189, 209, 219
  training, 189, 207, 209, 219
Negotiating skills, 145, 176

O

Occupational psychologist, 150, 168
Occupational psychology, 151
Organisational behaviour, 23, 132, 142
Organisational culture, 132, 151
Organisational reengineering, 165

P

People model, 149, 184, 261-319
People's Capabilities Evaluation,
  activities, 149-151
  method, 157-163, 193-199
  stages, 160-163, 194-199
Peopleware, 9
  areas, 23
  incorporation into the software process, 21
  lines of research, 19
  modelling, 16
  principles, 10
Person,
  definition, 140
  profile, 185, 189, 190
Person/roles match table, 188, 189
Personality factors,
  correspondence with people's capabilities, 154
  16 PF test, 151, 194, **253-260**
    administration elements, 256-260
    global dimensions, 152, 256
    primary scales, 152, 254-255
    questionnaire, 194, 253, 255, 256, 258
    response style index, 253, 255
    pole, 253, 254, 255, 256, 260
    ratio, 188, 189, 199
Personality factors model, 161, 196, 263, 269-293
Personnel selection, 253
Planner, 168, 172, 173, 174
Planning and organisation, 145, 174
Process documentation, 190
Process engineer, 150
Product, 32, 140
Profile,
  person, 185, 189, 190
  role, 185, 186, 187, 189, 190

Q

Quality engineer, 168, 172, 174

R

Requirements specifier, 168, 177, 178
Retirement manager, 168, 179
Risk management, 145, 173
Role,
  definition, 31, 140

  profile, 185, 186, 187, 189, 190
Role assigner, 169, 172, 174
Roles profile,
  development, 177-179
  integral, 180-181
  pre-development, 175-177
  post-development, 179-180
  project management, 172-175
  software life cycle model selection, 170-172
Role/capabilities table, 169
Role/people table, 190

S

SLCM selector, 168, 170, 171, 172
Self-organisation, 145, 173, 178, 179, 180
Skills,
  interpersonal, 144
  intrapersonal, 144
  management, 144
  organisational, 144
Sociability, 145, 174, 176
Software life cycle, 2
  definition, 2
  models, 2
Software process, 3
  definition, 3
  models, 9, 28, **37-127**
    activity-oriented, 9, **37**
    assessment of, 130
    ALF, 29, 30, **113**, 130
    CMMI, 29, 30, **85**, 130
    definition, 3
    descriptive, 9, **28**, 37, 93, 131
    eXtreme Programming, 99
    FUNSOFT, 29, 30, **39**, 130
    IEEE STD 1074, 29, 30, **67**, 130, 167, 183
    IPSE 2.5, 29, 30, **49**, 130
    ISO/IEC 12207, 29, 30, **53**, 130
    ISO 9001, 29, 30, **76**, 130
    Marvel, 29, 30, **47**, 130
    People CMM, 29, 30, **121**, 130
    people-oriented, 9, **93**
    PMDB+, 29, 30, **111**, 130
    prescriptive, 9, **28**, 44, 110, 131
    PRISM, 29, 30, **42**, 130
    Process Cycle, 29, 30, **95**, 130
    SOCCA, 29, 30, **115**, 130
    SPADE, 29, 30, **50**, 130
    STATEMATE, 29, 30, **40**, 130
    Systems Dynamics-Based, 29, 30, **93**, 130
    TAME, 29, 30, **38**, 130
    TRIAD, 29, 30, **45**, 130
    Unified Process, 29, 30, **118**, 130
    Win-win model, 29, 30, **106**, 130
Software process evaluation, 4, 37
Software process improvement, 5, 37
Software process modelling, 4, **7**
  definition, 4
  elements, 31
  environments, 32
  information perspectives, 33
  notational characteristics, 34
  objectives, 7
Software process prediction, 37

Stress tolerance,
   145, 171, 173, 175, 177, 178, 180, 181
System operator,   168, 179
Systems analyst,   168, 175, 176, 177, 178

T

Table of correspondence,   **154**, 184
Tenacity,   145, 178, 179
Team,
   performance measurement,   212
   primary and supporting,   150
Team leader,   168, 172, 173, 174

Teamwork/cooperation,
   145, 172, 174, 176, 177, 178, 181
Technique,   140
Trainer,   168, 181

W

Win-Win Spiral Model,   29, 30, **106**, 130
Workforce participants,   149, **154**

X

XP,   29, 30, **99**, 130